RECOMMENDED REFERENCE BOOKS

for Small and Medium-sized Libraries and Media Centers

2003

RECOMMENDED REFERENCE BOOKS

for Small and Medium-sized Libraries and Media Centers

2003

Dr. Martin Dillon, EDITOR IN CHIEF

Shannon Graff Hysell, ASSOCIATE EDITOR

LIBRARIES UNLIMITED
UNLIMITED
A Member of the Greenwood Publishing Group

Westport, Connecticut • London

LIBRARIES UNLIMITED
A Member of Greenwood Publishing Group, Inc.
88 Post Road West
Westport, CT 06881
1-800-225-5800
www.lu.com

Library of Congress Cataloging-in-Publication Data

Main entry under title:

Recommended reference books for small and medium-
    sized libraries and media centers.

    "Selected from the 2003 edition of American
reference books annual."
    Includes index.
    1. Reference books--Bibliography.   2. Reference
services (Libraries)--Handbooks, manuals, etc.
3. Instructional materials centers--Handbooks,
manuals, etc.   I. Dillon, Martin II. Hysell, Shannon Graff
III. American reference books annual.
Z1035.1.R435   011'.02   81-12394
ISBN 1-59158-055-2
ISSN 0277-5948

Contents

Contents

Part IV
SCIENCE AND TECHNOLOGY

29—Science and Technology in General

30—Agricultural Sciences

31—Biological Sciences

32—Engineering

33—Health Sciences

34—High Technology

35—Physical Sciences and Mathematics

Introduction

Recommended Reference Books for Small and Medium-sized Libraries and Media Centers (RRB), now in its twenty-third volume, is designed to assist smaller libraries in the systematic selection of suitable reference materials for their collections. It aids in the evaluation process by choosing substantial titles in all subject areas. The increase in the publication of reference sources in the United States and Canada, in combination with the decrease in library budgets, makes this guide an invaluable tool.

Following the pattern established in 1981 with the first volume, *RRB* consists of book reviews chosen from the current edition of *American Reference Books Annual*. This nationally acclaimed work provides reviews of reference books, CD-ROMs, and Internet sites published in the United States and Canada within a single year, along with English-language titles from other countries. *ARBA* has reviewed more than 56,500 titles since its inception in 1970. Because it provides comprehensive coverage of reference sources, not just selected or recommended titles, many are of interest only to large academic and public libraries. Thus, *RRB* has been developed as an abridged version of *ARBA*, with selected reviews of resources suitable for smaller libraries.

Titles reviewed in *RRB* include dictionaries, encyclopedias, indexes, directories, bibliographies, guides, atlases, gazetteers, and other types of ready-reference tools. General encyclopedias that are updated annually, yearbooks, almanacs, indexing and abstracting services, directories, and other annuals are included on a selective basis. These works are systematically reviewed so that all important annuals are critically examined every few years. Excluded from *RRB* are regional guides in the areas of biological sciences, travel guides, and reference titles in the areas of literature and fine arts that deal with individual authors or artists. All titles in this volume are coded with letters which provide worthwhile guidance for selection. These indicate that a given work is a recommended purchase for smaller college libraries (C), public libraries (P), or school media centers (S).

The current volume of *RRB* contains 521 unabridged reviews selected from the 1,561 entries in *ARBA 2003*. These have been written by more than 200 subject specialists throughout the United States and Canada. Although all titles in *RRB* are recommended acquisitions, critical comments have not been deleted, because even recommended works may be weak in one respect or another. In many cases reviews evaluate and compare a work in relation to other titles of a similar nature. All reviews provide complete ordering and bibliographic information. The subject index organization is based upon the 22d edition of the *Library of Congress Subject Headings*. References to reviews published in periodicals (see page xxi for journals cited) during the year of coverage are appended to the reviews. All reviews are signed.

The present volume contains 37 chapters. There are four major subdivisions: "General Reference Works," "Social Sciences," "Humanities," and "Science and Technology." "General Reference Works," arranged alphabetically, is subdivided by form: bibliography, biography, handbooks and yearbooks, and so on. The remaining three parts are subdivided into alphabetically arranged chapters. Most chapters are subdivided in a way that reflects the arrangement strategy of the entire volume: a section on general works and then a topical breakdown. The latter is further subdivided, based on the amount of material available on a given topic.

RRB has been favorably reviewed in such journals as *Booklist*, *School Library Media Quarterly*, *Journal of Academic Librarianship*, *Library Talk*, and *Reference Books Bulletin*. For example, *Library Talk* (Jan/Feb 2002, p. 54) states the *RRB* is "the answer to the prayers of librarians of small to medium-sized facilities who need to buy reference materials." The editors continue to strive to make *RRB* the most valuable acquisition tool a small library can have.

In closing, the editors at Libraries Unlimited would like to express their gratitude to the contributors whose reviews appear in this volume. We would also like to thank the staff members who have been instrumental in the preparation of this work.

Contributors

Gordon J. Aamot, Head, Foster Business Library, Univ. of Washington, Seattle.

Stephen H. Aby, Education Bibliographer, Bierce Library, Univ. of Akron, Ohio.

Anthony J. Adam, Reference Librarian, Prairie View A & M Univ., Coleman Library, Tex.

January Adams, Asst. Director/Head of Adult Services, Franklin Township Public Library, Somerset, N.J.

Donald Altschiller, Reference Librarian, Boston Univ.

Elizabeth L. Anderson, Part-Time Instructor, Lansing Community College, Mich.

Frank J. Anderson, Librarian Emeritus, Sandor Teszler Library, Wofford College, Spartanburg, S.C.

Robert T. Anderson, Professor, Religious Studies, Michigan State Univ., East Lansing.

Charles R. Andrews, Dean of Library Services, Hofstra Univ., Hempstead, N.Y.

Helene Androski, Reference Librarian, Univ. of Wisconsin—Madison.

Melvin S. Arrington Jr., Assoc. Professor of Modern Languages, Univ. of Mississippi, University.

Susan C. Awe, Asst. Director, Univ. of New Mexico, Albuquerque.

Mary A. Axford, Reference Librarian, Georgia Institute of Technology, Atlanta.

Suzanne I. Barchers, *Weekly Reader*, Stamford, Conn.

David Bardack, Professor, Dept. of Biological Sciences, Univ. of Illinois, Chicago.

Mark T. Bay, Electronic Resources, Serials, and Government Documents Librarian, Hagan Memorial Library, Cumberland College, Williamsburg, Ky.

Leslie M. Behm, Reference Librarian, Michigan State Univ. Libraries, East Lansing.

Sandra E. Belanger, Reference Librarian, San Jose State Univ. Library, Calif.

Laura J. Bender, Science Librarian, Univ. of Arizona, Tucson.

Kenneth W. Berger, Team Leader, Reference/ILL Home Team, Perkins Library, Duke Univ., Durham, N.C.

John B. Beston, Professor of English, Santa Fe, N.Mex.

Barbara M. Bibel, Reference Librarian, Science/Business/Sociology Dept., Main Library, Oakland Public Library, Calif.

Adrienne Antink Bien, Medical Group Management Association, Lakewood, Colo.

Terry D. Bilhartz, Assoc. Professor of History, Sam Houston State Univ., Huntsville, Tex.

Susanne Bjorner, Consultant, Bjorner & Associates, Franconia, N.H.

Richard Bleiler, Reference Librarian, Univ. of Connecticut, Storrs.

Edna M. Boardman, Bismark, N.D.

Michael S. Borries, Cataloger, City Univ. of New York.

Christopher Brennan, Assoc. Director, Drake Memorial Library, SUNY, Brockport, N.Y.

Georgia Briscoe, Assoc. Director and Head of Technical Services, Law Library, Univ. of Colorado, Boulder.

Janet Dagenais Brown, Assoc. Professor and Education and Social Sciences Librarian, Wichita State Univ., Kans.

Patrick J. Brunet, Library Manager, Western Wisconsin Technical College, La Crosse.

Frederic F. Burchsted, Reference Librarian, Widener Library, Harvard Univ., Cambridge, Mass.

Robert H. Burger, Assoc. Univ. Librarian for Services, Univ. of Illinois, Urbana-Champaign.

Joanna M. Burkhardt, Head Librarian, College of Continuing Education Library, Univ. of Rhode Island, Providence.

Hans E. Bynagle, Library Director and Professor of Philosophy, Whitworth College, Spokane, Wash.

E. Wayne Carp, Professor of History, Pacific Lutheran Univ., Tacoma, Wash.

Joseph Cataio, Manager, Booklegger's Bookstore, Chicago, Ill.

Bert Chapman, Government Publications Coordinator, Purdue Univ., West Lafayette, Ind.

Boyd Childress, Reference Librarian, Ralph B. Draughon Library, Auburn Univ., Ala.

Dene L. Clark, (retired) Reference Librarian, Auraria Library, Denver, Colo.

Joshua Cohen, Director for Outreach and Continuing Education, Mid-Hudson Library System, Poughkeepsie, N.Y.

Donald E. Collins, Assoc. Professor, History Dept., East Carolina Univ., Greenville, N.C.

Barbara Conroy, Career Connections, Santa Fe, N.Mex.

Rosanne M. Cordell, Head of Reference Services, Franklin D. Schurz Library, Indiana Univ., South Bend.

Kay O. Cornelius, (formerly) Teacher and Magnet School Lead Teacher, Huntsville City Schools, Ala.

Paul B. Cors, Catalog Librarian, Univ. of Wyoming, Laramie.

Gregory A. Crawford, Head of Public Services, Penn State Harrisburg, Middletown, Pa.

Mark J. Crawford, Consulting Exploration Geologist/Writer/Editor, Madison, Wis.

Gregory Curtis, Director, Northern Maine Technical College, Presque Isle.

Dominique-René de Lerma, Professor, Conservatory of Music, Lawrence Univ., Appleton, Wis.

Scott R. DiMarco, Director of Library Services, Herkimer County Community College, N.Y.

Tara L. Dirst, Technology Coordinator, Abraham Lincoln Historical Digitization Project, Northern Illinois Univ., DeKalb.

Margaret F. Dominy, Information Services Librarian, Drexel Univ., Philadelphia.

John A. Drobnicki, Assoc. Professor and Head of Reference Services, City Univ. of New York—York College, Jamaica.

David J. Duncan, Reference Librarian, Humanities, Wichita State Univ., Ablah Library, Kans.

Joe P. Dunn, Charles A. Dana Professor of History and Politics, Converse College, Spartanburg, S.C.

Bradford Lee Eden, Head of Cataloging, Univ. of Nevada at Las Vegas.

Marianne B. Eimer, Interlibrary Loan/Reference Librarian, SUNY College at Fredonia, N.Y.

Karen Evans, Instruction and Reference, Indiana State Univ., Terre Haute.

Lorraine Evans, Instruction and Reference Librarian, Auraria Library, Denver, Colo.

Elaine Ezell, Library Media Specialist, Bowling Green Jr. High School, Ohio.

Ian Fairclough, Cataloger, Marion Public Library, Ohio.

Judith J. Field, Senior Lecturer, Program for Library and Information Science, Wayne State Univ., Detroit.

Virginia S. Fischer, Reference/Documents Librarian, Univ. of Maine, Presque Isle.

James H. Flynn Jr., (formerly) Operations Research Analyst, Dept. of Defense, Vienna, Va.

Michael A. Foley, Honors Director, Marywood College, Scranton, Pa.

Lynne M. Fox, Information Services and Outreach Librarian, Denison Library, Univ. of Colorado Health Sciences Center, Denver.

David K. Frasier, Asst. Librarian, Reference Dept., Indiana Univ., Bloomington.

Susan J. Freiband, Assoc. Professor, Graduate School of Librarianship, Univ. of Puerto Rico, San Juan.

David O. Friedrichs, Professor, Univ. of Scranton, Pa.

Ronald H. Fritze, Assoc. Professor, Dept. of History, Univ. of Central Arkansas, Conway.

Thomas K. Fry, Assoc. Director, Public Services, Penrose Library, Univ. of Denver, Colo.

Sandra E. Fuentes Riggs, Librarian, Montgomery Library, Cambellsville Univ., Campbellsville, Ky.

Jeanne D. Galvin, Chief of Reference, Kingsborough Community College, City Univ. of New York, Brooklyn.

Zev Garber, Professor and Chair, Jewish Studies, Los Angeles Valley College, Calif.

Denise A. Garofalo, Director for Telecommunications, Mid-Hudson Library System, Poughkeepsie, N.Y.

John T. Gillespie, College Professor and Writer, New York.

Lois Gilmer, Library Director, Univ. of West Florida, Fort Walton Beach.

Edwin S. Gleaves, State Librarian and Archivist, Tennessee State Library and Archives, Nashville.

Barbara B. Goldstein, Media Specialist, Magothy River Middle School, Arnold, Md.

Anthony Gottlieb, Asst. Clinical Professor, Univ. of Colorado School of Medicine, Denver.

Richard W. Grefrath, Reference Librarian, Univ. of Nevada, Reno.

Arthur Gribben, Professor, Union Institute, Los Angeles, Calif.

Laurel Grotzinger, Professor, Univ. Libraries, Western Michigan Univ., Kalamazoo.

Patrick Hall, Assoc. Librarian for Public Affairs, Penn State Univ., Middletown, Pa.

Ralph Hartsock, Senior Music Catalog Librarian, Univ. of North Texas, Denton.

Karen D. Harvey, Assoc. Dean for Academic Affairs, Univ. College, Univ. of Denver, Colo.

Lucy Heckman, Reference Librarian (Business-Economics), St. John's Univ. Library, Jamaica, N.Y.

Carol D. Henry, Librarian, Lyons Township High School, LaGrange, Ill.

Mark Y. Herring, Dean of Library Services, Winthrop Univ., Dacus Library, Rock Hill, S.C.

Ladyjane Hickey, Head of Cataloging and Business, Management and Marketing Bibliographer, Newton Gresham Library, Sam Houston State Univ., Huntsville, Tex.

Marquita Hill, Cooperating Professor of Chemical Engineering, Univ. of Maine, Orono.

V. W. Hill, Social Sciences Bibliographer, Memorial Library, Univ. of Wisconsin, Madison.

Christopher J. Hoeppner, Reference Instruction Librarian, DePaul Univ., Chicago.

Susan Tower Hollis, Assoc. Dean and Center Director, Central New York Center of the State Univ. of New York.

Leslie R. Homzie, Reference Librarian, Brandeis Univ., Waltham, Mass.

Sara Anne Hook, Assoc. Dean of the Faculties, Indiana Univ., Purdue Univ., Indianapolis.

Mihoko Hosoi, Public Services Librarian, Cornell Univ., Ithaca, N.Y.

Shannon Graff Hysell, Staff, Libraries Unlimited.

David Isaacson, Asst. Head of Reference and Humanities Librarian, Waldo Library, Western Michigan Univ., Kalamazoo.

D. Barton Johnson, Professor Emeritus of Russian, Univ. of California, Santa Barbara.

Richard D. Johnson, Director of Libraries Emeritus, James M. Milne Library, State Univ. College, Oneonta, N.Y.

Dorothy Jones, Reference Librarian, Founders Memorial Library, Northern Illinois Univ., De Kalb.

Florence W. Jones, Librarian, Auraria Campus Library, Denver, Colo.

Elaine F. Jurries, Coordinator of Serials Services, Auraria Library, Denver, Colo.

Thomas A. Karel, Assoc. Director for Public Services, Shadek-Fackenthal Library, Franklin and Marshall College, Lancaster, Pa.

John Laurence Kelland, Reference Bibliographer for Life Sciences, Univ. of Rhode Island Library, Kingston.

Vicki J. Killion, Asst. Professor of Library Science and Pharmacy, Nursing and Health Sciences Librarian, Purdue Univ., West Lafayette, Ind.

Christine E. King, Education Librarian, Purdue Univ., West Lafayette, Ind.

Svetlana Korolev, Science Librarian, Golda Meir Library, Univ. of Wisconsin, Milwaukee.

Janet J. Kosky, Mukwonago Community Library, Wis.

Lori D. Kranz, Freelance Editor; Assoc. Editor, *The Bloomsbury Review*, Denver, Colo.

Betsy J. Kraus, Librarian, Lovelace Respiratory Research Institute, National Environmental Respiratory Center, Albuquerque, N.Mex.

Marlene M. Kuhl, Library Manager, Baltimore County Public Library, Reisterstown Branch, Md.

Sharon Ladenson, Social Sciences Bibliographer and Reference Librarian, Michigan State Univ. Libraries, East Lansing.

Linda L. Lam-Easton, Assoc. Professor, Dept. of Religious Studies, California State Univ., Northridge.

Charles Leck, Professor of Biological Sciences, Rutgers Univ., New Brunswick, N.J.

Hwa-Wei Lee, Dean of Libraries, Ohio Univ., Athens.

Polin P. Lei, Silver Springs, Md.

Michael Levine-Clark, Reference Librarian, Univ. of Denver, Colo.

Tze-chung Li, Professor, Graduate School of Library and Information Science, Rosary College, River Forest, Ill.

Koraljka Lockhart, Publications Editor, San Francisco Opera, Calif.

Jeffrey E. Long, Interlibrary Loan/Photocopy Services Library Asst., Lamar Soutter Library/Univ. of Massachusetts Medical Center, Worcester.

Barbara MacAlpine, Science Librarian, Coates Library, Trinity Univ., San Antonio, Tex.

Theresa Maggio, Head of Public Services, Southwest Georgia Regional Library, Bainbridge.

Glenn Masuchika, Senior Information Specialist, Rockwell Collins Information, Iowa City, Iowa.

John Maxymuk, Reference Librarian, Paul Robeson Library, Rutgers Univ., Camden, N.J.

George Louis Mayer, (formerly) Senior Principal Librarian, New York Public Library and Part-Time Librarian, Adelphi, Manhattan Center and Brooklyn College.

Peter H. McCracken, Serials Solutions, LLC, Seattle, Wash.

Dana McDougald, Lead Media Specialist, Learning Resources Center, Cedar Shoals High School, Athens, Ga.

Glenn S. McGuigan, Reference Librarian, Penn State Abington, Abington, Pa.

Peter Zachary McKay, Business Librarian, Univ. of Florida Libraries, Gainesville.

Lynn M. McMain, Instructor/Reference Librarian, Newton Gresham Library, Sam Houston State Univ., Huntsville, Tex.

Constance A. Mellon, Assoc. Professor, Dept. of Broadcasting, Librarianship, and Educational Technology, East Carolina Univ., Greenville, N.C.

Lillian R. Mesner, Mesner Information Connections, Lexington, Ky.

Michael G. Messina, Assoc. Professor, Dept. of Forest Science, Texas A & M Univ., College Station.

Elizabeth M. Mezick, CPA/Asst. Professor, Long Island Univ., Brookville, N.Y.

Robert Michaelson, Head Librarian, Seeley G. Mudd Library for Science and Engineering, Northwestern Univ., Evanston, Ill.

Ken Middleton, User Services Librarian, Middle Tennessee State Univ., Murfreesboro.

Bill Miller, Director of Libraries, Florida Atlantic Univ., Boca Raton.

Richard A. Miller, Professor of Economics, Wesleyan Univ., Middletown, Conn.

Terri Tickle Miller, Slavic Bibliographer, Michigan State Univ. Libraries, East Lansing.

Jim Millhorn, Head of Acquisitions, Northern Illinois Univ. Libraries, DeKalb.

Paul A. Mogren, Head of Reference, Marriott Library, Univ. of Utah, Salt Lake City.

Janet Mongan, Research Officer, Cleveland State Univ. Library, Ohio.

Craig A. Munsart, Teacher, Jefferson County Public Schools, Golden, Colo.

James M. Murray, U.S. Courts Library, Spokane, Wash.

Valentine K. Muyumba, Monographic Cataloging Librarian, Indiana State Univ., Terre Haute.

Madeleine Nash, Reference Librarian, Spring Valley, N.Y.

Rita Neri, Health Sciences Librarian, Long Island Univ., Brooklyn Campus, N.Y.

Charles Neuringer, Professor of Psychology and Theatre and Film, Univ. of Kansas, Lawrence.

Deborah L. Nicholl, Asst. Professor, Coates Library, Trinity Univ., San Antonio, Tex.

Shawn W. Nicholson, State Documents and Social Sciences Librarian, Michigan State Univ., East Lansing.

Danuta A. Nitecki, Assoc. Univ. Librarian, Yale Univ., New Haven, Conn.

Christopher W. Nolan, Asst. University Librarian, Elizabeth Huth Coates Library, Trinity Univ., San Antonio, Tex.

Carol L. Noll, Volunteer Librarian, Schimelpfenig Middle School, Plano, Tex.

Marshall E. Nunn, Professor, Dept. of History, Glendale Community College, Calif.

Peggy D. Odom, Grants Resource Center Librarian, Waco-McLennan County Library, Tex.

James W. Oliver, Chemistry Librarian, Michigan State Univ., East Lansing.

Ray Olszewski, Independent Consultant, Palo Alto, Calif.

Rona Ostrow, Chief Librarian and Professor, Lehman College Library, CUNY, Bronx.

John Howard Oxley, Faculty, American Intercontinental Univ., Atlanta, Ga.

Robert Palmieri, Professor Emeritus, School of Music, Kent State Univ., Ohio.

J. Carlyle Parker, Librarian and Univ. Archivist Emeritus, Library, California State Univ., Turlock.

Phillip P. Powell, Asst. Reference Librarian, Robert Scott Small Library, College of Charleston, S.C.

Varadaraja V. Raman, Professor of Physics and Humanities, Rochester Institute of Technology, N.Y.

Jack Ray, Asst. Director, Loyola/Notre Dame Library, Baltimore, Md.

Nancy P. Reed, Information Services Manager, Paducah Public Library, Ky.

Allen Reichert, Electronic Access Librarian, Courtright Memorial Library, Otterbein College, Westerville, Ohio.

Robert B. Marks Ridinger, Head, Electronic Information Resources Management Dept., Univ. Libraries, Northern Illinois Univ., De Kalb.

Cari Ringelheim, (formerly) Staff, Libraries Unlimited.

Alice A. Robinson, Adjunct Professor, LaGuardia Community College, Long Island City, N.Y.

Deborah V. Rollins, Reference Librarian, Univ. of Maine, Orono.

John B. Romeiser, Professor of French and Dept. Head, Univ. of Tennessee, Knoxville.

Michele Russo, Acting Director, Franklin D. Schurz Library, Indiana Univ., South Bend.

Nadine Salmons, Technical Services Librarian, Fort Carson's Grant Library, Colo.

Steven J. Schmidt, Assoc. Librarian, Indiana Univ./Purdue Univ. at Indianapolis Libraries.

Willa Schmidt, (retired) Reference Librarian, Univ. of Wisconsin, Madison.

Ralph Lee Scott, Assoc. Professor, East Carolina Univ. Library, Greenville, N.C.

Karen Selden, Catalog Librarian, Univ. of Colorado Law Library, Boulder.

Susan K. Setterlund, Science/Health Science Librarian, Florida Atlantic Univ., Boca Raton.

Ravindra Nath Sharma, Library Director, West Virginia State College, Institute.

Esther R. Sinofsky, Library Media Teacher, Alexander Hamilton High School, Los Angeles, Calif.

Kennith Slagle, Asst. Director for Collection Management, Jackson Library, Univ. of North Carolina at Greensboro.

Richard Slapsys, Umass Lowell Reference Coordinator, Fine Arts Librarian, Umass Lowell, Mass.

Mary Ellen Snodgrass, Freelance Writer, Charlotte, N.C.

Sandhya D. Srivastava, Asst. Professor, Serials Librarian, Hofstra Univ., Hempstead, N.Y.

Kay M. Stebbins, Coordinator Librarian, Louisiana State Univ., Shreveport.

Martha E. Stone, Coordinator for Reference Services, Treadwell Library, Massachusetts General Hospital, Boston.

John W. Storey, Professor of History, Lamar Univ., Beaumont, Tex.

William C. Struning, Professor, Seton Hall Univ., South Orange, N.J.

Timothy E. Sullivan, Asst. Professor of Economics, Towson State Univ., Md.

Philip G. Swan, Head Librarian, Hunter College, School of Social Work Library, New York.

Paolina Taglienti, Head of Acquisitions, Long Island Univ., Brooklyn Campus Library, N.Y.

Nigel Tappin, (formerly) General Librarian, North York Public Library, Ont.

Marit S. Taylor, Reference Librarian, Auraria Libraries, Univ. of Colorado, Denver.

Mary Ann Thompson, Asst. Professor of Nursing, Saint Joseph College, West Hartford, Conn.

David A. Timko, Head Reference Librarian at the U.S. Bureau of Census Library.

Diane J. Turner, Science/Engineering Liaison, Auraria Library, Univ. of Colorado, Denver.

Robert L. Turner Jr., Librarian and Asst. Professor, Radford Univ., Va.

Nancy L. Van Atta, Dayton, Ohio.

Mark van Lummel, Librarian, Elkhart Public Library, Ind.

Leanne M. VandeCreek, Social Sciences Reference Librarian, Northern Illinois Univ., DeKalb.

Vang Vang, Reference Librarian, Henry Madden Library, California State Univ. Fresno.

Anthony F. Verdesca Jr., Reference Librarian, Florida Atlantic Univ., Boca Raton.

Graham R. Walden, Assoc. Professor, Information Services Dept., Ohio State Univ., Columbus.

Kathleen Weessies, Maps/GIS Librarian, Michigan State Univ., East Lansing.

Karen T. Wei, Head, Asian Library, Univ. of Illinois, Urbana.

Arlene McFarlin Weismantel, Reference Librarian, Michigan State Univ., East Lansing.

Andrew B. Wertheimer, Doctoral Student, Univ. of Wisconsin—Madison.

Lucille Whalen, Dean of Graduate Programs, Immaculate Heart College Center, Los Angeles, Calif.

Robert L. Wick, Asst. Professor and Fine Arts Bibliographer, Auraria Library, Univ. of Colorado, Denver.

Agnes H. Widder, Humanities Bibliographer, Michigan State Univ., East Lansing.

Mark A. Wilson, Professor of Geology, College of Wooster, Ohio.

Terrie L. Wilson, Art Librarian, Michigan State Univ., East Lansing.

Julienne L. Wood, Head, Research Services, Noel Memorial Library, Louisiana State Univ. in Shreveport.

Hope Yelich, Reference Librarian, Earl Gregg Swem Library, College of William and Mary, Williamsburg, Va.

Henry E. York, Head, Collection Management, Cleveland State Univ., Ohio.

Courtney L. Young, Social Sciences Librarian, The Pennsylvania State Univ. Libraries, University Park.

Louis G. Zelenka, Jacksonville Public Library System, Fla.

L. Zgusta, Professor of Linguistics and the Classics and Member of the Center for Advance Study, Univ. of Illinois, Urbana.

Anita Zutis, Adjunct Librarian, Queensborough Community College, Bayside, N.Y.

Journals Cited

FORM OF CITATION	JOURNAL TITLE
AG	*Against the Grain*
BL	*Booklist*
BR	*Book Report*
C&RL	*College and Research Libraries*
C&RL News	*College and Research Libraries News*
Choice	*Choice*
JAL	*Journal of Academic Librarianship*
LJ	*Library Journal*
RUSQ	*Reference & User Services Quarterly*
SLJ	*School Library Journal*
TL	*Teacher Librarian*
VOYA	*Voice of Youth Advocates*

Part I
GENERAL REFERENCE WORKS

1 General Reference Works

ACRONYMS AND ABBREVIATIONS

C, P

1. **Acronym Finder. http://www.acronymfinder.com/.** [Website]. Free. Date reviewed: Jan 03.

The *Acronym Finder* is a useful, free site that provides users with the definitions of 266,000 acronyms—both those well known and some that are not. The search mechanism is simple. The user puts in the acronym in the right-hand search box and selects whether they would like to search for the exact acronym or the acronym that begins with the specified letters in the left-hand box. The site limits search results to 300 acronyms. If the site comes up with too many hits, the user can then sort the results by most common, slang, organizations and schools, or by field (e.g., information technology, science and medicine). Each acronym links to Amazon.com for titles that may be of interest to the user. Hence, the downside of this site: Because it is a free site it is heavily sponsored by advertisers. The user will have to sort through the many advertisements that continually pop up while waiting for their results. Nevertheless, this site will be useful for librarians working the reference desk.

—**Shannon Graff Hysell**

ALMANACS

C, P, S

2. *The New York Times* **Almanac 2002.** John W. Wright, ed., with the editors and reporters of *The Times* New York, Penguin Books, 2001. 1002p. maps. index. $25.00. ISBN 1-57958-348-2. ISSN 1523-7079.

The New York Times Almanac provides extensive data and detailed factual information on topics including (among many others) U.S. and world history, government organization, science and technology, and sports. The great strength of the almanac is its timely coverage and thorough textual analysis of domestic and international events. Effective writers and researchers, the editors of *The New York Times Almanac* utilize their investigative abilities, as well as the resources of a major news organization.

General topics covered are comparable to those of the previous edition (see ARBA 2001, entry 5). Significant updates include results of the 2000 Census and a clear and concise report on the terrorist attacks and aftermath of September 11, 2001. The Census 2000 report includes an in-depth description and analysis of population trends and changes at the state and national levels, such as population growth in metropolitan areas and the increasing diversification of the U.S. population. The report on the September terrorist attacks covers domestic and international political, social, and military responses, and includes a discussion of the anthrax attacks in the United States. The almanac is clearly organized, easy to use, and includes a 29-page index with cross-references as well as a 16-page color map section. It is highly recommended for school, public, and academic libraries.

—**Sharon Ladenson**

P, S

3. **Scholastic Book of World Records 2002.** New York, Scholastic, 2001. 320p. illus. $9.95. ISBN 0-439-31398-8.

Answers to questions researchers might have relating to record-holders in seven broad categories are accessed through a loosely defined table of contents page and an eight-page, end-of-the-book index. The categories—or sections of the book—named in the table of contents are "Nature Records," "Human-Made Records," "U.S. Records," "Science and Technology Records," "Money and Business Records," "Sports Records," and "Popular Culture Records." Entries in some of the sections are alphabetized while in others they are not. One page is devoted to each world record presented.

No rationale is given for inclusion in this book of world records. However, the following explanation is given for the graphs accompanying the text on each page: "In most cases, the graphs in this book represent the top five record holders in each category. However, in some graphs, we have chosen to list well-known or common people, places, animals, or things that will help you better understand how extraordinary the record holder is . . ." (verso of the title page).

World records can be found in other sources, but the graphs, text, and color pictures illustrating each of the 306 entries in this book make it unique. Unlike most reference books, it is fun to browse and its low price makes it very affordable for school, public, and home libraries.—**Lois Gilmer**

BIBLIOGRAPHY

National and Trade Bibliography

International

C, P

4. **Global Books in Print. http://www.globalbooksinprint.com.** [Website]. New Providence, N.J., R. R. Bowker. Price negotiated by site. Date reviewed: Jan 03.

Global Books in Print provides all of the information librarians find with *Books in Print Online* but with additional listings from Australia, Canada, Great Britain, and New Zealand. The site now holds more than 5 million print titles as well as reviews from such publications as *Publisher's Weekly* and *Library Journal*. The site is searchable by several different means, including an advanced search, a Boolean search, a quick search, and a browse search through 17 indexes.

Along with full bibliographic information of all print titles, the site offers several other features. The site provides access to lists of best-selling authors and titles, award-winning authors and titles, and biographies of more than 6,000 authors. For those who want to narrow their search further, Bowker has provided a fiction room, children's room, and a forthcoming releases room. These rooms offer the same easy search capabilities but will narrow the search to these specific topics.

The site also provides information that will be especially useful to librarians. A link to the "Hooks to Holdings" site will inform both librarians and library patrons if the title searched for can be found in their library. Users can also create lists of titles they are interested in. Once compiled the lists can be edited and can then be downloaded to programs that accept ASCII data, downloaded into MARC format, or downloaded into vendor-specific formats for electronic ordering. Finally, librarians looking for publisher, distributor, or book agent information can search for them by name, address, ISBN prefix, or company type.

This title will be valuable for all types of libraries for a variety of reasons—to locate book titles and publishers, find books on specific topics, and to aid in collection development, just to name a few. *Books in Print Online* offers much of the same information, along with bibliographic information on video listings, audiocassettes, and out-of-print titles, but only for works published in the United States. Both offer easy search options and reliable data and can be recommended for all types of libraries.—**Shannon Graff Hysell**

United States

C, P, S

5. **CD-ROMs in Print: An International Guide to CD-ROM, CD-I, 3DO, MMCD, CD32, Multimedia, Laserdisc, and Electronic Products.** 16th ed. Alan Hedblad, ed. Farmington Hills, Mich., Gale, 2002. 1940p. index. $185.00pa. ISBN 0-7876-5524-4. ISSN 0891-8198.

This 16th edition of *CD-ROMs in Print* remains a useful compendium of CD-ROMs and other electronic products available worldwide. It lists more than 20,000 titles complete with full descriptions and contact data for each product. The volume also includes contact information for companies involved in CD-ROM development and distribution, including profiles of more than 4,500 companies associated with this industry. Nearly 1,700 of the title listings are new to this edition, as are 138 of the company profiles. The volume also contains indexes by geographical area, multimedia features, Macintosh compatibility, electronic books and other formats, audience level, and subject. A wide variety of subject areas are covered, including: business and industry; science and the professions; entertainment, games, and hobbies; and culture, history, and education. Each descriptive listing includes information on dates covered, audience level, language, subject, specification, price, and availability. Defunct and out-of-print CD-ROMs are also included and appropriately designated because the editor feels that these products may still be available through other vendors. This work compares favorably overall with the CD-ROM product *Multimedia & CD-ROM Directory on CD-ROM* published by TFL Publishers. This work under review is also available for licensing and deliverable on disk or CD-ROM at www.galegroupcom/bizdev.—**Rona Ostrow**

BIOGRAPHY

International

C, P, S

6. **Biography Resource Center. http://www.gale.com/BiographyRC.** [Website]. Farmington Hills, Mich., Gale. Price negotiated by site. Date reviewed: Mar 02.

The *Biography Resource Center* will be of use to students and researchers in the areas of literature, multi-cultural studies, entertainment, politics, government, history, the arts, and science and technology. This database from Gale uses reputable sources such as *The Complete Marquis Who's Who, Contemporary Authors, Encyclo-pedia of World Biography, Newsmakers*, and Debrett's People of Today. The site provides some 13,000 images of biographees and links to nearly 7,000 corresponding Websites.

The easiest way to search the site is by entering a person's name in the search box. This will lead users to names that match the criteria and then to a list of sources that contain information about the person. The user can choose from several different content types, including journal and periodical articles, thumbnail biographies, narrative biographies, additional resources, and Websites. Full citations for each article are provided. Users can also do a "Custom Search" by providing data on ethnicity, birth or death dates, occupation, or gender. A "Full Text Search" can be conducted when a user only knows keywords about the person being researched or is searching for a person who has done a specific task. Here, the user can search by all of the keywords, any of the keywords, or by use of Boolean operators. Other features of this database allow users to print the data found, e-mail it to themselves or someone else, bookmark it for later use, or use the "Citation Generator" to produce a correct citation for the work.

This resource will be especially useful in high school and undergraduate libraries where students will be researching specific people for reports and term papers. The database is extremely useful to use and the information is easy to comprehend. This source, however, should be used as a beginning point and not as a sole point of research. School and college and university libraries will find it of great use to their patrons.—**Shannon Graff Hysell**

C, P

7. **The International Who's Who 2003.** 66th ed. Florence, Ky., Europa Publications, 2002. 1809p. $365.00. ISBN 1-85743-154-5.

C, P

8.   **The International Who's Who Online. http://www.worldwhoswho.com/register.html.** [Website]. Florence, Ky., Europa Publications. Free with purchase of print edition. Date reviewed: Jan 03.

This 66th edition of *The International Who's Who* provides biographical information for nearly 20,000 influential people from around the world. Some 1,000 of these names are new to this edition and many others have been updated to reflect the changes in the lives of the biographees. The people gathered here come from a variety of professions; most of them are well known in their country. The people listed here include government and political officials, business professionals, artists, journalists, medical professionals, scientists, athletes, and entertainers in theater and film. As with most "who's who" publications, the information is gathered directly from the biographees so the quality varies from person to person. In general, the following information is included: name, birth date and birth place, family, a list of positions held, a list of achievements and awards, and contact information. Supplementary material includes a list of abbreviations, international telephone codes, a list of royal families, and a list of obituaries from the past year.

With the purchase of the book users are given single-user access to *The International Who's Who Online*. The site provides the same information as the print volume but is updated regularly to reflect the most recent changes. Users can search by name, nationality, place and date of birth, and occupation. The obituary and a list of new entrants is also provided.—**Shannon Graff Hysell**

C, P

9.   **Marquis Who's Who on the Web. http://www.marquiswhoswho.com/ontheweb.asp.** [Website]. New Providence, N.J., Marquis Who's Who/Reed Reference Publishing. Price negotiated by site. Date reviewed: Jan 03.

Marquis Who's Who has been providing biographical information on influential people for over 100 years. It has been a standard resource in all types of libraries as well as a favorite among researchers from all fields. This online database provides the most up-to-date information for more than one million individuals from all fields, including government, the arts, science and technology, business, and entertainment. The site is updated each day with new biographies and updated information of current biographies. The site allows the researcher to search in one of two ways—with a basic name search or with an advanced search. With the basic search users can enter the first or last name of the person being researched (or both names). The search results are provided on the next screen and include the name of the biographee, occupation, city where they were born, and their state or country of residence. Users can then click on the name to get further information. A typical biography includes information on the person's family, education, career highlights, awards, memberships, and contact information. It also indicates which Marquis' title(s) they were listed in. The advanced search allows users to search under 13 different search criteria, including name, occupation, university, religion, or keyword. Search results are arranged in alphabetic order and can be screened 20 per page.

This resource brings together a lot of information that will be of use to many library patrons. The electronic format will save libraries a lot of space that would be taken up by many volumes. Because the site is updated daily the reliability of the information given is greatly enhanced. This resource is recommended for large academic and public libraries.—**Shannon Graff Hysell**

C, P

10.   Sherby, Louise S. **The Who's Who of Nobel Prize Winners 1901-2000.** 4th ed. Westport, Conn., Oryx Press/Greenwood Publishing Group, 2002. 277p. index. $69.95. ISBN 1-57356-414-1.

For the latest edition of this work, Sherby has taken over the role of general editor from the retired Bernard and June Schlesinger (see ARBA 97, entry 30; ARBA 92, entry 28; and ARBA 88, entry 33, for reviews of previous editions). There are 62 new entries added to this edition, covering the years from 1995 to 2000. However, the format of the book remains unchanged. Each of the six prizes is alphabetically listed starting with chemistry and concluding with physics. Prizes are then chronologically listed within each section. In addition, there are four indexes—by name, education, nationality, and religion. In short, it is easy to locate information on prize winners.

Each entry has up to 15 potential fields of biographical and bibliographic information, and concludes with a brief commentary. The individual portraits are best described as minimalist and, in this regard, the book well fits the mold of the ready-reference volume. Although a variety of sources were used in verifying information, Sherby particularly credits the Nobel Museum Website at http://www.nobel.se. Indeed, the material at the

Website is fuller and more up to date than the volume under review. Nonetheless, Sherby's volume is valuable for anyone who needs quick access to Nobel Prize information.—**Jim Millhorn**

P, S

11. **U*X*L Encyclopedia of World Biography.** Laura B. Tyle, ed. Farmington Hills, Mich., U*X*L/Gale, 2003. 10v. illus. index. $399.00/set. ISBN 0-7876-6465-0.

This resource, designed with middle school and high school students in mind, provides biographical information for 750 influential people worldwide—both historical and contemporary. The 750 chosen are those believed to be the most studied figures at the middle and high school levels. The biographees come from a wide range of fields, from American and world history and government to the sciences, literature, and arts and entertainment.

Arranged alphabetically throughout 10 volumes beginning with Hank Aaron and ending with Paul Zindel, each individual is covered in two to three pages and each has a black-and-white photograph accompanying the text. Information includes their birth and death dates (if applicable), profession, information on their childhood and personal lives, career highlights, and a list for further reading. The biographies are well written and, although brief, provide information that will be interesting to young adults. An alphabetic list of individuals is listed in the table of contents, followed by a list of individuals by nationality.

School and children's public library collections have many sources to choose from for their biographical reference information. For those needing to expand their resources in this area or for those needing updated information, this will be a good selection.—**Shannon Graff Hysell**

United States

C, P

12. **The Scribner Encyclopedia of American Lives: The 1960s.** William L. O'Neill, ed. New York, Charles Scribner's Sons/Gale Group, 2003. 2v. illus. index. $375.00/set. ISBN 0-684-80666-5.

The Scribner Encyclopedia of American Lives: The 1960s (SEAL: The 1960s) is a comprehensive, two-volume work that is arranged alphabetically and contains 647 biographies. O'Neill, a prominent social historian, has brought together 201 contributors, including biographers writing about their own subjects, historians, journalists, scholars in other fields, attorneys, and freelance writers. The latter group of 25 individuals contribute from 1 to 27 biographies, 146 of the total (22 percent). O'Neill's criteria for inclusion in SEAL: 1960s is broad. Figures who helped define the decade or "in some other way are connected to it in the public mind" qualify (p. viii). In addition to including figures associated with the turbulent times of the 1960s, O'Neill wanted to present a cross section of American life—people "who were not of the period in the sense of helping to shape it" (p. viii). Thus, the reader will find biographies of people involved in commonplace activities, such as "making and selling goods, producing art and music, doing research, and playing and viewing sports" (p. viii). Although the subjects are mostly restricted to Americans, O'Neill included other nationalities, such as the poet W. H. Auden and the film director Alfred Hitchcock, who significantly influenced American art and culture.

The comprehensiveness of SEAL: The 1960s is quite successful. From Buffy Sainte-Marie to Curtis Emerson LeMay, Eldridge Cleaver to Paul Samuelson, Linus Carl Pauling to Bella Abzug, the entries are wide-ranging and of very high quality, each accompanied by a photograph and bibliography. The overwhelming majority of the photographs are appropriate; some even have the capacity to startle, such as the lithe, muscular Abbie Hoffman, but the one of the Beach Boys with beards was probably taken in the 1970s and seems inappropriate (many of the photographs are not dated). One could carp about the omission of such important figures as Saul Alinsky, Robert Coles, A. J. Muste, Dave von Ronk, Michael Walzer, and Richard Wright, but as O'Neill admits, the selection was difficult and other informed readers might have chosen differently. These minor quibbles aside, SEAL: The 1960s is a delight and will become an indispensable resource for biographical information about the 1960s.
—**E. Wayne Carp**

C, P

13.   **Who's Who of American Women 2002-2003.** 23d ed. New Providence, N.J., Marquis Who's Who/Reed Reference Publishing, 2002. 1172p. $279.00; $251.10 (standing order). ISBN 0-8379-0428-5. ISSN 0083-9841.

Since last reviewed in ARBA 2000, the number of women featured in *Who's Who of American Women* provides biographical data for more than 7,000 more women (21st ed.; see ARBA 2000, entry 21). According to the front matter of this volume, nearly 13,000 of the entries are new to this volume and close to 10,000 have been revised from the previous edition. This title provides information on women who are successful in a variety of professions, including business, government, education, art and culture, and those who have received prestigious honors or have been selected for honorary institutions. The biographical data are provided by the women themselves so the quality varies. In general it includes name, occupation, birth date, education, career history, publications, professional activities, awards, and home and office addresses. This has long been a standard source in many public and academic libraries and this new edition deserves a place on these reference shelves as well.—**Shannon Graff Hysell**

DICTIONARIES AND ENCYCLOPEDIAS

C

14.   **The American Heritage College Dictionary.** 4th ed. New York, Houghton Mifflin, 2002. 1636p. illus. maps. $25.00. ISBN 0-618-09848-8.

The 4th edition of *The American Heritage College Dictionary* adds 7,500 new words and senses to its vocabulary since the 3d edition that was published 9 years ago (see ARBA 94, entry 1075, for a review). Many new computer and Internet terms have been added, as well as newly coined words in science, politics, and the arts. There are also biographical entries for newly prominent persons and updated entries for U.S. towns, cities, and states with statistics from the 2000 census. The text is enhanced by more than 2,500 graphic images, including photographs, drawings, and maps.

Entries begin with the entry word in bold type, inflected and divided into syllables. Pronunciation is shown, then part of speech and variants, if applicable. The definitions follow. For words with more than one possible meaning or sense, definitions are arranged by order of sense, beginning with the most central or common sense. Etymologies appear in square brackets following the definitions. Cross-references are given for those words that have additional information in another entry. Some entries contain explanatory notes and examples of usage.

A special feature of this dictionary is its use of notes. "Word History" notes are given for some entries whose etymologies are of particular interest. Other types of notes include regional notes for hundreds of words whose occurrence is restricted to certain areas of the United States; synonym notes for synonyms of special interest; usage notes that present important information and guidance on matters of grammar, diction, pronunciation, and usage; and "Our Living Language" notes that discuss the social aspect of a word.

Other special features include a style manual that discusses the basic, generally accepted stylistic conventions of American English, abbreviations and pronunciation guides, and guidewords at the top of every page. Type size is comfortable for easy reading and extra-wide margins give the dictionary a very uncluttered appearance that is pleasing to the eye. Most libraries will want to have one or more copies of this dictionary for ready-reference as it is up to date and easy to use. It is an excellent choice for a home or student dictionary as well. [R: Choice, Jan 03, p. 789]—**Dana McDougald**

C, P

15.   **Cambridge International Dictionary of English on CD-ROM.** [CD-ROM]. New York, Cambridge University Press, 2002. Minimum system requirements: Pentium processor running at 166MHz. CD-ROM drive. Windows, 95, 98, NT4, 2000, or ME. 32MB RAM. 20MB hard disk space. SuperVGA, 16-bit color monitor (800x600 resolution). SoundBlaster-compatible sound card with speakers or headphones. Mouse. $65.00. ISBN 0-521-77575-2.

This CD-ROM version of the *Cambridge International Dictionary of English* contains approximately 50,000 definitions and 100,000 examples, including several hundred new words that were not defined in the print version.

All of the terms are defined using a controlled vocabulary of 2,000 words, making this a reasonable tool for students of English.

The dictionary can be searched or browsed for a given term. Additionally, filters allow users to limit searches to particular types of words in six broad areas: part of speech, label (e.g., American English, medical), grammar, category (e.g., idioms), frequency (from rare to very common), or related words. While the filter option is very handy, it can be confusing for first-time users.

Although this is a British dictionary, it does an excellent job of catering to an American audience. Audio clips of pronunciations are available in American and British English, and although terms are typically defined using British English, there are always links from American spellings or terms to the equivalent British versions.

There are numerous interactive features giving users the ability to annotate terms, to try out pronunciations (if the computer is equipped with a microphone), to complete exercises, and to jump from any word in the dictionary to its definition. Users can also easily look up words by clicking on the term in a word processor or Internet browser. The dictionary is easy to install and fairly easy to use. The only real problem is that the software opens up separate windows for searches and definitions. On a computer with multiple windows open, this can get very confusing.

The *Cambridge International Dictionary of English on CD-ROM* is recommended for any library serving ESL students. Although the interactivity of the CD-ROM is helpful, the print version will probably be adequate for most libraries.—**Michael Levine-Clark**

P, S

16.   **The Encyclopedia Americana 2002.** international ed. Danbury, Conn., Grolier, 2002. 30v. illus. maps. index. $1,049.00/set. ISBN 0-7172-0135-X.

Encyclopedia Americana has been a well-respected resource for academics for more than 173 years. This edition marks the sets 67th consecutive revision. After reading the set's preface as well as a review of the 2000 edition (see ARBA 2001, entry 24), it is easy to see that only moderate updates and no expansive revisions have been made to this latest edition.

Hundreds of experts have contributed to this encyclopedia over the years, which boast 45,000 entries to date. The entries are both authoritative and objective and it is obvious there is collaboration between the editors and the experts as the reviews are written in an easy-to-understand language. Articles that have been updated by the editors of the publication have an asterisk by the author's name. After a brief preface, an extensive list of contributors, and a key to pronunciation and abbreviations, the entries are arranged in alphabetic order. The longer, more extensive entries provide a table of contents; for example, the entry on Africa is divided by geography, the economy, the people, the arts, and history. Many entries also provide cross-references to related articles (either within the article or at the end) and a bibliography listing resources for further research. A glossary of terms accompanies some of the more technical articles (e.g., electricity, stock exchange). There are thousands of black-and-white and color illustrations, photographs, and maps sprinkled throughout the volumes. Although the illustrations are not as extravagant as in other notable encyclopedias such as *World Book Encyclopedia* (see ARBA 2003, entry 41), they do add significantly to the text.

This resource will continue to be a significant tool at the reference desk of academic and public libraries. Available in both print and electronic form (see ARBA 2002, entry 29) libraries will have their choice of how to retrieve its information.—**Shannon Graff Hysell**

P, S

17.   **Encyclopedia Americana. http://www.go.grolier.com.** [Website]. Bethel, Conn., Grolier Educational. Price negotiated by site. Date reviewed: Aug 02.

This new online edition of the well-respected *Encyclopedia Americana* is exceptionally easy to use and provides a wealth of information at the fingertips of the user. One of six online publications currently available from Grolier and Scholastic Library Publishing, this resource provides 45,000 articles written by more than 6,000 contributors. Many of these articles link directly into OCLC's WorldCat bibliographic database—up to 25 bibliographic citations per entry. This resource also gives users access to journal articles from the *Americana Journal*. About 250 articles are added weekly and many include photographs from the Associated Press.

Users can either browse the encyclopedia or they can search for specific topics either by article or journal. Users are first given the option to browse by specific subject (e.g., arts, society, geography, history), editors' pick (specific articles or Websites that the editors have found to be particularly useful or newsworthy), journal articles (which links to features stories or online news), and profiles (biographical portraits of 1,500 of *Encyclopedia Americana*'s most frequently searched people). For those needing to narrow their search, an advanced search option is also available.

Added features of this resource include cross-references and links to related articles, bibliographic citations to print and online resources, relevant periodical literature (access to the full text of more than 1,000 periodical articles from EBSCO), and a teacher's guide and student's guide for those articles found in *Americana Journal*. The teacher's guide and student's guide will be useful for those teaching at the high school level. The teacher can take one of the featured articles (or one of those in the archives) and have access to an introduction they can give their class, articles they can assign, activities they can assign, and lists of useful vocabulary. By using this as a teaching tool, one's students will not only learn more about current events but about the history behind them, how to research online and in printed volumes, and critical thinking skills.

Beginning with this online edition of *Encyclopedia Americana* Grolier is in the process of making this resource compliant with the rules of the Americans with Disabilities Act. They have provided a text-only version of this product, which includes all of the photographs, illustrations, maps, and flags, but excludes video and sound files. They are in the process of providing narration for video and animated content.

This encyclopedia will be well received in all high school, undergraduate, and some graduate libraries. It is easy to use and provides an incredible amount of information from credible sources. Those who can afford it should seriously consider its purchase.—**Shannon Graff Hysell**

P, S

18.   **Grolier Multimedia Encyclopedia 2002.** deluxe ed. [CD-ROM]. New York, Scholastic, 2002. Minimum system requirements: Pentium 100 or higher processor. Double-speed CD-ROM drive. Windows 95, Windows 98, Windows 2000, Me, XP, NT 4.0, or later. 16MB RAM, 25MB hard disk space. 16-bit color (640 x 480 resolution). 16-bit stereo Sound Blaster compatible card and speakers. Apple QuickTime 4.0 or higher. Direct X version 3.0 or higher. Mouse or compatible pointing device. $29.95. ISBN 0-439-35767-5.

The reasonable price of this two-disk CD-ROM set is only one of the attractive features of the 2002 edition of the *Grolier Multimedia Encyclopedia*. Unlike many other electronic databases, the set displays easy and intuitive navigation. Boasting material suitable for three reading levels, it is an effective reference resource for all age groups. The search system supports Boolean searching and is heavily cross-referenced. In the individual articles highlighted blue words lead the reader to further materials in related subjects. Many of the articles link to online resources selected particularly for research on the subject in question as well as articles in the *Encyclopedia Americana* (2002 ed.; see entry 16) and *The New Book of Knowledge* (2000 ed.; see ARBA 2001, entry 26). "Ballet," for example, has five Internet sites linked to the article.

The multimedia is excellent, boasting still pictures, videos, and sound clips. All the media ran well, except for the Jesse Owens video, which performed an illegal operation. Particularly fascinating are the cutaways. For example, the cutaway of the White House shows the interior of the building a floor at a time. The accompanying teacher's guide crosses the curriculum in providing activities and projects developed for the three grade levels. Unfortunately, the manual is a looseleaf binder with poorly punched pages. It will not stand up to regular use without some reinforcing.

The encyclopedia is updated on the Internet regularly. A cursory check of the "Ballet" articles showed no major changes. There is an alphabetic listing entitled "New Articles," which is material that apparently did not make it onto the CD-ROM. All in all, this is an excellent multimedia encyclopedia and is recommended for purchase for public and school libraries.—**Nancy P. Reed**

C

19.   **Oxford Reference Online. http://www.oxfordreference.com.** [Website]. New York, Oxford University Press. Price negotiated by site. Date reviewed: Jan 03.

This new site from Oxford University Press, launched in the Spring of 2002, provides users with information from 100 of their most successful titles. By 2004, some 30 new and updated titles will be added to this resource. The site provides access to over 1.5 million entries, with topics ranging from general reference, architecture, medicine, mythology, politics, the social sciences, and many more. Users can search for specific topics, quotations, or from one of Oxford's many bilingual dictionaries.

Users can search the database in a variety of ways. If one has a specific term they would like to research the easiest search is the "Quick Search." An "Advanced Search" is available for those needing to narrow the results. With the "Advanced Search" users can use the option of an "extended search" (finds plurals, derivatives), "Boolean," or "Spell-check Search" (which finds results with closely related spellings). Users can search by subject: Oxford has provided 23 subjects on the introductory page (e.g., Economics & Business, Biological Sciences, Law, Quotations). Users can also search within one of the 100 titles provided. Search results are automatically ranked by relevance (although users can select to have results organized by subject, title, or alphabetically), and for each the source book and subject are noted. Each entry provides cross-references to related terms; users need only click on the entry to go to that term.

This site provides the researcher with many simple ways to search the site. The layout is easy to navigate, with a simple design and no advertisements. All service buttons—information on how to cite the book, abbreviations, and acknowledgements—are conveniently found at the top of the screen and "Help" buttons are readily available. *Oxford Reference Online* has been a much-anticipated online resource, which has been well worth the wait. This site is highly recommended for academic and public libraries of all sizes.—**Shannon Graff Hysell**

C, P

20.   **The Oxford World English Dictionary Shelf on CD-ROM.** [CD-ROM]. New York, Oxford University Press, 2002. Minimum system requirements: PC Pentium-class processor with 166MHz. CD-ROM drive. Windows 95, Windows 98, Windows NT4.0. 64MB RAM. 80MB hard disk space. SVGA monitor with 16-bit color. Internet access. $99.95. ISBN 0-19-860445-9.

This new CD-ROM includes the text of four separate Oxford dictionaries: *The New Oxford Dictionary of English, The New Oxford American Dictionary, The Australian Oxford Dictionary,* and *The Canadian Oxford Dictionary*. The CD-ROM comes with a short explanatory booklet, which unfortunately contains no information at all about the contents of each dictionary. The CD-ROM is installed on the hard drive, and one need not insert the CD-ROM again after the first installation. To install the tool, the user must type in a unique registration number in the menu that pops up automatically when the CD-ROM is inserted. The number is provided on a card that comes inside the CD-ROM case. Windows 95 or better is required for this installation, along with 64MB of RAM and 80MB of free hard disk space.

Along with the dictionaries, this CD-ROM includes "iFinger" software, which is also installed automatically on the user's computer, and remains as an icon on the Windows taskbar unless put into "sleep mode," or until the software is uninstalled. This software enables the user to type in a word at any time and receive back separate definition screens from each of the four dictionaries, or from as many as have defined the word. The iFinger software also allows the user to double-click on words or highlight them with the mouse, and obtain definitions that way also, either in Windows text documents or in Web pages. One can choose to register with iFinger by filling out a form and transmitting it; this will bring the user information about software updates and other product information.

These four dictionaries are not clones of each other. For instance, searching on the word "Oxford" reveals that *The New Oxford Dictionary of English* cites the city in central England (as do the three other dictionaries), with a 1991 population of 109,000; whereas *The Canadian Oxford Dictionary* gives the same location information but states that the 1991 population was 132,000. *The New Oxford Dictionary of English* also cites "Oxford" as "a type of lace-up shoe with a low heel," while *The Canadian Oxford Dictionary* defines it as "a low, sturdy shoe laced over the instep." *The Australian Oxford Dictionary* is the only one of the four that does not offer a definition for the oxford shoe. *The New Oxford American Dictionary* is the only one of the four to offer a third definition for "Oxford": "a heavy cotton cloth chiefly used to make shirts."

Looking up the word "dictionary" reveals that all four dictionaries offer the same basic definition, but *The New Oxford Dictionary of English* and *The New Oxford American Dictionary* offer the phrase "have swallowed a dictionary," which means to "use long and obscure words when speaking." However, the prize-winner for "dictionary" is *The Australian Oxford Dictionary*, which omits "have swallowed a dictionary," but which is the only one of the four to include a 52-line history of dictionaries, starting with Greek glossaries of the first century, and ending with *The Australian National Dictionary* of 1988. It would be desirable in future iterations of this tool to offer one conflated entry that could include all the elements present in one or the other of the different tools, perhaps with an indication where the entry is specific to a geographic area.

The software is sophisticated enough to take different forms of a word and bring one to the base form (e.g., typing in or clicking on "haikus" will take you to "haiku"). The searches are not case-, punctuation-, or accent-sensitive. It is possible to copy or print dictionary entries. There is also a utility with which one can add words to the dictionary, or edit it.

Various Websites exist that provide free access to one dictionary or another. Overall, however, this is a reasonably priced, easy-to-use tool that provides the user with simultaneous access to several current and reliable abridged dictionaries that will reside right on the user's computer until they decide otherwise.—**Bill Miller**

DIRECTORIES

C, P

21.   **Directories in Print: A Descriptive Guide to Print and Non-Print Directories, Buyer's Guides, Rosters and Other Address Lists of All Kinds.** 21st ed. Terrance W. Peck, ed. Farmington Hills, Mich., Gale, 2002. 2v. index. $545.00/set. ISBN 0-7876-5314-4. ISSN 0899-353X.

Directories in Print (DIP) lists 15,740 publications from around the world, grouped into 26 broad categories. The indexes (alternate formats, subject, and title and keyword) help guide users to the directories that will be of interest to them. As the name implies, the directories are primarily ones in print, but when a directory appears in more than one format or has accompanying material in a different format, this is noted. There are also listings for directories that are published only online. Each listing includes a brief description, scope, and publication information. Information is also provided on defunct and out-of-print directories and on some publications that do not contain directory-type information but may be thought of as directories. DIP is kept up-to-date by supplements and is available in various electronic formats (with similar Gale publications included). Its citation as an "Outstanding Reference Source" by the American Library Association is well deserved.—**Michael S. Borries**

C, P

22.   **Headquarters USA 2003: A Directory of Contact Information for Headquarters and Other Central Offices of Major Businesses & Organizations in the United States and Canada.** 25th ed. Jennifer C. Perkins, ed. Detroit, Omnigraphics, 2002. 2v. index. $175.00/set. ISBN 0-7808-0459-7. ISSN 1531-2909.

Formerly published under the titles *National Directory of Addresses and Telephone Numbers* and then the *Business Phone Book USA*, this edition contains more than 119,000 listings on 2,485 pages. Arranged much like a telephone directory, it is easy to use. Volume 1 is an alphabetic listing of organization names, and volume 2 is a listing by subject. The title covers a great variety of businesses and organizations in the United States and Canada. For-profit businesses, nonprofit organizations, government agencies and offices, colleges and universities, libraries, publications (such as magazines, newsletters, and newspapers), military bases, political organizations, sports organizations, television programs, Internet resources, and more than 4,000 high-profile people can be accessed through this work. Contact information includes a mailing address, telephone number, fax number, toll-free number, Web address, and stock symbols for each organization listed.

Research and verification are ongoing. Published criteria for inclusion are scattered throughout the subject volume. Selection criteria include industry rankings from lists compiled by associations and found in business publications. Most ranking schemes are based on annual sales. Other criteria are used for other listings. For example, libraries are chosen on the basis of population (public libraries) or by volumes owned.

Special features offered by this work are a U.S. map showing time zones and various charts and tables listing abbreviations, area codes, and conglomerates. The index contains useful *see* and *see also* references. Several online or print sources would have to be consulted for the information found in this one reference set.—**Lois Gilmer**

C, P, S

23.   **iTools. http://www.itools.com.** [Website]. Free. Date reviewed: Oct 02.

Formerly known as *Research It!* and *Find It!*, *iTools* is a quick ready-reference resource that will provide users with access to a plethora of information right at their fingertips. The site is organized into six basic categories: Search Tools, Language Tools, Research Tools, Financial Tools, Map Tools, and Internet Tools. By using "Search Tools" one has access to search engines, subject directories, and personal and business phone directories. "Language Tools" gives users access to dictionaries (e.g., *Merriam-Webster's*, *Cambridge International Dictionary*), thesauri, and foreign-language translations. "Research Tools" allows users to access encyclopedias, newspaper and journal articles, biographies, and quotations. "Financial Tools" will convert currency, while "Map Tools" gives directions between two locations and provides topographical maps. Finally, "Internet Tools" gives users access to search networking, html, and Web sources. This source provides a lot of information that will be helpful at a busy reference desk.—**Shannon Graff Hysell**

GOVERNMENT PUBLICATIONS

C, P

24. **Guide to U.S. Government Publications.** 2002 ed. Donna Batten, ed. Farmington Hills, Mich., Gale, 2002. 1690p. index. $360.00. ISBN 0-7876-5455-8. ISSN 0092-3168.

For more than four decades librarian John Andriot's *Guide to U.S. Government Serials & Periodicals* (1959-1972) and *Guide to U.S. Government Publications* (1973-), collectively known to documents librarians simply as "Andriot," have been standard reference sources both for researchers seeking information about current and former federal serial titles and for librarians managing federal documents collections. Recent editions, published by Gale, consistently have provided a useful overview of the Superintendent of Documents classification system; detailed agency-by-agency lists of ongoing, irregular, and past periodical publications; and essential information about changed or ceased titles, Government Printing Office depository program item numbers, and altered classification numbers. The valuable Agency Class Chronology yields Superintendent of Documents classification numbers presently or formerly assigned to particular agencies. Librarians and library patrons alike appreciate the more than 36,000 entries in the massive agency, title, and keyword and title indexes.

Larger federal depository libraries will need to purchase the *Guide* annually. Given its cost, smaller depository libraries and nondepository libraries may choose to purchase it less frequently. Although the *Guide* includes electronic documents, all users will need to supplement its contents with data available on selected university and federal documents Websites, most notably the Federal Depository Library Program (FDLP) Desktop at http://www.access.gpo.gov/su_docs/fdlp/. [R: Choice, April 02, p. 1388]—**Julienne L. Wood**

HANDBOOKS AND YEARBOOKS

C, P

25. **The Essential Desk Reference.** New York, Oxford University Press, 2002. 815p. illus. maps. index. $30.00. ISBN 0-19-512873-7.

This ready-reference volume of facts and lists is claimed by the editors to be a universe of information not found in any other book or resource. It certainly does contain a lot of lists and quick information on numerous subjects, and seems to be quite authoritative, but whether it has more information than, say, the *New York Public Library Desk Reference* (3d ed.; see ARBA 2000, entry 47) or even *Information Please Almanac, Atlas, & Yearbook* (49th ed.; see ARBA 97, entry 6) or the *World Almanac and Book of Facts* (2001 ed.; see ARBA 2002, entry 5) remains to be seen.

That said, the Oxford folks have put together a handy quick information book. It contains facts, concepts, terms, lists, timelines, diagrams, topical overviews, and follow-up bibliographies. The subject-based table of contents, with detailed subheadings, allows a reader to get to any section of the book easily, facilitating browsing. In fact, the browsing capacity of this book is half the fun. One thing does lead to another and soon the reader has discovered informative facts hitherto unknown. The comprehensive index helps readers find specific facts quickly and efficiently.

The frequent question with all reference books nowadays is are they needed? Does the Internet provide the information just as readily? In fact, virtually all the bibliographic citations following the entries in this book are Websites. Is there convenience in a handheld book? Is a Google-type search too vast and vague? Has book information been screened for reliability? *The Essential Desk Reference* does respond to such questions and makes a strong case for its purchase. The indexing here is excellent, the choice of topics is thorough, and the data have been authenticated by experts. The issue of outdatedness has long been a concern with paper reference sources, but the supplied Websites not only offer opportunities for further study, but make any fact easy to update or verify. Best of all, the $30 price of *The Essential Desk Reference* makes it highly affordable for libraries, schools, and homes. It is recommended for all types of libraries. [R: LJ, 1 Sept 02, pp. 164-166; SLJ, Nov 02, p. 100]

—**Paul A. Mogren**

MUSEUMS

C, P

26.	**The Official Museum Directory 2002.** 32d ed. New Providence, N.J., National Register, 2001. 2v. index. $259.00pa./set. ISBN 0-87217-906-0. ISSN 0090-6700.

The 32d edition of *The Official Museum Directory* is a 2-volume work containing listings on more than 8,100 museums operating in 87 different fields, ranging from science museums to zoos to historic homes to fine arts. It is one of the most trusted and accessible sources for museum professionals to identify vendors, access unique collections and exhibitions, and contact directors and curators. Volume 1 lists institutions by state, and contains a number of indexes: an alphabetic index to institutions, an index to personnel, an index to institutions by category, an index to institutions by collection, and new listings. Volume 2 is a guide to more than 2,100 vendors, their products, and their services, subdivided by category. An alphabetic index to vendors is provided at the beginning of this volume, as well as page numbers to their listings.

This product is one of the most useful and up-to-date reference works in the area of museums, especially in relation to current personnel and exhibitions. The continual publication and updating of this book is a tribute to its popularity and trustworthiness.—**Bradford Lee Eden**

PERIODICALS
AND SERIALS

C, P, S

27.	**MasterFILE Premier. http://search.epnet.com.** [Website]. Birmingham, AL, EBSCO Publishing. Price negotiated by site. Date reviewed: Mar 02.

MasterFILE Premier is a database of 1,890 periodicals covering a multitude of subjects, such as general reference, business, consumer health, science, and much more. In addition to the full text of the 1,890 periodicals, indexing and abstracts to more than 2,500 periodicals is provided as well. The full text files go back as far as January 1990 and the indexing and abstracts go as far back as January 1984. Users can search for words or terms in the entire database, with the option of using Boolean operators, or they can limit their search to full text entries, specific publications, or periodicals published during a specific date. A "Subject Search" function allows users to search for entries that cover specific topics. Users can also browse for terms in all of the subject listings or under "People," "Products & Books," "Companies," or "Subjects" categories. Unfortunately, only one listing can be selected at a time. So if users want to view articles under more than one listing they will have to go back and forth between the pages. This drawback, of course, can be time consuming, especially if the user has a slower Internet connection.

The "Dictionary Search" provides dictionary-type information (syllable breakdowns, parts of speech, and definitions) while also providing connections to entries with that term. Unlike the "Subject Search," the "Dictionary Search" does allow users to select more than one term. In the "Publication Search" page, periodical titles can be searched with "Beginning With," "Match Any Words," and "Match Exact Phrase" options. Articles can be viewed in text only or in a full-page image from the periodical using Adobe Acrobat. This database will be very useful to librarians, teachers, and students, but it may be difficult to navigate if the user is unfamiliar with the Internet.

—**Cari Ringelheim**

QUOTATION BOOKS

C, P

28.   **People on People: The Oxford Dictionary of Biographical Quotations.** Susan Ratcliffe, ed. New York, Oxford University Press, 2001. 481p. index. $35.00. ISBN 0-19-866261-0.

This interesting collection of quotations from famous people about famous people covers the gamut, from the profound to the frivolous, and has its share of invective snipes. Entries include names from history, politics, the arts, sports, literature, and pop icons. Primarily American, Canadian, and European personalities are profiled and a full range of historical periods and interest areas are given—everyone from Homer to Richard Gere. The selections provide keen insights into the individual spotlighted. For example, Sir Walter Scott, who many regard as a popular romanticist of his time, gains new respect in the eye of today's reader when we hear Jane Austen, Lord Byron, and Thomas Carlyle speak highly of his writing ability and personal character. William Hazlitt said of Scott, "His works (taken together) are almost like a new edition of human nature. This is indeed to be an author!" The editor blends serious quotes with amusing images. The notations for Charles de Gaulle include Churchill who is reported as saying "What can you do with a man who looks like a female llama surprised while bathing?" In addition to the alphabetic listing of quotes by subject name, there is an index that cross-references the originator of the observation to the observed. For example, in the author index under Alistair Cooke there are a range of comments he penned on luminaries from Greta Garbo to Dwight D. Eisenhower. This is a good resource to add spice to research on prominent figures as well just an entertaining volume to browse. [R: LJ, 15 Oct 01, p. 68; Choice, June 02, p. 1740]—**Adrienne Antink Bien**

Part II
SOCIAL SCIENCES

2 Social Sciences in General

GENERAL WORKS

Dictionaries and Encyclopedias

C, P

29. **Dictionary of the Social Sciences.** Craig Calhoun, ed. New York, Oxford University Press, 2002. 563p. $75.00. ISBN 0-19-512371-9.

While there is an abundance of dictionaries on individual social sciences, surprisingly there are few works that attempt to cover the whole spectrum. Calhoun, along with several associate editors (Joseph Karaganis and Paul Price) and 11 others listed under "Editors and Contributors," has produced a volume that covers anthropology, sociology, political science, economics, human geography, cultural studies, Marxism, and "dozens of other important fields." Basic terms, concepts, theories, schools of thought, methodologies, techniques, topics, issues, and controversies are covered in 1,800-plus entries ranging from 50 to 500 words.

The presentation is designed for general readers, the "educated lay person," students, and scholars. There are 275 biographical entries for major figures who had a "profound impact." Words appearing in an entry that are defined elsewhere in the dictionary appear in capital letters. The words defined are in English, except for cases in which the foreign word is used in English—mostly German and French words.

A 37-page bibliography is provided, which also is perhaps the least useful resource in the volume. The entries do not state the sources used, nor do the items listed in the bibliography state with which word they are associated. The reader, therefore, has an interesting list of further reading with no guidance as to what any of it relates to. This is an unfortunate situation, which renders the value of this portion of the project somewhat in doubt.

Individual entries read well, and are certainly stated in a way in which the average reader would have little trouble comprehending. By the very nature of the undertaking, space limitations restrict depth. For example, the term "survey research" is included, with what amount to *see* references to "sampling," "census," and "validity." However, the word questionnaire does not appear in the dictionary, nor do a number of significant other terms from the area of survey research. For purposes of becoming familiar with the general language of a number of disciplines, this volume is useful. For beginning-level undergraduates this book is a good starting point. For upper-level undergraduates and for graduate students, this volume will be appropriate for reading in an area of the field of major concentration. Again, for scholars this would only be valuable when reading in unfamiliar territory.

Overall, the contribution is a good current dictionary. A future volume would be rendered more valuable through the association of the works researched to the terms defined. This work is recommended for undergraduate social science programs, public libraries, and community colleges. [R: LJ, 1 Sept 02, pp. 162-164]

—**Graham R. Walden**

C, P

30.   Gallup, George, Jr. **The Gallup Poll: Public Opinion 2001.** Wilmington, Del., Scholarly Resources, 2002. 316p. index. $90.00. ISBN 0-8420-5001-9. ISSN 0195-962X.

People have been counting on the Gallup Poll as a measuring device for public opinion since 1935. In that time, there have been 26 volumes in this ongoing project, which has published the results of nearly 10,000 survey reports. The latest edition is George Gallup Jr.'s *The Gallup Poll: Public Opinion 2001*. As in past editions, this volume documents public opinion in five distinct areas: response to major news events, support for political parties and candidates, attitudes concerning issues in society, changing lifestyle in trends, and the overall public mood. Suggestions for poll questions come from a variety of sources, such as the media, newspapers, politicians, and university professors.

Prior to the actual poll questions there are four short sections geared to help the reader. The first section, titled "The Sample," describes the design of the sample questions for telephone and personal surveys. Polls usually consist of approximately 1,000 interviews. Weighing procedures and sampling tolerances are also considered in connection with sampling error. The remaining three sections include Gallup Poll accuracy record for presidential elections since 1936, a chronology of specific events from December 16, 2000 until December 13, 2001, and a listing of Gallop regions. The poll questions are arranged chronologically with date of interview followed by source of question, survey number, question, poll results, and a lengthy analysis of the results. The book concludes with a general index.

Many of the questions are appropriate and interesting to the average citizen. This edition in particular focuses on questions concerning the war on terrorism. Of all the polling systems around today, the Gallup Poll may be the most famous, and with the level of acceptance on scientifically based opinion polls on the rise, most libraries will probably have this series in their reference collections, making the purchase of this new edition mandatory.

—**Richard Slapsys**

3 Area Studies

GENERAL WORKS

C, P, S

31.   **E-Conflict World Encyclopedia. http://www.countryreports.org.** [Website]. Free. Date reviewed: Aug 02.

This Website provides facts on all of the countries of the world based on information provided from the International and Pan-American Conventions. The homepage offers a drop-down menu for all of the countries. Users can click on the country they would like to learn more about and are taken to a page containing a map (with surrounding countries) and links to information on the country's economy, defense, geography, government, and people. Also provided are links to the countries national anthem (with purchasing information) and a page containing relevant links containing information on the same country. Weather information for the day and the exchange rate in U.S. dollars are also supplied. Researchers can also perform a subject search on this site. For example, this reviewer entered the keyword "castles" and was given two additional sites: one to the Slovakia national anthem, and the second to the flag of Gibraltar, which features a castle.

This site will be popular with both tourists and middle and high school students. It provides very basic almanac-type information on each country. This is not a site for in-depth information, but the links provided to other complementary sites will give more advanced statistics and history. This should be a popular site in school and public libraries.—**Shannon Graff Hysell**

UNITED STATES

General Works

S

32.   **The Blackbirch Kid's Visual Reference of the United States.** Woodbridge, Conn., Blackbirch Press, 2002. 336p. illus. maps. index. $49.94. ISBN 1-56711-659-0.

This colorful, fact-filled work will be an ideal addition to elementary and middle school libraries as well as children's reference collections in public libraries. Everyone is bound to find something of interest here as well as learn something new about their own state. The work begins with a section titled "A Look at the 50 States," which shows with illustrative maps the most and least populated states, the states and cities with the highest and lowest temperatures, the largest and smallest states, the states with the longest rivers, the states with the highest and lowest per capita incomes, and even the cities with the worst traffic. From here the book alphabetically lists each state, providing each with a four-page entry. First readers will find information on the state's nickname, population, statehood, electoral votes, and capital. It then discusses the geography, its history, and how it is today. The information is supplemented with color photographs of the city and its people, charts and maps, and sidebars with facts. After the states are discussed the work also looks at the U.S. territories of American Samoa, Guam, the Northern Mariana Islands, Puerto Rico, and the U.S. Virgin Islands. A short list of resources for further information follows, which includes books and Websites, and an index.—**Shannon Graff Hysell**

C, P

33. **City Profiles USA, 2003: A Traveler's Guide to Major US and Canadian Cities.** 6th ed. Detroit, Omnigraphics, 2003. 929p. maps. $130.00. ISBN 0-7808-1429-5. ISSN 1082-9938.

This guide provides information for travel-related services, facilities, attractions, and events for 250 cities in the United States and Canada. This helpful and useful work is organized alphabetically, with cities arranged in a state-by-state format (including nine Canadian cities). Each city has the following information: population, a brief historical description, the average temperature and precipitation, information sources (including online resources), transportation services, accommodations, restaurants, shopping, media (publications, television, and radio), colleges and universities, hospitals, attractions (including sports teams), and major events (with dates). Contact information is present, which includes addresses, telephone numbers, and sometimes fax and toll-free numbers; where applicable, World Wide Web addresses are provided. All cities have a description and basic informational facts: population, county, latitude and longitude, area codes, time zones, elevation, and area in land and water (in square miles). Climate information is also presented, including temperature average highs and lows per month and the average precipitation in inches per month.

Several special features are included along with the table of contents and the abbreviation codes. They include area codes in both geographic and numerical order, airlines, airports in code order and city order, AAA offices, business services, car rental agencies, convention centers and visitor information, hotel information, mileage tables, weather information, maps, and a calendar of events. This well-done work is especially useful for those needing contact information on any one of the 250 profiled cities. It should be included in all types and levels of libraries. It is informative, easy to use, and well written.—**Scott R. DiMarco**

New York

C, P

34. Kroessler, Jeffrey A. **New York Year by Year: A Chronology of the Great Metropolis.** New York, New York University Press, 2002. 367p. illus. index. $55.00; $19.95. ISBN 0-8147-4750-7; 0-8147-4751-5pa.

Kroessler, a specialist in New York City local history and historic preservation, has prepared a chronology of the Big Apple from 1524 to 2001, although the bulk of the volume pertains to the twentieth century. The text is enhanced throughout by black-and-white illustrations and photographs, many of them from the often-overlooked Queens Borough Public Library's Long Island Division (which holds the photograph morgue of the old *New York Herald-Tribune*). The entries are well written and cover a broad range of topics, including political, social, and cultural, and the reader often cannot help but utter, "I didn't know that." Some entries, however, lack the detail that one hopes for in a reference work; for example, some researchers might not be content to know that St. George's Episcopal Church in Flushing was dedicated in 1854 when no mention of the month or date is given. On the other hand, the fact that the author avoided a strict timeline approach, which can often be repetitive and tedious for the reader, has resulted in a book that is fascinating to both read and browse through, and which should therefore also appeal to a popular audience. The index is not very detailed, however, and there is no bibliography. Most young adults should be well served by the similarly arranged *A Short and Remarkable History of New York City* by Jane Mushabac and Angela Wigan (Fordham University Press, 1999), which contains illustrations from the Museum of the City of New York, while Kroessler's volume is best suited for adults and college students. The trade paperback price is quite a bargain.—**John A. Drobnicki**

AFRICA

C

35. **World Bank Africa Database 2002.** [CD-ROM]. Herndon, Va., World Bank, 2002. Minimum system requirements: IBM-compatible Pentium computer. CD-ROM reader (ISO 9660). Windows 95, Windows 98, Windows 2000, or WinNT 4.X. Excel 97 (or higher). 12MB RAM. 12MB hard disk space. 64K color display recommended. $95.00 (single user); $190.00 (multiple users). ISBN 0-8213-5059-5.

This latest edition of a valuable World Bank statistical product initiated in 1999 offers 1,154 indicators of social and macroeconomic data covering 53 African countries with populations over 1 million and 20 regional and local groupings. Time series data depth has been expanded over previous editions to cover the period from 1965 to 2000, presented in two component tables. "Country at a Glance" (also accessible via country outlines on the global "Map" option) presents two pages of summary data tracing key trends in economic and social development. "African Development Indicators 2002" offers all tables available in the print versions, although the title is somewhat inaccurate, as the general cut-off date for the CD-ROM was November 2001. Factors can be correlated to produce spreadsheets, which can then be saved or exported. Logical organization, clearly written headings, and ample prefaces to each section significantly aid users. Issuing these data sets in compact disk form guarantees wider accessibility of multifaceted baseline information. This resource is recommended for college, university, and large public library networks.—**Robert B. Marks Ridinger**

ANTARCTICA AND
THE POLAR REGIONS

C, P

36.   **Encyclopedia of Antarctica and the Southern Oceans.** B. Stonehouse, ed. New York, John Wiley, 2002. 391p. illus. maps. $350.00. ISBN 0-471-98665-8.

This is an excellent and comprehensive encyclopedia of the coldest and remote regions on earth. The volume was first thought of 15 years ago and took over 5 years to compile. The editor, based at the Scott Polar Research Institute at Cambridge, had an especially difficult time because of communication difficulties with a number of the contributors who spent large amounts of time in the Antarctic. On the other hand, their location gave them first-hand knowledge of the area they were writing about. Some 27 individuals contributed to the encyclopedia; however, the bulk of the articles are unsigned. The volume is arranged in the standard encyclopedia format followed by five appendixes, eight "study guides," a bibliography, and an A-Z index of entries. The appendixes cover: "Agreed Measures for the Conservation of Antarctic Fauna and Flora;" "Convention for the Conservation of Antarctic Seals"; "Convention on the Conservation of Antarctic Marine Living Resources"; "Protocol on Environmental Protection to the Antarctic Treaty"; and "Text of the Antarctic Treaty." "Study guides" are included for: "Climate and Life," "Exploration," "Geography," "Geology and Glaciology," "Information Sciences," "National Interests in Antarctica," "Protected Areas under the Antarctic Treaty," and "Southern Oceans and Islands."

The volume is attractive and easy to read and is illustrated with black-and-white maps and photographs. There is a large color fold-out map of Antarctica and the Southern Oceans. The bibliography, called "Further Readings," is very good. The "study guides" are essays that enable one to locate articles in the encyclopedia on the study guide topic. There are some minor inconsistencies in the literal A-Z index, which lists every entry including cross-references. This means, for instance, that when one looks in the index under "Belgrano II Station" instead of referring the reader to the article on the General Belgrano Station on page 112, they are referred to the cross-reference on the Belgrano II Station on page 26 where they are then sent to the correct page. The binding is very attractive and colorful, but seems a little loose. This is largely due to the heavy text block being attached by too light end pages. The encyclopedia is "printed on acid-free paper responsibly manufactured from sustainable forestry in which at least two trees are planted for each one used for paper production," according to the verso of the title page.

This is a very attractive volume that most libraries will want to own for their general reference collections. Alas, it is $350, but it is money well spent.—**Ralph Lee Scott**

ASIA

China

C, P

37.   **The New Cambridge Handbook of Contemporary China.** By Colin Mackerras. New York, Cambridge University Press, 2001. 313p. illus. maps. index. $59.95; $24.95pa. ISBN 0-521-78143-4; 0-521-78674-6pa.

Focusing on the events of the 1990s, *The New Cambridge Handbook of Contemporary China* is completely revised and updated from its earlier version which emphasized the 1980s (see ARBA 92, entry 94, for a review). The book begins with a chronology of significant events from 1949 to 2000, followed by chapters on politics and law, eminent contemporary figures, a bibliography, foreign relations, economy, population, gazetteer, minority nationalities, and education. The "Eminent Contemporary Figures" chapter provides brief biographies of 106 figures who were influential in the People's Republic of China (PRC) during the 1990s. The chapter titled "Bibliography" contains more than 200 classified and annotated titles of mostly English-language materials published since 1990, including reference books, scholarly journals, newspapers, and Websites relevant to the scope of this volume. An alphabetic listing of countries with diplomatic relations with the PRC is offered in the "Foreign Relations" section. Dozens of helpful tables, figures, and maps are used to illustrate information pertinent to each chapter. Unfortunately, the chapter on culture and society, one of the best chapters from the earlier volume, is omitted entirely in this edition. With the return of Hong Kong and Macau to China in the late 1990s, both places are still excluded for reasons of manageability. A comprehensive index completes the volume. Pinyin is used throughout. There are inconsistencies in providing names in Wade-Giles and pinyin and cross-referencing in the index section. Some names have Wade-Giles romanization with references provided to their pinyin forms and vice versa while others do not. Nonetheless, this is a useful handbook for quick reference on contemporary China. It is suitable for the general public as well as academic libraries.—**Karen T. Wei**

Korea

C, P, S

38.   Connor, Mary E. **The Koreas: A Global Studies Handbook.** Santa Barbara, Calif., ABC-CLIO, 2002. 305p. illus. maps. index. (Global Studies, Asia). $55.00. ISBN 1-57607-277-0.

This well-researched and well-written introductory book on North and South Korea is intended for general readers who are not specialists on Asia in general and on Korea in particular, but who would like to gain a general knowledge of the two divided Korean nations. The four chapters in part 1 cover such topics as geography and history, economic development since 1945, political development since 1945, and contemporary culture and social problems. Part 2 includes many useful reference materials, such as a chronological table; a section on significant people, food, and etiquette; a list of organizations; an annotated bibliography of recommended works on Korea; and an index. In addition to the recommended books, journals, and literature, the annotated bibliography also includes relevant Websites, CD-ROMs, films, and videos. Because of the richness of reference materials covered in part 2, this handbook on the Koreas can also serve as a quick reference tool for public and school libraries and for general area studies collections in academic and special libraries.—**Hwa-Wei Lee**

AUSTRALIA AND THE PACIFIC AREA

C, P

39.   **The Pacific Islands: An Encyclopedia.** Brij V. Lal and Kate Fortune, eds. Honolulu, University of Hawaii Press, 2000. 664p. illus. index. $115.00 (w/CD-ROM). ISBN 0-8248-2265-X.

This impressive work is the outcome of nearly a decade's work, with entries from more than 200 contributors in various countries, but chiefly within Australia. Assembled at the Australian National University in Canberra, it testifies to the efficiency with which Australia has assumed its natural place as the center for Pacific Island studies, by reason of its geography, population, and educational and financial resources.

The encyclopedia contains much useful and accurate information on the major aspects of Pacific Island life, including the physical environment, the various peoples, the history of settlement and European contacts, the languages and religions, politics, economy, society, and culture. The focus is on the three traditional cultural groups—Melanesian, Polynesian, and Micronesian—but there is a discernible bias in favor of island groups where English is spoken; French Polynesia (especially the Marquesas) and New Caledonia get rather short shrift. The entries are arranged thematically (not alphabetically as in most encyclopedias) in a series of chapters. This arrangement, with so much material to include, can be awkward at times; the extensive subject index is likely to be more useful in the long run. The chapter on history is the most immediately interesting and informative, especially in its account of the effect of World War II on the islands. The volume is accompanied by a CD-ROM that supplements the text and includes a help guide. It contains a map library in Adobe Illustrator format.

—**John B. Beston**

EUROPE

General Works

P, S

40.   **Peoples of Europe.** Tarrytown, N.Y., Marshall Cavendish, 2003. 11v. illus. maps. index. $329.95/set. ISBN 0-7614-7378-5.

These volumes are targeted at the middle school level and describe the 44 European nations, including how they are different and how they are similar. The profiles introduce each country by highlighting its geography, history, religions, and life-style information (language, health conditions, cuisine, family life, the arts, music, and social customs). The narrative also describes the nation's current political situation. Each chapter has a gazetteer of demographic statistics, major cities, languages, currency, and so on. A useful feature is the historical timeline covering major events in each country's history. Although the sections are short, as appropriate to the target audience, a substantive amount of information is provided. These sketches portray the individual flavor of each country and its impact on life today. For example, the reader learns that in the 1500s the Italians invented the musical notation we still use today and that Jan Van Eyck of Belgium invented oil painting in the 1400s.

Each volume has a glossary and a bibliography for further reading for each country. The set concludes with a general index as well as specialized indexes by biographical names, geography, arts, music, festivals, food, people and culture, religions, and sports. There is also a pronunciation guide and a list of National Days.

This is a useful reference to whet the appetite of young students of European history and instill an appreciation for the many contributions these countries have made to the world's culture.—**Adrienne Antink Bien**

Ireland

C, P

41.   Dunn, Seamus, and Helen Dawson. **An Alphabetical Listing of Word, Name, and Place in Northern Ireland and the Living Language of Conflict.** Lewiston, N.Y., Edwin Mellen Press, 2000. 309p. (Symposium Series, v.57). $99.95. ISBN 0-7734-7711-X.

An Alphabetical Listing of Word, Name, and Place in Northern Ireland and the Living Language of Conflict is a subject dictionary of personalities, institutions, significant dates, and lore and language of "the Troubles," as the Northern Ireland conflict of the last 30 and more years is known. It is a veritable ready-reference work for those new to the study of Northern Ireland in the late twentieth century and for comparatively knowledgeable journalists, historians, social scientists, news junkies, and interested others. The authors, Dunn and Dawson, work at the Centre for the Study of Conflict at the University of Ulster, the foremost think tank on the island of Ireland devoted to study of the Troubles. Dunn is author, co-author, or editor of at least 17 publications primarily dealing with education and the conflict in Northern Ireland as well as works about politics, criminal justice, and ethnic minorities in Northern Ireland. Dawson is a frequent collaborator with him; it is difficult to know in this and other works exactly what her contribution has been. They are both among the most respected and objective experts on the Troubles in Northern Ireland according to the author of the foreword, Vice-Chancellor of the University of Ulster.

A comparable work, *Northern Ireland: A Chronology of the Troubles 1968-1999*, by Paul Bew and Gordon Gillespie, was reviewed in ARBA 2001, entry 450. The work under review is a dictionary with entries from a few lines to a page or so in length. Thus, the two books complement each other. The purpose of the work is to provide a detailed, comprehensive list of the language of the conflict as it is used in the everyday speech of the community. It will be a great help to students trying to do research papers who must quickly grasp the topic from reading books, periodical articles, and newspaper stories on the Internet that are full of personal names, organization names, places, and unfamiliar concepts. The entries are written by the authors. There are four pages of unannotated, bibliographic references at the end of the book, published from the 1970s to the 1990s, which will be useful to those using the dictionary as well as for library collection development. The work has no maps or other graphics.—**Agnes H. Widder**

MIDDLE EAST

C, P, S
42.   Asante, Molefi Kete. **Culture and Customs of Egypt.** Westport, Conn., Greenwood Press, 2002. 168p. illus. index. (Culture and Customs of Africa). $44.95. ISBN 0-313-31740-2.

Molefi Kete Asante, a professor in the department of African American Studies at Temple University, has authored more than 50 books, including *The Egyptian Philosophers* (African American Images, 2000). This book on Egypt is a fine addition to Greenwood Press's Culture and Customs of Africa series.

The work is divided into seven well-developed chapters. They include: land, people, and a historical overview; government, economy, education, and tourism; religion and worldview; architecture and art; social customs and lifestyles; the media and cinema; and literature, the performing arts, and music. These chapters address all relevant areas and provide the reader with a well-rounded picture of the culture and customs of Egypt. Chapter 4, "Architecture and Art," serves as a typical example of what to expect. Architecture from the days of the pyramid through the physical expressions of Islamic art to present day are represented. "Fine Arts" is next, then "Cairo Museums," "National Galleries," "Key Artists," "Graphic Arts," and finally, "Textiles and Fashion."

Toyin Falola gives the series foreword. A very useful chronology that ranges from 639 C.E. to the present is included. This work also has a glossary, a fine bibliography, and a useful index. In addition, numerous black-and-white photographs contribute to the highlighted points.

This work will be of considerable help to students interested in both ancient and modern Egypt. It is able to give the reader a unique view into everyday life and the rich cultural heritage of the people of Egypt. It should be included in all libraries at all levels.—**Scott R. DiMarco**

C, P
43.   Goldscheider, Calvin. **Cultures in Conflict: The Arab-Israeli Conflict.** Westport, Conn., Greenwood Press, 2002. 228p. index. $45.00. ISBN 0-313-30722-9.

Goldscheider's volume provides an overview of the conflict between Israelis and Arabs. Concentrating on various issues, the author shows how the two are often widely divergent in their viewpoints and how this contributes to the conflict. A dense chapter on the history of the area provides background for the reader on the beginning of the conflict. Highlighting the Jewish immigration, Arab nationalism, the establishment of the Israeli state, and the resultant wars instigated by the Arab neighbors of the new state, the reader is taken through years of history that contribute pivotal information on the conflict.

Goldscheider describes issues he believes contribute to the conflict: economic dependence of the Arabs upon Jews, lack of education and opportunity for Arabs, the population numbers and land holdings of each group, and the traditional social mores of the Arabs that prevent them from fully participating in a modern society. The author details reasons why these factors have contributed to the economic and social failure of Arabs to achieve a satisfactory lifestyle within Israel. Goldscheider neglects to mention Hamas or other terrorist activities as reasons for the continuing conflict. A check of the index reveals the lack of any in-depth mention of terrorism. Readers must ask how a balanced view of the situation in Israel can be presented without addressing the terrorist activities of Arab groups. Surely the continuing violence against Israel and Jewish citizens contributes to the conflict.

A timeline, index, annotated bibliography, and a selection of official documents aid the reader in understanding the current tensions. This work is recommended for high school and university levels. [R: VOYA, Oct 2002, p. 311]—**Karen Evans**

4 Economics and Business

GENERAL WORKS

Bibliography

C, P

44.   **Encyclopedia of Business Information Sources: A Bibliographic Guide to More Than 34,000 Citations Covering over 1,100 Subjects of Interest to Business Personnel.** 16th ed. James Woy, ed. Farmington Hills, Mich., Gale, 2002. 1177p. $355.00. ISBN 0-7876-3494-8. ISSN 0071-0210.

In its 16th edition, the *Encyclopedia of Business Information Sources* is intended to be a convenient and accessible volume for business managers and information professionals to use to locate key sources for a variety of topics. It includes references to more than 34,000 citations grouped into over 1,100 specific topics. The wealth of topics covered by the volume makes it an interesting publication. Many specific types of industries are covered, including the cheese industry, the musical instrument industry, and the greeting card industry, along with professional groups, geographic regions, government and regulatory agencies, and current issues. According to the publisher, this edition of the volume has been extensively updated.

A typical entry in the *Encyclopedia* begins with cross-references to other subject entries in the volume. Sources for an entry are then divided into broad categories of types of works, with general works listed first, followed by almanacs and yearbooks, directories, financial ratios, handbooks and manuals, Internet databases, online databases, periodicals and newsletters, statistics sources, trade and professional associations, and other sources. Other categories in entries cover abstracts and indexes, bibliographies, CD-ROM databases, encyclopedias and dictionaries, price sources, research centers, and institutes. The titles and names of individual sources, such as publications or organizations, are then listed under each category in alphabetic order. The information included with these source listings can include contact information, prices, frequency of publication, and a brief annotation. Entries are easy to use and there is also a helpful user's guide at the front of the volume, along with an outline of the contents that alphabetically lists the topics with page numbers.

The final 266 pages of the *Encyclopedia of Business Information Sources* provide an alphabetic listing of the sources cited in the volume. Sources are listed by publication or organization name, with contact information (including e-mail and Website addresses), price, updates, and a brief annotation. This section may be useful for collection development librarians selecting materials for public, academic, and special libraries that cover business, government, financial, and environmental issues. The *Encyclopedia of Business Information Sources* would be a good addition to reference collections in public, academic, and a wide variety of special libraries. It is comprehensive, well organized, attractively produced, and easy to use.—**Sara Anne Hook**

Biography

P, S

45.   Carey, Charles W., Jr. **American Inventors, Entrepreneurs, and Business Visionaries.** New York, Facts on File, 2002. 410p. illus. index. (American Biographies). $65.00. ISBN 0-8160-4559-3.

This volume contains 264 biographical entries in alphabetic order, each 800 to 1,500 words with 2 to 5 "Further Reading" sources on 280 individuals. There are 16 double entries (e.g., the Duryea Brothers, Hugh and Christie Hefner). Included are "people from all categories of American life"; some are lesser known but interesting people who made contributions in new and imaginative ways. Their contributions include a corn refining machine (1715), the octant (1731), the cotton gin (1793), a paper bag machine, steel, steel plow, automobiles, linotype and adding machines, peanut butter, AOL, Ben and Jerry's ice cream, and the disposable diaper. Included are entrepreneurs in television production (Oprah Winfrey), conglomerates, organized crime, soap, ladies' hats, prostitution, and the slave trade. Among the well-known names are Henry Flagler, Jay Gould, Pinkerton, Pullman, Vanderbilt, Westinghouse (railroads); Eastman, Land (photography); Ray Kroc (fast foods); Morgan, Hetty Green, Michael Milken (finance); du Pont, Frasch, Hall (chemicals); Case, Gates, Hollerith, Wang, Wozniak, Jobs (computers); Field, Walton, Ward (mercantile activity); and Whitney (agriculture). This fun-to-read source will add spice for economics and business classes. Appendixes include entries by 53 invention/business types and by year of invention. A 7,000-word introduction weaves most of the entries into a historical narrative and an excellent index concludes the volume.—**Richard A. Miller**

P, S

46.   **Leading American Businesses: Profiles of Major American Companies and the People Who Made Them Important.** Farmington Hills, Mich., U*X*L/Gale, 2003. 3v. illus. index. $135.00/set. ISBN 0-7876-5428-0.

Leading American Businesses: Profiles of Major American Companies and the People Who Made Them Important is intended for use by middle school students, although nothing in the volumes themselves makes that clear. The editors chose 45 of "today's most successful and influential corporations" representing "the best of the energized, creative spirit that has shaped the American economy for more than 165 years." All three volumes have the same cover, featuring pictures of Oprah Winfrey, Bill Gates, and Henry Ford. Each volume begins with the same "Words to Know" (from *acquisition* to *wholesale*) and ends with the same cumulative index. Each entry includes a narrative article about the business, relevant sidebars, and photographs, as well as a timeline.

Among the 45 businesses chosen are standard industrial giants like Boeing and General Electric and General Motors. However, the majority of the entries deal with companies like Ben & Jerry's Ice Cream, Eddie Bauer, The Gap, Inc., Levi Strauss & Company, and Dream Works SKG (Steven Spielberg's studio), no doubt chosen to pique the interest of young consumers.

While these volumes are attractive and well researched, some of the information will rapidly become outdated. As an early introduction to American capitalism and economy, *Leading American Businesses: Profiles of Major American Companies and the People Who Made Them Important* serves a useful purpose; however, the degree to which these volumes fit the interests and needs of its target readers is perhaps debatable.—**Kay O. Cornelius**

P, S

47.   Logan, Rochelle, and Julie Halverstadt. **100 Most Popular Business Leaders for Young Adults: Biographical Sketches and Professional Paths.** Westport, Conn., Libraries Unlimited/Greenwood Publishing Group, 2002. 419p. illus. index. (Profiles and Pathways Series). $60.00. ISBN 1-56308-799-5.

There are 100 popular business leaders, many of them household names, included in this biographical reference source. Successful people from television, finance, Internet start-up companies, beauty and modeling businesses, and retail are among the interesting fields covered. The inclusion of unusual entrepreneurs such as Steven Jobs, Spike Lee, Laura Ashley, Paul Newman, Eileen Ford, and Quincy Jones, as well as the more traditional names such as Bill Gates and Donald Trump indicates how useful this book is. Each businessperson's picture, career highlights, important contributions, career path, and key dates are given. Each entry also includes advice from the person, an inspiring quote, and suggested further readings.

Clearly written, this book should be useful for all elementary and high school libraries as well as the children's department of public libraries. Another book in the series, *100 Most Popular Scientists for Young Adults* (see ARBA 2000, entry 1277), might also be another useful addition.—**Carol D. Henry**

Chronology

C, P

48.   **Notable Corporate Chronologies.** 3d ed. Julie A. Mitchell, ed. Farmington Hills, Mich., Gale, 2001. 2v. index. $450.00/set. ISBN 0-7876-5049-8. ISSN 1078-3865.

The 3d edition of *Notable Corporate Chronologies* provides succinct histories of more than 1,800 worldwide business organizations. Significant events in the growth and development of each organization are chronologically ordered by key dates. Among events included are incidents related to the founding of each corporation, major products handled, key executives and their tenures of office, major mergers and acquisitions, notable scandals and other newsworthy events, financial milestones, and major stock offerings. Each presentation offers corporate location and access data, such as address and telephone and fax numbers as well as, where appropriate, URL and e-mail address and cable and telex numbers. Suggestions for further reading, primarily recently published articles in business journals, are given at the end of each history.

In addition to the individual corporate chronologies, which comprise the major portion of the two volumes, listings are provided for key corporate events (by year from the early 1700s through 2000), significant anniversaries, and forthcoming events (for the period of 2001 through 2021). An immensely useful master index not only includes entries for the corporations presented, but also former and alternative names, major acquisitions, product names, key executive officers, and selected important events. A brief introduction gives general comments, including an overall format of individual histories and tables of abbreviations utilized in the text. The data provided are largely of a factual nature without evaluation.

Criteria for inclusion of entries are not given. However, the included corporations appear to represent those most likely to be of general interest. These carefully edited volumes provide easy access, in a single source, to much information of interest to a wide audience, including researchers, students, executives, and investors.
—**William C. Struning**

Dictionaries and Encyclopedias

C, P
49.   Botto, Francis. **Dictionary of E-Business: A Definitive Guide to Technology and Business Terms.** New York, John Wiley, 2000. 334p. $49.95pa. ISBN 0-471-88145-7.

The title of this work promises more than it delivers. At the same time, however, the author delivers more than he promises. Despite claiming to definitively cover both technology and business terms, this short work focuses almost exclusively on the technological side of e-business—from *3-D* to *Zoom options*. Of the approximately 2,500 entries, only a handful pertain to nontechnical topics. On the other hand, the information provided for many of the terms is more exhaustive than a typical dictionary entry and many entries are accompanied by informative essays. Some of these longer entries include *data warehouse, firewall*, and *MPEG-1*. At the very reasonable price of $49.95, this work provides a lot of bang for the money. It is recommended for business reference collections supporting users with research or applied interests in e-business.—**Gordon J. Aamot**

C, P
50.   **Encyclopedia of Busine$$ and Finance.** Burton S. Kaliski, ed. New York, Macmillan Reference USA/ Gale Group, 2001. 2v. illus. index. $240.00/set. ISBN 0-02-865065-4.

The stated purpose of the *Encyclopedia of Busine$$ and Finance* is to "summarize the body of knowledge we know as business in a single place and in a language accessible to the layperson." This encyclopedia presents more than 300 entries covering areas of accounting, economics, finance, management, marketing, information systems, and law. Special attention is given to topics of careers and ethics; for instance, entries may be found for "Careers in Accounting" and "Careers in Management." Specific topics covered range from consumer behavior to ethics in finance to management and leadership styles.

Entries are arranged in alphabetical order and extensive cross-referencing is provided. A brief bibliography is provided for each entry. Articles are signed and are written by contributors primarily from colleges and universities. Illustrations, photographs, and statistical charts are included with some of the articles. An index is provided, with pages for specific articles in bold face. Entries are clear and concise, some using company-specific case studies to illustrate a concept. For instance, the entry "Discount Stores" presents the history of these business enterprises, describing development of key companies including K-Mart and Wal-Mart, plus statistical figures for net sales for the aforementioned companies. Key people are also discussed (e.g., Adam Smith, Max Weber, Fred Luthans).

The encyclopedia was prepared with various users in mind, from high school students to college students to faculty researchers and business practitioners. It can serve as both a starting point to research or provide basic background reading on a business topic for the layperson. With this audience in mind, the *Encyclopedia of Busine$$*

and Finance is recommended to school, public, and academic library collections. [R: Choice, April 01, p. 1446; BL, June 01, p. 1934; LJ, 1 Sept 01, pp. 162-164; RUSQ, Fall 01, pp. 72-74]—**Lucy Heckman**

C, P

51.   **Gale E-Commerce Sourcebook.** Deborah J. Baker, ed. Farmington Hills, Mich., Gale, 2003. 2v. index. $195.00/set. ISBN 0-7876-5750-6. ISSN 1542-1120.

The *Gale E-Commerce Sourcebook* is an interesting and attractive reference set that is intended to be a practical and comprehensive source of information for a broad range of patron groups, from high school students to researchers. It includes a directory of more than 4,700 organizations, associations, and agencies related to e-commerce. Its breadth of coverage and its many special features make it a worthy resource for the fast-changing field of e-commerce.

The *Sourcebook* is divided into two volumes. The first volume includes an introduction and a combination of preface and user's guide. This is followed by 93 separate "how-to" topics. The bulk of the volume is then a directory of organizations, associations, and consultants working in e-commerce, including educational programs, government regulatory agencies, publications, trade shows and conventions, Website designers, and Website hosting companies. These entries continue into the second volume. Volume 2 also includes brief profiles of 250 leading e-commerce companies worldwide. A typical entry in the *Sourcebook* includes entry number, title, mailing address, telephone number, fax number, e-mail address, and URL. In some cases, the entry may also include the name and title of a contact person. A concise one-paragraph description is provided with each entry. Entries for e-commerce companies include the year the company was founded, company revenue in U.S. dollars, and the number of employees. Entries are arranged in a two-column format with plenty of white space and generous margins, making the *Sourcebook* easy to use and to photocopy. Dividing the *Sourcebook* into two parts will also be appreciated by patrons, since they will not have to wrestle with a single thick and heavy volume.

An interesting and valuable feature of the *Sourcebook* is the section of "how-to" topics. These are concise and easy-to-read essays on a variety of subjects related to e-commerce, ranging from accounting practices to XML. Subheadings are used generously in the essays and many essays include a bibliography. Taken as a whole, the "how-to" topic section presents an excellent overview of the legal, technological, and financial issues related to e-commerce. However, one of the individual "how-to" topic essays may be just what a patron needs to begin research on a particular aspect of starting or managing an e-commerce business. There are two rankings lists in the *Sourcebook*. The first of these lists is a ranking by annual revenue and the second list is a ranking by number of employees. The *Sourcebook* also has an extensive general index; however, it has an unusual arrangement. Instead of referring to the page number of the entry, the *Sourcebook* uses a combination of a single-letter section abbreviation and entry number. This took a few minutes to figure out and get comfortable with.

The *Gale E-Commerce Sourcebook* is an appropriate resource for many types of libraries, but would be a particularly good addition to public, academic, and corporate library collections. Although many dot.com companies may not survive, the number of entries in the *Sourcebook* and the "how-to" topics make this resource an excellent way to learn more about e-commerce even if a few entries are for companies that no longer exist. In addition, since the majority of the entries are for associations, organizations, and consultants, these entities are more likely to survive and would be of most interest to patrons who are exploring opportunities in the e-commerce arena. [R: LJ, 1 Feb 03, pp. 74-76]—**Sara Anne Hook**

C, P

52.   Hillstrom, Kevin, and Laurie Collier Hillstrom. **Encyclopedia of Small Business.** 2d ed. Farmington Hills, Mich., Gale, 2002. 2v. index. $425.00/set. ISBN 0-7876-4906-6.

The *Encyclopedia of Small Business* consists of 600 well-written entries on a wide range of topics important to new and established small business owners and entrepreneurs. Many of the entries are actually thoughtful essays tailored to the specific concerns a small business has. Following each entry are lists of references for further reading. A master index at the end of the 2d volume is a helpful resource for finding terms, related entries, organizations, and other material. Entries from the 1st edition have been revised and updated. More than 100 new entries cover emerging topics, such as the trend toward casual business attire, data encryption, licensing, online auctions, and the portability of benefits. A list of the entries is included in the front of each volume. Although some entries have *see also* references at the end, there are not enough. The usefulness of the entries would be improved with bold references in the text to related entries.

The articles cover the entire range of topics relevant to starting a small business, developing a business plan, market analysis, management, marketing, accounting, advertising, legal and insurance aspects, government regulations, selling and distribution, employee relations, retirement plans, taxes, and a myriad of other matters. There are many entries on specialized topics, such as banner advertisements, bar coding, comp time, credit history, Internet domain names, nepotism, the Patent and Trademark Office, promissory notes, *spam* (e-mail), tuition assistance programs, the U.S. Chamber of Commerce, workplace anger, and zoning ordinances. There are also unexpected entries. For example, "Office Romance" discusses the conditions in the modern workplace that foster these relationships, the different kinds of relationships, the complications that frequently follow co-workers becoming intimate, and how the small business should deal with them. A separate entry discusses sexual harassment. The selection of topics appears to have benefited from active participation by the advisory board. The *Encyclopedia* is an important contribution to the literature on small business and will be useful to the ingénue as well as the experienced entrepreneur. The Hillstroms are experienced reference book authors and have delivered another quality work.—**Peter Zachary McKay**

Directories

P

53.   **World Directory of Business Information Web Sites 2002.** 5th ed. Chicago, Euromonitor International, 2000. 288p. index. $690.00pa. ISBN 1-84264-141-7.

This straightforward but expensive directory lists approximately 2,000 business Websites from 133 countries. Sites are chosen from trade associations and trade magazines, stock exchanges, and government offices and NGO's for their utility to the business researcher. The sites emphasize statistical, marketing, and company information as well as agriculture, consumer, industrial, and financial data. Each entry lists site name; originator; Web address; a description of services offered; an outline of the type of statistics (if applicable); and charging structure. This edition appears to list more fee-based sites than earlier editions but the majority of sites are free. There is also an Internet version. Most entries are listed by country, although there are both international and regional chapters. It has both an alphabetical index by name and an index that is alphabetical by country, subdivided by business or service sector. This second index by sector will be very useful for researchers of international statistics. A test comparison of these sites against general searches in Google, Yahoo!, and AlltheWeb found that a little more than half the sites can be found within the first two screens of each of the services, although none were as efficient as using the URL from the sector index. Address accuracy was quite good considering the volatility of the Web. Third world, regional, and international-based sites are a real strength of this work.

As far as content goes, this title is recommended. There are two caveats. Libraries really have to ask themselves if the information is worth $690; only if the agency does serious work in third world or regional economies will the library gets its value. The second caveat is that it has a statement on the verso of the title page that reads, "Reproduction in any form whatsoever is prohibited and libraries should not permit photocopying without prior arrangement. Unauthorized use will result in immediate proceedings against the offending party." Libraries will have to consider if they can live with this restriction.—**Patrick J. Brunet**

Handbooks and Yearbooks

C, P

54.   **Business Rankings Annual, 2002: Lists of Companies, Products, Services, and Activities.** Amy Brooks, Lynn M. Pearce, and Deborah J. Untener, eds. Farmington Hills, Mich., Gale, 2002. 2v. index. $315.00/set. ISBN 0-7876-4029-8. ISSN 1043-7908.

The *Business Rankings Annual* is a handy reference book that provides, in one resource, nearly 5,000 lists and rankings for a wide variety of business activities and outcomes. This volume is an updated edition that provides top 10 lists, for both domestic and international business activities, that were compiled from more than 300 original online and print sources. The arrangement and presentation of these business activities as top 10 lists is an easy and accessible method of organization that is both entertaining and informative. The use of lists permits not only detailed and explicit applications but also encourages casual users who may simply wish to browse through this thorough and interesting summary of relative commercial activities.

The layout of the entries is logical and easy to use with numbered entries are grouped by alphabetically arranged subjects. Entries are identified first by a descriptive phrase and the year for which the list applies along with the criteria by which the list was compiled, the total number of observations in the ranking source, and any pertinent remarks from the ranking source that help to define the list for users and provide context for the listed information. Also, individual items listed often include relative data such as scores, sales figures, or rates of change, in addition to bibliographic citations that identify original sources. A comprehensive index is provided so that individuals, products, and firms can be identified and cross-referenced. Other useful features include a four-digit Standard Industrial Classification (SIC) index that outlines subject categories, a SIC to North American Industry Classification System (NAICS) conversion table, and a bibliographic listing of the original sources used to compile these rankings and lists.—**Timothy E. Sullivan**

C, P

55.   **Hoover's MasterList of Major U.S. Companies 2002: The Facts You Need on More Than 5,200 Leading Public and Private Enterprises.** 8th ed. Austin, Tex., Hoover's, 2001. 987p. index. $134.95. ISBN 1-57311-070-1.

As with its other directories, Hoover's presents this material in an attractive format with alphabetically arranged entries printed in bold, easy-to-read fonts. This 8th edition of *Hoover's MasterList of Major U.S. Companies* packs a lot of information into 1 volume, listing over 5,000 companies and organizations in the United States. Public companies with sales over $125 million are included in the directory. Entries are brief due to the large number of listings in one volume. Each entry includes a summary of the company's products and operations, the mailing and Web address of the firm, the top three executives (CEO, CFO, and human resources contact), an indication if the company is publicly traded or privately held, and a selection of recent company financials. The financial information, when available, includes sales, net income, market value, and number of employees for the previous five years, and also indicates the percentage change from the previous year for each category.

Valuable features include company rankings lists arranging the top 500 U.S. companies by sales, employees, 5-year sales growth, and market value. Useful indexes include the "Index by Industry," which allows one to browse for companies by major and specific industry grouping, and the "Index by Headquarters," which lists by state and city the corporate headquarters of each of the companies included in the directory. Another less useful listing, "Index by Stock Exchange Symbol," shows the stock exchange and lists the page number of the entry for each of the public companies listed in the directory. Unlike the *Dun & Bradstreet Million Dollar Directory* (Dun & Bradstreet Information Services) and other business directories, the Hoover publications do not list industrial classification codes such as the SIC code or the newer North American Industrial Classification System code (NAICS). The *MasterList* does provide an index by industry, however, if one wanted to search for companies based upon this criteria.

A unique quality of this publication, the directory lists many private companies and nonpublic entities, such as foundations, sports teams and leagues, universities, not-for-profits, and major government-owned entities such as the United States Postal Service. This inclusion of many organizations that would not normally be listed in a business directory provides a scope of content rarely seen in similar publications. This guide is recommended for all libraries, especially those with small business reference collections in need of a current directory.

—**Glenn S. McGuigan**

C, P

56.   **Small Business Sourcebook: The Entrepreneur's Resource.** 16th ed. Sonya D. Hill, ed. Farmington Hills, Mich., Gale, 2002. 2v. index. $365.00/set. ISBN 0-7876-6762-X. ISSN 0883-3397.

From sign shops, shoe stores, and sewing centers to green houses, gardening centers, and golf shops; animal clinics, art galleries, and auctioneers; calligraphy, campgrounds, and candy shops—more than 300 small businesses are covered in the *Sourcebook*. The *Sourcebook* is a standard reference work for identifying information resources for starting, developing, and growing 341 specific small businesses as well as for finding information on general small business topics and sources of assistance at the state and federal levels and by Canadian province. The *Sourcebook* is divided into four main sections: "Specific Small Business Profiles," "General Small Business Topics," and "State Listings and Federal Government Assistance."

The "profiles" are not narrative descriptions of small businesses but rather directory listings of information sources specific to one of the small businesses covered. For each kind of small business the *Sourcebook* provides start-up information, associations and other organizations, educational programs, directories of educational programs, reference works, sources of supply, statistical sources, trade periodicals, videocassettes/audiocassettes, trade shows and conventions, consultants, franchises and business opportunities, computerized databases, computer systems/software, libraries, and research centers. Many of the entries are enhanced with descriptive annotations in addition to the essential identifying and contact information, including addresses, telephone and fax numbers, e-mail addresses, and URLs for Websites.

The first half of the second volume contains annotated entries on general small business topics arranged in 99 chapters (with up to 14 subheadings) ranging from accounting, business plans, and customer service to electronic commerce, entrepreneurship, management, manufacturing, publicity, venture capital, and workplace safety. The second volume also contains listings of resources for small business development by state, including small business development centers, chambers of commerce, minority business assistance programs, educational programs, and publications. Sections on Canadian and U.S. Federal Government Assistance follow.

The "Master Index" lists alphabetic references to the organizations, publications, products, services, and other materials covered in the 25,000 numbered entries. Other features include a user's guide, a glossary of small business terms, a Standard Industrial Classification Index (SIC), listings for licensing assistance programs, and a guide to publishers that is new to this edition.

The *Sourcebook* is valuable for identifying sources of information but the task of actually locating and accessing the sources is left to the researcher. One must also keep in mind that it is not comprehensive. For example, while there is a listing for the National Restaurant Association Educational Foundation there is not a listing for the National Restaurant Association (www.restaurant.org), which is the leading trade group for restaurateurs. The Association's Website is replete with detailed information in most of the categories covered in the *Sourcebook*. Librarians may use the *Sourcebook* to develop their collections of small business information sources. The strength of the reference work lies in its catalog of resources for specific kinds of small businesses as well as the variety of sources covered and the copious annotations. It will aid entrepreneurs who need both general and specific information to help them solve problems.—**Peter Zachary McKay**

ACCOUNTING

C, P

57. Collin, P. H., David York, and Adrian Joliffe. **Dictionary of Accounting.** 2d ed. Oak Park, Ill., Peter Collin, 2001. 294p. $15.95pa. ISBN 1-901659-85-2.

This handy terminological dictionary, the 1st edition of which appeared in 1992, "provides basic vocabulary of terms used in the fields of accounting, bookkeeping and general finance." Each of the terms, reflecting both British and American usage, is defined in simple English and examples are provided to show how the term in question is used in context. A useful supplement includes common abbreviations used, list of documents in both countries that are essential for the practice of accounting and auditing (e.g., Statements of Standard Accounting Practice and Financial Reporting Standards for the UK and Statements of Auditing Standards and Financial Accounting Standards Board [FASB] Statements of Financial Accounting Standards for the U.S.), as well as explanations of "T" accounts, and the basic accounting equation and sample UK financial statements.

By and large the dictionary is accurate and comprehensive. It does not include terms related to not-for-profit and governmental accounting, and occasionally omits terms that are basic to American accounting, auditing, and financial practice (e.g., chart of accounts, GAAS—Generally Accepted Auditing Standards, time value of money, and Black-Scholes Option Pricing Model). The definitions of terms are simple and straightforward and are not intended to provide an in-depth explanation, but in some cases the definition is so simple that it fails to explain (e.g., reversing entry). This work would be useful for business, finance, and accounting students and for both American and British accounting and finance specialists who might be confused by each other's terminology.

—**Robert H. Burger**

BUSINESS SERVICES AND
INVESTMENT GUIDES

Directories

P

58.   Jiao, Qun G. **Internet Guide to Personal Finance and Investment.** Westport, Conn., Oryx Press/Greenwood Publishing Group, 2002. 344p. index. $55.00pa. ISBN 1-57356-470-2.

According to the press release, *Internet Guide to Personal Finance and Investment* is intended to be a "road map for finding the sharpest personal finance information available online." This attractive volume, compiled by an associate professor/reference librarian at Baruch College, City University of New York, contains information on more than 1,400 Websites that cover nearly every aspect of personal finance and investment. The volume takes a broad view of personal finance and includes sites chosen on the basis of ease of use, timeliness, scope, sponsorship, and the level of free access to information on the site, with almost all of the sites offering free access.

The volume is divided into three parts. Part 1, titled "Financing Your Goals," includes chapters on employee benefits and financial planning for college costs, family-owned or small businesses and retirement, personal finance services, and tools and Websites to meet the needs of specific populations (such as children and minorities). Part 2 covers a myriad of investment options, with chapters on bonds, commodities, currencies, futures and options, mutual funds, stocks, global markets, and real estate with an additional chapter on investment resources and services. Part 3 is devoted to chapters on the management and protection of assets, including consumer protection, debt management, insurance, legal information and services, family law matters, online banking, tax and estate planning, and unclaimed assets. Within each chapter, headings and subheadings are in clear, bold print, making it simple to locate individual Website entries. Entries are arranged in an attractive two-column format, making the volume quite appealing and easy to read.

A typical entry includes the title of the Website in bold print, its URL, and a brief paragraph describing the site including the name of the sponsor of the site. Descriptions are concise and give the reader enough information to decide whether a site offers content and services that would be useful. Although Website directories can often be outdated, many of the sites included in this guide are provided by large organizations and corporations that are more likely to stay in operation.

Three indexes are provided. One of the indexes lists the Websites by title and another index is for sponsors. The third index is a simple subject index. The volume also features a short overview of financial planning, with brief sections on such important topics as buying a house and saving for retirement. A short preface offers assistance in using the volume, including scope and content.

At a cost of $55, the *Internet Guide to Personal Finance and Investment* would be an excellent addition to public libraries as well as other libraries, such as those in nonprofit agencies that serve patrons who need assistance with financial planning and investment decision-making.—**Sara Anne Hook**

Handbooks and Yearbooks

P

59.   **NASDAQ-100 Investor's Guide 2002-2003.** Paramus, N.J., Prentice Hall, 2002. 293p. illus. index. $20.00pa. ISBN 0-7352-0322-9.

The NASDAQ-100 is a stock market index that includes the 100 largest domestic and international companies, based upon market capitalization, that trade on the NASDAQ Stock Market, excluding those in the financial services and utility sectors. The *NASDAQ-100 Investor's Guide* is intended to serve as a tool for investors interested in incorporating the NASDAQ-100 into their own investment portfolio.

Written with the editors of the *New York Institute of Finance*, the guide provides an overview of this popular, although often volatile, index. For the most part, it consists of profiles of the individual component stocks that make up the index. Each profile includes a discussion of the company's primary business, key products, and recent acquisitions as well as a discussion of the company's earnings and revenues, key ratios, and charts provided by Baseline Financial Services (a leading provider of information products and services to the investment community).

Profiles are found in chapters 4 and 5 of the guide, with the difference being that those found in chapter 4 represent the 25 companies from the index viewed as being most attractive for the year ahead by Michael P. Byrum, CFA. Byrum is chairman of the investment strategy committee that manages the Rydex OTC Fund, a mutual fund that invests exclusively in NASDAQ-100 companies with the goal of replicating the performance of the index.

The *NASDAQ-100 Investor's Guide* is a useful primer for anyone interested in learning about the NASDAQ-100 index, its tracking stock, or related mutual funds. While the guide does provide helpful background on the index and its component stocks, investors should be careful to consider just where a company is at the point in time they are ready to buy it. Additional research, such as reviewing current quarterly and annual reports, should be undertaken before making any investment decisions. This guide is recommended solely for public library collections.

—**Elizabeth M. Mezick**

CONSUMER GUIDES

P

60.   **Consumer Sourcebook.** 15th ed. Sonya D. Hill, ed. Farmington Hills, Mich., Gale, 2002. 1213p. index. $305.00. ISBN 0-7876-5277-4. ISSN 0738-0518.

Consumers should be able to make informed choices and have adequate recourse if products or services prove to be less than satisfactory. The 15th edition of Gale's *Sourcebook* aims to do just that by providing more than 18,000 references to consumer interest, organized into 17 subject chapters, ranging from general consumerism to education, insurance, health care, and utilities. Groups that primarily promote a single product or industry are excluded. This edition was compiled through contact with the agencies, as well as from government publications and Gale databases, and contains more than 5,000 new entries.

Two informative and useful sections precede the main text. "Chapter Descriptions" informs readers of each chapter's scope, issues, and resources, and "Consumer Tips" offers suggestions for each subject chapter. Individual chapters may include these subsections: "Internet Databases," "Government Agencies," "Associations and Organizations," "Publications," "Multimedia Resources," and "Media and Corporate Contacts." Sequentially numbered entries, although necessarily short, supply sufficient data for identification and, often, a brief description. Two appendixes, dealing with hotlines and clearinghouses and testing laboratories, and alphabetic and subject indexes provide additional access.

The two sections preceding the chapters might be even more useful if incorporated into their respective chapters. Otherwise, the comprehensive nature of this directory makes it a valuable reference tool. As comments are welcome, so are future editions, expanded to accommodate growing consumer issues.—**Anita Zutis**

FINANCE AND BANKING

Handbooks and Yearbooks

C, P

61.   **Plunkett's Financial Services Industry Almanac 2002-2003.** Jack W. Plunkett, ed. Houston, Tex., Plunkett Research, 2002. 713p. index. $229.99pa. (w/CD-ROM). ISBN 1-891775-23-5.

Plunkett's almanacs for various industries, including this one, have been reviewed favorably in past editions of *American Reference Books Annual* (see ARBA 2001, entry 144, for a review of the 2000-2001 edition of this source). This edition continues with much the same format. Single-page profiles characterize each of the editor's "Financial Services 500." These are the "biggest, most successful" U.S.-based public companies active in one or more areas of the financial services industry. Each profile includes, among other items, listings of corporate officers and brands, divisions or affiliates, sales and earnings figures for the most recent five years, and a one-paragraph narrative focusing on the company's plans for growth or other notable features.

The firms are indexed by industry sector, headquarters location, and by those with operations in particular U.S. regions and internationally. In addition, several introductory chapters provide surveys of particular sectors and of the industry as a whole. More than 40 data tables are included here, making this source a useful starting point for statistics concerning the industry. A CD-ROM version is included. This continues to be a recommended source for company and industry information available at a reasonable price.—**Christopher J. Hoeppner**

INDUSTRY AND MANUFACTURING

Handbooks and Yearbooks

C, P

62.   Troy, Leo. **Almanac of Business and Industrial Financial Ratios, 2002.** 33d ed. Paramus, N.J., Prentice Hall, 2002. 801p. index. $150.00pa. (w/CD-ROM). ISBN 0-13-042369-6. ISSN 0747-9107.

There are certain reference sources that form the essential core of materials for a business reference collection. This serial is indisputably one of those items. Meeting a common research need for business people and college students seeking industry-wide financial ratios, the *Almanac* provides access to data by industry classification and by size of firms within those industries. The 50 items of financial data issue from the calculations of tax returns for all active public and private companies within those industries in the United States. The accompanying CD-ROM version delivers access to the content of the volume in the scanned image PDF format. Within this electronic version, it is possible to open up data tables in Excel spreadsheets.

A useful feature of the *Almanac* is the ability to view the data by asset size of firms. Certain reference sources may provide similar financial data but all of the calculations are generated from the firms of various sizes grouped together within an industry. The *Almanac*, on the other hand, divides the calculations for various firms based upon the size of assets in 13 categories. This division includes firms with approximately zero assets to those possessing over $250 million in assets. This feature allows a more detailed view of the financial breakdown of large and small firms within various industries.

Reflecting a major change in the 33d edition, the industries are now categorized using the North American Industrial Classification System (NAICS). This new system expands the number of industries, particularly those in the area of technology, communication, and service. Examples of new industry categories included in this volume are computer systems design, computer and peripheral equipment, and scientific research and development services. The implication of this change is that it is not possible to follow the trend analysis of certain past calculations. The *Almanac* is highly recommended for all business reference collections.—**Glenn S. McGuigan**

INTERNATIONAL BUSINESS

Dictionaries and Encyclopedias

C, P

63.   **Worldmark Encyclopedia of National Economies.** Jeffrey Lehman and Rebecca Parks, eds. Farmington Hills, Mich., Gale, 2002. 4v. illus. maps. index. $295.00/set. ISBN 0-7876-4955-4.

The editors of this encyclopedia believe the study of national economies enables countries to learn from each other when solving current and future problems. The country overviews were written by an international group of experts in the areas of economics and politics. The set is divided into four volumes, one for each of the main continental areas of the world: Africa, the Americas, Asia and the Pacific, and Europe. There are 198 alphabetic country entries with data on currency, chief exports and imports, gross domestic products, balance and trade, and exchange rates. The articles provide black-and-white maps, graphs, and charts for statistical information. A bibliography of sources used is provided at the end of the entry. The information for each country is current and has been gathered from the World Bank, the United Nations, and the International Monetary Fund.

One of the best features of the encyclopedia is the "Introduction to World Currency," color plates that depict the current currency for 169 countries. A glossary and a cumulative index are provided in each of the four volumes. This work is recommended for corporate, academic, and public libraries' business collections. The information will be helpful to the students of business and economics as well as businesspeople working with companies that have international interests. [R: SLJ, Nov 02, pp. 104-105]—**Kay M. Stebbins**

Handbooks and Yearbooks

C

64.   **Economist Country Briefings. http://www.economist.com/countries/.** [Website]. Free. Date reviewed: Nov 02.

The "Country Briefings" section of the *Economist* Website should be seen as a subset of the much larger Economist Intelligence Unit (EIU) database, which contains economic and political information on approximately 200 countries. When users open this page they will find information on 60 countries, which includes countries that are members of the European Union, those countries being considered for European Union membership, and other countries representative of the rest of the economic world. At the end of the list of countries with briefings the user will find reference to approximately a half-dozen recent forecast update articles that can be clicked on. In the upper right-hand corner is a search box that will allow the user to search for other countries; this information is available for an additional fee.

Users will find a great deal of quality information available on the free portion of this site. Each country briefing starts with an excerpt from the EIU's *Country Forecast* publication, the *Economist Global Agenda*, or an article from the print version of the *Economist*. These articles were less than 6 weeks old and most were less than 10 days old at the time of this review. The rest of the page is divided into three columns entitled "Recent Articles," "Country Profile," and "Related Items." The "Recent Articles" section includes articles that have appeared in the *Economist* in the last two to three years. Some of these are available for free but others require that the user have an existing subscription to the *Economist* or have a premier subscription to the EIU publications in order to read the articles.

A lot of the content in the "Country Profile" section will remind users of the *Background Notes* published by the Unites States Department of State. The user will find a small outline map and the following section headings: "Forecast," with information on the political and economic outlook; "Factsheet," with basic data; "Economic Data," which covers 10 selected economic indicators over four years that can be downloaded as a spreadsheet; "Political Structure," with a description of the country's system and the names of all cabinet members; "Political Forces," which identifies political parties and groups, plus the names and roles of key political figures; "Economic Structure," which discusses economic strengths and weaknesses, products and markets, and comparisons with similar economies. There is a currency converter and a list of the EIU available for sale that will provide more detailed information.

The "Related Items Section" includes a link to the EIU store and links for backgrounder articles on relevant topics. The next segment in this section is devoted to Websites, including government sites for the country being profiled, associations, and companies in the country. This is a very extensive listing and the links tested worked. The last segment is a list of articles from the Web dealing with the country being profiled, which is also very extensive. This site also has some links to research tools, titled "Articles by Subject," which is an alphabetic list by topic, city, and country; a glossary of Internet terms; and a business database that includes an economic dictionary among other resources.

The user could spend hours browsing through the information on an individual country. It is easy to navigate and the page layout is well done. For more comprehensive information the user needs to acquire a premier membership or purchase individual EIU publications. Every screen provides purchase information for these publications. In addition to this, users will find some other advertisements as a header to each screen shot and also on the initial country briefings page.

This is a good site to refer business and economic students to and for businesspeople who are considering doing business in a particular country. However, if the user needs to do some serious economic analysis or information on the rules and regulations for doing business with a particular country, they will need to purchase the relevant materials.—**Judith J. Field**

C, P

65.   **Hoover's Handbook of World Business 2002: Profiles of Major Global Enterprises.** Austin, Tex., Hoover's, 2002. 720p. illus. index. $129.95. ISBN 1-57311-074-4.

This is the 9th edition of this handbook, which fills a need for the small academic and public libraries that have occasional queries about non-U.S.-based companies. In this edition they have identified 300 of the world's most influential companies. Some of the industries included are telecommunication firms, banks, chemical firms, petroleum companies, and airlines. The contents of the book include a two-page description of the elements that are included in the profile template used for the companies; a 50-page compendium of various lists of the largest, most profitable companies by assets within their industries; the 2-page profile of each company; and 3 indexes.

The profiles provide an informative snapshot of each company. One of most popular sections in the profile is a short list of major competitors. Other information included in the profile include a brief overview of the company, some history about the company, a list of officers, their corporate location, a list of their major product lines and operations, and some financials. There is an index by industry; by headquarters location; and a very detailed index by brands, people, and companies.

This can be purchased separately or as part of a four-title series available as an indexed set. The other titles in the set are *Hoover's Handbook of American Business* (see ARBA 2003, entry 148), *Hoover's Handbook of Emerging Companies* (see ARBA 2003, entry 149), and *Hoover's Handbook to Private Companies* (see ARBA 2003, entry 150). Whether purchased individually or as a set, smaller business collections will find that this title is well worth the money.—**Judith J. Field**

C, P

66.   **Hoover's MasterList of Major International Companies 2002: The Facts You Need on 3,000 Leading Private and Public Enterprises Worldwide.** Austin, Tex., Hoover's, 2001. 552p. index. $149.95. ISBN 1-57311-071-X.

Hoover's MasterList of Major International Companies covers approximately 3,000 private, public, and government-owned companies from more than 60 countries. Selected for coverage are "the largest and most-well-known non-U.S. business enterprises" (preface) and data are taken from Hoover's own internal database of company information. Each entry contains the company's name, address, CEO, CFO, fiscal year, type of company, telephone and fax numbers, Website address, exchange, sales, net income, and employees for 1996-2000. A one-paragraph capsule description of the company itself, including its products or services is provided as well. Companies are listed alphabetically. A symbol next to the company name indicates that a profile of it is available through Hoover's Online (http://www.hoovers.com). Additionally, many company profiles also appear in the Hoover's Handbook Series, which includes *Hoover's Handbook of American Business* (see ARBA 2003, entry 148) and *Hoover's Handbook of Emerging Companies* (see ARBA 2003, entry 149). Also available is a company rankings section by sales and by employees, which provides a comparison study of the companies. The helpful indexes arrange companies by industry, by headquarters (i.e., name of country where the company's headquarters is located), and by short name (which cross-references names such as JAL to it full name of Japanese Airlines Company Ltd.).

This informative source provides basic information about leading non-U.S. companies and is comparatively inexpensive. This volume complements the online edition of Hoover's and provides ready-reference data for patrons in both public and academic libraries. Those libraries that do not subscribe to online Hoover's should purchase this volume, along with the other print editions. This volume, as well as the entire series, is highly recommended and continues the excellent standards of Hoover's.—**Lucy Heckman**

LABOR

General Works

Dictionaries and Encyclopedias

C, P, S

67.   Morkes, Andrew. **Encyclopedia of Careers and Vocational Guidance.** 12th ed. Chicago, Ferguson, 2003. 4v. illus. index. $159.95/set. ISBN 0-89434-418-8.

Each edition of this basic career source broadens its scope of usefulness to the career seeker. This edition devotes substantial introduction to preparing for a career, finding and applying for a job, and key aspects of being hired. Throughout each section, key resources and Websites are noted to enable readers to further their search.

The background, structure, and outlook of 93 career fields are compiled in the first volume to provide an overview and estimates of future performance. In addition, an appendix lists organizations and associations that assist in training and job placement for people with disabilities. Another compiles books and lists organizations that deal with internships, apprenticeships, and training programs.

The 3 additional volumes contain 677 career articles that put each occupation in context and describe its duties, requirements, and earnings. In addition, the most successful job-search strategies and career-management moves for that occupation are described. An outlook section views future prospects. Informational resources are indicated for greater depth.

This tool is fundamental for the use of career counselors, academic advisors, and human resource personnel. As an initial exploration, it provides a sound basis for professional, technical, specialty, and support positions. It also encourages strategic mid-life individuals who seek to make optimal career moves.—**Barbara Conroy**

C, P, S

68.   **O*Net Dictionary of Occupational Titles.** 2d ed. Indianapolis, Ind., JIST Works, 2002. 688p. index. $39.95pa. ISBN 1-56370-845-0.

This 2d edition of the *O*Net Dictionary of Occupational Titles* is based on the Department of Labor's release of the O*Net database—a computerized database of information on occupations. *O*Net* is short for *The Occupational Information Network*, the database's formal name. This work is designed to replace the *Dictionary of Occupational Titles* (DOT; JIST Works, 1993) by merging the DOT with the O*Net database. It condenses the list of jobs formerly in the DOT, only listing significant jobs and not covering obscure jobs.

The 2d edition covers 1,112 jobs, with 1,094 updated from the 1999 edition, and covers 100 percent of the workforce. The data for earnings and projected growth and the number of openings have all been updated to 2000 numbers. The *O*Net Dictionary of Occupational Titles* is cross-referenced to the DOT and the *Complete Guide to Occupational Exploration* (JIST Works, 1993), a system for organizing jobs based on interests.

Each entry contains the O*Net number, occupational number, O*Net occupational title, and OES (Occupational Employment Survey) title, along with information on education required, U.S. employment totals, job openings, projected growth percentages, and average earnings. There is also a helpful alphabetic job title index. This edition is recommended for academic and business libraries' career and human resources collections. It can be used for assessing the kinds of jobs needed for a business and it is helpful in writing job descriptions. Students can use it to determine what kind of education and training they will need to obtain the jobs they want.—**Kay M. Stebbins**

Directories

P

69.   **The Directory of Outplacement & Career Management Firms 2001-2002.** 12th ed. Fitzwilliam, N.H., Kennedy Information, 2001. 579p. index. $129.95pa. ISBN 1-885922-65-5.

Businesses needing to downsize or lay off employees frequently employ outplacement consultants to provide support to employees losing their jobs. The focus of the 12th edition of the *Directory of Outplacement & Career Management Firms 2001-2002* is to identify leading firms worldwide that provide corporate sponsored outplacement services. Since the 10th edition, the directory also provides information on firms offering a variety of other career-management-related services.

The work is comprised of three main sections. A 20-page introductory section provides short essays on topics of interest to client companies, individuals involved in career changes, and industry-related professional associations. The bulk of the work is devoted to providing information about the nearly 500 outplacement firms included in the directory. The alphabetic listing is divided into two sections. The first, and largest, section covers firms that work primarily or exclusively on a corporate-paid basis for outplacement services. The second section includes firms that provide outplacement and career management services to both corporations and individuals. Each entry is about one page long and consists of standard sections. These include address and contact information, principals, fee information (percentage of salary and minimum fee), whether group outplacement services are available, whether fees are paid by company or individuals, revenue breakdown by areas of business, geographical areas and industries served, staff size, and founding date. Most of the firms listed are based in the United States, but there is also a good representation of international outplacement firms. Finally, useful indexes provide a means to identify firms serving broad industries and geographic regions. One can also find firms by the personal names of key principals and affiliations with professional associations.

Given the state of the economy, it seems likely there will be a growing demand for the kinds of outplacement and career management services offered by the firms included in this directory. This resource is recommended for business reference collections focusing on career resources, especially those in large public libraries.

—**Gordon J. Aamot**

Handbooks and Yearbooks

C, P, S

70.   Derks, Scott. **Working Americans 1880-1999. Volume III: The Upper Class.** Lakeville, Conn., Grey House Publishing, 2001. 567p. illus. index. $135.00. ISBN 1-930956-38-X.

An amalgam of business history, economic history, labor history, and sociology, this fascinating volume gives the reader a "decade by decade" (the final two decades of the nineteenth century are lumped together) snapshot of the upper class in the United States from 1880 to 1999. Following an introduction for each decade, the author gives the reader three family profiles per decade (three family profiles for the final two decades of the nineteenth century). While the family profiles read like condensed historical novels, the author created each fictional family from governmental studies and statistics. Each fictional family is placed in a real geographical locale. These locales cover every part of the country from east to west and north to south. The locales add depth and human interest to the profiles. They include annual income, life at home, life at work, and life in the local geographical community. Each family profile is followed by a historical snapshot, an economic profile, and a news profile. The economic profile provides such information as annual income by profession, standard jobs, and selected prices of household goods for the time. It serves a framework by which the reader may judge the family's lifestyle. Each chapter includes a wealth of photographs depicting the fictional families and their geographic locales. There are also innumerable facsimiles of clothing, household goods, inventions, illustrations from newspapers and magazines, and advertisements from every decade. The author has finished the work with bibliographic sources, by decade, and a detailed index.

This volume is highly recommended for every public library of whatever size. It should be purchased by school libraries for grades seven through senior high. It should also be on the shelves of every college library serving an undergraduate student body.—**Dene L. Clark**

C, P

71.   **Plunkett's Companion to the Almanac of American Employers: Mid-Sized Firms 2002-2003.** Jack W. Plunkett, ed. Houston, Tex., Plunkett Research, 2002. 684p. index. $179.99pa. (w/CD-ROM). ISBN 1-891775-26-X.

As indicated by its title, *Plunkett's Companion to the Almanac of American Employers: Mid-Sized Firms 2002-2003* is intended to complement its volume covering firms with more than 2,500 employees. This volume emphasizes mid-size firms, defined as those with 150 to 2,500 employees, that are primarily U.S.-based, for-profit companies with publicly held stock. The volume's purpose is to assist job-seekers in finding quick and meaningful information about potential employers, with individual company entries and supplemental materials that permit comparison within and across industry groups. *Plunkett's* can also be differentiated from other sources of information on corporations because this volume's view of companies is tailored to what potential employees need to know rather than to the information needs of investors, accountants, or financial analysts.

Each entry in this guide is presented on a single page, divided into segments that make it easy to find and compare the information. The top box provides the industry group code, the URL for the company's Website, a ranking of sales and profits within the industry groups, and a salary and benefits rating. The second box lists a variety of subject backgrounds, such as technical writing and hardware development, arranged into six categories, with an indication of whether the company hires people with these types of backgrounds. On the left side of the page, a series of boxes contain information on type of business, brands, divisions and affiliates, and names and titles of top officers and their telephone numbers, along with the company's toll-free number, fax number, and address. On the right side of the page, a brief, concise narrative provides information on the growth potential of the company and any special features of the company that would bode well for future employees. The bottom of the page contains boxes for financial information.

A "Salaries/Benefits" box lists the various plans available to employees, along with the salaries and bonuses for the top and second executive positions. A separate box includes comments on the company's competitive advantage, with another box for additional thoughts about the company. There is also a space for the number of women officers or directors, a space to note whether the company is a "hot spot" for the advancement of women and minorities, and boxes to check the location of the company that are divided regionally rather than by state. The information presented in the entries is clear and well organized and will be useful to job-seekers in targeting the employers that will offer the best opportunities for long-term career growth and stability.

In addition to the individual company entries, this guide has a number of special features that make it a particularly valuable research tool for job-seekers and others who have a particular interest in a company or industry group. Beginning chapters not only cover how to use the volume, but discuss major trends affecting the employee marketplace and ideas for doing research on potential employers. A directory of contacts for job-seekers and a composite view of 498 companies included in the volume and why they were selected are also provided along with an industry list with codes, a ranking of the companies within industry groups, an alphabetic list of the companies with industry codes, and three geographical indexes. Additional indexes are provided at the end of the volume. All of these indexes make it simple to find information on specific companies and to see how they compare to companies within and outside of their own industry groups. *Plunkett's* also includes a number of interesting tables, including one on female CEOs and another on the top 20 employers with women officers and directors.

This work will be a useful addition to nearly any public or academic library, as well as libraries that serve companies or agencies that assist people looking for jobs. The page-long entries will be easy for patrons to photocopy and the supplemental directory and statistical information will be handy for ready-reference. The chapters covering major trends that will affect those seeking new jobs and techniques for effective job hunting are particularly timely and well written.—**Sara Anne Hook**

Career Guides

Directories

C, P

72.   **Job Hunter's Sourcebook: Where to Find Employment Leads and Other Job Search Resources.** 5th ed. Amy Darga, ed. Farmington Hills, Mich., Gale, 2002. 1180p. index. $115.00. ISBN 0-7876-5933-9.

Serving job-seekers and career-changers at all levels, this resource serves as a clearinghouse by organizing a wide range of information (see ARBA 2000, entry 201; ARBA 98, entry 233; and ARBA 92, entry 222, for reviews of past editions). A somewhat lengthy introductory section explains the categories of data and entry contents. The volume continues to contain two sections. Part 1 consists of more than 200 alphabetically arranged profiles of high interest occupations from accountants to writers. The number of occupational categories, drawn from the *Occupational Outlook Handbook* (2000-2001 ed.; see ARBA 2001, entry 197), continues to rise with each new edition—from 155 in 1992 to 193 in 2000. Entries offer seven easy-to-use categories of information, such as sources of help wanted ads, employment agencies, and job referral services. It should be noted that occupational descriptions are not comprehensive; for example, the one for librarians does not include references to two publications routinely used in job-hunting (i.e., *American Libraries*, and *C&RL News*). While a category for Web-based resources is not included, links are identified where the Web page is part of the organization. Previously noted concerns about more frequent updates are partially addressed by the inclusion of Web addresses.

Part 2 continues to focus on job-hunting topics (over 30 with this edition) that will be useful to everyone (e.g., interviewing skills, government publications) or describe opportunities for specific groups of individuals (e.g., women, minorities, ex-offenders). Each topical section contains six easy-to-use categories of information (e.g., reference works, software, databases). An alphabetic master index of occupations profiled, with appropriate *see also* references, and an index to all references cited in both parts complete the volume.

This resource has been successful in the past and the format and scope are continued with this edition. A major limitation is that the editors assume that library patrons know the job-hunting process already or have access to knowledgeable reference librarians. New editions should consider pairing with an author of a how-to book to show how the resources are best used for specific professions, such as the importance of the résumé, the curriculum vitae, networking, and the use of local or regional newspapers. The cost of the print version continues to be reasonable;

however, more library patrons are focused on Internet resources. The editors should consider moving the publication toward a Web version that can be updated more frequently and link directly to the important resources available on the Internet. Those public and academic libraries that have found the print version helpful in the past will welcome the new edition.—**Sandra E. Belanger**

Handbooks and Yearbooks

C, P

73.   Damp, Dennis V. **The Book of U.S. Government Jobs: Where They Are, What's Available, and How to Get One.** 8th ed. McKees Rocks, Pa., Brookhaven Press; distr., Ada, Mich., KSB Promotions, 2002. 286p. index. $21.95pa. ISBN 0-943641-21-7.

     This 8th edition is a sourcebook on employment opportunities available with the federal government and how to look and apply for positions. A comprehensive handbook, it provides background, job classifications, federal résumé styles, material on Civil Service Exams, and much more. Guidance on new decentralization of hiring initiatives and widespread use of the Internet postings and in hiring processes is also included. The preface outlines federal employment changes since the last edition and the September 11th terrorist attack's impact on prospects.

     The first chapter gives an overview of federal employment. The second outlines the process involved in applying for positions, including competitive examinations, tests, salaries, and eligibility. The third deals with information sources on postings, including periodicals, hotlines, commercial directories, books, and software; specialized opportunities for students and interns; Washington, D.C. department and agency telephone numbers; and refers to appendixes for lists of Websites and job centers nationwide. Following chapters discuss the following: interviews; examinations; completing applications; employment with law enforcement and with the postal service; veteran and military dependent preferences; opportunities for the disabled; and key things to remember. Appendixes not already mentioned include checklists for job-hunters, federal occupations (general schedule and wage grade classifications), and a list matching occupations to general schedule and wage grade classes and agencies and departments. Other access is provided by a detailed contents and index. This thorough, useful guide deserves strong consideration for career collections in U.S. public and academic libraries. [R: LJ, 1 Sept 02, p. 162]

—Nigel Tappin

C, P

74.   Lauber, Daniel, and Kraig Rice. **International Job Finder: Where the Jobs are Worldwide.** River Forest, Ill., Planning/Communications, 2002. 348p. index. $32.95; $19.95pa. ISBN 1-884587-11-9; 1-884587-10-0pa.

     The purpose for this book is to collect online and off-line resources for finding international jobs. Some 1,200 resources are discussed, which include a mix of job-listing and job-finding tools. Online tools include gateways (Internet sites that compile lists of other sites on a topic) and job source sites (Internet sites that list openings for specific jobs). Print sources include books about specific geographic locations and jobs in those locations, journals that advertise job openings, directories of companies, and trade association publications. Resources are listed in order by the number of jobs available. Each listing contains the title of the Website or job source and the URL or publication information. Each entry gives a 50-250 word description of the source and what it contains. A free electronic update sheet is available online to keep this work current.

     Chapter 1 contains general information about the book and how to use it. It also includes general information and references to more complete information on danger zones, tax considerations when working abroad, health information, advice about avoiding Internet job scams, and brief information about local customs and mores of the country in question. Chapter 2 gives step-by-step instructions on how to set up a computer; how to obtain an Internet Service Provider; how to use the Internet, e-mail, and newsgroups; and PDR files. Chapter 3 covers sources of information about jobs available worldwide. Chapters 4 through 11 cover one continent each, listing the job-seeking resources relevant to their respective geographic locations. Chapter 12 includes a bibliography of the print resources referenced throughout the book and provides an order form, should the reader care to obtain any of these titles.

Two indexes are available: alphabetical and topical. The topical index contains several categories, such as job title, industry, and geographic location. Brief biographies of the authors complete the book. There are a few scattered advertisements of relevance. Also included are screen shots of many of the Web pages indexed. This book is recommended for large career collections and libraries that support international programs. [R: LJ, 1 Oct 02, pp. 83-85]—**Joanna M. Burkhardt**

C, P

75.   Plunkett, Jack W. **Plunkett's Employers' Internet Sites with Careers Information 2002-2003.** Houston, Tex., Plunkett Research, 2002. 695p. index. $199.99pa. (w/CD-ROM). ISBN 1-891775-19-7.

For job-seekers searching for corporate employment, this volume is invaluable. It targets the search to corporate Websites in specific industries. General information opens the guide, such as how to apply for a job online, major Websites, what factors to search for, and key resources for researching major corporate employers and specific industries. Following this section, data from more than 500 company Websites from leading nation-wide industries are presented. The selection focuses on mid-size to large companies that provide extensive career information on the Internet in a user-friendly format.

Corporate employers are listed in a standard format that provides comparable data on each company's employment process (listings, procedures, and so on), contact personnel, financials, and benefits. In addition, the company's corporate culture is described, its locations are listed, and information is provided on how to best use their Website. Some companies are noted for the advancement of women and minorities. Various lists and indexes permit accessing specific companies by their industry sector, brand names, or subsidiaries; by their geographic location; and by types of positions (writing, consulting, sales, research, and so on). The print volume comes with a CD-ROM version that periodically updates tagged sites for quick checking by the job-seeker.—**Barbara Conroy**

MANAGEMENT

C

76.   **The Directory of Management Consultants 2002.** 10th ed. Washington, D.C., BNA Books, 2001. 981p. index. $295.00. ISBN 1-885922-69-8.

This comprehensive, compilation of U.S. management consulting firms represents more than 20 years of experience and research in the field. Listings are taken from Kennedy Information's files, with information provided by the firms and authenticated as much as possible. There is no listing fee. Firms of poor reputation, with incomplete information at press time, or that do not fall within the publisher's definition of management consultants are not included. Thorough, accurate listings include name, contact information, a general description, individual consultant specialties, geographic concentration, year founded, staff size and revenue, memberships, services and industries covered, branch office contact information and specialties, and international branch locations.

The introduction includes sections on how to use the directory, how to read a listing, and an overview of management consulting today. The 2d section is entitled "Advice to Clients on the Selection and Use of Management Consultants," and includes chapters on why projects fail and how to avoid failure as well as fees. The next section, "Of Related Interest," covers professional associations and includes an essay entitled, "On Becoming a Management Consultant." After the alphabetic "Primary Listings," five indexes provide access points by services, industry, geographic location, key principals, and advertisers. In sum, this listing of 2,400 firms in North America, with the locator for 4,300 key principals in the industry, is an indispensable resource for buyers of management consulting services, management consultants themselves, and aspiring management consultants. Although not inexpensive, this resource will be well used by business students, researchers, and owners.—**Susan C. Awe**

MARKETING AND TRADE

Directories

C, P

77. **Directory of Business Information Resources, 2002.** 10th ed. Millerton, N.Y., Grey House Publishing, 2002. 2500p. index. $275.00; $250.00pa. ISBN 1-930956-76-2. ; 1-930956-75-4pa.

C, P

78. **Directory of Business Information Resources. http://www.greyhouse.com.** [Website] Millerton, N.Y., Grey House Publishing. $495.00/year subscription. Date reviewed: May 02.

     Now in its 10th edition, this directory has proven its value as a resource to accurately identify important information sources in 98 industries and professions. Among the industries covered are accounting, advertising, banking, biotechnology, computers and data processing, food and beverage, libraries, marketing, motion pictures, printing, publishing, real estate, travel, and wholesaling. Sources covered include associations, newsletters, magazines and journals, special issues of magazines, trade shows, directories and databases, and Websites. Arranged by industry, entries include mailing address, telephone and fax numbers, Website and e-mail addresses, key contacts, and a brief description. Additional information provided includes number of members, dues, and founding year for associations; physical description, price, and frequency for publications; and date, location, and number of attendees for trade shows. The total number of listings is now almost 22,000. The introductory material has a user's guide that explains the entries and a cross-reference table correlating Standard Industrial Classification (SIC) codes with the industries covered. Indexes include an alphabetic entry index keyed to the sequentially numbered listings, a publisher index, and a magazine special issues index. Grey House Publishing also sells subscriptions to an Internet version of the directory for $495 per year. The major competing product is Gale's *Business Organizations, Agencies, and Publications Directory* (14th ed.; see ARBA 2003, entry 140), priced at $480.

     In the listings for accounting, there are some troubling omissions. For instance, there is no entry under Associations for the American Institute of Certified Public Accountants (AICPA)—it is included under trade shows. There is no mention of the *CPA Journal*, published by the New York State Society of Certified Public Accountants, which is a vital source for current accounting news and analysis. There are also no listings for the Rutgers Accounting Web (RAW; http://accounting.rutgers.edu/), a leading Internet accounting directory, and CPA2Biz (http://www.cpa2biz.com/CS2000/Home/default.htm), a joint portal of the AICPA and their state CPA partners. Furthermore, while there is an entry for the Financial Accounting Foundation there is not an entry for the Financial Accounting Standards Board (FASB) Website (http://www.fasb.org), the accounting profession's standard setter where information is published about matters currently under consideration. These serious omissions raise the question of whether the compilers are knowledgeable about the industries covered.—**Peter Zachary McKay**

Handbooks and Yearbooks

C, P

79. **Plunkett's E-Commerce & Internet Business Almanac 2001-2002.** Jack W. Plunkett, ed. Houston, Tex., Plunkett Research, 2001. 518p. index. $249.99pa. (w/CD-ROM). ISBN 1-891775-21-9.

     This 2d edition of *Plunkett's E-Commerce & Internet Business Almanac* is similar in format and content to the 1st edition (see ARBA 2001, entry 209). However, due to the volatile nature of e-commerce, there have been significant revisions for this edition. The number of companies profiled has increased from 330 to 386 (referred to as the "E-Commerce and Internet 400") and each receives a full-page entry. Included in the company profile is a description and "growth plan," brief financial data, salaries and benefit plans, and contact information. There are several indexes; the most useful is an index of company rankings within the industry groups. The editor has also provided an introductory overview of online retailing and a discussion of business-to-business trends with some key statistical tables. Another narrative chapter explores the impact on business of recent trends in personal computers and Internet access. Finally, there is a list of Websites, organizations, and publications that are most relevant to the e-commerce arena. A CD-ROM accompanies the book, with data that can be downloaded and customized. This is a recommended purchase for most academic business collections as well as for public libraries that actively support the business community.—**Thomas A. Karel**

OFFICE PRACTICES

C, P

80.   Jaderstrom, Susan, Leonard Kruk, and Joanne Miller. **Complete Office Handbook: The Definitive Reference for Today's Electronic Office.** Edited by Susan W. Fenner. 3d ed. New York, Random House, 2002. 596p. index. $21.95pa. ISBN 0-375-70929-0.

In less than a generation, the duties of office support staff have metamorphosed from secretary to administrative or executive assistant. Technology is the agent that has transformed the office from a typewriter and filing cabinet to a complex electronic environment. The 3d edition of the *Complete Office Handbook* is designed to assist the individual who serves as an administrative assistant, executive assistant, or project manager in this twenty-first century office structure. It covers, in detail, every facet of office operations, from office supplies and financial record keeping to complex operations, including computers, dictation equipment, and telecommunications equipment. The authors recognize that an administrative assistant may perform a broad variety of duties depending on the office in which he or she works so they devote entire chapters to such topics as records management, travel planning, and Web publishing. This handbook is just as useful for the entry-level office worker as it is for the professional advancing to the level of executive assistant. It includes sections on such basic topics as business etiquette; written and oral communication; maintaining calendars; and word processing. A particularly useful feature of the handbook is a nine-page glossary of computer terms.

At the price of $21.95 this book is within the financial means of every person entering the office workplace; likewise, every office, no matter its size, should purchase the handbook. Colleges and schools offering associate or four-year degree programs in the office management field most certainly need to acquire this handbook as well. Public libraries (mid-size to large) may also want to make it available to their patrons.—**Dene L. Clark**

5 Education

GENERAL WORKS

Directories

P, S

81.   **Guide to Summer Camps and Summer Schools 2002/2003.** 28th ed. Boston, Porter Sargent Publishers, 2002. 639p. index. $45.00; $27.00pa. ISBN 0-87558-145-5; 0-87558-146-3pa.

Summer camp is not just rowboats, swimming, and horseshoes anymore. For parents and school-age students interested in summer recreational and educational opportunities, there is a wide and growing variety of summer camp opportunities. This directory provides useful descriptions of more than 1,000 such camps in the United States and abroad.

The guide is arranged into a number of sections reflecting the particular focus of the summer camps or schools. There are academic program categories for the United States, other countries, the learning disabled, specialized subjects (e.g., computers, debate, oceanography), music and the arts, and other special interests (e.g., community service, wilderness camping, nature studies). Other programs are listed for instructional sports; students with special needs (e.g., emotional disorders, cancer, HIV/AIDS); and for boys, girls, and coeducational recreational camps. Within these sections, camps are usually listed by region, state, and then camp name, although occasionally they are simply alphabetic by name. The camp descriptions themselves include addresses; telephone numbers; e-mail addresses; names of directors; and information on ages and grades accepted, enrollment, number of students and faculty, fees, type of instruction, courses, amenities, and duration and frequency of programs along with a paragraph description of the camp. There is also a supplementary section of illustrated announcements with full-page camp descriptions written by the schools themselves. In addition, there are indexes to military training, religious affiliation, and camp name.

This directory is almost identical in layout and level of detail to *The Handbook of Private Schools* (see ARBA 2001, entry 218), which is also published by Porter Sargent Publishers. Many of the camps are somewhat expensive, limiting the market to the more affluent. Overall, the information compiled should be invaluable to parents, students, and school advisors looking into such programs. This guide is recommended for public libraries.

—**Stephen H. Aby**

Handbooks and Yearbooks

C, S

82.   Williams-Boyd, Pat. **Educational Leadership: A Reference Handbook.** Santa Barbara, Calif., ABC-CLIO, 2002. 341p. index. (Contemporary Education Issues). $45.00. ISBN 1-57607-353-X.

This new title in the publisher's Contemporary Education Issues series is organized into eight chapters: "Overview"; "Chronology: Shifting Perspectives—Involvement," "Ownership, and the Business of Community Building;" "Shifting Styles, Changing Metaphors: The Art of Creating Effective Leadership;" "The Community of Leaders and Learners;" "Competing Models: Leaders Initiating Change;" "Directory of Organizations, Institutes, Associations, Government Agencies, and Leadership Academies;" and "Selected Print and Nonprint Resources." An extensive index is provided as well.

The author describes education leadership styles and the manner in which leadership might be practiced by students, families, teachers, school-level administrators, system-level administrators, local school boards, professional developers, researchers, and state and federal political officials. The chronology is a good starting place for identification of legislation and events that exemplify and set trends in the public perception of educational leadership. Although it is difficult to do justice to such a broad definition of educational leadership and its history in an introductory volume written at the high school or freshman college level, the chapter bibliographies, directories, and selected list of resources make this a useful starting place for further research. *Educational Leadership* is recommended for high school and undergraduate libraries supporting teacher preparation programs.

—**Rosanne M. Cordell**

COMPUTER RESOURCES

S

83. Buckleitner, Warren, Ann Orr, and Ellen Wolock. **Complete Sourcebook on Children's Interactive Media 2002. Volume 10.** Flemington, N.J., Children's Software Revue, 2002. 655p. $62.95pa. ISBN 1-891983-06-7.

The subtitle of this 10th annual edition indicates the overall scope of the work: "5400 critical reviews of educational software, web sites, interactive toys, and popular videogames." Shareware, most overseas software, and videogames inappropriate for children are not covered. Since the suggested level of materials covered is for ages 1 to 15 (up to 9th grade), games that are popular with kids in the middle grades, but officially aimed at adult audiences, are not included (e.g., Grand Theft Auto). New to this edition are 615 reviews, written by a variety of teachers and parents.

Section 1 lists entries alphabetically by software title, with one to five stars ("dud" to excellent) as well as a more specific decimal point rating. Age levels and Entertainment Software Rating Board (ESRB) ratings (e.g., teen, everyone) are listed. Entries note platform (e.g., Win 95, Mac OS, PlayStation), publisher contact data, copyright date, price, educational summary (e.g., logical thinking, alphabetization, strategy, a utility for designing Internet surveys), and a review of one or more paragraphs. Sample titles that may be familiar are "Myst," "Furby," "Print Shop Deluxe," "Grolier Multimedia Encyclopedia," "SimCity 3000," "Reading Rabbit," "Oregon Trail," and "Math Blaster." Most reviews include evaluative statements, and often note problems or unique features, although some are merely descriptive. It is clear that the software has actually been used in the evaluation process. Sentences like "our testers loved the zany characters," "we learned several new solitaire games, and are now completely addicted," "we'd recommend a game controller," and "children who need a little external reward may not stick with the program" will help the would-be purchaser. Products are often compared to similar choices, which may or may not be reviewed in the book. For instance, the "Super Poo-Chi Interactive Puppy" entry mentions the more popular "Rocket Dog," but there's no review of "Rocket Dog" in the book. Sections 2, 3, and 4 list "just the best," programs that have received ratings from 4.2 to 5, by subject (e.g., mathematics, art and creativity, spelling), grade, and platform. The final two sections are directories for publishers, catalogs, and online stores.

A password provides one year's access to a continually updated Internet review database, plus selected articles from the bimonthly *Children's Software Revue*. Subscribers to the magazine already have access to the database and thus the contents of the book under review. There are other reference works that review children's multimedia, but none are as comprehensive as this. It will be a welcome addition to school and public library collections.

—**Deborah V. Rollins**

S

84. **CLCD Instructional Materials Database. http://www.childrenslit.com.** [Website]. Bethesda, Md., CLCD Company LLC, $249.95/year (for 1st subscription); $200.00/year (for 2d subscription); $150.00/year (for 3d subscription); $100.00/year (for 4th and subsequent subscriptions). Date reviewed: Mar 02.

Designed to complement the *Children's Literature Comprehensive Database* (CLCD; see entry 374), the *CLCD Instructional Materials Database* (CLIMD) contains reviews of teaching and instructional materials from the California Instructional Technology, Eisenhower, and ERIC Clearinghouses. The search design of this database is also similar to CLCD. That is to say, users can search for words or phrases with the option of choosing various qualifiers. For example, the database can search for singular or plural forms of the specified word or phrase as well as word variants and exact matches. Furthermore, users can opt to search in a specified entry field: "Author," "Title," "Subject," "Contents," "ISBN," or "Summary." Other qualifiers, such as age group, language, author/illustrator, publisher, and publication date are also available. Works in English, French, Spanish, German, Italian, Russian, Chinese, Japanese, and Vietnamese are included.

Also similar to CLCD, users can select one or more items from the search results list to be saved into a separate list. These selections can then be sorted by year of publication, clearinghouse, author, title, or language in ascending or descending order. Cataloging information for the materials can also be downloaded in brief, full, or MARC format. Another feature of CLIMD is that users can specify a search in one or more of the clearinghouses, such as ERIC CIJE (Current Index to Journals in Education) or ERIC RIE (Resources in Education). Other ERIC Clearinghouses are available, such as the clearinghouses for assessment and evaluation, community college, education management, and rural and urban education materials. The review entries contain title, publisher, publication date, clearinghouse, and source data, along with an indication of recommended grade levels and available formats. Contact and product information, a summary of the item, and a list of contents (or the table of contents if appropriate) are also provided as well as links to entries for related materials. Overall, this database can be very useful for teachers and librarians who work with elementary age students. Navigating the database is fairly easy, but may be more difficult for users who do not have much experience with the Internet or computers.

—**Cari Ringelheim**

S

85.   **Educators Guide to Free Internet Resources 2002-2003: Elementary/Middle School Edition.** Kathleen Suttles Nehmer, ed. Randolph, Wis., Educators Progress Service, 2002. 291p. index. $39.95pa. ISBN 0-87708-363-0.

S

86.   **Educators Guide to Free Internet Resources 2002-2003: Secondary Edition.** 20th ed. Kathleen Suttles Nehmer, ed. Randolph, Wis., Educators Progress Service, 2002. 317p. index. $39.95pa. ISBN 0-87708-362-2.

Each of these books is a listing of educational materials—some for use by teachers, some for use by students. It was compiled by the editor writing thousands of letters to companies inquiring about materials they are willing to offer free to educators and others. In the case of Websites, each and every site is visited to make sure it still exists as well as being checked for content. The materials are intended to "help teachers teach," not only to make their jobs easier but also to help students learn more. This is especially useful when it comes to free computer materials, for computers really are the tool of the future. Easy-to-find information tells readers just what they may expect to find at each Website visited. The body of the *Guide* gives full information on each of the titles. This includes descriptive information along with suggested grade level and format of material to give preliminary information about the teaching materials found at that particular Website. The complete Web address is included. The title index enables readers to locate any item whose title is known. It guides users directly to any specific item in the resource, where you can read the description of the material and find all ordering information. The subject index guides users to all materials relating to topics of a more specific nature than the general subject heading categories in the body of the *Guide*. The source index provides an alphabetic list of the names of the organizations from which materials can be obtained.—**Janet Mongan**

S

87.   **EvaluTech. http://www.evalutech.sreb.org./search/index.asp.** [Website]. Atlanta, Ga., Southern Regional Education Board. Free. Date reviewed: Jan 03.

Originating in 1997, this site is a free resource designed to provide reviews of instructional materials for educators. It is sponsored by the Southern Regional Education Board's Educational Technology Cooperative and the Educational Resources Evaluation Services of the North Carolina Department of Public Instruction. The site reviews computer software, CD-ROMs, books, and videos for K-12 educators and only products that are recommended are critiqued.

The site is searchable through a variety of criteria, including keywords, subject, format, levels, title, author, series, and copyright date. Users can easily narrow or broaden their search by adding or eliminating certain criteria. After conducting a search the user is presented with the results in table format that includes the name of the author/ title/series, publisher, copyright date, grade, and format. After clicking on the title they would like more information on, the user will find a one-paragraph review of the work. Reviews are written by media specialists, teachers, and other education professionals, and reviewers are instructed to use the specific criteria laid out by the Website's sponsor. (Criteria are listed on the Website.) Reviews are well written and evaluate the organization, accuracy, and strengths and weakness of the work as well as list the appropriate subject and grade level for its use.

This site will be extremely useful to educators and media specialists from all states. In the coming year the materials reviewed will be correlated with state student academic standards, making the site even more useful for K-12 educators.—**Shannon Graff Hysell**

S

88.   **NetTrekker. http://www.nettrekker.com.** [Website]. Thinkronize. $1,295.00/school (includes standards content). Date reviewed: Aug 02.

NetTrekker is a search engine that has been designed specifically with K-12 students and educators in mind. The Websites and links featured here have been selected due to their academic nature and have been evaluated by a team of 400 educators. The search engine provides access to both elementary and secondary sources and is searchable by grade level.

After supplying a user name and password the user can search by either keyword or by the subject areas provided (science, language arts, technology, religion, social studies, mathematics, health and physical education, and the arts). When one clicks on the main subject a page with related subject appears; for example, "Science" sends the user to the subtopics of animals, earth science, space science, and so on. If the user is looking for a person of this specialty they can click on "Famous People" at the bottom of the page, which directs them to a list of featured noteworthy people. There is also a list of general sites on the subject listed at the bottom. All sites have been rated and signed by the reviewer and given a short description. The user can then either select to go to that site or choose another on the page. The sites are given symbols for how reliable they are; the appropriate grade level; whether they have audio, illustrations, bibliographies, charts/maps, formulas/examples, lesson plans, or learning exercises; and what language they are in (English, Spanish, German, or French). Users can customize their searches in several different ways. They can use the "Timeline" feature to create a timeline for specific periods. They can set their results so that they show a detailed view (with URL, reviewers ratings, additional features) or a limited view (just the site name and URL).

What makes this tool especially useful for schools is the fact that it incorporates state curriculum standards into the site. This feature provides lesson plans, learning exercises, and Websites that meet each state's benchmarks. This feature is provided at additional cost.

For schools that can afford this site, it will save educators, media specialists, and students a lot of time wading through the information on the Web. It will be a useful research tool for elementary, middle, and high schools. [R: BR, Sept/Oct 02, p. 82]—**Shannon Graff Hysell**

ELEMENTARY AND
SECONDARY EDUCATION

Bibliography

S

89.   Beck, Peggy. **GlobaLinks: Resources for World Studies, Grades K-8.** Worthington, Ohio, Linworth, 2002. 148p. index. $39.95pa. ISBN 1-58683-040-6.

Although resources are numerous and readily available, Americans are often accused of being provincial and out of touch with the rest of the world. Beck's bibliography promotes a more global, multicultural, and diverse view of the world. The book is divided into three areas: print and nonprint, Websites, and key pal/pen pal projects. These areas are further divided into a wide range of subjects that fit under the umbrella of "World Studies."

Each alphabetically arranged entry includes complete bibliographic information plus the ISBN and a suggested age range for which the item is best suited. Websites obviously include their URLs. The author's strength, however, lies not only in her selections, but also in her consistently high-quality annotations. The mention of the occasional quirky bits of information is apparent proof that Beck has reviewed each of the sources included in the bibliography. True to a librarian's heart, almost 35 pages (out of 148) are devoted to indexes—Website title, author/illustrator, title, and subject. This compilation is highly recommended for the professional collection of young adult sections and school media centers. [R: BR, Mar/April 02, p. 70; SLJ, Mar 02, p. 263]—**Phillip P. Powell**

Directories

S

90.   **Funding Sources for K-12 Education 2002.** Westport, Conn., Oryx Press/Greenwood Publishing Group, 2002. 910p. index. $49.95pa. ISBN 1-57356-566-0.

Funding Sources for K-12 Education 2002 is an outstanding source for anyone who is serious about finding funds to help advance their educational agendas, whether for schools, libraries, museums, or social or welfare agencies. This directory is the 4th edition researched and published by Oryx Press. The book's impact will be very favorable especially among those educators, researchers, and community-based organizations whose funding is depleted or been cut due to inflation or political and economic problems.

The book contains both a foreword and an introduction. The former is written by an education practitioner who graciously shares her insights with the readers. She states that the job of a grant writer is not magical nor is it easy. She delineates some of the processes involved in finding and receiving funds, the knowledge and the competitive edge that the grant writer must possess to be successful. The one-page introduction emphasizes the connection between government, nonprofit, private, and local sources. It also explains the four types of indexes found in the guide. The indexes are the most efficient way to locate funding in this directory.

The very brief "How to Use This Directory" explains the format and layout of the written text. Immediately after these 2 pages are 10 pages of Websites arranged in alphabetic order by sponsoring organization. There is a well-written chapter titled "A Guide to Proposal Writing," which will be an invaluable tool to grant writers. Moreover, it features an excellent example of a proposal letter sent to a private foundation soliciting funds for a project to improve police-community relations. The main section of the guide is the "Grants Program Section," which lists programs in alphabetic order and includes grant titles, application deadlines, contact details, and other pertinent information. There are four indexes. These are the subject index, the sponsoring organizations index, the grants by program type index, and the geographic index. The geographic index includes not only grants available in the 50 states, but also Puerto Rico, Canada, Europe, the Asiatic countries, Israel, and the United Kingdom. There is no glossary to demystify specialized terms, similarly there is neither an appendix nor a bibliography. However, the discerning educator may not even notice, since the directory's extensive listing, superb writing, and well-detailed guide definitely overcome this lack. This is an appealing book and will be a worthwhile source for schools, educators, and educational organizations (both secular and religious). Basically any entity seeking to acquire or to enhance funds for curriculum and teacher development, technology, the library, arts enrichment, sports, health, human services, the environment, community development, and a myriad number of other programs should invest in this book.—**Alice A. Robinson**

Handbooks and Yearbooks

C, S

91.   Campos, David. **Sex, Youth, and Sex Education: A Reference Handbook.** Santa Barbara, Calif., ABC-CLIO, 2002. 316p. index. (Contemporary Education Issues). $45.00. ISBN 1-57607-776-4.

The goal of ABC-CLIO's Contemporary Education Issues series is to provide balanced overviews of current and controversial education topics. This latest volume in the series achieves that goal by describing the full range of sex education programs, from the most conservative (abstinence-only) to the most liberal (comprehensive), in use in American schools today. A "Chronology of Sex Education" is included, which highlights statistics, people, and events key to the development of modern sex education in the United States. A separate chapter provides an in-depth discussion and a more detailed decade-by-decade look at this development. Important issues related to sex education for youth are also explored, including sexual abuse and harassment, sexual orientation, and sex education for youth with disabilities. Although chapters are dedicated to issues of diversity in sexual orientation and ability/disability, none are devoted to issues related to ethnic or cultural diversity. This seems surprising, given the comprehensive nature of the book. A couple of useful features round out the volume: a directory of organizations that provide information or assistance on general sex education, abuse and harassment, sexual orientation, and youth with disabilities; and a lengthy bibliography of relevant book, journal, and Internet resources.

The author of this book has skillfully condensed a tremendous amount of information into one very usable volume. The work is thoroughly documented, and will provide administrators, teachers, teachers in training, and parents with an excellent overview of the subject. It will also offer researchers an excellent starting point for further study. This volume is recommended for academic and public libraries.—**Janet Dagenais Brown**

S

92.   Hall, Susan. **Using Picture Storybooks to Teach Literature Devices.** Westport, Conn., Oryx Press/ Greenwood Publishing Group, 2002. 349p. index. (Recommended Books for Children and Young Adults, v.3). $32.50pa. ISBN 1-57356-350-1.

Using recently published picture books (through 2000), Hall has compiled a practical, useful resource that teachers and librarians of all ages will appreciate. From alliteration to understatement, Hall provides succinct definitions of more than 40 literary devices. Each book includes bibliographic information, a brief summary, a discussion of the use of the key devices, examples of other devices, a description of the style of the art, and identification of the curriculum tie-in.

Picture books are an easily understood source for teaching literary devices. The stories are compact, the art is absorbing, and older students will appreciate the economy of style that comes with a well-told picture book. Tackling the teaching of literary devices becomes easy with Hall's resource. The teaching is left to the user—this book is not an in-depth treatment or step-by-step manual for teaching literary devices. The entries are brief, leaving the user to determine how best to develop the understanding. The beauty of Hall's book is that it provides an abundance of choices, excellent books, and an extremely user-friendly format for the busy teacher or librarian who needs to explore analogy, motif, serendipity, and the like.

The appendixes, including resources identified in a variety of ways, are particularly useful. A very minor improvement for the next edition would be a more complete table of contents with the page numbers provided for the literary devices. This work is an extremely useful, intelligent resource.—**Suzanne I. Barchers**

Indexes

S

93.   **Multicultural Projects Index: Things to Make and Do to Celebrate Festivals, Cultures, and Holidays Around the World.** 3d ed. By Mary Anne Pilger. Westport, Conn., Libraries Unlimited/Greenwood Publishing Group, 2002. 130p. $55.00. ISBN 1-56308-898-3.

Introducing young learners to holidays, festivals, and customs of cultures from around the world with projects ranging from decorations to costumes, handicrafts, foods, songs, and dances has never been easier and more exciting thanks to Pilger's *Multicultural Projects Index*. Educators will find this *Index* very useful. Arranged by subject and project area, each entry describes the activity and guides readers to source pages that have complete bibliographic information. Pilger's *Index* also has an author index and a key at the beginning explaining exactly how the *Index* is to be used. From popular activities such as origami folding and kite making to how to play a Vietnamese elephant march game, one will find what they are looking for.

Providing quick and easy access to a wide range of activities is the aim of this book and it does exactly that. Having Pilger's *Multicultural Projects Index* will prove to be a gem for any school librarian and libraries that have a curriculum collection.—**Vang Vang**

HIGHER EDUCATION

General Works

Directories

C, S

94.　**The College Blue Book.** 29th ed. Eric Hoss, ed. New York, Macmillan Reference USA/Gale Group, 2002. 6v. index. $300.00/set. ISBN 0-02-865624-5.

This six-volume reference work is one of the research collection staples of all major academic libraries. The 29th edition follows the same format as previous editions, organizing information into the following volumes: Narrative Descriptions; Tabular Data; Degrees Offered by College and Subject; Occupational Education; Scholarships, Fellowships, Grants, and Loans; and Distance Learning Programs. This comprehensive reference guide to colleges and universities in the United States and Canada is invaluable, and is also essential in most high school counseling offices. Vocational and distance learning programs within and outside higher education are listed as well. Essential information is provided on degrees, entrance requirements, financial aid, and statistics, along with descriptions and historical information on each institution listed. This is one of the primary sources for current information related to higher education and educational institutions in the United States and Canada.

—**Bradford Lee Eden**

S

95.　**Complete Book of Colleges.** 2003 ed. New York, Princeton Review/Random House, 2002. 1330p. index. $24.95pa. ISBN 0-375-76256-6. ISSN 1088-8594.

This source provides brief information on more than 1,700 colleges and universities plus more in-depth profiles of 180 institutions that paid a fee for inclusion. An introduction offers advice in finding the right match between a prospective student and a university. This is followed by a very useful "Admissions Wizard" section, which has readers answer five basic questions about their college preferences (selectivity, geographic region, cost, size, and environment). The answers generate a search string that can then be matched to a list of colleges meeting all given preferences. This is a exceptionally quick way to begin narrowing the list of colleges a prospective student needs to consider.

The main section of this book discusses each institution, providing contact information, including Web address, facts on admission standards, enrollment, tuition, financial aid availability, size of library, athletics, make-up of student body, religious affiliation (if any), academic requirements, facilities, and so on. There are indexes by location, size, environment (urban, suburban, rural), cost, and selectivity.

The information about the institutions is as up-to-date and complete as possible; Web addresses were accurate as of time of publication. The Princeton Review Website provides further helpful information. This source is highly recommended for any library serving high school students.—**Michele Russo**

Handbooks and Yearbooks

S

96.　**Competitive Colleges, 2001-2002: Top Colleges for Top Students.** Lawrenceville, N.J., Peterson's Guides, 2001. 487p. index. $18.95pa. ISBN 0-7689-0557-5. ISSN 0887-0152.

College sponsors of the book and Web resources designed for college-bound students are identified. The major portion of the book is devoted to one-page descriptions of the colleges, arranged in alphabetic order. Following the same format throughout, a statement pertaining to college setting and various contact information for admissions directors are provided at the top of the page followed by college descriptions subdivided by the following topics: academics, students, facilities and resources, campus life, campus safety, and applying.

Statistical information appears in the margins of the pages. These figures paint pictures of students when they enter, as they become part of the student body, and as they graduate. Financial data are also presented. Statistics relating to the previous year's entering class tell the number who applied, the percentage of that number who were accepted, the percentage who enrolled, ACT and SAT scores, and financial matters. The student body is statistically described by classification, gender, and nationality. The "Graduation and After" section tells how long it took students to graduate, whether they pursued further study, and job-related statistics. Financial matters refer to the amount spent on tuition and fees and the amount of financial aid received.

Seven appendixes identify colleges by cost of attending, size, sex of student body, religious affiliation, public colleges, and colleges accepting fewer than half of their applicants. The appendixes are followed by two indexes—a majors by college index and a geographic index.—**Lois Gilmer**

Financial Aid

Directories

C, S

97.   **The Scholarship Book 2003: The Complete Guide to Private-Sector Scholarships, Fellowships, Grants and Loans for the Undergraduate.** Paramus, N.J., Prentice Hall, 2002. 550p. index. $30.00pa. (w/CD-ROM). ISBN 0-7352-0367-9.

"Need Money for College? You'll Find It Here!" screams the headline on the back cover of this reference work published by Prentice Hall. The information contained in this bulky 8-by-11-inch paperback was compiled from the databank at the National Scholarship Research Service, which, according to the editors of the volume, is "the largest private sector financial aid research service in the world" (p. v). In the introduction, the editors provide encouragement to the prospective college students for whom this work is intended, stating that the private sector offers some $50 billion annually to support education in the United States, that the average undergraduate scholarship is about $5,000 per year, that much of this money remains unclaimed every year, that 80 percent of the scholarships are not need-based, and that 90 percent are not concerned primarily with grades. Moreover, the editors assert that the average student will find in this volume at least 20 private sector scholarship sources for which he or she is eligible to apply.

For each of the 3,600-plus scholarship sources listed, the editors provide a brief description of the award, including its amount and its eligibility requirements, the deadline date for the application, and an address where one can get more information or request application materials. At the end of the volume are references to other books and Internet sites that the editors recommend to students preparing for college life, as well as an alphabetic index of all the scholarship sources. The volume also comes with a CD-ROM that features the entire text of the book, plus direct Internet links to the home pages of thousands of private sector financial aid sources.

Any reference work that seeks to provide readers with information about thousands of items needs to have an attractive and user-friendly format. Unfortunately, this source, although data-filled, is not particularly easy to read. Consequently, users should not be misled by the promise on the book's back cover or by the publisher's promise that with the CD-ROM "you can point-and-click your way to college financial aid in seconds!" Those willing to exploit this goldmine of data, however, may find that their hard work was not performed in vain.

—**Terry D. Bilhartz**

C, S

98.   **Scholarships, Fellowships, and Loans: A Guide to Education-Related Financial Aid Programs for Students and Professionals.** 18th ed. Chrystal Rózsa, ed. Farmington Hills, Mich., Gale, 2002. 1215p. index. $199.00. ISBN 0-7876-5292-X. ISSN 1058-5699.

A tradition of excellence continues in the 18th edition of *Scholarships, Fellowships, and Loans.* Detailed information on more than 4,200 awards is listed for students ranging from undergraduate and vocational/technical education to post-doctoral and professional studies. The preface includes three pages of useful tips on how to find financial aid that students should be encouraged to study.

The main body of the text includes entries that are alphabetically arranged by administering organization. In addition to contact information, each entry provides information about purpose, qualifications and restrictions, selection criteria, award amounts, number of awards granted, and application details.

The addition of six extremely useful indexes makes this resource stand out above similar sources. The vocational goals index is arranged by levels of study and broad subject categories to give the reader a quick overview of each award's purpose and eligibility requirements. Other indexes classify awards by fields of study, legal residence and place of study requirements, special recipients, and sponsors. These indexes allow users to further refine their search for appropriate awards.

While *Scholarships, Fellowships, and Loans* does not discuss financial aid programs administered and funded by individual colleges or universities, it does include useful information about state and federal programs, including the AmeriCorps. Although not inexpensive, *Scholarships, Fellowships, and Loans* is a valuable resource for anyone seeking financial aid. It is highly recommended for all libraries.—**Michele Russo**

INTERNATIONAL EXCHANGE PROGRAMS AND OPPORTUNITIES

C

99.   **Institute of International Education Passport. http://www.iiepassport.org/.** [Website]. New York, Institute of International Education. Free. Date reviewed: Oct 02.

The Institute of International Education (IIE) is a well-respected organization that promotes higher education throughout the world and administers the Fulbright program for the U.S. government. Its Website claims it is "the most complete guide to planning academic year and short term study abroad." The program listings are taken from IIE's two well-known reference publications: *Academic Year Abroad* (30th ed.; see ARBA 2002, entry 288) and *Short-term Study Abroad* (see ARBA 2002, entry 291), and appear to include all the listings from the printed works.

IIE Passport has simple and advanced search modes. The basis of both is searches by country, field of study, and language. The advanced search allows the user to add the type of program they are interested in and length of time involved. The additional useful features of the printed works are here too: a student guide to studying abroad that includes planning a trip and what to expect in the country. There are lists of Internet resources on studying and living abroad, publications, organizations, and travel Web pages.

The Website has a link to a very similar site StudyAbroad.com. In fact the IIE site is the product of an alliance with Educational Directories Unlimited, which owns StudyAbroad.com. Both sites have a similar look and feel, and also contain much of the same advertising. The advertisements for study abroad programs are grouped in large blocks, and take up a larger amount of space than the usual advertising sidebar. This is a bit distracting. The content of *IIE Passport* is excellent, and this should be the first stop when trying to identify study abroad programs on the Web.—**Christine E. King**

LEARNING DISABILITIES AND DISABLED

C, P, S

100.   Turkington, Carol, and Joseph R. Harris. **Encyclopedia of Learning Disabilities.** New York, Facts on File, 2002. 304p. index. (Facts on File Library of Health and Living). $60.00. ISBN 0-8160-4075-3.

Intended to help parents, teachers, physicians, and students, the *Encyclopedia of Learning Disabilities* will meet its goal for many questions. Alphabetically arranged entries cover general topics and concepts (e.g., learning style, college admission, learning disabilities), treatments and strategies (e.g., corporal punishment, whole language approach), organizations, disabilities and problems (e.g., dyslexia, traumatic brain injury, learned helplessness), court cases and laws, people, assessment techniques and instruments, physiology, and more. Length varies from a sentence or two to two or more pages. Longer articles on disabilities have convenient headings that make it easy to find information on symptoms, cause, prognosis, diagnosis, and treatment. The writing is accessible to general readers. No references are provided for any entries. Some common terms are not defined at all, or may be mentioned only in passing. There is also no entry for Pervasive Developmental Disorders, also known as PDD, but there are entries for autism and Asperger's syndrome that note that they are forms of PDD. Furthermore, there are no entries for *inclusion* or *inclusive education*, concepts that are often differentiated from *mainstreaming*, which does merit an entry. There are also no statistical tables showing the extent of learning disabilities, either in general or by type, although individual articles may note the percentage of the population affected.

Appendixes cover national organizations (arranged by disability), government agencies and information sources, assistive technology resources, telephone hotlines, Websites for companies that sell assistive technology, listservs, and a short bibliography for general readers that is arranged by audience level. A brief glossary explains specialized terms that may be unfamiliar to the lay audience. A longer bibliography of research articles and texts and an index round out the book. Indexing and cross-references could be improved. For instance, the commonly used acronyms IEP (Individualized Education Plan) and LRE (Least Restrictive Environment) have no *see* references among the entries, nor are they in the index. Entries for them exist, but they are filed under the full phrase. The entry for stimulant medications points to those on ADHD and Ritalin, but not those on Cylert, Dexedrine, and Adderall. Also, the index does not list the individual drug names under the heading "Stimulant Medications," and omits some of the relevant page references.

Despite its problems, this work will be used—according to the introduction, learning disabilities affect one in seven Americans. Libraries that already own the more comprehensive and scholarly three-volume *Encyclopedia of Special Education* (Wiley, 2000) can forgo this purchase. The *Learning Disabilities Sourcebook* (Omnigraphics, 1998) is a readable compilation of government and other reports reprinted in chapter format. The *Special Education Dictionary* (LRP, 1997) has brief but clear definitions and a wealth of acronyms, and may be sufficient for many needs.—**Deborah V. Rollins**

6 Ethnic Studies

GENERAL WORKS

Dictionaries and Encyclopedias

C, P, S

101. **Multicultural Reference Center. http://www.marshallcavendish.com.** [Website]. Tarrytown, N.Y., Marshall Cavendish. Price negotiated by site. Date reviewed: Jan 03.

The *Multicultural Reference Center* is the product of the combined efforts of Marshall Cavendish and EBSCO. The source pulls together four key resources from Marshall Cavendish's works in multicultural studies: *The African American Encyclopedia* (2d ed.; see ARBA 2002, entry 309), *The Asian American Encyclopedia* (see ARBA 96, entry 394), *The Latino Encyclopedia* (see ARBA 97, entry 337), and *Encyclopedia of Multiculturalism* (see ARBA 95, entry 396).

With the use of EBSCO's point-and-click interface, users can easily search the database for relevant information. The site is searchable by entering a keyword, by entering a category (e.g., African Americans) or subject, by entering the title of an entry, or by entering a personal name. More than 2,000 main articles can be found here and each article has additional links to related newspaper or magazine articles, Websites, and images. The site provides additional features that will be especially useful in academic settings, including: "Reference Links" to related books, films, and organizations; "Ideas for Educators," which provides lesson plans for teachers; "Student Resources," which includes biographies and features on current events; a section where users can write notes on the subject and print them out; and a "Citation Builder," which creates citations of articles used and stores them in the "Notes" section.

This site is filled with useful information for high school and undergraduate college students. Libraries interested in purchasing this site should contact the publisher for a free 30-day trial.—**Shannon Graff Hysell**

Handbooks and Yearbooks

C, P

102. Brownstone, David M., and Irene M. Franck. **Facts About American Immigration.** Bronx, N.Y., H. W. Wilson, 2001. 818p. illus. index. $95.00. ISBN 0-8242-0959-1.

H. W. Wilson has a series of quick reference works known as the "Facts about . . ." series. These books are the telephone reference librarian's best aide because they deliver facts quickly and without undue ornamentation. The latest volume, *Facts About American Immigration*, is a worthy addition to this collection. The layout of the book is designed for speed. The book is separated into seven parts and six appendixes. Part 1 is an overview of immigration to the United States and this is the longest essay in the book. The authors heavily weighted the narrative with graphs and statistical tables, placing the emphasis on data presentation instead of data interpretation. Parts 2 through 6 cover immigration data from Europe, Africa, Asia, the Americas, and Oceania. The subsection in each part is separated by "Immigrants from . . ." a specific country, making it very easy to look up the immigration statistics from whatever country the researcher or student is interested in studying. Each "Immigrants from . . ." subsection ends with a listing of Internet and print resources. The six appendixes augment the volume by covering information such as immigration and naturalization legislation, estimates of illegal immigrants, and tips on how to do genealogical research. Also included are a comprehensive immigration chronology, a glossary of immigration terms, and a handy index. This book is a welcome resource and should be included in any public or academic library that serves patrons interested in immigration matters. It should be placed within easy reach for the telephone reference librarian.—**Glenn Masuchika**

P, S

103.   Mason, Antony. **People Around the World.** New York, Kingfisher, 2002. 256p. illus. maps. index. $24.95. ISBN 0-7534-5497-1.

People Around the World is designed with middle school age children in mind to introduce them to the various cultures and landscapes around the world. The book's introduction discusses the evolution of mankind and how different cultures have influenced each other through travel and trade. It also looks at those cultures that have kept much the same way of life for thousands of years and why.

The book is arranged by continent, beginning with the Arctic and Subarctic and ending with Australia and the Pacific. For each continent various countries are discussed so that a wide representation of cultures are described. For the most part topics of interest to children are discussed, including food, entertainment and play, city life and country life, and education. For some countries, political and economic strife is described. The publisher has used color photographs and well-written captions throughout the volume to supplement the text and these may prove more educational for children than the text itself. Each section ends with a list of countries located in the featured continent in a sidebar, which includes an illustration of the flag, and information on the capital, area in square miles, population, population density, life expectancy, religions, languages, adult literacy rate, and currency.

This work will be a good addition to public and school libraries. At the relatively low price of $24.95 many libraries will be able to purchase one for both the reference and circulating collections.—**Shannon Graff Hysell**

C, P

104.   Russell, Cheryl. **Racial and Ethnic Diversity: Asians, Blacks, Hispanics, Native Americans, and Whites.** 4th ed. Ithaca, N.Y., New Strategist, 2002. 974p. index. $99.00. ISBN 1-885070-45-4.

The inclusion of the 2000 U.S. Census numbers makes this 4th edition an important update over the recent previous edition (see ARBA 2001, entry 273) as it presents a racial and ethnic portrait of the United States at the beginning of the millennium. A few basic statistics reveal the demographic changes that have occurred since the 1990 census. The non-Hispanic white share of the population fell from 76 to 69 percent during those years. Some 31 percent of Americans are now minorities. And the trend continues. Among the 4 million babies born in 2000, only 58 percent were born to non-Hispanic white women. There were 20 percent born to Hispanics and 15 percent to blacks.

The bulk of this nearly 1,000-page book details these data in a series of chapters, each focusing on a different ethnic or racial group: American Indians and Alaska Natives, Asians, Blacks, Hispanics, Native Hawaiians and Other Pacific Islanders, Whites, and Total Population. For each group there are statistics on business, education, health, housing, income, and living arrangements as well as spending and wealth for some. The first page of each section features an overview of the most important data. The numbers come primarily from the Census Bureau and other federal agencies such as the Bureau of Labor Statistics, the National Center for Education Statistics, and the National Center for Health Statistics. In a minority of cases the latest data were from the late 1990s. In all cases, careful documentation as been provided for the sources of the statistics. The editor states that extensive data extraction and analysis has been performed on the government information.

The last chapter is an interesting exception. It deals with the attitudes and behavior of Americans regarding racial and ethnic groups. Most of the data are from the 2000 General Social Survey taken by the University of Chicago's National Opinion Research Center. Although most or all of the statistics provided here are available somewhere else in published sources or on Websites, most users will find this well-organized, systematic presentation well worth the price.—**Henry E. York**

AFRICAN AMERICANS

Biography

C, P

105.   Asante, Molefi Kete. **100 Greatest African Americans: A Biographical Encyclopedia.** Buffalo, N.Y., Prometheus Books, 2002. 345p. illus. $49.00. ISBN 1-57392-963-8.

As one of the most prominent figures in African American studies today, Temple University's Molefi Kete Asante has written extensively on the black experience in America. His latest work strives to reach a wider audience by profiling relatively well-known (and some lesser-known) figures of the last 200 years in the fine arts, science, literature, politics, and medicine. Selections were based on five basic criteria, including a "consistent posture" toward the social, cultural, and economic uplift of African Americans. Naturally, any such listing of "the greatest" is highly subjective, but Asante's choices are judicious and tend to avoid individuals who excel but do not rise above the crowd in terms of "uplifting the race." Thus, Shirley Chisholm and Tiger Woods are included, but not Michael Jordan or BET's Robert Johnson. Arranged in alphabetic order, each profile is two to four pages long and provides brief biographical information and an illustration (photographs when available, but many are pencil sketches). The prose is generally straightforward and aimed at a senior high or undergraduate audience; this volume is suitable primarily for the general reader rather than researcher. Although there is nothing new in Asante's book, undergraduate academic and public libraries will want to purchase it for its scope and balance. This will be a good companion volume to Henry Louis Gates Jr. and Cornel West's *The African-American Century: How Black Americans Have Shaped Our Century* (Simon & Schuster, 2000).—**Anthony J. Adam**

C, S

106.   Gubert, Betty Kaplan, Miriam Sawyer, and Caroline M. Fannin. **Distinguished African Americans in Aviation and Space Science.** Westport, Conn., Oryx Press/Greenwood Publishing Group, 2002. 319p. illus. index. (Distinguished African Americans Series). $59.95. ISBN 1-57356-246-7.

Distinguished African Americans in Aviation and Space Science is the third title in the Distinguished African Americans Series by Oryx Press. This title is a long-awaited reference source that chronicles the lives of some very important African American men and women in the field of aviation and space science. Some of these people were far more advanced in their time than many books would have us believe. The volume is very well written, devoting several pages to each person and ending with a list of sources for further reading. One could always find the information offered in *Distinguished African Americans in Aviation and Space Science* within the pages of other sources, but this would require the user to take the time to leaf through several volumes to come up with what is presented within this one volume. The list of names is impressive—80 men and 20 women—from George W. Allen to Yvonne Cagle (the second African American woman to be selected for the space program) to Ronald E. McNair (the astronaut who lost his life in the explosion of the *Challenger* in 1986). The presentation of early African American women such as Willa Brown, Bessie Coleman, and others who were involved in aviation before it was available to many women is very important.

A minor discrepancy that should not distract from the rest of the content can be found on page 48 where the authors list Indiana State Normal School as part of Indiana University. Willa Brown obtained an A.B. degree at Indiana State Normal School in 1931, which became Indiana State University in 1965.

This remains a fascinating book that is well put together by the authors. It offers the reader a fascinating bibliography, which includes print and nonprint materials to supplement the ones at the end of each biographical profile. Just as important as the other titles in this series, this is a unique source and a must-have reference tool even if the institution does not offer a program in African American studies. This reviewer would also like to see senior high school librarians invest in this source.—**Valentine K. Muyumba**

C, P

107.   **The Malcolm X Encyclopedia.** Robert L. Jenkins and Mfanya Donald Tryman, eds. Westport, Conn., Greenwood Press, 2002. 643p. illus. index. $74.95. ISBN 0-313-29264-7.

Now that Malcolm X appears to have taken his rightful place in American history, this encyclopedia by Mississippi State political science professor Mfanya Donald Tryman and history professor Robert L. Jenkins is a welcome and important guide for both researchers and undergraduates to the growing body of literature on the subject. More than 70 scholars have contributed to the 500-plus alphabetically arranged brief (typically one page), signed entries in the volume, which cover all aspects of the civil rights leader's life. Most of the entries are what one would expect in such a volume (e.g., biographies, organizations) but it is the unexpected entries such as "Malcolm as a Fund-Raiser" or "Malcolm X and Humor" that make for interesting browsing. The writing is generally straightforward and factual, with commentary kept to a minimum, and most entries are filled with cross-references. Each entry also includes a "Selected Bibliography." The concluding "Bibliography" is very good and will serve libraries well for collection development in this area. Black-and-white photographs are scattered throughout the text, and special features include a short timeline of his life, an introductory essay by Hanes Walton, 10 short (2-6 page) theme essays (e.g., "Malcolm X and the Role of Women"), and a concluding index. This encyclopedia is an excellent companion to Lenwood Davis' *Malcolm X: A Selected Bibliography* (see ARBA 85, entry 349) and Timothy Johnson's *Malcolm X: A Comprehensive Annotated Bibliography* (see ARBA 87, entry 680). This volume is highly recommended for all academic and public libraries. [R: LJ, 1 June 02, p. 132; BR, Sept/Oct 02, p. 69; VOYA, Oct 02, p. 318]—**Anthony J. Adam**

C, P

108.   **Who's Who Among African Americans.** 14th ed. Ashyia N. Henderson, ed. Farmington Hills, Mich., Gale, 2001. 1605p. index. $185.00. ISBN 0-7876-3635-5. ISSN 1081-1400.

The latest edition of this popular resource features biographical data on over 20,000 African American men and women of achievement from all fields of endeavor. Black persons who are not American citizens were also considered eligible for inclusion if they live or work in the United States and contribute significantly to American life. Most of the data have been gathered directly from the nominees, but secondary sources have been mined if the nominees declined to furnish data. Entries are alphabetically arranged by last name and include data on occupation, personal information, educational background, career information, organizational affiliations, honors, special achievements, military service, and business/home contact information. A separate "Obituaries" section provides entries on recently deceased newsworthy African Americans. Geographic and occupation indexes conclude the volume. This resource is also available from the publisher on diskette/magnetic tape or online via LEXIS-NEXIS as part of the Gale Biographies file. The typeface is large enough for easy reading, and the single-volume format remains convenient. As it also appears that this resource will be released in a new edition annually, libraries should begin to budget accordingly. This is an excellent resource to complement other annual "Who's Who" guides, including the complete Marquis series. This resource is highly recommended for all academic and public libraries.—**Anthony J. Adam**

Handbooks and Yearbooks

C, P, S

109.   **African-American Culture and History: A Student's Guide.** Jack Salzman, ed. New York, Macmillan Reference USA/Gale Group, 2001. 4v. illus. index. $375.00/set. ISBN 0-02-865533-8.

Based on the original five-volume *Encyclopedia of African-American Culture and History* (see ARBA 97, entry 331) and its supplements, this new set is designed for a wider audience, especially public library and high school patrons. The *Student's Guide* incorporates the same editorial criteria of the original encyclopedia—the 852 alphabetically arranged unsigned articles include 597 three- to five-paragraph short biographies of notable African Americans, events, historical eras, legal cases, areas of cultural achievement (such as music, professions, and sports), data on all 50 states, and 12 major cities, and 15 historically black colleges. Although most of the articles are based on entries from the original set, contemporary popular topics and individuals have been added. Entries were chosen to reflect the school curriculum and are updated through the summer of 2000. Most of the articles include cross-references, and sidebars and quality black-and-white photographs are featured throughout. Half of volume 4 is concluding matter: a chronology of African American history from 1444 to 2000, a glossary, an extensive list of suggested resources, and an index.

School and public library patrons will find the set extremely readable without being patronizing. Naturally, with a work of this scope, the writing can vary from entry to entry, but all in all the information is useful, timely, and informative. This set compares favorably with other relatively new general interest African American encyclopedias, including Williams' *The African American Encyclopedia* (see ARBA 94, entry 402) and the *Reference*

Library of Black America (Gale Research, 1990). This set is highly recommended for all high school and public library collections. Academic libraries will also find it useful for undergraduates. [R: BL, July 01, p. 2035]

—**Anthony J. Adam**

ASIAN AMERICANS

C, P

110.   **The Columbia Documentary History of the Asian American Experience.** Franklin Odo, ed. New York, Columbia University Press, 2002. 590p. index. $65.00. ISBN 0-231-11030-8.

Researchers, students, general readers, and reference librarians will welcome this publication. It is the first one to offer ready access to the actual documents of Asian American history gathered together in one volume. It also serves as a companion volume to Gary Okihiro's *The Columbia Guide to Asian American History* (see ARBA 2002, entry 316).

There are 155 documents, dating from "Naturalization Act, March 26, 1790" to "U.S. Catholic Bishops Welcome Asian Pacific Americans, July 2001." Each one is accompanied by a brief interpretive essay and bibliographic note. The editor contributes interpretive essays for the book's six parts as well as an introductory overview.

The editor does a very impressive job of summarizing the complex themes and events in Asian American history. He is the director of the Asian Pacific American Program at the Smithsonian Institute and the author of several important publications in Asian American studies.

The range and variety of the documents are amazing. Along with the expected important court decisions and state and national legislative acts, users have access to songs, political cartoons, poetry, letters, executive orders, army instructions, and a most curious *Life* magazine article titled "How To Tell the Japs [sic] from the Chinese." This mixture is lively, rich, and rewarding reading. There is an index but no bibliography; the reader is directed to Gary Okihiro's work for this information.—**Marshall E. Nunn**

INDIANS OF NORTH AMERICA

Biography

C, P, S

111.   Johnson, Troy R. **Distinguished Native American Spiritual Practitioners and Healers.** Westport, Conn., Oryx Press/Greenwood Publishing Group, 2002. 293p. illus. index. (Distinguished Native Americans Series). $69.95. ISBN 1-57356-358-7.

This biographical dictionary provides information on the lives and leadership roles of 100 spiritual leaders and healers in Native North American societies. Compared to other biographical dictionaries, this compendium has fairly lengthy entries (2 to 4 pages) for each individual. Covering persons from the sixteenth through the twentieth centuries, a summary, description of the person's early life, their leadership, and a section on further reading are provided. Both well-known and more obscure leaders are included, and there is a balance between more Native traditional leaders, and those who adapted somewhat to white society yet were still activists within their communities for preserving culture, land and resource protection, and education.

Black-and-white images of individuals and important documents add to the collection. A unique inclusion in this work is the addition of quotes from the leader. A map that illustrates the locations of the different tribes whose leaders were covered would have made an excellent addition to this work. An appendix is included, however, which arranges the leader by nation or group. This work is recommended for high school, public, and academic libraries.—**Tara L. Dirst**

Dictionaries and Encyclopedias

C, S

112.   **American Indian History.** Carole A. Barrett, ed. Hackensack, N.J., Salem Press, 2002. 2v. illus. maps. index. (Magill's Choice). $55.00/set. ISBN 1-58765-067-3.

These two new volumes add to two other publications provided in the Magill's Choice series of core teaching tools for public, school, and college libraries. They contribute 224 essays describing the major events and developments in the history of Native Americans in North America. All but 16 essays or entries have been previously published.

There is much for students and scholars to like about these volumes. First, and very importantly, for each entry the author is listed and his or her academic affiliation is provided in the list of contributors in the first volume. This gives the reader reasonable confidence in the accuracy of the information. The format of the entries is exceptionally practical and convenient. Each entry is introduced with name of the event or topic, the date of its occurrence, founding, locale, tribes involved, categories to which it belongs (for further investigation), and significance of the incident or event. Every entry concludes with a *see also* section for the reader's convenience, and the longer entries also have a section listing sources for further study. Some of the major topics also provide annotations.

Having established that the essays provided about historical events in American Indian history are credible and convenient, it is essential to note that there are over 200 pages devoted to providing additional information of importance to students. The essays cover battles, treaties, legislation, court cases, protest movements, organizations, and institutions. The appendixes and indexes are intended as research tools for the student. Included are a gazetteer of historic places; a list of historic Native Americans; a directory of museums, archives, and libraries; a list of organizations, agencies, and societies; a timeline of major events in the history of Native Americans; a list of tribes by culture area; a lengthy bibliography; and a list of Web resources and addresses. There are five indexes: a categorized index, a geographical index, a personages index, a tribes index, and a subject index. While there are scattered photographs and maps, these have lesser importance. These volumes are ideally suited for school and college libraries.—**Karen D. Harvey**

Handbooks and Yearbooks

C, P, S

113.   Cutler, Charles L. **Tracks That Speak: The Legacy of Native American Words in North American Culture.** New York, Houghton Mifflin, 2002. 255p. illus. index. $22.00; $14.00pa. ISBN 0-618-06509-1; 0-618-06510-5pa.

So often when people speak of "gifts" given by America's indigenous people to the European explorers, they refer primarily to corn and tobacco. Several books have been written in the last decade that expand this limited view to the concepts of democracy, women's rights, and even environmentalism. Some authors and critics believe that the use of the word "gifts" is either erroneous or just ignorance of what happens when two cultures come in contact. Nonetheless, the contributions of American Indians to our contemporary culture are many and often unrecognized. In this interesting reference, Cutler has focused on the Indian words that remain a part of American English. Undoubtedly, they were not merely gifts, but significant contributions that remind readers who the first North Americans were.

The introduction provides a broad overview of the book, including some important information such as why the Algonquian language contributed more words to English than any other Indian language family and the tragic loss of many Indian languages. Place-names, such as states (e.g., Connecticut) and rivers (e.g., Mississippi) are not included; their numbers are beyond the scope of this book. Nor are Latin American words (e.g., barbecue) included.

The table of contents is clearly divided into categories with the Indian words within each category listed, making it a simple index. Whatever the name, it is very useful. The background and significance of each work is explained. The strength of this reference book seems to be in the way the words are presented. The entries combine fascinating storytelling and sound historical documentation that are exceptionally engaging. They are considerably richer than brief encyclopedia-type entries. What a resource this work would be for elementary teachers who are usually just equipped with a rather sterile list of Indian words. As is expected for a reliable reference book, the notes, bibliography, and index are thorough and helpful. A few black-and-white photographs are also included.—**Karen D. Harvey**

JAPANESE

C, P

114.   **Encyclopedia of Contemporary Japanese Culture.** Sandra Buckley, ed. New York, Routledge, 2002. 634p. index. $140.00. ISBN 0-415-14344-6.

The last two decades have witnessed the publication of several one-volume encyclopedias and handbooks on Japan of varying qualities. However, Buckley's *Encyclopedia of Contemporary Japanese Culture* (ECJC) is a most welcome contribution to the literature with more than 750 topical and biographical entries exploring the "lived experience of everyday Japanese life" for the postwar period (p. xiii). This view of cultural life not only includes coverage of popular culture, such as musicians, directors, fashion designers, writers, and artists, but also interesting articles on such diverse topics as smoking, day workers, cross-dressing, and so on that are not unique in Japan but have different social meanings and histories there. Buckley also succeeds in breaking the myth of Japanese homogeneity by incorporating articles on minorities in Japan and the Japanese Diaspora in the Americas. Most notably, ECJC features excellent coverage of Japanese women and consistently introduces critical feminist perspectives that are rarely seen in other reference works on Japan.

Although scholarly, ECJC is eminently readable for undergraduate and public library readers, and is an ideal reference tool thanks to its excellent index and cross-referencing (although the latter is less consistent). Entries are signed by scholars, including many by the editor, a visiting professor at McGill University. Unfortunately, only about half of the entries contain references or suggestions for further reading. There are some inevitable typographical errors, such as the cross-reference from baseball to *Zenkyoto* (p. 43) and the claim that the first Japanese emigrant to North America came in 1977 rather than 1877 (p. 358). Some entries, perhaps due to space constraints, missed current scholarship, such as how Karen Tei Yamashita's entry on Japanese American literature ignores first generation writings in Japanese, or how June Gordon's article on "literacy" neglected to mention how scholars have questioned Japanese claims for functional literacy in the early postwar years. More fundamentally, coverage of political and corporate culture is minimal. For these areas, as well as pre-1945 Japan, librarians should turn to the nine-volume *Kodansha Encyclopedia of Japan* (see ARBA 84, entry 305) or Kodansha's 1993 *Japan: An Illustrated Encyclopedia* (see ARBA 94, entry 115). Despite the aforementioned reservations, ECJC is one of the year's best reference works and should be widely purchased and enjoyed for the diversity and quality of writing it makes accessible. [R: LJ, 15 Feb 02, pp. 134-135; Choice, April 02, p. 1400]—**Andrew B. Wertheimer**

JEWS

C, P

115.   Medoff, Rafael. **Jewish Americans and Political Participation: A Reference Handbook.** Santa Barbara, Calif., ABC-CLIO, 2002. 371p. index. (Political Participation in America). $55.00. ISBN 1-57607-314-9.

The Political Participation in America series documents the role of groups or "blocs" of citizens in the political process of the United States. The newest volume covers Jewish Americans. Medoff, a historian who has written several books on Jewish history and edits the journal *American Jewish History*, has divided the book into five chapters that provide an overview of American Jewish political life. The first covers demographics and the history of the Jews in the United States. The second documents political activism, which, for the most part, is on the left. Jews have been active in the labor movement, the civil rights movement, the antiwar movement, and the struggles to liberalize immigration. They fought on both sides in the Revolutionary and Civil Wars. They have lobbied for support of Jews who wanted to leave the Soviet Union, for the state of Israel, and for social issues ranging from abortion and the environment to equal rights for gays and women. They have been elected to office and appointed to cabinet and Supreme Court positions. Medoff provides a look at the major issues and key people involved. Each chapter has a reading list in addition to the annotated bibliography at the end of the book. A most useful section after the text contains primary source documents such as George Washington's letter to the Hebrew Congregation of Newport, Rhode Island, and Ulysses S. Grant's Order 320 expelling Jews from the Kentucky-Tennessee-Mississippi region (rescinded by President Lincoln). In addition to these documents, there is a list of key people, laws, and terms; a chronology; and a resource list of organizations. This book is a nice companion to more comprehensive sources such as *Jews in American Politics* (Rowman & Littlefield, 2001) and *The Congressional Minyan: The Jews of Capitol Hill* (Ktav, 2000). It is a useful resource for academic and public library collections.

—**Barbara M. Bibel**

LATIN AMERICANS

C, P, S

116.   Garcia, Alma M. **The Mexican Americans.** Westport, Conn., Greenwood Press, 2002. 220p. illus. index. (New Americans). $44.95. ISBN 0-313-31499-3.

The Mexican Americans is a recent title in the Greenwood Press series, New Americans, designed to introduce high school students and general readers to United States immigrant groups. The book has a comprehensive scope given its length of only 185 pages—220 pages including the appendix, glossary, references, and index. Along with the expected historical background and demographic portrait, the book's 13 chapters present information on immigration periods, culture, gender issues, political identity, and U.S.-Mexico relations.

Alma Garcia is a knowledgeable author who handled co-editing duties for the well-received book *Chicana Feminist Thought* (Routledge, 1997). Unfortunately, Garcia does not connect well with the primary target audience of high school students. The reading level seems correct for the group, but the tone is sometimes too dry or seems aimed at an older group. The book has a rough historical organization, so topics, such as music or education, are discussed in a variety of chapters according to the context. The table of contents includes both chapter and section titles, which is a plus to both user and librarian. However, it is still worthwhile to use the index in the back of the book.

The physical layout of the main text does not help to draw in the reader. There are several black-and-white photographs, including some personal photographs from the author, but most are too heavily contrasted or poorly reproduced. The glossary is too short, and the few terms that are selected, such as *quinceañera*, are well identified within the book. Bolding of terms in the text, side boxes for concepts or definitions, or footnotes would have been more useful than the glossary. There is an appendix containing 12 brief biographies of "Notable Mexicans and Mexican Americans," which may be helpful to students in choosing a paper topic. Garcia includes her references, which contain scholarly books and journal articles. While the references give authority and are helpful to have, a "Further Reading" list geared specifically toward high school students would have been welcome.

To those of us who are minorities within a minority group, the issue of representation is often foremost in mind. As a Mexican American with a Protestant background, this reviewer's only reservation regarding content is the feeling that Garcia does not give a full picture of religious experience. In chapter 6, "Family Culture, and Life Cycle Rituals" Garcia gives a one-sentence caveat that "other religious denominations such as evangelical Protestant groups have been gaining a following among Mexicans." However, Garcia immediately chooses to relate only Catholic baptismal, wedding, and funeral rituals to describe Mexican and Mexican American religious culture.

Overall, the content of the book is sound, and it is a good source for historical and statistical information on Mexican Americans. The book will serve as a useful aid to a high school student with a special report or assignment, despite some inconsistency of tone. Some changes to how the information is presented would make the series more approachable to students, and librarians might feel that they were getting a bit more for their money. After all, at $44.95 for this work, and with similar pricing on the other series titles, The New Americans series could become an expensive investment. This source is recommended for high school and public libraries. College libraries serving undergraduates and educator resource centers may also give this title consideration.

—**Sandra E. Fuentes Riggs**

7   Genealogy and Heraldry

GENEALOGY

Directories

P

117.   **RootsWeb.com. http://www.rootsweb.com.** [Website]. Provo, Utah, MyFamily.com. Free. Date reviewed: Nov 02.

    RootsWeb.com and its counterparts continue to feed the popular misperception that all genealogical information may be found on the Internet. For here one can find 225 million ancestor names, a registry of over 1 million surnames, 25,000 mailing lists, and 10 million postings on 175,000 message boards—all for free. Of course, this information is only as complete and as accurate as the suppliers of the data. A simple search in the site's World Connect database for this reviewer's great-great-great-grandfather, Charles N. Clark (1816-1878), located records for him and his forbearers, yet neither his son (my great-great-grandfather, George Congress Clark, 1830-1898), nor George's children were found. Such a finding does not surprise the experienced researcher, yet the site does nothing to discourage those new to genealogical research.

    For patrons willing to research their own family trees, *RootsWeb.com* includes a plethora of information they will need to get started: suggestions on interviewing family members, documents to consult, where to locate data for various ethnic groups, various databases, and so on. The volume of information often can intimidate the novice, and the arrangement does nothing to dispel this perplexity. For example, under the initial heading "Getting Started" is an immediate subheading titled "Getting Started at Roots Web." Clicking on this link leads to suggestions about sharing one's research with *RootsWeb.com*, joining a mailing list or message board, and so forth. All this can be overwhelming for those who need orientation and bare bones advice. Although the arrangement of the site is problematic, given the amount of information available the site is recommended for novice and experienced genealogists alike.—**Christopher Brennan**

Handbooks and Yearbooks

P

118.   Kovacs, Diane K. **Genealogical Research on the Web.** New York, Neal-Schuman, 2002. 194p. illus. index. (Neal-Schuman NetGuide Series). $55.00pa. ISBN 1-55570-430-1.

    This publication is a workshop in a book. It started out as the author's workshop titled "Genealogical Research on the Internet." Now it is the front end for that experience. Individuals can sign up for the online version of this book and can work through the exercises online. They also have access, via e-mail, to the author. In order to participate in these online activities the user should know how to use basic Internet access and have some e-mail software and a recent Web browser. No prior genealogical experience is necessary since this work is designed to teach the user about several of these resources.

The book is divided into four parts. Part 1 deals with how to get started. Part 2 talks about how to find and use genealogical references on the Web. It includes the author's 10 best genealogical sites on the Web and a good discussion of each. Part 3 deals with how to network online with other family members, researchers, and so on. Part 4 deals with some of the more specialized resources available on the Internet, such as African American and Native American ancestry. There is also a section on sources that is divided into three parts. The first is a genealogy ready-reference e-library; the second, a list of more readings about genealogical research, including a fun list that deals with fiction in which real genealogical research plays a role; and the last is a glossary of genealogy and Internet terms.

The text is generally quite good with clear explanations. The advantage of the online portion is that most of the URLS discussed are a click away. There are, naturally, some problems, such as site locations changing. Information on the pages of the site may have been rearranged since the author wrote about those pages. Correcting the links is taken care of in the online version. There are occasional typographical errors in the text. It is not clear where this work should be placed in a library's collection. It is a reference item, but in order to use it effectively it is important to be connected to the online version so that the user can work through the exercises. This aspect would argue for putting the work in a circulating collection. It takes some time to go through all the exercises, but it is quite educational and enjoyable. In her preface, the author gives permission to download the learning activities and adapt them to local staff and patron training as long as the copyright statements remain intact. This feature should be very useful to those contemplating such a task.—**Robert L. Turner Jr.**

P

119.   Neafsey, Edward. **Surnames of Ireland: Origins and Numbers of Selected Irish Surnames.** Kansas City, Mo., Irish Genealogical Foundation, 2002. 224p. maps. index. $32.00pa. ISBN 0-940134-97-7.

Neafsey's creative inspiration for this work of 203 surnames (only 28 percent of them are Irish surnames) was sparked by his interest in genealogy. However, its usefulness for genealogical research is marginal. His other interests were the origin of names and their spellings. For each surname he has also created a population distribution country outline map with a dot for every surname's household. The study for the maps was based on telephone listings in 1992, plus an estimate of families and persons without telephones. However, there is no mention of the consideration of people with unlisted numbers or the formula for the estimates.

Neafsey's preface reports that the origins of his selected 203 surnames were taken from multiple sources, including Patrick Hanks' and Falvia Hodges' *A Dictionary of Surnames* (see ARBA 90, entry 401), which covers more than 70,000 British and European surnames, and Patrick Woulfe's *Irish Names and Surnames* (Irish Genealogical Foundation, 1992). Neafsey also states that he used works from Edward MacLysaght, but he does not disclose which works were consulted. MacLysaght's latest title is *The Surnames of Ireland* (6th ed.; see ARBA 86, entry 389). Most libraries that subscribe to *Names*, the journal of the American Names Society, may want this book in their collection.—**J. Carlyle Parker**

Indexes

P

120.   **AncestryPlus. http://www.gale.com.** [Website]. Farmington Hills, Mich., Gale. Price negotiated by site. Date reviewed: Aug 02.

With the increase in interest among the American population in genealogy, this online product from the Gale Group is sure to be useful in many public libraries. Gale formed a partnership with Ancestory.com, the popular source for family history research, to create a tool designed specifically with libraries in mind. This site provides access to one billion names located within 3,000 databases. It also provides the information for Gale's popular three-volume *Passenger and Immigration Lists Index* (see ARBA 82, entry 465) and its supplements (2002 supplement, see entry 121; and 1996 supplement, see ARBA 97, entry 367), which lists 2.8 million passengers who arrived in the United States during the seventeenth, eighteenth, and nineteenth centuries. Information from the *Biography and Genealogy Master Index* (see ARBA 99, entry 404), which provides 13 million indexed biographical sketches, is also provided. Information on immigration, military, court, church, and ethnic records as well as information from the Social Security Death Index, Periodical Source Index (PERSI), and the Civil War Pension Index are provided as well. More than 700 historical maps are shown in detail on this Website.

This site is fairly easy to use and very attractive to look at. The easiest way to conduct a search is by using the name search option and selecting a state. Results are than posted by featured database. The user can then click on the type of information they are searching for from the applicable database. Those needing to narrow their search can perform an advanced search by providing dates, keywords, or record type. A "sound-alike" option is provided for those not knowing the exact spelling of the person's name they are searching for. Users can also search by type of record (e.g., census records, vital and church records, military records) or by state or county.

It is hard to imagine that a researcher would not be able to find something of value using this source. The only problem may be sifting through the many records that a search will provide. Large public libraries and those in communities with a large interest in genealogical research will definitely want to consider the purchase of this database.—**Shannon Graff Hysell**

P

121.　**Passenger and Immigration Lists Index. 2002 Supplement, Part 2: A Guide to Published Records of More Than 3,931,000 Immigrants ....** P. William Filby and Katherine H. Nemeh, eds. Farmington Hills, Mich., Gale, 2001. 555p. $260.00. ISBN 0-7876-3454-9. ISSN 0736-8267.

This is the 26th supplement to the *Passenger and Immigration Lists Index* that was first published in 1981 (see ARBA 82, entry 465). It follows the same format as the previous volumes (1996 supplement; see ARBA 97, entry 367). The citations in the main body of the work contain the name of the immigrant as originally spelled in the published source, the immigrant's age when given, the place of arrival, naturalization or other record of immigration, the year of arrival, a code that refers to the source where the list can be found, and the page number in the source where the name can be found. Entries also list accompanying family members, if any, with each person's relationship to the primary listee and their age with cross-references from these accompanying relatives to the primary listee. There is a section on how to locate the sources indexed and a bibliography.

There are some minor, although annoying, problems with this volume. In a section titled "Highlights" it is mentioned that there are more than 125,000 immigrants who arrived in the New World between the sixteenth and the mid-twentieth centuries taken from over 40 sources, but there are only 38 sources listed. The editors also had a problem with some of their printing. In most of the introductory material, an apostrophe appears as either an "o" with an acute symbol or an "i" with a grave symbol, a comma becomes an "o" with an acute symbol, and so on. This error does not appear to have happened in the listings of the names or sources. However, the editors should have proofread their material before sending it out. Nevertheless, this work is still a highly useful source for immigration information and will be very useful in libraries that have genealogical research questions.

—**Robert L. Turner Jr.**

HERALDRY

P

122.　Hannings, Bud. **The Story of the American Flag.** Glenside, Pa., Seniram Publishing, 2001. 128p. illus. $8.95pa. ISBN 0-922564-02-7.

The Story of the American Flag is a handy, inexpensive volume that discusses much more than just the history of Old Glory; it also includes interesting tidbits of American military history throughout. The book begins with a short introductory history of the flag and then goes into more detail with a historical chronology of flag-related events in U.S. wars, including the American Revolution, the Civil War era, World War II, and the post-Korean War era and Vietnam War. The remainder of the book provides notable facts about the flag, quotes about the flag, and several miscellaneous related lists (i.e., presidents and vice presidents of the United States, lists of flags [with illustrations] that flew over America, and holidays when all Americans should fly the flag). Hannings also provides copies of the Declaration of Independence, the U.S. Constitution, the "Star Spangled Banner," and, of course, the Pledge of Allegiance. Some of the more interesting, and more difficult to find, information is included in chapters on how to fold the flag, the history of the Medal of Honor, and proper ways to display the flag and personal salutes.

This small, 128-page volume could easily be used as a ready-reference source in a busy library. It pulls a lot of U.S. patriotic history into one volume. At the inexpensive price of $8.95, libraries needing this type of information could easily afford this easy-to-browse reference.—**Shannon Graff Hysell**

PERSONAL NAMES

P

123.   Room, Adrian. **Dictionary of First Names.** New York, Sterling Publishing, 2002. 670p. $14.95pa. ISBN 0-304-36226-3.

Another addition to the many first name books available is Adrian Room's *Dictionary of First Names.* This 2d edition of the *Dictionary of First Names* has been updated with charts of naming patterns in England and Wales from 1944 to 2001. It notes the top 10 names for girls and boys over a 30-year period, as well as the top 50 names from 1998-2001.

What makes this name book a little different than most is that it not only identifies the meaning of the name, but also its use in literature and perhaps the reason why the name became popular. At the end of each entry, famous contemporary men and women with each name are also listed. The added bits of trivia and literary lore make this an appealing and intriguing book from which to choose a baby name. It is recommended for public libraries and expectant parents who want something a little more unusual.—**Deborah L. Nicholl**

8 Geography

GENERAL WORKS

Atlases

C, P, S

124.   **Compact Peters World Atlas.** updated ed. Union, N.J., Hammond, 2002. 231p. maps. index. $19.95. ISBN 0-8437-1832-3.

The 43 topographic maps in this atlas represent all countries and continents at the same scale. The underlying principle of this representation is based on the equal status of all peoples. Each double-page topographic map shows ½₀ of the Earth's surface, allowing for direct comparisons. The scale for all of the topographic maps is 1 square centimeter on the maps equals 6,000 square kilometers in reality. Scale is also given in miles.

The latest computer technology was used to adapt the world map to the 43 double spreads in the topographic section. The three-dimensional relief was accomplished by photographing specially made plaster relief models and blending those photographs with hand-rendered coloring. The green represents vegetation, the brown represents barren land, and a mixture of the two colors represents thin or scattered vegetation. The 1,000 largest and most important cities and towns are shown. Because the maps are in a two-page spread, there is the problem of what ends up in the center, but this book's binding is flexible enough to be able to press down and see the entire map. Scale is given at the bottom of the right-hand page of each topographic map. Each map features a locater world map for easy reference.

The 2d part of the atlas includes 246 individual world thematic maps under 45 subject headings. Each of the subject headings is given a double-page spread; when more than one topic is covered under any subject, separate maps are provided. The thematic maps have been revised for this edition using the latest available data obtained from published materials of the United Nations and other international organizations. The easy-to-use index provides both a page number and a locater letter, which can be found either at the top or at the bottom of each map frame.

The slick, hard-backed binding is colorful and eye-catching. The size—8½-by-12½-by-½—makes the book comfortable to hold and to use. The sharp graphics and multicolored maps are visually appealing, and generous margins and large page numbers contribute to the ease of use. All in all, this is an economical atlas that provides a true representation of the world's countries and valuable, up-to-date statistical information, and will be a welcome addition to most libraries. [R: LJ, 1 Nov 02, pp. 76-78]—**Dana McDougald**

P, S

125.   **Dorling Kindersley Concise Atlas of the World.** New York, DK Publishing, 2001. 350p. illus. maps. index. $29.95. ISBN 0-7894-8002-6.

If indeed the primary function of a world atlas is to help pinpoint places on the globe, then most atlases published today do this well. The *Dorling Kindersley Concise Atlas of the World* does a good job for the money, perhaps the only reason for selecting the concise edition, as it is an update of its parent, the *DK World Atlas* (see ARBA 2001, entry 328). Easy access to the contents of this 34-centimeter volume arranged by continent is assured through map and flag keys printed on the endpapers. Main-entry maps on each slick and colorful page are surrounded by a repeated series of diminutive satellite-like, "at-a-glance" facts, diagrams, and photographs. These thumbnail color photographs help to illustrate a country's physical and cultural characteristics and serve as little windows into lands near and far. Some atlases you consult; this atlas, with its straightforward prose, you can pour over or peruse. [R: LJ, 15 Sept 01, p. 69]—**Anthony F. Verdesca Jr.**

S

126.   **Maps on File.** 2002-2003 ed. New York, Facts on File, 2002. 2v. maps. index. (Facts on File Library of World History). $250.00 looseleaf w/binder. ISBN 0-8160-5006-6.

S

127.   **Outline Maps on File.** updated ed. New York, Facts on File, 2002. 1v. (various paging). maps. index. (Facts on File Library of World History). $185.00 looseleaf w/binder. ISBN 0-8160-4996-3.

This edition of *Maps on File* retains the clear, concise layout of previous editions (see ARBA 2002, entry 350, for a review of the 2001 edition, and ARBA 2002, entry 351, for a review of the online edition). This edition is presented in 2 volumes and features 500 reproducible maps that are ideally suited for middle and high school students writing reports or preparing presentations. Volume 1 provides country maps of the world's regions, including Africa, Asia, Australia and Oceania, Europe, North and Central America, South America, and the Canadian provinces. Each country map provides major cities, borders with neighboring nations, a scale in miles and kilometers, and names of major rivers and roads. The second volume provides detailed maps of the U.S. states as well as maps representing each country's demographics, natural resources, politics and military, education and social issues, and statistics.

Outline Maps is much like volume 1 of *Maps on File*, but without the map lables. Presented here are reproducible blank maps of countries and regions throughout the world. This set is ideal for teachers teaching a geography lesson or testing their students. A "Teacher's Guide" is provided at the back of the volume, which provides the answer key to all maps. Because the volume is presented in a looseleaf format with a three-ring binder, the "Teacher's Guide" can easily be removed from the volume.

These sets are an ideal addition to middle and high school libraries. Each map is reproducible, ensuring that the volume will be used frequently. Available for an additional $75.00 annually are the replacement maps for *Maps on File* that reflect changes within the past year.—**Shannon Graff Hysell**

C, P

128.   **The National Atlas of the United States of America. http://www.nationalatlas.gov.** [Website]. Free. Date reviewed: Oct 02.

This ambitious, largely Web-based resource is an update of the print *National Atlas of the United States* (U.S. Geological Survey, 1970). The original book lived out the limitations of a print national atlas in that it was large and colorful (and therefore expensive) but contained quickly dated thematic content. The new *Atlas*, begun in 1997, is issued not as a book but as a coordinated ongoing program. Umbrellaed under the one URL, the varied components range from entirely digital to print format. The scope of the project is broader, as are the audience and the variety and utility of output. In spite of this it manages to stick to its stated purpose of providing a "reliable summary of national-scale geographical information," while also furnishing links to more detailed sources of information on many topics.

The *Atlas* consists of five major components: an interactive map engine, several multimedia maps, a data warehouse, printed maps, and printable maps. The interactive map engine allows the user to zoom in and pan around a map of the United States, adding themes of information from a long list ranging from agriculture to population characteristics to hazardous waste. The seven multimedia maps depict somewhat random topics, including animations of U.S. geology over 2.6 billion years, avian cholera, volcanoes, and 2,000 incidents of West Nile virus. To view all seven animations it is necessary to download and install the viewing plug-ins Shockwave, Flash Player, and QuickTime Player. The Data Warehouse is intended for researchers who can utilize data files that underlie many of the thematic maps. Most files are only usable in GIS software packages. A few others are in .dbf format, usable in a number of database programs. Since 1970 update maps of the *National Atlas* have been published and sold as looseleaf sheets. The "Printed Maps" page provides ordering information for dozens of these sheets and provides a link to scanned images of the entire original atlas. The "Printed Maps" section presently provides reduced versions of West Nile Virus and President Election maps, ready to print on standard color printers.

The drawbacks to online maps in general are the limitations of bandwidth and screen size. Viewing graphics on the Internet requires good access speed, and the small viewing window makes map analysis difficult over a large area. Print output is limited to whatever options the end user possesses, which is almost always of lower quality than a professionally published map. Overall, the site is strong in content with some room for improvement on navigability. Since 20 federal agencies and 1 private partner provide the content, each component possesses a different arrangement and logic. It is an enjoyable tool if one takes a few minutes to become acquainted with atlas content and navigation. This site is recommended both as a resource and as a pointer to further resources for the upper elementary to graduate levels.—**Kathleen Weessies**

C, P

129.   **Oxford Atlas of the World.** 10th ed. New York, Oxford University Press, 2002. 304p. maps. index. $75.00. ISBN 0-19-521919-8.

Because of its reasonable price, clear maps, and large and useful reference sections, the *Oxford Atlas of the World* has been a staple of reference collections since it was first introduced a decade ago. The atlas consists of 3 pages of basic statistics on the world, followed by 16 beautiful satellite images (mostly of cities), a 32-page "gazetteer of nations," and a large "introduction to world geography." The latter section, which runs to 47 pages, contains maps, text, and images explaining the geography of the universe, oceans, climate, population, cities, trade, and 17 other topics.

The bulk of the atlas, of course, is taken up with maps and their indexes. A section of almost 70 city maps is useful only for providing a general sense of the size and shape of major cities. For most purposes, it will be necessary to consult more detailed city maps. The sections on the world and each of the continents contain broad physical and political maps, followed by more detailed regional maps. One flaw of the atlas (and of many other atlases) is that countries or states included on the detailed regional maps are often split onto two or more separate maps. Denver is thus part of the middle United States while the western half of Colorado is part of the western United States. Although state and country boundaries are artificial, they do represent important geographical connections. Denver's important association to the Rocky Mountain region is obscured by its position on a map of the plains states. There are many similar examples. Despite these minor criticisms, the *Oxford Atlas of the World* is one of the best atlases available and is highly recommended for all reference collections. [R: LJ, 1 Feb 03, p. 76]—**Michael Levine-Clark**

S

130.   **World Almanac Atlas of the World.** Mahwah, N.J., World Almanac Books, 2002. 192p. maps. index. $18.95; $12.95pa. ISBN 0-8343-0117-2; 0-8343-0118-0pa.

The 192 maps in this atlas represent every continent, country, U.S. state, and Canadian province. The maps, even the smallest ones, are sharp and easy to read, although only major cities, towns, or waterways are shown. The scale of each map is given, and each map includes a visual scale for measuring distance. Insets feature information on the national capital; the country or state's flag; population; language; largest city; monetary unit; and locations of major cities, rivers, islands, or other important features.

The atlas is divided by major divisions of the world. After the introductory material, there is a world map followed by major sections on Asia and Oceania, Europe, Africa, South America, North America, the Polar Regions, and the United States. A full page is devoted to maps of major countries and each state of the United States, but maps for smaller countries are placed from two to five per page. Surprisingly, even pages with five maps look uncluttered because of the quality of the graphics. A two-page spread is devoted for the introductory maps of the continents, with thematic maps and graphs provided for each.

Introductory material for the atlas includes thematic maps, graphs, and tables of information based on the 2000 U.S. census. There are also maps, graphs, and tables of statistics that examine the growing world population and the latest trends in health and mortality. There are two indexes: a world index and an index of the U.S. states. This publication is a very easy-to-use atlas with maps that are sharp and clear. The largest and most detailed maps are those of the U.S. states. It is quite inexpensive and thus would be ideal for students and even home use.—**Dana McDougald**

Handbooks and Yearbooks

C, P

131.   Hudson, John C. **Across This Land: A Regional Geography of the United States and Canada.** Baltimore, Md., Johns Hopkins University Press, 2002. 474p. illus. maps. index. (Creating the North American Landscape). $29.95pa. ISBN 0-8018-6567-0.

Hudson taught a course on North America at Northwestern University for many years. This book is a product of those years in which the course was constantly revised and updated. It is a readable and informative volume that is not limited to one phase of geography, but which includes the physical, historical, economic, human, and political aspects of the topic. It is divided into 10 parts consisting of 27 chapters. Starting with a consideration of Atlantic Canada and Quebec, the work proceeds through the various sections of the United States and Canada, rounding out with Hawaii as the last chapter. Lists of references abound, including time-tested works and recently published books. A list of general works follows the preface. Then, each chapter has 10 or more pertinent books listed that relate to the chapter's area. The volume is illustrated with maps and photographs that enhance understanding. This work will be useful for general readers as well as geography students.

—**Frank J. Anderson**

P, S

132.   **Junior State Maps on File.** New York, Facts on File, 2002. 1v. (various paging). maps. index. $185.00 looseleaf w/binder. ISBN 0-8160-4752-9.

In keeping with Facts on File's On File series, this title offers more than 400 reproducible state maps and fact sheets in a looseleaf, three-ring binder format for grades 4 through 10. The nine tabbed dividers teamed with the table of contents provide easy access to the maps. After a general section on the United States and its regions, the maps are arranged by geographic region: New England, Mid-Atlantic, Midwestern, Mountain and Prairie, Southern, Southwestern, and Western and Pacific. Five maps and a fact sheet are provided for each state: major cities, outline map, physical features, industry, agriculture, and state facts and flag. Printed on heavier paper stock, the crisp black-and-white sheets make excellent masters for photocopying supplemental instructional materials, creating overhead transparencies, or simply enhancing research reports. This is an excellent U.S. geography resource for school and public libraries that do not subscribe to the online version.—**Esther R. Sinofsky**

S

133.   **Mapping the World.** Danbury, Conn., Grolier, 2002. 8v. illus. maps. index. $239.00/set. ISBN 0-7172-5619-7.

Maps are often viewed as superficial pieces of paper that show where to make a left or right turn. In reality, they are an integration of technology and art that have played a critical role throughout history, both on Earth and beyond. Whether going on vacation or landing on the moon, maps are necessary, but they can be difficult to understand. Maps are the result of an often complex progression of data gathering, interpretation, and portrayal, which are the focus of this set.

Each of the 8, 48-page volumes contains front matter consisting of a table of contents, general information about the entire set, and an introduction to the particular volume. End matter contains a volume-specific glossary, a listing of further reading and Websites, and a comprehensive index for the entire set. Volume titles are "Ways of Mapping the World," "Observation and Measurement," "Maps for Travelers," "Navigation," "Mapping New Lands," "Mapping for Governments," "City Maps," and "Mapping for Today and Tomorrow." The many drawings and photographs in each volume are all in color. In many cases, an aerial photograph and map are drawn side-by-side to improve interpretation skills. The text incorporates both English and, in parentheses, SI or metric units. In the volume "Observation and Measurement," these two measurement systems are referred to as imperial and metric, respectively.

The greatest problem with this set is one that comes from the nature of the subject itself. The fact that a map results from an integration of so many processes means that a study of maps does not lend itself to alphabetic, encyclopedic entries or a neat, linear progression of study. To obtain maximum benefit, the user of this set will probably need to integrate information from multiple entries in the same volume or entries in several volumes. Cross-referencing between volumes is accomplished through the set index at the back of each volume and by marginal notations across the bottom of the left page.

Technological and mathematical applications addressed range from the logic of Eratosthenes to measure the Earth's circumference over 2,000 years ago to today's global positioning and geographic information systems. While not designed specifically as a history book, the maps and discussions of the Crusades (volume 2); Columbus, Magellan, and Captain James Cook's travels (volume 4); and explorations of Africa (volume 5) provide useful historical information.

The edition reviewed was published exclusively for the school and library market. While a primary-grade student may benefit from some of the illustrations, intermediate and middle school students and older would learn the most from the set. Mapping is a perpetual process. Today, satellites enable scientists to determine centimeter changes in sea level to fuel the debate over global warming or to determine minute elevation changes in Mt. Everest as the duel continues between plate tectonics and erosional forces. This set can provide students with a strong background into what mapping is and how the mapping process can be applied to a variety of interests (other than going on vacation). [R: SLJ, Nov 02, pp. 102-104]—**Craig A. Munsart**

C, P, S

134.   Shearer, Benjamin F., and Barbara S. Shearer. **State Names, Seals, Flags, and Symbols: A Historical Guide.** 3d ed. Westport, Conn., Greenwood Press, 2002. 495p. illus. index. $65.00. ISBN 0-313-31534-5.

There is a perennial interest in factual information and lore about the 50 states along with the territories and districts that comprise the United States. This respected title is now in its third edition and contains three new chapters on state and territory universities, governors, and professional sports teams. The preexisting 14 chapters have all been extensively updated since the last edition. All information is documented from various state statutes, official documents, and other relevant publications. Color plates of state seals, flags, flowers, trees, birds, stamps, and license plates are included in a center section of the volume. There is also a select bibliography of state and territory histories that unfortunately fails to list the magnificent *The New Handbook of Texas* (Texas State Historical Society, 1996) that is also available online. A detailed index concludes the volume.

The two Shearers and Greenwood Press have once again produced an attractive and useful reference work that is fascinating just to browse. A perusal of the "Official Designations" chapter reveals that 13 states have designated English as their official language, a trend that started with Illinois in 1969 but did not really take off until 1984 when 2 more states followed suit with 10 more joining them between 1987 and 1998. Other equally intriguing information can be found throughout this attractive volume.—**Ronald H. Fritze**

9   History

ARCHAEOLOGY

Dictionaries and Encyclopedias

C, P

135.   **The Concise Oxford Dictionary of Archaeology.** By Timothy Darvill. New York, Oxford University Press, 2002. 506p. $45.00. ISBN 0-19-211649-5.

The Concise Oxford Dictionary of Archaeology is quite possibly one of the finest single-volume reference works in the field of archaeology currently available. Compiled by Darvill, professor of archaeology at Bournemouth University in Great Britain, it covers a wide array of archaeological topics in comfortably sized, easy-to-understand entries. The coverage is very broad, explaining archaeological terms, cultures, people, and artifacts from Asia, Africa, the Americas, and the Pacific Rim in addition to Europe and the Mediterranean area. All of the entries are as current as possible. While some illustrations would have added even more to this resource, without them it is still a great purchase for any library.

The entries are alphabetically arranged, with the term printed in bold face for ease of scanning and the entry written for a non-archaeological audience. Some excellent quick reference resources, including treaties covering the handling of archaeological and cultural artifacts, timelines of major areas of the globe, listings of rulers and emperors, and a complete timeline of ancient Egyptian dynasties and their rulers are included in the appendixes. In the introduction, a scheme is detailed classifying each entry by type (i.e., deity, artifact, biography, equipment, and so forth), and each entry carries an abbreviation telling the user what type of entry they are reading. *The Concise Oxford Dictionary of Archaeology* will be useful in all sorts of libraries for all sorts of patrons, from children writing book reports to university students preparing research papers to readers of historical fiction curious about terminology and authenticity. It is recommended as a vital reference resource for all types of libraries.

—**Mark T. Bay**

AMERICAN HISTORY

General Works

S

136.   Hanes, Sharon M., and Richard C. Hanes. **Great Depression and New Deal: Almanac.** Farmington Hills, Mich., U*X*L/Gale, 2003. 278p. illus. index. (U*X*L Great Depression and New Deal Reference Library). $55.00/vol.; $145.00/set. ISBN 0-7876-6588-9.

S

137.   Hanes, Sharon M., and Richard C. Hanes. **Great Depression and New Deal: Biographies.** Farmington Hills, Mich., U*X*L/Gale, 2003. 241p. illus. index. (U*X*L Great Depression and New Deal Reference Library). $55.00/vol.; $145.00/set. ISBN 0-7876-6534-7.

S

138.   Hanes, Sharon M., and Richard C. Hanes. **Great Depression and New Deal: Primary Sources.** Farmington Hills, Mich., U*X*L/Gale, 2003. 260p. illus. index. (U*X*L Great Depression and New Deal Reference Library). $55.00/vol.; $145.00/set. ISBN 0-7876-6535-5.

The Great Depression of the 1930s and President Roosevelt's introduction of the New Deal was a defining moment in American history. These three volumes combine to provide a historical analysis of this time in history. The set is designed for middle school students and is written and arranged to fit their educational needs.

The *Almanac* provides a background for the Great Depression and New Deal. It includes 16 chapters, each of which focuses on a specific topic. The book begins with a timeline, a glossary, and research and activity ideas (e.g., exploring the Internet, political debates, creating political cartoons). The volume then provides 16 chapters, which address such topics as the causes of the Great Depression, farm relief, industry and labor, women and minorities in the Great Depression, and prohibition and crime.

The *Biographies* volume introduces students to key figures of the time, including politicians such as Eleanor and Franklin Roosevelt and J. Edgar Hoover, and activists such as Molly Dewson and Hallie Flanagan. The biographies run several pages in length and include personal and professional information, interesting sidebars, a black-and-white photograph, and resources for further information.

Primary Sources is divided into eight chapters, each of which focuses on a different theme (e.g., "A New Deal for Americans," "Women's Voices"). Each chapter begins with an overview and then provides excerpts from speeches, letters, and essays. The authors help students research by following up with information of what happened next, facts on the document and its author, and posing questions for the reader to ask themselves. Each of the volumes concludes with its own list of books and Websites for further information and an index.

This set will be useful in middle school libraries and children's reference collections in public libraries. The information is straightforward but also includes tips for further research and interesting activities to put them in the time of the Depression and New Deal era.—**Shannon Graff Hysell**

Atlases

C, P, S

139.   **Civil War Maps. http://lcweb2.loc.gov/ammem/gmdhtml/cwmhtml/.** [Website]. Washington, D.C., Library of Congress. Free. Date reviewed: Jan 03.

This Website, sponsored by the Geography and Map Division of the Library of Congress, provides users access to 2,240 Civil War maps and charts and 76 atlases and sketchbooks. The majority of the maps shown here are from Richard W. Stephenson's *Civil War Maps: An Annotated List of Maps and Atlases in the Library of Congress* (2d ed.; see ARBA 90, entry 648). The maps and charts depict battles, engagements, troop movements, and fortifications. There are also a handful of reconnaissance maps, coastal charts, and theater of war maps. Many of the maps are reproductions of the original maps used between 1861 and 1865, although a few were created later to help explain specific events. Maps from both the northern Federal side as well as the southern Confederates are represented. Along with presenting these historical maps and charts, the work also offers essays about mapping during the Civil War and presents a list of further resources. Most entries provide a brief paragraph describing the map, but there is no attempt to analyze or evaluate them critically.

The site is searchable by keyword, geographic location, subject index, and creator index. Along with each displayed map is information on when it was created, the scale, links to other similar subjects, the call number and control number, and the name of the repository. There is a wealth of information located here for both scholars of the Civil War and students doing research on this historical time period. The site's source is extremely reliable and the site is easy to navigate, which makes this Website a worthwhile resource for school, public, and academic libraries.—**Shannon Graff Hysell**

Biography

C, P

140.   Fredriksen, John C. **America's Military Adversaries: From Colonial Times to the Present.** Santa Barbara, Calif., ABC-CLIO, 2001. 621p. illus. index. $85.00. ISBN 1-57607-603-2.

Fredriksen, independent historian and author of *American Military Leaders: From Colonial Times to the Present* (see ARBA 2000, entry 596) and *Warbirds* (see ARBA 2000, entry 611), has written an excellent biographical encyclopedia of the various military adversaries (naval, air, and land) America has faced since colonial times. A few individuals included are such well-know figures as the French and Indian War's Montcalm; the Revolutionary War's Joseph Brant, Cornwallis, and Burgoyne; the Civil War's Lee and "Stonewall" Jackson; Cochise; Geronimo; Poncho Villa; Nazi Germany's Galland, Rommel, and Kesselring; Imperial Japan's Tojo and Yamamoto; and Iraq's Saddam Hussein. The Revolutionary War British General Simon Fraser is a fine example of the typical entry. Included items are: dates of life and death, a portrait, a two-page entry that includes a biography, an individual bibliography, and a *see also* section that highlights other military figures.

The material is divided into a preface, 223 entries for military adversaries of the United States, an appendix listing all by occupation, and an appendix divided by conflict. Additionally, a 50-page bibliography is provided as well as a useful index. This work is especially strong in frontier wars, the American Revolution, the War of 1812, the Civil War, and World War II. A shortfall seems to be the lack of depth in modern conflicts such as the Korean War, the Vietnam War, the Gulf War, and Somalia. This well-done work is especially useful for those looking to begin research into those who led America's military adversaries. It should be included in all libraries. [R: BL, 15 May 02, pp. 1624-1626; Choice, May 02, p. 1562]—**Scott R. DiMarco**

C, S

141.   **Lifetimes: The Great War to the Stock Market Crash. American History Through Biography and Primary Documents.** Neil A. Hamilton, ed. Westport, Conn., Greenwood Press, 2002. 328p. illus. index. $74.95. ISBN 0-313-31799-2.

This publication is another book about the 1920s that emphasizes the transforming effects of World War I. As such, there is nothing new here, especially for scholars. Still, using 60 biographical sketches to illuminate prominent themes, the study adequately calls attention to the decade's contrasts. The 1920s were years of prosperity, rapid change, incredible optimism, and some acceptance of international responsibility. They were also years of grinding hardship for many Americans, oppressive conformity, intellectual despair, and a return to pre-war isolationism. These paradoxes become apparent through the portrayals of such personalities as Henry Ford, William Haywood, William Jennings Bryan, Clarence Darrow, Bruce Barton, F. Scott Fitzgerald, A. Mitchell Palmer, and Emma Goldman.

It would be easy to fault the editor for certain omissions—such as Sinclair Lewis, Billy Sunday, or Zane Grey—but, in fairness, the attempt was to be representative rather than all-inclusive. So the biographies include business leaders and labor organizers, conservative and liberal politicians, popular sports heroes, and radical social reformers. Women, exemplified by Aimee Semple McPherson and Alice Paul, and other minorities, seen in Louis Armstrong and Anna May Wong, are not neglected. Accompanying each biography is a brief bibliography and a sampling of original documents, as in "Mr. Bryan's Last Speech" at the famous Monkey Trial of 1925, or in an excerpt from Ernest Hemingway's *The Sun Also Rises*. Overall, the volume's appeal is enhanced by numerous photographs; two useful appendixes (one listing all the documents and the other providing a time from June 1914 to October 24, 1929); an extensive, topically organized bibliography; and an exhaustive bibliography. For high school and college undergraduates researching the 1920s, this work will be a helpful study tool. [R: SLJ, Nov 02, p. 100]—**John W. Storey**

Chronology

C, S

142.   Zeman, Scott C. **Chronology of the American West: From 23,000 B.C.E. Through the Twentieth Century.** Santa Barbara, Calif., ABC-CLIO, 2002. 381p. illus. index. $85.00. ISBN 1-57607-207-X.

The human dramas that have been played out in the American West are extraordinary. This extensive chronology, which is studded with thoughtful essays and figures, attempts to capture this broad swath of history, from 23,000 B.C.E. (when the Bering Land Bridge was exposed) to events of 2000. For the most part it succeeds in conveying the framework of that story in accessible, attractive, and interesting prose. The American West is defined in this book as the lands west of the 98th meridian, including the states it intersects. The author curiously includes Hawaii in this chronology; despite his brief explanation, it still shares little with the rest of the western stories. Parts of Mexico and Canada are also covered when they are essential to cultural and historical events.

The book is divided into four parts, each with important events briefly described in chronological order and with short essays in boxes. The first part is "The Native West," which is western history from the earliest occupied sites to the kingdom of Montezuma. "The Imperial West" follows, being the account of various European explorations and conquests. "The Incorporated West" covers the increasing dominance of the United States in western history, from 1840 to the 1932 Summer Olympics in Los Angeles. The last part is "The Contested West," which starts with the Great Depression and continues to the first year of the 21st century. This last part is especially interesting because it includes new and diverse perceptions of the American West that transcend the traditional cowboy and Indian images at the center of western mythology. There is a bit of a leftward slant in some ways (every "marginalized" group is included at least once and labor unions are always heroic), but overall the entries and essays are balanced and informative.

The author adds a long bibliographic essay at the end of the text, giving hundreds of references for his entries and essays. This essay and the resources it cites elevates this text far above the skeletal chronologies that are common in bookstores. This is a professional work that will interest the public because of its clarity and scope.

This book is highly recommended for all libraries with history collections. It will be useful for many constituencies, from schoolchildren writing research reports to historians who need to see the broad outlines and contexts of historical events.—**Mark A. Wilson**

Dictionaries and Encyclopedias

S

143.   **American History. http://www.americanhistory.abc-clio.com/.** [Website]. Santa Barbara, Calif., ABC-CLIO. $599.00/year. Minimum system requirements: Internet access with a version 4.0 or later browser. Browser must be cookie and JavaScript enabled. ISSN 1531-1260. Date reviewed: Mar 02.

This electronic resource from ABC-CLIO is designed specifically with teachers and students in mind. Designed much like the other social studies databases from ABC-CLIO, this Website focuses on American history from the early exploration to the American Revolution and the establishment of the 13 original colonies. It covers westward expansion, the Civil War, the Industrial Revolution, and the current threat of terrorism, with much more in between.

The layout of the site is easy to follow. Students can research independently by using the "Reference" section. This page allows the user to search by text (keyword or phrase), topic (a chronological listing of periods throughout U.S. history), or category (e.g., essays, documents, images, maps, quotes). The essays on each topic are thorough and will be easy for middle to high school students to understand and the photographs and maps are clear. A "cybrarian" is available online to answer any questions the user might have using the sight and a Merriam-Webster dictionary is readily available for those having vocabulary problems.

One of the most valuable assets of this reference for the use in schools is that it allows teachers to create a calendar of events and assignments that will specifically meet the needs of their classroom. Under the section titled "Administration" teachers or school media specialists can create research assignments for their students, as well as create subject-specific tests and a class syllabus. Both a student access code and an administrator access code are provided so that students will not have access to the "Administration" page. This also allows students to have access to the Website from school or home and will give parents the opportunity to keep up on their children's assignments.

The *American History* Website is a remarkable tool that will give learning U.S. history new appeal to young adults. Students will enjoy using it and it will give teachers the opportunity to teach U.S. history in a new and exciting format. The cost may keep some schools from purchasing this remarkable tool, but for all of the topics covered and the use it will have in the library, the classroom, and in students' homes this product deserves careful consideration.

—**Shannon Graff Hysell**

C, P, S

144.　Atkins, Stephen E. **Encyclopedia of Modern American Extremists and Extremist Groups.** Westport, Conn., Greenwood Press, 2002. 373p. illus. index. $74.95. ISBN 0-313-31502-7.

Extremists have been in America as long as America has been around. "Nothing exceeds like excess," Oscar Wilde is reported to have said, and extremists have certainly been excessive in this country. The *Encyclopedia of Modern American Extremists and Extremist Groups* stands as a sad testament to this country's homegrown hotheads, lunatics, and guttersnipes.

"What is objectionable, what is dangerous about extremists," the late Robert Kennedy once opined, "is not that they are extreme, but that they are intolerant. The evil is not what they say about their cause, but what they say about their opponents." It is also what they do to those perceived opponents. Consider Marshall Applewhite, resident kook of the kookier Heaven's Gate. The comet Hale-Bopp was a signal for something, causing Applewhite to renounce lust, embrace (if one can use that word in this context) castration, and send himself and just over three dozen members to a new age by mixing phenobarbital sleeping pills in applesauce, pudding, or vodka. Other groups are less easy to dismiss. ACT-UP has the cache of Hollywood and the politically correct crowd even though its tactics are no different from dozens of other routinely denounced groups. Atkins covers them all: offbeat "religious" groups, militia, the KKK, David Koresh, the Unabomber, and more.

Entries range in length from a few hundred words to nearly a thousand. Cross-references and bibliographies ("Suggested Readings") enhance the volume's usefulness. This is an excellent reference tool and should place Atkins in line for a second *Booklist* Editor's Choice Award.—**Mark Y. Herring**

S

145.　**Encyclopedia of American History.** Gary B. Nash, ed. New York, Facts on File, 2003. 11v. illus. maps. index. $935.00/set. ISBN 0-8160-4371-X.

This 11-volume encyclopedia is designed with high school students in mind. The general editor, Gary B. Nash, was co-director of the National Standards for United States History Project, and has brought his experience with education to this multivolume set. Unlike other encyclopedic volumes it is not organized in the standard A-Z format. Instead, each volume covers a different era of American history and the terms, events, and people relevant to that era are featured in that volume. Each volume provides a list of the entries and an introduction of the time period covered. Entries are typically several pages in length and include biographies of important people and black-and-white photographs and maps. Each volume concludes with a chronology, a list of important documents, a bibliography, and an index to that specific volume. Along with biographies, entries cover topics on events, movements, political developments, the economy, literature, business, art and architecture, and science and technology of the time. Many of the entries provide lists of further reading so students can expand on their research. The use of illustrations and maps is extensive, and they successfully enhance the text. Volume 11 provides a comprehensive index to the set, which serves to pull the 11 volumes together.

This set will be useful in school libraries—its intended audience. Unfortunately, at $935 it may be too expensive for some.—**Shannon Graff Hysell**

C, P

146.　Jones, Terry L. **Historical Dictionary of the Civil War.** Lanham, Md., Scarecrow, 2002. 2v. (Historical Dictionaries of War, Revolution, and Civil Unrest, no.18). $245.00/set. ISBN 0-8108-4112-6.

This reviewer, a former reference librarian and current Civil War historian, finds little to criticize and much to praise in this work. As a historical dictionary, it is superior. The author, however, a professor of history and an author of several books on the Civil War, gives readers much more. Part narrative history, part chronology, part bibliography, but mainly an encyclopedic dictionary, he presents users with a superb companion to Civil War literature that should become a standard in libraries and in the homes of both professionals and amateurs with an interest in the Civil War.

The 38-page chronology that begins this title is excellent. Starting with a brief listing of events of the years 1820 to 1859 that up led to the war. The following years 1860 through 1865 are wonderfully detailed, including many items not normally found in standard chronologies of the war. This is followed by a 76-page narrative history that is equally well done. The author, Terry L. Jones, presents users with a comprehensive treatment of the topic that is as free of sectional bias as one could expect in a field that is rife with one-sided publications. The narrative is conveniently divided into subheaded sections covering the coming of the war, secession, domestic events, diplomacy, military campaigns by year, and postwar effects. The chronology and narrative together are important additions that give users background to the specifics presented in the alphabetic dictionary segment that forms the main body of this title. If there is a disappointment in this work, it is the all-to-brief atlas section. The three maps add little, and the too-small printing requires good eyes to read.

The main dictionary segment measures up to the two previous sections in content and comprehensiveness. The scope is broad. Although biographical entries tend to dominate, the inclusion of other topics is plentiful, including battles, weapons, ammunition, equipment, medicine, prisons, ships, topography, and many others. This reviewer tested the contents by searching small battles and lesser-known subjects and was never disappointed. Of particular interest are the individual entries for each state of the Union and Confederacy, illustrating how the war affected that state. While there is no subject index, information is still easy to locate through the profuse use of bold type within entries that leads users to related topics elsewhere in the two volumes. This title concludes with a very good 75-page bibliography, grouped by main topics, which leads users to additional information on the war.

This is an outstanding contribution to the reference literature of the Civil War. Civil War enthusiasts and libraries of any type with an interest in this topic should seriously consider this work for inclusion in their collections.
—**Donald E. Collins**

C, P, S
147.   Olson, James S. **Historical Dictionary of the Great Depression, 1929-1940.** Westport, Conn., Greenwood Press, 2001. 355p. index. $90.00. ISBN 0-313-30618-4.

Americans today have little if any comprehension of the Great Depression's hardship, or of its revolutionary impact on American politics and society. At the depth of this economic earthquake, industrial productivity had fallen by 50 percent, foreign trade was off by about 70 percent, unemployment stood around 25 percent, and the stock market had lost approximately 90 percent of its value. This catastrophe once and for all shattered the heretofore illusion of a self-regulating economy behaving in accordance with impersonal natural laws, such as supply and demand. Brushing aside obsolete notions of laissez faire, Franklin D. Roosevelt's New Deal utilized federal power to an unprecedented degree, initially seeking to fashion a centrally directed economy through the National Industrial Recovery Act (1933), placing government squarely on the side of organized labor for the first time in American history through the National Labor Relations Act (1935), and attempting to protect ordinary Americans from want through the Social Security Act (1935).

This useful dictionary by Olsen, a Texas historian with considerable experience at producing such studies, documents this pivotal period. The 500 or so entries, varying in length from a few sentences to a page or 2, cover not only politics and economics, but also intellectual currents and popular culture. So, in addition to expected features on people and subjects such as Herbert Hoover, John Maynard Keynes, Bull Market, and Hundred Days, one also finds entries on Shirley Temple, Lou Gehrig, Scottsboro Case, and Superman. A helpful chronology and a thorough index make for easy access to the material. The volume's only shortcoming is the absence of a brief introductory essay providing some perspective and assessment. Still, this study would be of value to high school and college studies, and reference librarians should add it to their collections.—**John W. Storey**

Directories

C, P
148.   **Directory of Historical Organizations in the United States and Canada.** 15th ed. By American Association for State and Local History. Walnut Creek, Calif., Alta Mira Press, 2002. 1358p. index. (American Association for State and Local History Book Series). $129.95pa. ISBN 0-7591-0002-0.

It has been 10 years since the last edition of this directory. Its comprehensive listing of state and local historical agencies, sites, and museums was compiled from survey responses and 13,000 history-related organizations and programs in the United States and Canada are included. The directory's broad scope covers historical museums of many types (maritime, sports, tribal, and so on), historic houses and gardens, and state and local genealogical societies.

There are four parts to the directory. The major section lists historical organizations in the United States. Entries are alphabetic by state and city. Each entry has been assigned a unique identifying number that can be used as a locator device from the index. Complete contact information is provided, including e-mail and URL addresses where appropriate. Information on the size of the group's membership, its collection focus, its publication titles, and a brief mission statement are also provided. Part 2 covers state National Archive and Records offices and presidential libraries. Universities offering degrees in public history and state history offices appear as well. Part 3 is dedicated to Canada's historical organizations and part 4 is made up of two indexes; one is a subject index and the other is alphabetic. Both of the indexes give the organization's name, entry identification number, and state or province.

A similar work is the three-volume *Directory of Genealogical and Historical Societies in the United States and Canada* (Iron Gate Publishing, 2000). Most of the historical societies appear in both titles, but this one includes not only state and local genealogical groups but also specific family history societies. The review title has the advantage of providing more information about each organization. The two directories complement one another nicely and both will be useful to genealogists and local history researchers. Tourists, hobbyists, and researchers will find the review title useful in locating subject specific collections. The disadvantage of any print directory is the rapidity with which information changes. Hopefully, with the financial support of the History Channel, the editors will not have to wait another 10 years to update this valuable resource. [R: Choice, June 02, p. 1746]—**Marlene M. Kuhl**

Handbooks and Yearbooks

S

149.   Brownstone, David M., and Irene M. Franck. **The Young Nation: America 1787-1861.** Bethel, Conn., Grolier Educational, 2002. 10v. illus. maps. index. $339.00/set. ISBN 0-7172-5645-6.

The Young Nation, a 10-volume set, provides an excellent history of the American Colonies, their development into a new nation, and the conflict involved in nation-building which led to the Civil War. The set ends in 1861. Organized thematically, the set examines the British, French, and Spanish roots of the United States; the expansion of the new nation; immigration; the conflict over slavery; Native American and women's issues; and many other events and concepts.

One real benefit of this set is the way in which the authors explain in clear terms the challenges that the forefathers had in conceiving of and creating the new nation. Instead of treating historical information as a list of facts, dates and events, the authors show how history happened. Accelerated learners will be able to synthesize and analyze philosophical issues in history. Each volume includes an index to the complete set. Within the text, there are references to related topics, either in the same volume or in another. The final volume includes a glossary, demographic data, and the U.S. Constitution. Each volume also includes references to high-quality, educational Websites and other print publications. The set includes many colorful images and maps, although some images are not placed well contextually. This valuable reference set is recommended for junior and senior high school libraries.—**Tara L. Dirst**

C, S

150.   Girard, Jolyon P. **America and the World.** Westport, Conn., Greenwood Press, 2001. 304p. maps. index. (Major Issues in American History). $55.00. ISBN 0-313-31292-3.

Excerpts or full-length documents related to U.S. foreign relations throughout its history are used to illustrate several consistent threads in this work in the Major Issues in American History series from Greenwood Press. The author sees these threads as isolationism, freedom of the seas, the Monroe Doctrine, the idea of pan-Americanism, and an open door policy. The purpose of this book, as is others in the series, is to assist teachers and students at all levels in classes that approach history "within a problem-solving framework." The documents, which are arranged chronologically, begin with George Washington's farewell address and end with the Reagan-Gorbachev Summit in Reykjavik, the conference that ended the Cold War. Each chapter begins with a historical essay by Girard; the documents follow. Each document has a brief introduction that sets it in context. The book includes careful documentation, a chronology, a selected bibliography, and an index. Greenwood Press has a long history of publication of books of this type and continues to exercise strong quality control on each title. *America and the World* is recommended for high school and university libraries.—**Edna M. Boardman**

C, P

151. *The New York Times* **20th Century in Review: The Vietnam War. Volume I: 1945-1969.** Mark Lawrence, ed. Chicago, Fitzroy Dearborn, 2001. 2v. illus. maps. index. $150.00/set. ISBN 1-57958-368-7.

Although the Vietnam War deeply divided the American people, both sides can agree that the media, and *The New York Times* in particular, played a significant role during the conflict. The "good gray lady" was not only the nation's paper of record, but also a key resource for policy-makers, an influential critic of the war, and, perhaps most famously, the publisher of the Pentagon Papers (the top-secret Defense Department's study of the war's origins). Because of the *Times'* singular importance during the Vietnam War, scholars will welcome this extraordinary 2-volume collection of some 600 articles about the war as recorded in the pages of *The New York Times*. Nevertheless, they constitute only a tiny proportion of the entire number of articles actually published during the war. Faced with a staggering amount of newsprint, the editors used strict criteria to emphasize four categories of material: basic news reporting of major events of the war that usually appeared on the front page, important editorials and commentary by *Times* columnists, investigative and analytical stories from distinguished reporters, and stories that had a significant impact on the history of journalism such as the initial reporting of the My Lai massacre. Within these constraints, the range in chronology and topics covered is remarkable.

The Vietnam War volume consists of nine parts and is chronologically organized. Part 1 begins in 1945 with the upsurge in Vietnamese nationalism and closes with the debacle at Dienbienphu and Geneva. Part 2 covers the nation-building years of 1954-1961, when the United States replaced France as the major Western power in Indochina. The bulk of the 2 volumes, some 75 percent, covers the decade of heaviest U.S. involvement, 1963-1973. Thus, part 3 looks closely at the Kennedy years and America's increasing commitment to Indochina in 1961-1963. Part 4 reveals the growing divide between the Johnson administration, which escalated the war, and the *Times* editorial writers, who called for negotiation. Part 5, "America at War, 1965-1968," the largest in the collection, gathers together a wide range of stories that cover the ground war, the failings of the South Vietnamese state, peace initiatives, and the antiwar movement. Part 6 chronicles how the Tet Offensive ended President Lyndon B. Johnson's presidency. Part 7 focuses on President Nixon's secret plan to end the war while preserving America's honor, his invasion of Cambodia and Laos, and the legal wrangling over the Pentagon Papers. Part 8, "The End of the American War, 1971-1975," concentrates on the war between the South and North Vietnamese armies and the eventual fall of Saigon to the Communists. Finally, part 10, "The Aftermath of War, 1975-2000," consists of 3 sections that cover Americans' initial retrenchment from Vietnam, the re-entry of Vietnam into national consciousness in the 1980s as Americans contested the legacy of the war, and the continuing divisions among Americans amidst political and economic reconciliation between the United States and Vietnam. This volume is a must-have for all libraries.—**E. Wayne Carp**

P, S

152. **U*X*L American Decades.** Tom Pendergast and Sara Pendergast, eds. Farmington Hills, Mich., U*X*L/ Gale, 2003. 10v. illus. index. $399.00/set. ISBN 0-7876-6454-5.

U*X*L American Decades is a 10-volume set designed to present a broad overview of the major events and people that helped shape American society throughout the twentieth century. Each volume contains a different image in the central panel of the cover reflecting an important icon from that decade. For example, the 1960-1969 volume features a flag bearing the "Peace" symbol. After an overall chronology and a brief essay titled "An Overview," eight chapters comprise each volume: "Arts and Entertainment"; "Business and the Economy"; "Education"; "Government, Politics, and Law"; "Lifestyles and Social Trends"; "Medicine and Health"; "Science and Technology"; and "Sports." Each chapter contains a timeline of significant events within the chapter's field, an overview summary of the events and people detailed in that chapter, short biographical accounts of key people and their achievements during the decade, a series of brief topical essays describing events and people within the chapter's theme, and a "For More Information" section that includes books and Websites. In addition, each volume concludes with a longer "Where to Learn More" listing of books and Websites, as well as an alphabetic subject index for that volume. A paperback cumulative index lists volume and page number for topics covered in all 10 volumes. *U*X*L American Decades* volumes contain many black-and-white photographs and a few scattered sidebars.

Designed for middle school students, this series should not be overlooked for high school use as well. Even reluctant readers could find the sports and pop music statistics fascinating. In fact, researchers of any age who need information about popular culture in a particular decade would probably find this series to be quick and convenient. The language is neither too difficult nor too simple for an average reader. Although *U*X*L American Decades* covers a lot of ground, as with any such series, some of the included material could be open to question as to its political biases or other biases simply because of what is included or excluded. The series is at its best when it quotes important figures and lets the readers draw their own conclusions about what they say. It is perhaps not quite always as successful in choosing the half dozen or so "key people" from each decade. As always, references to Websites will tend to be outdated long before the bibliographic information. For those, however, who can afford the price, *U*X*L American Decades* is an interesting and unique reference.

—**Kay O. Cornelius**

Quotation Books

C, P

153.   **America in Quotations: A Kaleidoscopic View of American History.** Howard J. Langer, comp. Westport, Conn., Greenwood Press, 2002. 463p. index. $79.95. ISBN 0-313-30883-7.

There is no question that *America in Quotations* is an interesting book that is packed full of vibrant quotes and descriptions about American history. The question is, however, how does one use it effectively? Gathering this material is a challenging task: 18 chapters are devoted to major periods of American history, such as pre-Columbus, the American Revolution, Westward expansion, the Civil War, industrialism, the Depression, World War II, and on through to the terrorist attacks on the World Trade Center in 2001. Greenwood Press describes the book as a "grassroots look at the country as real people tell the story of America." Although this is true, it is difficult to use the book as a history of America because the passages are sometimes unsupported by adequate historical background or are taken out of context and hard to understand. For example, in chapter 4 on the American Revolution, there is very little explanation of the causes of the conflict and no mention of the Boston Tea Party or the hardships of Valley Forge. There are only four entries that cover the Mexican-American War. Because it is out of context, the relationship of entry 323, a quote by James Garfield, is unclear. Brief biographies of the 350 people quoted in the book, as well as a chronology of U.S. history and a bibliography, are also provided.

America in Quotations is a noble effort to capture the breadth of U.S. history in first-person narrative, but the scope of the project really requires multiple volumes. There are many evocative passages that make the reader want to learn more, and for the curious reader the source material is listed at the end of each entry. [R: SLJ, Nov 02, p. 102]—**Mark J. Crawford**

AFRICAN HISTORY

C

154.   Lye, Keith, with the Diagram Group. **Encyclopedia of African Nations and Civilizations.** New York, Facts on File, 2002. 400p. illus. maps. index. (Facts on File Library of World History). $75.00. ISBN 0-8160-4568-2.

This volume mentions countless African civilizations and nations. Because it has maps, chronologies, and pictures, all with text and independent text, redundancy is rampant. Like many encyclopedias, the pictures are profuse and add interest, but are small and dark; and the maps are often difficult to understand. Sobering political history, with a little disturbing natural history to boot, is emphasized here. Not the glorious cultures or terrains or even lifestyles, the journalist author of this history seems to teach that good intentions of indigenous or foreign people are rarely significant for long. The general progress of hundreds of parts of Africa is the same—2,000 years ago nearly everyone was hunting and gathering when iron-using settled life was introduced by migrating Bantu peoples. Some ensuing cultures developed indigenous empires that suppressed or enslaved others. Encroaching do-gooders or business people took advantage of offended people to make in-roads that led to competing international empires that evolved to abusiveness. The resulting idealistic revolutions typically progress to tyrannies. This encyclopedia well identifies data, places, and personae of these stages. Unfortunately, there are many typographical errors, multiple spellings (Omayyad and Umayyad), other errors (the sides of the step pyramid are said to be smooth), and unusual opinions (Nefertiti emphasized over Akhenaton for reducing the gods to one god). Users must be familiar with underdeveloped countries in order to use this reference.—**Elizabeth L. Anderson**

ASIAN HISTORY

Handbooks and Yearbooks

C, P, S

155.   Benn, Charles. **Daily Life in Traditional China: The Tang Dynasty.** Westport, Conn., Greenwood Press, 2002. 317p. illus. index. (The Greenwood Press "Daily Life Through History" Series). $49.95. ISBN 0-313-30955-8.

Based on a college course taught by the author, this curriculum-oriented book, *Daily Life in Traditional China: The Tang Dynasty*, introduces students of varied disciplines to ancient China during the Tang period, 618-907. Known as the golden age of Chinese culture, Tang China produced the greatest literature, arts, music, dance, law code, and Buddhism during its 300-year history. The book begins with a map of Tang China and its capital Changan and a listing of the tang emperors. There is a wealth of information about historical life that is divided into 12 topics: history, society, cities and urban life, house and garden, clothes and hygiene, food and feasts, leisure and entertainment, travel and transportation, crime and punishment, sickness and health, life cycle, and death and the afterlife. There are more than 40 illustrations throughout. A list of suggested English-language readings by topics and an index complete the volume.

The text of the book heavily derives from original Tang sources or secondary studies. However, notes of the original sources have been omitted that will undoubtedly diminish the value of the book as a serious scholarly work. However, undergraduates, high school students, and the general public will enjoy the lively account in this excellent introductory work to an ancient time and a faraway place, and gain a better understanding of Tang China. This work is recommended for public, high school, and undergraduate libraries.—**Karen T. Wei**

C, P

156.   McLeod, John. **The History of India.** Westport, Conn., Greenwood Press, 2002. 223p. maps. index. (The Greenwood Histories of the Modern Nations). $39.95. ISBN 0-313-31459-4.

India is a vast and complex country with a long and fascinating history. It has suffered countless foreign invasions, but its resilience has been remarkable. Its ancient traditions and values have not been obliterated by proselytizing religions. Rather, the intruders have been "Indianized" in the process. In linguistic and cultural expressions, India is impressively rich. Countless volumes have been written on the history of India.

In this slender volume John McLeod does a good job of presenting in broad outlines some of the major events and episodes that make up India's history. So many kings, regimes, and governments have shaped Indian history that there is little room for the author to dwell on the cultural and religious dimensions of the Indian people. The Ramayana and the Mahabharata are mentioned, but their role in the molding of Indian values and worldviews, such as adherence to truth, obedience to father, and keeping one's word of honor, is not discussed. The Bhagavad Gita is used as a springboard for discussing castes. There is no mention of Thomas Babington Macaulay in the book, although his introduction of English into India has had a greater impact on modern India than any other single factor.

With all that, this is a useful compilation of important facts relating to Indian history. Its strength lies primarily in the last six chapters in which brief narratives of the struggle for independence and post-independence India down to the close of the twentieth century are nicely presented. All in all, this is a book that all libraries should have.—**Varadaraja V. Raman**

C, P

157.   **Vietnam: Yesterday and Today. http://servercc.oakton.edu/~wittman/.** [Website]. By Sandra M. Wittman. Skokie, Ill., Oakton Community College. Free. Date reviewed: Oct 02.

The lessons learned from America's misadventure in Vietnam continue to be relevant in the emerging political landscape of the twenty-first century, from the anti-terrorism mission in Afghanistan to the possible invasion of Iraq. The consequences of military intervention remain an important topic of study in schools and colleges, and students pursuing research of Vietnam War-related issues can benefit from consulting Professor Sandra Wittman's carefully compiled Website, which is specifically designed for students and teachers.

Wittman (Emeritus, Oakton Community College) brings a teacher's enthusiasm to much of the subject matter, as in the introduction, where she conveys a sense of immediacy by discussing the veterans who still suffer from Post Traumatic Stress Disorder and Agent Orange exposure, and the Amerasian children and Vietnamese refugees who now live in the United States. Helpful "Tips for Students" offer advice on how to pick a topic, and offer good topic suggestions that include "drug use in Vietnam" and "Vietnam: Lost or Won?," as well as how to consult reference librarians; use Interlibrary Loan; avoid the pitfalls of plagiarism and copyright; and search, evaluate, and cite information. The chronology is particularly detailed and provides a solid foundation for research.

The majority of the site's content is comprised of bibliographies of sources, both books and films. The categories include "Vietnamese Perspective" and "Women," and there are subdivisions by literary genre. Wittman's experience as a bibliographer in this field, having previously published *Writing About Vietnam: A Bibliography of the Literature of the Vietnam Conflict* (see ARBA 91, entry 512), yields a well-chosen collection of citations. However, there are no annotations, either synoptic or analytic, which is a decided shortcoming for the novice scanning the long lists of books and films. For instance, Robert Mason's classic *Chickenhawk* is listed under "Personal Accounts," but how is the user to know that it is one of the best memoirs by a helicopter pilot? Many of the mere titles fail to reveal the book's subject matter. It would have been more helpful to have a shorter list with annotations; even brief annotations giving an overview would be much preferable to the bare bones of an unannotated bibliography.

Visually, the site is conservative in graphical presentation, almost to a fault. Illustrations and period photographs, which would help bring the subject to life for students accustomed to the graphics of many contemporary Websites, are minimal.

Numerous links to other Vietnam-related Websites are provided, which, unlike the bibliographies, feature excellent annotations describing each site. The several recognitions and awards earned by *Vietnam: Yesterday and Today* are listed, including being recommended by the History Channel and The Discovery Channel School.

—**Richard W. Grefrath**

AUSTRALIAN AND PACIFIC HISTORY

P, S

158.   Clarke, Frank G. **The History of Australia.** Westport, Conn., Greenwood Press, 2002. 236p. maps. index. (The Greenwood Histories of the Modern Nations). $44.95. ISBN 0-313-31498-5.

The history of Australia has always been a very popular topic. Since the 1960s numerous histories of Australia have been published, beginning with Manning Clark's pioneering study *A History of Australia* (Cambridge University Press, 1962) right through to Phillip Knightley's *Australia: Biography of a Nation* (Jonathan Cape, 2002). In 1987, Robert Hughes published the popular *The Fatal Shore* (Knopf, 1987) that eventually resulted in a fine documentary film. In the area of reference, three major works have been published. The year 1984 saw the publication of John Shaw's *Australia Encyclopedia* (Collins, 1984), followed shortly by Jan Bassett's slim *Concise Oxford Dictionary of Australian History* (see ARBA 88, entry 525). More recently, Graeme Davison has edited *The Oxford Companion to Australian History* (Oxford University Press, 1998).

As part of The Greenwood Histories of the Modern Nations series, Clarke has published *The History of Australia*. Clarke's intention is to present an objective, layperson snapshot of Australian history up to current times. Although the author is successful, this slim volume feels condensed and basically reads as a straightforward narrative. It begins with a timeline of historical events. The first chapter is a very short overview of Australia (geography, climate, culture, and so on). The rest of the text is a chronological study in short, concise chapters beginning 60,000 years ago with Aboriginal Australia and ending with 2001 and beyond. Each chapter is broken down into smaller sections, with headings, covering such essential topics as colonization, war, government, and politics. The work ends with smaller sections for notable people, notes, a bibliographic essay, and an index.

Although this work is an admirable concentrated study of Australian history, if reference collections are already sound in this area then they will not need this book. It could be considered for circulating collections, but may be more suitable for small public library reference collections.—**Richard Slapsys**

C, P

159.   Craig, Robert D. **Historical Dictionary of Polynesia.** 2d ed. Lanham, Md., Scarecrow, 2002. 365p. (Asian/Oceanian Historical Dictionaries, no.39). $65.00. ISBN 0-8108-4237-8.

It has taken an extraordinarily wide and deep knowledge to assemble this information about the 14 Pacific Island states that constitute Polynesia and, probably, only Craig could have done it, by virtue of his experience in the field from traveling and teaching and through his positions as editor of *Pacific Studies* and director of the Pacific Rim Studies Center at Alaska Pacific University.

The book begins with a useful chronology from 1300 B.C.E., when Tonga was first colonized, to mid-2001. Entries are brief until they flesh out in the 1980s and become quite full in the 1990s. The entries themselves are alphabetic, as implied by the dictionary nature of the book, so that important figures and institutions appear alphabetically alongside complete entries on the island groups. The chief emphasis in the island entries is historical, but there is also ample information on their political systems and economies. The information is always interesting and sometimes quite moving, as in the tragic history of tiny Nauru. When the Japanese occupied it during World War II, they moved its population of 1,200 to Truk, where 500 died. Mining of its phosphate deposits has caused massive ecological damage, and the money from the mining has been badly invested.

This 2d edition is more complete than the 1st edition published in 1993 (see ARBA 94, entry 120), updating material on contemporary events and adding new information. The comprehensive bibliography of 1,200 books has dropped some entries from the 1993 edition and added others—nearly 40 percent are newly published books. This work is, necessarily, the standard reference work on Polynesia.—**John B. Beston**

EUROPEAN HISTORY

General Works

Atlases

C

160.   Magocsi, Paul Robert. **Historical Atlas of Central Europe.** rev. ed. Seattle, Wash., University of Washington Press, 2002. 274p. maps. index. $75.00; $40.00pa. ISBN 0-295-98193-8; 0-295-98146-6pa.

Maps have forever captured the imagination of the intrepid explorer and armchair traveler. When well-designed maps are accompanied by cogent analysis that contextualizes and interprets the social, political, and historical dimensions they illustrate, the researcher or interested reader stands to gain immeasurably from the encounter. Paul Robert Magocsi's *Historical Atlas of Central Europe* provides precisely that kind of experience for the student or scholar. This edition is an extensively revised and updated version of *The Historical Atlas of East Central Europe*, first published in 1993 by the University of Washington Press and the University of Toronto Press as volume 1 in the series (see ARBA 94, entry 520). The maps themselves are beautifully executed by the University of Toronto's Office of Cartography.

The atlas covers the area from Poland, Lithuania, and the eastern part of Germany to Greece and western Turkey, and extends in time from the early fifth century to the present. The linguistic borders on the west are those of the German and Italian-speaking peoples. On the east, they are situated at the border of Russia and the states of the former Soviet Union.

Since the fall of the Roman Empire, Central Europe has served as a kind of nexus for powerful military, political, and social forces that have literally forged much of the Europe we know today. The seedbed for the two World Wars of the twentieth century, Central Europe's incessant volatility over the centuries has left a tragic scar on the face of the modern world. Nevertheless, as the author reminds us, the countries of "Middle Europe" have also transformed and enriched the Western world through their intimate connections with key intellectual and religious movements, like the Renaissance, Reformation, Humanism, and most recently, in the political realm, the fall of Soviet-style communism, which had enslaved many of their citizens. The final chapter, "Central Europe, 2002," vividly illustrates the momentous changes to this part of the world since the peaceful revolutions starting in 1989.

The *Historical Atlas of Central Europe* offers 21 new and 41 revised maps since the 1993 edition. In addition, there are 11 new chapters and 8 fresh thematic maps covering such topics as population changes, ethnolinguistic distribution, and Catholic and Orthodox churches. This is a masterfully done book that will be a necessity for college and university libraries, geographers of the European continent, as well as those, like this reviewer, who have a passion for maps of any kind. [R: LJ, 15 Nov 02, p. 62]—**John B. Romeiser**

C, P, S

161.   **The Routledge Atlas of the Holocaust.** 3d ed. By Martin Gilbert. New York, Routledge, 2002. 282p. illus. maps. index. $75.00; $19.95pa. ISBN 0-415-28145-8; 0-415-28146-6pa.

First published in 1982 as *The Dent Atlas of the Holocaust* and revised in 1993, the 3d edition of *The Routledge Atlas of the Holocaust* documents one of history's most horrible events. Distinguished British historian Sir Martin Gilbert uses 317 maps, text, and photographs to document Hitler's attempt to destroy Europe's Jews. He begins by showing the birth and death places of 17 people: historians, scientists, artists, and workers. The maps that follow demonstrate, in chronological sequence, the destruction of Jewish communities, acts of resistance and rebellion, paths of escape and rescue, and the fates of individuals.

New to this edition is a map that shows, country by country, where non-Jews recognized as rescuers by Yad Vashem risked their lives to save Jews. The *Atlas* also documents the murders of many non-Jewish civilians, Gypsies, homosexuals, euthanasia victims, and political prisoners. Gilbert notes that despite the meticulous German records the *Atlas* will never be complete because it is impossible to know everything that happened during the war.

The maps trace each phase of Hitler's plan, from the conquests of territories through the liberation of the death camps. Each one illustrates an event. Commentary offers statistical information, historical background, and something about the people of the area. Archival photographs bring the events to life. A bibliography and indexes of places and individuals help users locate specific material. This small but effective work demonstrates the magnitude of the Nazi terror by bringing it down to a personal level. It is highly recommended for academic, public, and school libraries.—**Barbara M. Bibel**

Bibliography

C, S

162.   **The Oryx Holocaust Sourcebook.** By William R. Fernekes. Westport, Conn., Oryx Press/Greenwood Publishing Group, 2002. 397p. index. (Oryx Holocaust Series). $55.95. ISBN 1-57356-295-5.

Divided into 6 main sections (for example, "General Print Resources," "General Electronic Resources"), this book is further subdivided into 17 narrower chapters ("Narrative Histories," "Film and Videotape"). Each chapter begins with an overview of its scope, and each citation gives full bibliographic information, including ISBN, number of pages, binding, total time (for audiovisual items), and contact information for organizations (address, telephone and fax numbers, URL, and e-mail address). The majority of the annotations are descriptive rather than evaluative. Although the author's criteria for inclusion might seem fairly broad—items must have been available at the time of the book's publication, be in English, and be scholarly and topical—this sourcebook is selective rather than comprehensive, emphasizing post-1990 materials (although including important older works). Although one could quibble over Fernekes' omission of Norman Finkelstein's *The Holocaust Industry* (2000), which received enormous press coverage, other important sources that one would expect to find are not included, such as Gerald Fleming's *Hitler and the Final Solution* (1984), Henry Friedlander's *The Origins of Nazi Genocide* (1995), and Deborah Lipstadt's *Denying the Holocaust* (1993). In discussing the Holocaust Teacher Resource Center Website (http://www.Holocaust-trc.org/), the author neglects to mention that it makes available online two valuable bibliographies published by the Holocaust Resource Center and Archives of Queensborough Community College: *Annotated Videography on Holocaust and Related Subjects* and *Educational Resource Guide on the Holocaust: A Selected Bibliography and Audio-Visual Catalogue* (neither of which is mentioned in this book). Also, curiously, Websites are not included in the book's subject index; thus, if a user looks under "Propaganda," one is not referred to the excellent German Propaganda Archive at Calvin College, although one finds it by browsing through the list of Websites. The substantial annotated bibliography in *The Columbia Guide to the Holocaust* by Donald Niewyk and Francis Nicosia (see ARBA 2001, entry 445) should serve the needs of most students, while serious researchers will still want to use *Bibliography on Holocaust Literature* by Abraham J. Edelheit and Hershel Edelheit (see ARBA 94, entry 532; ARBA 91, entry 519; ARBA 87, entry 522), a project which will hopefully continue in the future.—**John A. Drobnicki**

Biography

C

163.   **The Rise of the Medieval World 500-1300: A Biographical Dictionary.** Jana K. Schulman, ed. Westport, Conn., Greenwood Press, 2002. 500p. (The Great Cultural Eras of the Western World). $99.95. ISBN 0-313-30817-9. ISSN 1534-9527.

This useful work compresses 800 years of (largely) European history into biographical entries of 400 figures of the medieval period. As one might expect, the focus is on the privileged few, such as royalty, nobles, churchmen, and intellectuals. Where sources allow, however, one also finds a smattering of women, Muslims, and Jews. The book opens with a brief sketch of the overall period, and is followed by a chronology. Individual entries are rarely over two pages in length, and generally cite one or two items in the attached bibliography. In other words, this is more of a ready-reference work than a source for detailed, scholarly information. However, for those with only a passing knowledge of the medieval period it is a good launching point. The work concludes with a solid name index and general index. This work is recommended for undergraduate libraries.—**Jim Millhorn**

C, S

164.   **Roman Emperors (De Imperatoribus Romanis). http://www.roman-emperors.org/.** [Website]. Free. Date reviewed: Oct 02.

The *Roman Emperors* Website, recently featured at Salve Regina University's conference "Ancient Studies—New Technology," presents scholarly essays about more than 100 emperors, from Augustus to Romulus Augustus to Irene Basilissa to Manuel II. Other emperors' biographies await essayists, and the site welcomes submissions.

Essays are peer reviewed by scholars. The Website itself, which has received awards from the Perseus site, *Encyclopaedia Britannica*, and The History Channel, was founded in 1996 by Professor Richard Weigel of Western Kentucky University and about two dozen faculty and graduate students from universities in the United States and abroad. Essays range from very brief (640 words) to extensive (14,000 words); most are from 1,500 to 4,000 words. Notes and a bibliography follow each essay.

The writers strive for readability so that students from high school through college can enjoy learning about the contribution each emperor made to the evolution of the Roman Empire. An invaluable and attractive resource is the photographic collection of sculpture and coins from Justin Paola's *Collection of Roman Emperors* (www.roman-emperors.com), used with permission. Other features of the *Roman Emperors* site include a timeline, genealogies, an index of battles, a virtual coin collection, maps, and links to other classics sites recommended by the editorial college.

Navigating the site's helpful indexes is fast and easy, tempting any user to read beyond the information he or she visited the site to find. Users can select, from three layout options, the format in which they prefer to access the material. This site is recommended for classicists and students of all ages and levels.—**Nancy L. Van Atta**

Dictionaries and Encyclopedias

C, P

165.   Nafziger, George F. **Historical Dictionary of the Napoleonic Era.** Lanham, Md., Scarecrow, 2002. 353p. (Ancient Civilizations and the Historical Eras, no.6). $89.50. ISBN 0-8108-4092-8.

Those familiar with Scarecrow Press's historical dictionaries series will be familiar with the general format and coverage of this book: it contains a chronology, paragraph-length articles, and an extensive bibliography at the end of the work. Unfortunately, like all of the other books in the series, this volume has no index or *see also* references, so finding entries can be a bit of a challenge. Treaties, battles, constitutions, and conventions are found under the name associated with it; thus, the Treaty of Amiens is found under "Amiens, Treaty of," and the Convention of El-Arisch under "El-Arisch, Convention of." With the large number of battles, treaties, and other diplomatic events included in this work, such an arrangement might be necessary, but it is awkward for the uninitiated.

Nafziger is a military historian, and this clearly comes across in the content of the dictionary. Battles and biographies of key military and political figures make up the largest portion of dictionary entries, and they are strong in their depth and detail. Military terminology is also explained throughout. The closing bibliography is outstanding in its depth. Treaties, conventions, and other diplomatic events, however, often get very short entries that give little more than a summary of the effects of the diplomatic agreement. Art, literature, culture, and science are treated only marginally. This volume is geared toward the military and political aspects of the era, which is perhaps fitting in an era so consumed by warfare and diplomacy. [R: Choice, June 02, p. 1750]

—**Terri Tickle Miller**

S

166.   **Renaissance.** Bethel, Conn., Grolier Educational, 2002. 10v. illus. maps. index. $345.00/set. ISBN 0-7172-5673-1.

Each of the 10 slim volumes in this young adult encyclopedic set that "tells the story of the Renaissance" is a delight to browse and read. Every page has lovely color reproductions of major art and architecture of the period. The narrative is engaging, accurate, and well written. The alphabetic entries in each volume run from 2-5 pages, with text insets drawing attention to key points. The initial paragraph of each entry is an easy-to-understand, bolded summary of the topic. Intriguing sidebars enhance understanding; for example, an illustrated sidebar on Leonardo da Vinci's notebooks explains that they are written back to front and are difficult to read because he was left-handed and wanted to avoid smudging the ink. A *see also* box for each entry makes cross-referencing easy.

Limited to 80 pages, each volume shares the same brief introduction, timeline, glossary, further reading list (with Websites), and set index, plus roughly 20 unique entries. The entries cover broad topics centering on Europe, such as "Artists Workshops, City-States, Inquisition, Fortifications, and Merchants." There are entries for major artists, authors, scholars, politicians, and movements of the period. Appropriately in this global age, there are also entries on Africa, China, India, and the Americas, including the interactions between them.

This set brings history alive for both young and old. While directed to a middle school audience (grades 5-10), it will bring knowledge and pleasure to all readers and is recommended for general libraries as well as school libraries.—**Georgia Briscoe**

Handbooks and Yearbooks

P, S

167.   **Renaissance & Reformation Almanac.** Peggy Saari and Aaron Saari, eds. Farmington Hills, Mich., U*X*L/Gale, 2002. 2v. illus. index. $99.00/2-vol. set; $225.00/5-vol. set. ISBN 0-7876-5467-1.

P, S

168.   **Renaissance & Reformation Biographies.** Peggy Saari and Aaron Saari, eds. Farmington Hills, Mich., U*X*L/Gale, 2002. 2v. illus. index. $99.00/2-vol. set; $225.00/5-vol. set. ISBN 0-7876-5470-1.

P, S

169.   **Renaissance & Reformation Primary Sources.** Peggy Saari and Aaron Saari, eds. Farmington Hills, Mich., U*X*L/Gale, 2002. 201p. illus. index. $55.00; $225.00/5-vol. set. ISBN 0-7876-5473-6.

The issue of providing students with a good textbook written at their level challenges teachers as they prepare their lesson plans. Peggy and Aaron Saari have offered one solution to this dilemma. In their *Renaissance & Reformation* set, students have a useful introduction to this period.

The *Almanac* serves students in several ways. It provides coverage of both the Christian and Muslim worlds. All endeavors, viewpoints, and social aspects receive attention here. The timeline grounds the reader in some medieval context for the events and people described in the work. Difficult terms are defined up front. Assignment suggestions and "Further Readings" lists are offered to users. The topical rather than chronological approach will make historical discussions easier for students to understand. There are concerns here, however. Although the forces leading up to the Renaissance and Reformation are discussed in detail here, some of the literary giants (e.g., Dante, Boccaccio, Petrarch) do not get the attention they deserve. The use of Websites in the "Further

Readings" section limits the volume's usefulness. Finally, this part of the set would have benefited from further editing as there are some factual errors in the text. For instance, Khayr al-Din was the Ottoman Empire's naval commander not the Ottoman leader; Suleyman the Magnificent held that role.

For the *Biographies* volumes the editors selected people from a wide range of disciplines. Their insight into their accomplishments, lives, and the forces that shaped them is commendable. The editors put certain difficult terms and their definitions in the front of the work. As with the other volumes in the bigger five-volume set, there are "Further Readings" sections available for users. These volumes do have three issues. First, the timeline in the front does not go back far enough. (One does not start discussing the Renaissance in 1377.) Because of this oversight, the user might miss the accounts of those who laid the foundations for these movements. Secondly, the other two works in the larger set mention important non-Western figures, which were omitted here. Finally, the use of Websites in the listing limits the set's shelf life.

The *Primary Sources* volume has several strengths. For example, the focus covers both Christian and Islamic topics. The source materials cover literary, philosophical, religious, and intellectual subjects. Women receive attention here as well. In addition, the editors have annotated the texts well with difficult words and their definitions set off in the margins.

This work has several benefits for the general user if one recognizes the shortcomings cited above. The work is recommended for junior high, high school, and public libraries.—**David J. Duncan**

P, S

170.   **The Usborne Internet-Linked Encyclopedia of the Roman World.** By Fiona Chandler, Sam Taplin, and Jane Bingham. Tulsa, Okla., EDC Publishing, 2001. 128p. illus. maps. index. $19.95. ISBN 0-7945-0117-6.

This book combines the storytelling of a history textbook and an encyclopedia's quick access to facts. The introduction explains to the young reader the types of sources of data about the Roman world, such as the traditional study of ancient texts and modern pollen analysis. Then readers can begin their journey at the founding of Rome, continue through the fall of the Western Empire in 476 C.E. and the endurance of the Byzantine Empire, as well as learn the many ways in which Roman culture exists today. A glossary; short biographies; a timeline; a table of the emperors; and short articles on the legal and monetary systems, mythology, and other topics complete the final quarter of the book. Every page is richly illustrated by photographs of artifacts or colorful line drawings, such as a cut-away plan of a Roman bath. The publisher's Website offers links to educational Internet sites for every page of text; the links include the highly respected Perseus Digital Library and Kentucky Educational Television's Distance Learning Website. The economical text nevertheless is surprisingly comprehensive, and students can learn about the daily life of citizens and noncitizens, the wealthy and the poor, and women as well as men. The authors are experienced writers of children's reference books; their tone is light, and even the appendixes are fun to read. Libraries needing a textbook for elementary readers may also want to purchase *Find Out About the Roman Empire: What Life Was Like in the Ancient World* by Phillip Steele (Southwater, 2000). This work is recommended for middle school libraries and public libraries' young adult collections.—**Nancy L. Van Atta**

Great Britain

C, P

171.   Arnold-Baker, Charles. **The Companion to British History.** New York, Routledge, 2001. 1391p. maps. $112.50; $39.95pa. ISBN 0-415-26106-7; 0-415-18583-1pa.

This is the 2d edition of a work that provides a comprehensive A-Z guide to the history of Britain and its peoples. It contains more than 1,400 pages presented in an encyclopedia fashion, with entries from early British history all the way up to the present. The author focuses on the history of Ireland, Scotland, and Wales as well. The author has omitted historians who are not historical sources, as well as the histories of the hundreds of individual military regiments that are a part of British history, since these two areas would have greatly expanded the scope of the book. Two appendixes are included, one of which lists "selected warlike events." There are also a number of English royal genealogies, maps, and other materials of interest provided at the end of the book. Overall, this is a well-constructed and important reference work on British history. [R: LJ, 15 Nov 01, p. 58]

—**Bradford Lee Eden**

C, P

172. **Cassell's Companion to Eighteenth Century Britain.** By Stephen Brumwell and W. A. Speck. New York, Cassell, 2001. 455p. $45.00. ISBN 0-304-34796-5.

Defining the period under review as extending from the Glorious Revolution (1688) to the Battle of Waterloo (1815), *Cassell's Companion to Eighteenth Century Britain* provides substantial coverage of the era that shaped modern Britain. Thus, the eager reader can find detailed articles on the union of England and Scotland (1707), the union of Britain and Ireland (1800), parties, Parliamentary reform, the American War of Independence (1775-1783), India, and influential British political leaders such as George III, Lord North, and both William Pitts. Readers will also find coverage of significant military engagements (e.g., the Battle of Culloden, the Battle of Trafalgar) and significant cultural figures (e.g., David Hume, William Wordsworth, Edward Gibbon). A general subject index, a chronology, and a bibliography extend the work's utility.

Both authors are English academics, with specialization in political and military history. It should come as no surprise, therefore, that their social history tends to be weak, and where it does appear, the focus tends to be on England. Thus, the article on Ireland is focused solely on the controversies surrounding the Irish parliament, ignoring such topics as the penal laws and the establishment of the Orange Order. No close examination is made of religious disabilities throughout the period, the highland clearances in Scotland, or of any events involving Wales. A greater balance of interests among the authors would have made this title even more useful. Nevertheless, the work is recommended for undergraduate academic and larger public libraries.—**Christopher Brennan**

C, P

173. **Cassell's Companion to Twentieth Century Britain.** By Pat Thane. New York, Cassell, 2001. 455p. $45.00. ISBN 0-304-34794-9.

Cassell's Companion to Twentieth Century Britain is part of a projected five-volume series chronicling the history of the British Isles from the medieval period to the present. One author is responsible for all of the articles, unlike most books set out in a dictionary format. Thus, while the breadth of coverage is not as comprehensive as might be found in similar volumes, a consistent style and tone throughout largely compensates for this lack of coverage. The alphabetically arranged articles generally consist of two short paragraphs that cover the essentials of the subject matter, provide cross-references embedded in the text (indicated by capital letters), and list suggestions for further reading. That said, there are some odd omissions that underscore the arbitrary nature of such an undertaking. V-1 rockets, which menaced Britain during World War II, are mentioned, but the *Spitfire* fighter planes that saved Britain are not. The Beatles get an entry, but the Sex Pistols do not. More inexplicable is the failure to discuss foot and mouth disease or the Millennium Dome, both major topics of national discussion at the close of the century.

An extremely useful subject index is provided at the end of the volume that groups subjects covered in the main body of the text under broad subject headings. There is also a chronology touching on the major events relating to Britain beginning in 1899 and ending in 2000. A one-page list of recommended general reading is also included. This volume should certainly be a part of any academic library's history collection.—**Philip G. Swan**

C

174. **Historical Dictionary of Late Medieval England, 1272-1485.** Ronald H. Fritze and William B. Robison, eds. Westport, Conn., Greenwood Press, 2002. 658p. index. $114.95. ISBN 0-313-29124-1.

The history of late medieval England can prove daunting to scholars of any level. As such, one always appreciates good starting points especially when, as Ronald Fritze and William Robison put it, a collaborative effort is utilized successfully (p. x). In compiling the *Historical Dictionary of Late Medieval England, 1272-1485*, Fritze and Robison have provided a useful reference tool.

This work has many positive attributes. It provides a comprehensive listing of the people, events, treaties, trends, and institutions important to medieval English society. Each kingdom related to this era has its own essay as well. Although their lengths vary, the articles contain exhaustive summaries on their respective topics. In addition, the reader will find further readings and the writer's name at the end of these pieces. Cross-references are printed in all capitals so that they will stand out in the text. At several points in the text, entries are cross-listed with *see also* references. This work contains a chronology and an index. The bibliography is well organized on several levels. There are listings by book type: reference, genera, primary, and secondary sources. The list also has works by historical subtopic. Trends such as the Hundred Years War, each monarch, and kingdoms also have their own sections. In short, Fritze and Robison have edited a great companion volume to Paul Szarmach's *Medieval England: An Encyclopedia* (see ARBA 2000, entry 420). This work is highly recommended for community college and academic libraries as well as those collections related to British studies and medieval studies.

—**David J. Duncan**

Russian

C

175.   Langer, Lawrence N. **Historical Dictionary of Medieval Russia.** Lanham, Md., Scarecrow, 2002. 288p. (Historical Dictionaries of Ancient Civilizations and Historical Eras, no.5). $70.00. ISBN 0-8108-4080-4.

This work covers the period from the founding of the Kievan state in the 860s to the accession of Peter the Great in 1682. A preliminary "Reader's Note" sorts out the confusing terminology for different nomenclatures and calendars. The volume opens with a bare-bones, 17-page chronology covering "Pre-Kievan Rus'," "Kiev Rus" (860-1240), "The Mongols and Medieval Muscovite Rus' " (1240-1462), "Early Modern Muscovy" (1462-1598), "The Time of Troubles" (1598-1613), and "Seventeenth-Century Muscovy." The tersely enumerated dates and events are set into a wider context in the introduction, which provides succinct narrative accounts of each period.

The dictionary, the heart of the book, is an alphabetic listing of persons, institutions, places, and events. The approximately 260 entries run from short paragraphs to 10-page essays. Virtually every entry has several boldfaced terms referring the reader to their further explication elsewhere in the dictionary. Boldface cross-referencing is also used in the earlier narrative sketches and in the chronology. The volume is well organized. The entries are well chosen, well written, and its various parts are nicely integrated with minimal duplication. The extensive, timely bibliography is organized in terms of the noted time periods. Additionally, short sections refer the reader to basic general works: "Geography and Maps," "Reference Works," "Art and Culture," and so on. An introduction to the bibliography provides a three-page sketch of Russian historiography, mentioning the names and views of major scholars.

This useful volume has the field to itself. This reviewer found only two deficiencies: the absence of maps (although the bibliography refers readers to selected atlases) and the absence of references to works not available in English. The reader should at least be alerted to the existence of major studies in a field relatively new here, but with a long tradition in Russia and Western Europe.—**D. Barton Johnson**

MIDDLE EASTERN HISTORY

C

176.   Ben-Dov, Meir. **Historical Atlas of Jerusalem.** New York, Continuum Publishing, 2002. 400p. illus. maps. index. $50.00. ISBN 0-8264-1379-X.

The author, an eminent archaeologist, tells the life story of the city of Jerusalem using text, photographs, and charts, with special emphasis on the results of archaeological evidence. The history of the place, that is, the size and location of the city in each period, is emphasized, but there is also a good presentation of the historical events. Jerusalem's location on trade routes, the obstacles to its development, and the struggle to maintain a secure source of water are all treated. The charts and site maps are very good.

Over the centuries, the original contours of the hills and valley upon which the city was built have been so overlaid with various constructions and their remnants that this guide is necessary to understand the levels of the city at different times. In addition, the boundaries of the city have changed in various time periods. The photographs are all soft black-and-white shots. There is a bibliography, but no footnotes. Much space in the latter part of the book is given to the Israeli-Palestinian crisis of the past century. Since there are passionately held alternative descriptions and interpretations of these events, this very controversial issue should be the focus of a separate book.—**Robert T. Anderson**

C, S

177.   Bertman, Stephen. **Handbook to Life in Ancient Mesopotamia.** New York, Facts on File, 2003. 396p. illus. maps. index. (Facts on File Library of World History). $50.00. ISBN 0-8160-4346-9.

This volume presents an excellent discussion about ancient Mesopotamian civilization (modern day Iraq), ranging from geography through government and society to religion and myth. Discussions of language, writing, and literature; art; architecture and building; economy; transportation and trade; military; and everyday life are also provided. In addition, the author has included chapters on archaeology and history (including place-names, maps, and the names of archaeologists), Mesopotamia and sacred scripture (including both the Bible and the Qu'ran), and Mesopotamia's legacy to the West. Illustrations abound, most of them quite standard but good to have in a volume such as this. Besides a solid and up-to-date bibliography for the further readings with which every chapter ends, the volume also contains a list of museums with major Mesopotamian collections.

The text reads well and is accessible for the average layperson, including the high school student (and even younger). Of particular interest to many may be the discussion of literature—epics and myths, poetry, and hymns—which is very nicely done and accurate. The one egregious error lies in the several references to ancient Sumer (so presented on the map) as Sumeria (the materials related to Sumer are Sumerian).

A very solid work, this volume belongs in public libraries as well as in high school and college libraries. Its accessibility and thoroughness make it a possibility for use as a course text.—**Susan Tower Hollis**

P, S

178.   **The Usborne Internet-Linked Encyclopedia of Ancient Egypt.** By Gill Harvey and Struan Reid. Tulsa, Okla., EDC Publishing, 2001. 128p. illus. index. $19.95. ISBN 0-7945-0118-4.

This volume presents lavish illustrations as it describes the major features of ancient Egyptian history and culture beginning in the late pre-Dynastic period and moves forward through the Ptolemaic period. After a brief survey of this history, the text segues into a description of royalty and religion, including discussions of government and its hierarchy, armies and wars, and trading and diplomacy, as well as providing materials on different aspects of religion, including gods, myths, temples, and all aspects of death and the afterlife. Completing the text section is an extensive discussion about everyday life covering houses, women, activities, clothing, education, and more. The volume concludes with a "Factfinder," which includes a timeline of history with contemporaneous events noted for other parts of the world, a list of kings and dynasties, a "who's who" including important non-Egyptian figures, a brief descriptive catalog of deities, a history of Egyptology (the science of the study of ancient Egypt), a list of museums containing major collections, a glossary, and an extensive index.

The unique aspect of this volume is its keyed reference to resources available on the Internet, linking the reader to many different Websites throughout the world where he or she may find pertinent and interesting materials related to the subject at hand. Since the volume seeks to serve children ages 9 to 12, it opens appropriately with caveats about the use of the Internet. Unfortunately, the information provided about needed resources to access the Internet links is out of date, and even the information provided on the Website has changed radically, as one cannot access by page number on Netscape 6.2, but rather one finds a list of site links by type on the home page. Some links that appear in the text seem to be missing from the current Web page (e.g., the Egyptian Museum in Cairo). Changes like these are to be expected when publishing Internet resources, but that they occur foregrounds the complete lack of any print-based references in the volume itself. Since most materials of any significance, even for the ages targeted, appear only in print resources and the targeted age group needs to learn to use print resources as well as the Internet, this omission is very serious. Nevertheless, the collection of sites comprises an excellent resource for anyone, and so the use of the book in public and school libraries is worth the investment.

—**Susan Tower Hollis**

WORLD HISTORY

Almanacs

C, P, S

179.   Ochoa, George, and Melinda Corey. **Facts About the 20th Century.** Bronx, N.Y., H. W. Wilson, 2001. 1004p. index. (The Wilson Facts Series). $95.00. ISBN 0-8242-0960-5.

The recent conclusion of the twentieth century and the beginning of the twenty-first century has resulted in the publication of reference and other works profiling the century and millennium. *Facts About the 20th Century* is a representative sample of this genre, reflecting public interest in a recently concluded historical period.

It is broken down into five specific sections including a year-by-year chronology of important twentieth-century developments, a reference dictionary of significant twentieth-century events and ideas, succinct biographical portraits of key personalities from various professions, listings of twentieth-century nations and vital statistics about these countries, and a historical gazetteer of nations existing during this century.

The entries for the section covering important events for each year feature developments in fields such as arts and entertainment, ideas, the military, politics, science and technology, society, and sports. Important events for 1903, as determined by the authors, include "Waltzing Matilda" becoming an unofficial Australian national anthem, publication of W. E. B. Du Bois' *The Souls of Black Folk*, Panama winning independence from Colombia, the United States and Canada resolving a border dispute, Marie Curie becoming the first woman to receive a Nobel Prize, an earthquake killing 2,000 in Constantinople, and Dorothea Douglass winning the first of 7 women's singles titles at Wimbledon (pp. 7-9). Key events and ideas receiving coverage include fundamentalism, China's Gang of Four, information revolution, and Sinn Fein. Entries on important personalities include American sculptor Alexander Calder, German World War II naval officer Karl Doenitz, Israeli Prime Minister Golda Meir, Cambodian leader Norodom Sihanouk, South African Anglican cleric Desmond Tutu, and British writer Evelyn Waugh.

Entries on individual nations include their main exports, listings of national leaders, and summaries of important twentieth-century developments in these nations. Examples of entries included and defined within the historical gazetteer include French Somaliland, Rhodesia, Rio de Oro, Slovenia, Transcaspian Region, and Upper Volta.

Facts About the 20th Century will be most beneficial to public libraries and lower division undergraduates. Although its scope of coverage is the entire twentieth century, its basic organizational structure is similar to annual almanacs such as *Annual Register* (see ARBA 2001, entry 711), *Statesman's Yearbook* (138th ed.; see ARBA 2003, entry 75), and the Central Intelligence Agency's *World Factbook* (2001 ed.; see ARBA 2002, entry 91). Succinctly written and augmented with significant secondary source research, *Facts About the 20th Century* provides a useful introduction to anyone desirous of a quick introduction to key twentieth-century events and personalities.—**Bert Chapman**

Atlases

C, P

180.   **Hammond Concise Atlas of World History.** Geoffrey Barraclough, ed. Union, N.J., Hammond, 2002. 184p. maps. index. $34.95pa. ISBN 0-8437-1750-5.

This concise atlas is not intended as a replacement, but a welcome update, of its hardbound larger editions—*HarperCollins Atlas of World History* (2001) and Hammond's *Times Atlas of World History* (4th ed.; see ARBA 94, entry 530). It does supersede, and is a revised edition of, the *Times Concise Atlas of World History* (5th ed.; 1998). Nevertheless, maps not included in new editions are still of value for researchers, and those other volumes should not be discarded. The HarperCollins edition is a slightly revised edition of the *Times Atlas*.

The *Hammond Concise Atlas of World History* begins with maps of human origins and the ice ages, and ends with "The World at the Millennium," which contains three world views of the "The Armaments Boom," "World Population Towards the Millennium," and "The Revival of Religious Conflict." It contains 112 illustrations and 344 maps and tables in vivid colors with supporting short essays, compared to its hardbound HarperCollins edition of 511 maps and tables. All of the editions include a very small print, three- or four-column, one-page bibliography of worldwide historical and general atlases and history, archaeology, economics, and geography books. The *Concise* edition's 31-page index is extensive, but not at all comprehensive. The same is true of indexes in all other hardbound and paperback editions. Also, unfortunately, its map of "The Expansion of the United

States 1802-1898" does not include the California Trail as one of its' "settlers' routes"; has Fort Crittenden as a "fur station" instead of a military post; and has Devil's Gate as a "pass" instead of a portal. All of these misprints are carryover errors from its earlier hardbound and paperback editions. This atlas is recommended for all libraries as a supplement to its earlier hardbound and paperback editions. It will also be a valuable addition for circulating collections.—**J. Carlyle Parker**

C, P, S

181.   Konstam, Angus. **Historical Atlas of the Crusades.** New York, Facts on File, 2002. 192p. illus. maps. index. $175.00. ISBN 0-8160-4919-X.

In the *Historical Atlas of the Crusades*, historian, archaeologist, and museum professional Angus Konstam provides a comprehensive, engaging look at the events and historical impact of the Crusades of Western Europe against the Eastern Mediterranean area during the Middle Ages. While most Americans have at least heard of the Crusades in school, this book gives the reader a far more complete view of their historical significance from both sides of the conflicts. In addition to describing personalities, battles, equipment, and tactics of all sides involved in the Crusades, Konstam examines some of the social and economic motivations for crusading, as well as the religious conflicts between the Roman and Byzantine Christian churches, and between the Islamic centers of Baghdad and Cairo, that influenced the Crusades and their aftermath. Konstam also examines the prejudices and beliefs of both sides of the Crusades and writes about how the Crusades led to the opening of the medieval mind and to the flowering of awareness of the outside world, which led to the Renaissance and had profound effects on our modern world.

The text is well written, in a style that undergraduates, secondary students, and most public library patrons should be able to read and understand. The book is beautifully illustrated with photographs, reproductions of illustrations, and well-rendered maps, which enhance the ability of the text to explain the Crusades. Also included are a glossary of useful terms, a chronology of the Crusades, and family trees of several of the most important dynasties involved. The book is well organized, and the index helps readers locate needed information quickly. The high quality of the *Historical Atlas of the Crusades*, coupled with its relatively low price, make it a useful addition to academic, high school, and public libraries.—**Mark T. Bay**

C, P

182.   **Oxford Atlas of World History.** concise ed. Patrick K. O'Brien, ed. New York, Oxford University Press, 2002. 312p. illus. maps. index. $45.00. ISBN 0-19-521921-X.

This atlas covers the scope of human history. It is divided into five broad subject areas: ancient, medieval, early modern, age of revolutions, and twentieth century. Each section has an introductory essay. All entries are on a two-page spread with text, multiple maps, and usually a small picture. Sometimes the picture could be a little larger. Map types (political, topographical) and projections (Mercator, conical) vary as needed. Maps are crisp and often dense with information. A few are affected by the book gutter. A current, well-selected bibliography and thorough index round out this work.

While valuable to a general audience, the editors obviously crafted this with the student in mind. Linkage between entries is ably provided within the descriptive text. Many entries detail political change, but there are also entries, particularly within the twentieth-century section, detailing social changes, such as the status of women, population, and human rights. Even within more traditional entries on empires there is often commentary or maps about trade, agriculture, or economy. The global inclusiveness is to be commended. Africa, Eastern Europe, Asia, and South America are well represented. It is clear from the editor's foreword to the end of the index that great care was taken to position this atlas within the current academic developments shaping the field of world history. Entries suggest possibilities and indicate scholarly debate rather than flatly stating one position. An excellent atlas, the *Oxford Atlas of World History* is highly recommended for all libraries. [R: LJ, Jan 03, p. 96]

—**Allen Reichert**

Chronology

S

183.   **Great Events: 1900-2001.** rev. ed. Hackensack, N.J., Salem Press, 2002. 8v. illus. maps. index. $475.00/set. ISBN 1-58765-053-3.

Great Events combines and updates two earlier reference works from Salem Press: *Twentieth Century: Great Events* (1992) and *Twentieth Century: Great Scientific Achievements* (1994). Nearly all of the entries from these previous works are included, while 283 new entries have been added. More than 200 of these new entries concern events from the mid-1990s up to the September 11th terrorist attack on the United States. All entries share the same format and are at least 1,000 words long. The title is followed by a brief summary, and basic facts are highlighted in a box. After the event is described in detail a concluding section discusses consequences. Most entries are signed, but unfortunately no bibliographies are included. A single black-and-white image or map may be included with an entry. The maps are generally more useful than the pictures. Salem provides five different indexes, arranged by category, timeline, geography, personages, and a general subject index.

This work most strongly covers political and scientific events. Overall, *Great Events* includes a fairly even distribution of global events, although U.S. events slightly predominate. Article quality varies, particularly in the discussion of consequences, but most give a solid account. Indexing quality also varies. The geographical index is very useful, with thorough *see also* references. However, the general subject index could be more robust. For example, while the Salt March and satyagraha are mentioned extensively in the entry concerning Mohandas Gandhi, neither makes the index. Finally, the desire for currency did lead to the inclusion of some events that do not have the magnitude of earlier events, such as the Bridgestone apology or Pets.com. Overall, this set is good and can be recommended for middle school and high school libraries. [R: SLJ, Nov 02, p. 100]—**Allen Reichert**

P, S

184.   Teeple, John B. **Timelines of World History.** New York, DK Publishing, 2002. 666p. illus. maps. $40.00. ISBN 0-7894-8926-0.

This reference shows at a glance what has happened in history across the globe, from 10,000 B.C.E. to September 11, 2001. Users see leaders take the stage, wars start and end, and ideas and technologies emerge and be replaced. Segmented by Asia, Africa, Europe, and the Americas/Australasia, full attention is given to all parts of the world and time periods. Each era is introduced with a narrative essay highlighting the major trends and influences and illustrated with photographs and fold-out maps. The sidebars add depth by featuring interesting individuals who may be politicians, artists, musicians, or cultural insights ranging from the milestones of the Industrial Revolution to the French Wars of religion, the first appearance of the Kabuki theater in seventeenth-century Japan, and the Flatiron Building (the New York City landmark built in 1901 and one of the earliest skyscrapers). In looking at the year 1678, across one page users see that at the same point in time the French explorer and missionary Louis Hennepin discovered Niagara Falls, John Bunyan published Pilgrim's Progress, the French seized Dutch forts in Senegal, and haiku poetry began to appear in Japan. This volume concludes with a concordance that serves as both index and glossary by listing major events and historical figures with page references. These timelines let the reader make connections within the full context of world history to appreciate the richness of its totality. This book is a treat to browse as well as a useful research tool.—**Adrienne Antink Bien**

Dictionaries and Encyclopedias

P, S

185.   **Ancient History: An On-Line Encyclopedia. http://www.fofweb.com/subscription.** [Website]. New York, Facts on File. Prices start at $299.00 (school libraries) and $450.00 (public libraries). Date reviewed: Feb 02.

Facts on File's *Ancient History: An On-Line Encyclopedia* is an excellent resource for beginning and intermediate study of ancient cultures. It provides an introduction for beginning scholars and lay readers and a quick reference for more advanced scholars. The database covers the ancient cultures of Africa, Egypt, Greece, Rome, and Mesoamerica. Obviously, much of the material for Egypt can also be found under Africa. The main menu is divided into seven sections: "Introductions," "Subject Entries," "Biographies," "Historical Documents," "Gallery," "Maps and Charts," and "Timelines." The "Introductions" are overview essays of the five ancient cultures, with linked cross-references to various subject entries. More than 6,500 entries for events, places, and cultural developments can be found under "Subject Entries." Users can browse the entries first by the individual civilizations or as a whole and then by additional breakdowns, such as era, topic, civilization, and geographical area. For example, users will find entries on slavery, architecture, deities, athletics and sports, poetry, and building techniques and materials. Users can also search for specific entries by keyword or phrase (exact or relative).

The database contains more than 3,000 biographies for ancient historical figures. Like the subject entries, users can locate the biographies by browsing lists of the entrants or by similar breakdowns used for the subject entries. Biographies for explorers, government officials, religious leaders, and warriors and military leaders are included. Under "Historical Documents" users will find ethnographical and historical materials along with excerpts from poems and novels. The "Gallery" provides access to several paintings, photographs, and coins of the ancient civilizations. Unfortunately, this area is not as extensive as many users would hope. In fact, only coin reproductions are available for the Ancient Rome civilization. Additional illustrations would have been helpful. The majority of the maps contained in the database are political and can by printed via Adobe Acrobat. The charts and tables would be ideal for classroom use, but they are not printable unless users want to try to use a screen print. The timelines are organized by era or topic and they are also not printable. This database is recommended for university and college libraries that support ancient history and mythology curriculums. [R: BR, Mar/April 02, p. 81; LJ, Jan 02, p. 166]—**Cari Ringelheim**

C, P

186.   **Encyclopedia of Holocaust Literature.** David Patterson, Alan L. Berger, and Sarita Cargas, eds. Westport, Conn., Oryx Press/Greenwood Publishing Group, 2002. 263p. index. (Oryx Holocaust Series). $54.95. ISBN 1-57356-257-2.

The Holocaust, a systematic attempt to wipe out an entire culture, is the most horrible event in modern history. Those who study it and those who lived through it have created a rich literature that tries to make sense of the appalling events. The importance of memory, an affirmation of life, and the need to speak for those who can no longer do so are major themes in the literature that bears witness to the Holocaust.

This encyclopedia profiles 128 authors of memoirs, diaries, novels, poems, and drama dealing with the Holocaust. All were alive during that time period and many survived Hitler's concentration camps. The alphabetic entries (two to four pages long) include brief biographies of the authors, information on the significance of their work, a critical appraisal of their work, and a selected bibliography. The authors covered include Cynthia Ozick, Elie Wiesel, Primo Levi, Arthur Miller, and Avraham Tory. Three appendixes list the authors by date of birth, by country of birth, and by birth name for those using pen names. Bibliographies of primary works of Holocaust literature and of critical studies of Holocaust literature complete the work.

This is an excellent resource for students in need of an introduction to Holocaust literature. Both academic and public libraries will find it useful. [R: LJ, 15 June 02, p. 56]—**Barbara M. Bibel**

P, S

187.   **World History. http://www.worldhistory.abc-clio.com/.** [Website]. Santa Barbara, Calif., ABC-CLIO, $599.00/year. Minimum system requirements: Internet access with a version 4.0 or later browser. Browser must be cookie and JavaScript enabled. ISSN 1531-1279. Date reviewed: Mar 02.

Designed with the same format as ABC-CLIO's other education Websites, *World History* provides more than 10,000 reference entries discussing cultures, events, inventions, religious movements, and personalities that have had an impact on history around the globe. The site lists topics chronologically, which will provide students with an overall concept of how history has developed. The site is designed mainly with teachers, school media specialists, and students in mind.

The home page provides a feature story (which changes regularly) and a note on historical things that happened on the day in history the site is being accessed. Students can then use the "Reference" page to research on specific topics of interest. The "Reference" page can be used in three different ways: by entering a keyword or phrase, by clicking on a specific time in history (arranged chronologically), and by category (requesting the information in a specific format, such as essay, image, map, documents, or events, just to name a few). When students find the topic they are researching they will also find related entries located in a sidebar, which will further their research. The site also features access to a Merriam-Webster dictionary and the added feature of contacting a "cybrarian" with specific questions about the site and how to better research a topic.

Teachers and media specialists will find the site useful because it allows them to create assignments, tests, and a syllabus on the "Administration" page. Only teachers and librarians will have access to this page because two user names and passwords are assigned to each school—one for teachers and librarians and one for students. This feature also allows students to access the Website from home and will allow parents to be aware of their children's homework and future assignments.

This database, much like the others from ABC-CLIO, will enhance any school's teaching curriculum. It will bring world history to life for many students and provide a new outlet for learning. The price may be a bit high for many schools, but the amount of material found here may make up for the expense.

—**Shannon Graff Hysell**

Directories

C, P

188.   **The History Highway 3.0: A Guide to Internet Resources.** 3d ed. Dennis A. Trinkle and Scott A. Merriman, eds. Armonk, N.Y., M. E. Sharpe, 2002. 688p. index. $89.95; $39.95pa. (w/CD-ROM). ISBN 0-7656-0903-7; 0-7656-0904-5pa.

Specialized print guides to resources available on the World Wide Web have become more important in recent years, supplanting the all-in-one guides that were popular when the Web was smaller in scope. However, they face the same core problem: keeping current as the availability of resources on the Web changes over time.

This guide passes the test for usability quite well; almost all of the URLs it refers readers to are still valid, displaying the information that the guide says they do. The only exception found was a site listed at www.geocities.com, probably a casualty of Yahoo!'s reorganization of its Geocities division (which replaced this base URL with geocities.yahoo.com). In general, however, this guide is quite good at emphasizing high-quality sites associated with universities and museums. It is a good source of reliable information of more popular presentations as well, such as www.pbs.org.

The book opens with two chapters on using the Internet, covering the usual mishmash of introductory topics, including browser selection, getting on the Internet, and e-mail "netiquette," all topics that are largely dispensable in a specialized directory of this sort. More useful is a brief, to-the-point discussion of how to evaluate the quality of a site's content; directories in general would benefit from including such discussion, especially one as good as the editors include here. The heart of the book is 41 chapters listing sites by either the geographical area they cover or by their theme. They include both the usual general themes (e.g., history of science, agricultural history, women's history) and some specialized ones (e.g., Holocaust studies, history of computers) for which the selection of Web resources is unusually rich. This reference would be an asset to anyone doing historical research, and is highly recommended. [R: LJ, 15 May 02, p. 84]—**Ray Olszewski**

Handbooks and Yearbooks

P, S

189.   **History of World War I.** Tarrytown, N.Y., Marshall Cavendish, 2002. 3v. illus. maps. index. $279.95/set. ISBN 0-7614-7231-2.

The recent outpouring of books and films related to World War II and the so-called "Greatest Generation," is now beginning to be rivaled by a parallel surge of interest in the Great War. Even though the vast majority of those who experienced World War I firsthand are no longer with us, the tempo of historical interest in the momentous event that created the modern era has quickened over the past few years. While it is tempting to make the case that World War II defined the twentieth century, an equally convincing argument can be made in favor of it having been World War I. In fact, some historians now consider the two conflicts to be a single struggle, punctuated by a brief 20-year period of relative peace.

Marshall Cavendish's three-volume *History of World War I* is the latest of the many fine treatments of the "war to end all war." Organized by three different themes, "War and Response, 1914-1916" (v.1), "Victory and Defeat, 1917-1918" (v.2), and "Home Fronts, Technologies of War" (v.3), this handsomely bound and richly documented work targets readers from the middle school through university levels. Of particular interest is the rich iconography, including colored maps of battlefields, photographs of participants and "key figures," as well as reproductions of newspapers and propaganda posters. In addition, inset boxes on "Eyewitnesses" and the "Political World" help to contextualize and enrich the treatment of World War I as something much greater than a military conflict. In many respects, this work makes it clear that the war, in addition to being the bloodiest struggle of the twentieth century, resulted in a cultural upheaval of monumental proportions.

The *History of World War I* will also be of particular interest to teachers of English, social studies, and history who are looking for new ways to present a war that brought us such "novelties" as the Zeppelin, poison gas, and Big Bertha, and colorful personalities like Mata Hari and the Red Baron. The American responses to World War I, and our brief participation in it, are highlighted, as are the sociocultural repercussions, such as the participation of African American soldiers and the entry of U.S. women into the workforce. The series further reminds us of the dense web of connections between the two world wars both in terms of weaponry and personnel. On the German side, we find the names of a future general like Erwin Rommel who is honing his strategic skills on the Western Front, as well as the twice-decorated and wounded Austrian corporal, Adolf Hitler. As Ian Kershaw has written, "the First World War made Hitler possible." On the American side, we learn of the skillful bravura of "Colonel" George S. Patton, their nemesis in Normandy and at the Battle of the Bulge slightly over two decades later.

Eminently readable and accessible to all, the ambitiously titled *History of World War I* does not disappoint either for the accuracy of its historical information or its lucid analyses. Despite occasional repetitions, which are inevitable in a work of this magnitude, the collection is bound to rekindle interest in the Great War as we approach the centennial of its outbreak in 1914. [R: BR, Sept/Oct 02, p. 68]—**John B. Romeiser**

S

190.　**The Kingfisher Book of the Ancient World: From the Ice Age to the Fall of Rome.** 2d ed. New York, Larousse Kingfisher Chambers, 2001. 160p. illus. maps. index. $22.95. ISBN 0-7534-5397-5.

This book explores civilizations around the world from prehistory to A.D. 600. The authors give interesting glimpses into the daily life of these past cultures to include religion, politics, commerce, food, and amusements. After a brief overview of man's evolution, each chapter focuses on a different region. In addition to the Fertile Crescent, Egypt, Rome, the Greeks and the Celts, ancient civilizations in India, the Far East, the Middle East, Africa, the Americas, Oceania and Europe are also featured. The reader learns such tidbits as that the wheel was originally invented by the Sumerians (5000-2000 B.C.E.) to make pottery and later adapted for carts, the Irish Celts (750 B.C.E.-A.D. 500) had a writing system based on straight lines called Ogam, and the earliest known rock art was done 45,000 years ago by Australian Aborigines. The structuring of the material by continents has logic, but it makes it difficult to understand parallel developments in diverse locations. Readers see a culture in isolation so understanding common themes is a challenge. The authors provide a chronology but it is not as helpful as it could be because it is divided by country and not aligned by the same starting date. A universal timeline would be more helpful but is not included. Appendixes include a glossary as well as an index. This resource will whet the appetite of the elementary school student to learn more about these long-gone but rich civilizations and the impact they have had on today's philosophies, religions, arts, and literature. [R: BR, May/June 02, pp. 71-72]
—**Adrienne Antink Bien**

C

191.　Rottman, Gordon L. **World War II Pacific Island Guide: A Geo-Military Study.** Westport, Conn., Greenwood Press, 2002. 477p. maps. index. $99.00. ISBN 0-313-31395-4.

The Pacific Ocean covers almost one-third of the circumference of the globe and comprises more area than all of the landmass of the planet combined. The Pacific theater of World War II was fought on thousands of islands, which (excluding Japan, New Zealand, New Guinea, the Netherlands East Indies, and the Philippines) constitute a total landmass smaller than the state of Ohio. Rottman, a retired Special Forces Army veteran who has written extensively on military history (including *U.S. Marine Corps World War II Order of Battle* [see ARBA 2003, entry 665]), has compiled the most definitive, comprehensive reference source imaginable on this vast, diverse, and fascinating theater.

Following a geo-military introduction to the theater and an excellent chronology, Rottman divides the Pacific into regions and addresses the war in each sector. Each island battle zone is treated extensively with information about the island, including physical characteristics, weather, historical background, native peoples, natural resources, and strategic/military import. This information is followed by detailed descriptions of the battles fought in each place, including units on both sides, tactics and strategy, casualties, deployment after liberation, and postwar sovereignty. Rottman concludes with brief treatment of the political status of each location today. The entries are lengthy, exceptionally detailed, and sophisticated, yet accessible to the lay person as well as the specialist. The 108 maps are invaluable, and the reading suggestions at the end of each section are an added feature should anyone wish to go beyond this remarkable source. It is an essential book for every library that deals with military history and it is one of the very best resources on any aspect of military history ever seen.—**Joe P. Dunn**

C, P

192.   Stearns, Peter N. **Cultures in Motion: Mapping Key Contacts and Their Imprints in World History.** New Haven, Conn., Yale University Press, 2001. 120p. illus. maps. index. $35.00; $15.95pa. ISBN 0-300-08228-2; 0-300-08229-0pa.

This book seeks to explore the impact of intercultural exchanges that have occurred throughout human history among the world's various civilizations. The author is interested in nothing less than the entire history of civilization. This study is a formidable task and, in view of the brevity of the volume, he is necessarily selective.

The book is divided into 14 chapters, each covering a historical theme. Representative themes include "The Hellenistic-Indian Encounter," "The Spread of Islam," "The African Diaspora," and "The Spread of Nationalism." Each chapter contains one or more maps accompanied by a few pages of text that tend to be little more than a general introduction to the topic. A shortcoming of the work is that the maps typically lack dates. For instance, the maps accompanying "The Jewish Diaspora" dutifully depict where the Jewish people have migrated, but give little information as to exactly when they did so (the text does provide some help). The maps throughout are limited to one color (various shades of red).

Each of the 14 sections contain a very brief list of suggested readings. Rather confusingly, a somewhat fuller bibliography, organized by chapter, is included at the end of the book. The titles found here tend to be highly idiosyncratic and are of only limited use. For instance, only four books are listed in the bibliography and suggested readings list accompanying chapter 12, "The Development of International Art." The bibliographic entries would also have been more useful if they had included brief annotations.

Some of the maps are more successful than others. Most effective are those that document the spread of religion, perhaps because these events most readily lend themselves to being represented on a map. The maps in other chapters, such as chapter 11 ("Imperialist Ideas About Women"), seem rather more arbitrarily chosen. While some will regret the absence of any maps detailing wars, the decision not to include such maps must be considered a good thing. Many other atlases that provide this sort of information are already available, and in any event the scope of this atlas is cultural, not military, history.

Atlases tend to be large and expensive. One of the chief virtues of this atlas is that it is neither. Although the atlas will be of limited use to advanced students and professionals, it will be of potential interest to most other readers.—**David A. Timko**

10 Law

GENERAL WORKS

Biography

S

193. Harer, John B., and Jeanne Harrell. **People For and Against Restricted or Unrestricted Expression.** Westport, Conn., Greenwood Press, 2002. 224p. illus. index. (The Greenwood Press "People Making a Difference" Series). $50.00. ISBN 0-313-31758-5.

This work looks at the lives and influences of 50 people who have been at the forefront of the freedom of speech law in this country. It is designed for use by students who are researching freedom of speech or preparing for a debate on the subject. The 50 people profiled became involved in the debate for different reasons. Some had careers that are affected by freedom of speech, including author Judy Blume and intellectual freedom advocate for the American Library Association Judith Fingeret Krug. Others became involved due to religious beliefs, such as the founder of the Christian organization Focus on the Family James C. Dobson and Martin Mawyer of the Christian Action Network. Many of the people listed here are concerned with pornography as it relates to children and the Internet. And others, such as Danny Goldberg and Frank Zappa, are fighting to keep music from censorship. Each biography is two to three pages in length and provides the education and career information for the individual, a history of their influence in the debate, and a list of suggested reading. Many of the individuals have black-and-white photographs. The work provides many supplementary materials for further research, including a reprint of the first amendment to the U.S. Constitution, historical documents related to the first amendment, a glossary of terms, a bibliography for further reading, a list of resources, and an index. This work will be useful in middle and high school libraries.—**Shannon Graff Hysell**

Dictionaries and Encyclopedias

C, P

194. Beyer, Gerry W., and Kenneth R. Redden. **Modern Dictionary for the Legal Profession.** 3d ed. Edited by Margaret M. Beyer. Buffalo, N.Y., William S. Hein, 2001. 987p. $82.00. ISBN 1-57588-659-6.

The *Modern Dictionary for the Legal Profession* is one of several sources for legal terminology—although this dictionary delves far beyond most legal dictionaries and lexicons in the scope of its content. Intended to be useful, informative, and entertaining, this 3d edition of the dictionary contains approximately 10,000 terms that the authors believe are essential to the modern practice of law and which are not easily located in other sources. The volume places particular emphasis on slang and colloquial references that may not be found in other legal dictionaries. It is intended for use by attorneys and judges, as well as by paralegals, students, legal secretaries, and researchers. The authors are a professor of law at St. Mary's University School of Law in San Antonio, Texas and a professor of law emeritus, now deceased, at the University of Virginia Law School.

In addition to coverage of standard legal terms, which are actually in the minority in the volume, the *Modern Dictionary for the Legal Profession* includes terminology from such diverse areas as finance, business, politics, sports, science and the environment, health care, and psychology. For example, one page includes the terms *greenmail, Green Party, Greenpeace, Grey Cup,* and the *Gridiron Club.* This page also list *Green-Speak,* a phrase developed to denote ambiguous remarks by Alan Greenpeace, Chairman of the Federal Reserve. The scope of the dictionary's content is evident by terms such as *BILY* (an acronym for "because I love you"), *Big House,* and *Big Iron* (slang for the mainframe computers that were prevalent during the 1980s). Most definitions are several lines in length and are clearly written, practical, and easy to understand. There are cross-references in italics. Abbreviations and acronyms are also included in the dictionary and a term printed in bold italics within a definition is put into context by having it as part of a main entry. The dictionary is attractively presented, with a two-column format and a dividing line between the columns. The typeface is large and crisp, making the dictionary easier to read than other sources.

The *Modern Dictionary for the Legal Profession* would be an appropriate addition to academic and public libraries, as well as for libraries that serve the legal community and other professional groups such as accountants and financial analysts. Its price is reasonable and it will be a useful source for terminology that is outside of the usual jargon for these professional groups.—**Sara Anne Hook**

C, P

195. **Legal Systems of the World: A Political, Social, and Cultural Encyclopedia.** Herbert M. Kritzer, ed. Santa Barbara, Calif., ABC-CLIO, 2002. 4v. maps. index. $425.00/set. ISBN 1-57607-231-2.

The scope of this work is very broad, encompassing 209 nations, 84 subnational areas of the world (both ancient and modern), and legal topics, for a total of 403 signed articles. Most articles are three to six pages in length and presented in alphabetical arrangement by topic heading. Geographic topics are placed in historic context with maps and a chart of the court structure. Subnational areas are listed separately for the United States, Canada, Australia, islands, and areas known to be diverse such as the Basque Region of France and Spain. Articles include references and lists for further reading to facilitate research.

U.S. law is usually divided into six main categories: administrative, constitutional, statutory, judicial, civil, and criminal. Because of its international emphasis, this work is organized differently. It has articles titled administrative law, civil law, and criminal law, while constitutional law, statutory law, and judicial review are treated as subheadings under civil law. Entries on individual countries cover constitutional law, judicial review, statutory law, and court systems where appropriate.

The topical entries explaining the civil law system and the common law system include the history of these two systems. The differences between the two systems and the characteristics necessary for each system are part of the articles, but the two systems are not contrasted in a chart or graph for ease in grasping the differences. In spite of this minor drawback, this work should be placed in collections that support pre-law, criminal justice, international law, and international commerce curriculums. Although in-depth works abound on individual topics, no other encyclopedia covers legal systems for the globe. [R: AG, Nov 02, p. 74]—**Ladyjane Hickey**

C, P, S

196. Maddex, Robert L. **The U.S. Constitution A to Z.** Washington, D.C., CQ Press/Congressional Quarterly, 2002. 646p. illus. index. (CQ's Ready Reference Encyclopedia of American Government). $125.00. ISBN 1-56802-699-4.

The 219 entries from this easy-to-use encyclopedia include terms from the text of the U.S. Constitution (e.g., domestic tranquility, full faith and credit), Constitutional topics (e.g., abortion, death penalty, equal protection), 17 significant Supreme Court decisions (including *Bush v. Gore* in 2000), and prominent people. (There is room for argument over the choices in this last category: why include Susan B. Anthony, Martin Luther King, and Edwin Corwin, but not Earl Warren or Felix Frankfurter?) The text is well written at a level intended for a wide audience. There are numerous cross-references that are embedded in the text, as well as *see also* references at the end of articles and separate *see* entries. Many articles feature illustrations, sidebars, and references to additional readings. Appendixes include a "Guide to the U.S. Constitution" that is in effect a concordance of Constitutional terms, a table of cases that are discussed in the text, and a list of Internet resources. Overall, this is another high-quality source that we have come to expect from CQ Press; it will be ideal for high school, public, and academic libraries.—**Jack Ray**

C, P

197.   **The Oxford Companion to American Law.** Kermit L. Hall and others, eds. New York, Oxford University Press, 2002. 912p. index. $65.00. ISBN 0-19-508878-6.

The Oxford Companion to American Law is an excellent resource for the layperson as well as the professional. This volume provides biographical information of important lawyers, judges, and justices, including their personal lives to their professional careers. It also contains entries that focus on the concepts that concern American legal institutions and current controversial cases that have affected America's legal history.

The volume is organized alphabetically with essays that offer a "historical and interpretive background . . . avoiding the use of arcane legal terminology" (p. ix). There are two indexes—one of case law and one of a topical nature that directs the user to the people, places, concepts, and institutions that are in the text. The text contains an integral system of cross-referencing that appears in each essay along with *see* and *see also* references after the piece. The true value in this text is that it is easy to use and functional for someone who does not understand law or for someone who wishes for a quick read on a legal topic or case law. I would recommend this volume for public libraries and college libraries. [R: LJ, 1 Sept 02, p. 170]—**Sandhya D. Srivastava**

Directories

P

198.   **Judicial Staff Directory, Winter 2002.** 19th ed. Washington, D.C., Congressional Quarterly, 2002. 1435p. index. $209.00pa. ISBN 0-87289-193-3. ISSN 1091-3742.

The 19th edition of the *Judicial Staff Directory* continues the title's tradition of offering a wealth of current and accurate information in a well-organized manner. This edition contains contact information for approximately 25,000 judges and court staff members at both the federal and state levels, including members of the Department of Justice. This work provides other useful information, such as a list of current nominees for federal judgeships and various judicial statistics.

The volume is organized into eight sections: federal courts; state courts; Department of Justice; a list of counties and cities and their corresponding federal courts; maps of federal court jurisdictions; indexes of federal judges (by appointing president, by year appointed, and alphabetical); brief biographies of 2,800 selected judges and court staff; and a comprehensive index of all individuals listed in the work. Listings are by court, and include the mailing address and, if available, Website address, as well as the title and telephone number of each judge and staff member. A star by a person's name indicates an entry exists for that person in the biography section. For fast and efficient use, the telephone number of each individual is included next to the name in the comprehensive index. Most sections begin with a table of contents and appropriate general material, such as a one-page explanation of the structure of the federal court system at the beginning of the federal courts section.

The prefatory materials are useful and aid access. In addition to a detailed table of contents, this section also includes a "Federal Court Locator," which lists the courts alphabetically by state for the convenience of users not familiar with the jurisdictions of the circuits. The one-page guide to using the volume is concise and helpful, while the page devoted to electronic public access to information in the courts provides brief descriptions of eight electronic services of various federal courts currently available to the public, such as PACER and the U.S. Supreme Court Electronic Bulletin Board System.

Since 1999, this title has been issued semi-annually (winter and summer). In addition, Congressional Quarterly also offers subscribers free access (password required) to the *Judicial Staff Directory* Website, which is updated daily. While this emphasis on providing information more speedily in a variety of formats is quite laudable, the paper version could be improved by specifically and prominently stating the exact date that the information is current through. Despite this small flaw, however, this comprehensive and well-organized volume is a worthwhile purchase for law libraries.—**Karen Selden**

P

199.   **The Sourcebook of Local Court and County Record Retrievers: The Definitive Guide to Searching for Public Record Information at the State Level.** 2002 ed. Michael L. Sankey, Annette Talley, and Peter J. Weber, eds. Tempe, Ariz., BRB, 2002. 634p. (Public Record Research Library). $39.95pa. ISBN 1-879792-67-2.

While increasing numbers of public records are available online, not all are, and often people need, for legal purposes, to acquire official physical copies of records from county courts or records offices. Such purposes may require, for instance, records affecting hiring, lending, litigation, or incorporations. This directory lists firms that physically visit such offices for those in need of this information, and have the expertise to search the records efficiently and supply copies of the needed documents. Entries are listed by county, with codes indicating which types of records they can provide and whether they serve process. A new feature in this edition is a listing at the beginning of each state section of firms that hand carry motor vehicle records and consent forms in that state. The second half of the book is an alphabetic listing of firms with more detailed information about each, including jurisdictions searched, turnaround time, and fee basis. Information is supplied by the firms in response to surveys and is listed for free, but some firms pay a fee to be listed as members of the Public Records Retrieval Network (PRRN). BRB lists these PRRN members in an online database at www.brbpub.com/prn. The online directory lists many fewer firms, and includes less information about each firm than this print version, which often contains, for instance, e-mail and Web addresses. This print directory also contains a useful introduction explaining the various types of public records and the kinds of firms that can supply them. *The Sourcebook of Local Court and County Record Retrievers* is recommended for all types of libraries.—**Marit S. Taylor**

Handbooks and Yearbooks

S

200.   Carleton, David. **Student's Guide to Landmark Congressional Laws on Education.** Westport, Conn., Greenwood Press, 2002. 227p. index. $49.95. ISBN 0-313-31335-0.

Perhaps it is the exasperation the law brings that manages to tease the best ripostes out of people when it comes to attorneys. It remains, nevertheless, that regardless of how we feel about law or lawyers, we still have to understand the courts, even when they speak out of both sides of their mouths.

The current volume attempts to distill one aspect of legalese: education. The coverage is not exhaustive. The cases considered have more to do with why we have education than with the legal means to secure it for given individuals. Hence, decisions that deal with the federal government's expanding role in education, or, to look at it more historically, the triumph of the federalists over the anti-federalists are covered here. Individual chapters treat the Land Ordinance of 1785, the Northwest Ordinance, the Morrill Acts, Smith-Hughes, The National Defense Education Act, the Elementary and Secondary Education Act, the disastrous Bilingual Education Act, and more.

In all, there are 18 bills discussed and thoroughly dissected. Students, especially those in education, will find this book especially helpful. Each chapter provides either a full reprint of the bill or key portions of it, a discussion of its background, and a few paragraphs or pages on the bill's impact. An index and a chronology help to place the acts in their proper historical landscape. [R: SLJ, Nov 02, p. 95]—**Mark Y. Herring**

P

201.   Jasper, Margaret C. **Elder Law.** 2d ed. Dobbs Ferry, N.Y., Oceana Publications, 2001. 174p. (Oceana's Legal Almanac Series: Law for the Layperson). $25.50. ISBN 0-379-11354-6. ISSN 1075-7376.

This series is written for the layperson, but law libraries also purchase these titles, which are written by attorneys who specialize in each subject. In this volume, four chapters discuss planning for retirement, for death (estate planning), and for health care, including long-term care and medical directives such as Durable Powers of Attorney for Health Care. The text focuses on issues that most seniors ask about, such as what Medicare does or does not pay for, the differences between types of life insurance policies, and the consequences of early or delayed retirement. The language is clear and to the point. The book has no index, but a detailed table of contents is sufficient for this concise survey (75 pages, excluding the appendixes) of laws affecting senior citizens. A glossary defines common legal terms briefly and simply. A short bibliography lists mainly Websites for government documents and organizations serving elders. The 20 appendixes include a sample will and living will, directories of government agencies, a table listing by state the factors judges consider when granting requests for grandparent visitation, and a table summarizing states' inheritance rules. Researchers wanting a more expansive discussion of elder law may wish to consult Jeffrey A. Helewitz' *Elder Law* (West/Thomson Learning, 2001), which includes forms. Jasper's book is recommended for public, academic, and law libraries.—**Nancy L. Van Atta**

P

202.   Jasper, Margaret C. **Juvenile Justice and Children's Law.** 2d ed. Dobbs Ferry, N.Y., Oceana Publications, 2001. 153p. (Oceana's Legal Almanac Series: Law for the Layperson). $25.50. ISBN 0-379-11356-2. ISSN 1075-7376.

Cases of child abuse and neglect, sometimes including extreme cruelty and torture, in addition to the increasing number of brutal gang killings in many cities, raise questions of the adequacy of our juvenile justice system to handle these cases. This legal almanac, part of Oceana's Law for the Layperson series, investigates the various methods society has developed to cope with these problems; how it has attempted to protect, educate, and discipline children; and the role the juvenile justice system plays in this endeavor. The author, a New York attorney, has the experience of having written and edited some 50 other legal almanacs aimed at the layperson.

Following an introductory chapter on various aspects of the juvenile justice system, including a historical overview, there are brief descriptive chapters on juvenile violence; drug and alcohol abuse; child abuse and neglect; the role of society; emancipation; teenage pregnancy; and other age-related issues, such as employment, smoking, and driving. The bulk of the volume is comprised of 24 appendixes, all in simple chart form. Some of the topics covered are statutory rape laws; compulsory education requirements; and minimum age requirements for marriage, employment, and purchasing cigarettes. Other addenda are a glossary of relevant legal terms with fairly simple definitions and a bibliography. A most useful feature—especially since there is no index—is the table of contents.

Each chapter is outlined in detail, with page numbers for each subtopic, making it possible, for example, to go directly to the page on strip searches in schools or to what is considered emotional neglect of a child. Particularly helpful for reference use are the charts listing requirements for each state regarding juveniles. The bibliography offers some useful material, but it is questionable whether the inclusion of so many works published in the 1970s and 1980s can be worthwhile since so many changes have taken place in the past 10 years. On the whole, however, the volume is concise, inclusive, and well written for the layperson; it should be especially valuable in school and public libraries where there may be few legal materials available.—**Lucille Whalen**

P

203.   Jasper, Margaret C. **More Everyday Legal Forms.** 2d ed. Dobbs Ferry, N.Y., Oceana Publications, 2001. 258p. (Legal Almanac Series). $25.50. ISBN 0-379-11361-9.

Oceana Publications' Legal Almanac Series is designed to provide educated laypersons with legal information that is pertinent to their everyday lives. The 2d edition of this volume contributes to the series by providing sample legal forms for many situations that will occur throughout the user's life. The work includes documents for arbitration and mediation, contracts, corporations and business associations, employee/employer relations, estate planning, financial matters, litigation, personal relationships, real estate, and copyright. Current topics of interest covered here include the legal issues for addressing living wills and copyright issues of software and hardware. More popular among most users will be the legal forms for prenuptial agreements, drawing up leases for rental properties, and preparing a will. This work is a handy addition to the Legal Almanac Series and will be useful in public and business libraries.—**Shannon Graff Hysell**

S

204.   Moore, Randy. **Evolution in the Courtroom: A Reference Guide.** Santa Barbara, Calif., ABC-CLIO, 2002. 381p. illus. index. $85.00. ISBN 1-57607-420-X.

More than 75 years ago Clarence Darrow defeated Williams Jennings Bryan at the Scopes Trial, clearing the way for the teaching of evolution in public schools and the triumph of the scientific worldview. True? Not necessarily. The actual history of the evolution-creationism controversy is far more complex and far less clear cut. Since the Scopes Trial, people on all sides of the issue—science teachers, civil libertarians, proponents of "scientific creationism," and, more recently, proponents of "intelligent design"—have challenged the various evolution-related laws. The resulting trials have tried to settle the issue, but the controversy continues.

This book, *Evolution in the Courtroom* includes overviews of the actions that led to the trials as well as analyses of the trials themselves. The book also includes discussions of the impact of court decisions on the teaching of evolution in public school. A biographical listing of the most important people in the history of the evolution-creationism controversy is included. There is also a detailed chronology of the entire history of the debate as well as an edited collection of the principal court decisions and a comprehensive biography. Illustrations enhance the discussion, and a thorough index rounds out the volume. This book will be a wonderful addition to a school library, preferably high school, as well as in a science classroom reference library.—**Barbara B. Goldstein**

S

205.   Pohlmann, Marcus D., and Linda Vallar Whisenhunt. **Student's Guide to Landmark Congressional Laws on Civil Rights.** Westport, Conn., Greenwood Press, 2002. 284p. index. (Student's Guide to Landmark Congressional Laws). $49.95. ISBN 0-313-31385-7.

This work, designed for high school and college undergraduate students, looks at the civil rights movement in the African American community by studying 36 individual laws. The authors have chosen to look at African American civil rights specifically because of their unique position in American history and because of the vast improvements made in the past three centuries. Each law is written in an edited form that will make it easier for students to understand. After an introduction from the author and a nine-page timeline of significant events in the movement, the work is broken down into three parts. Part 1 provides an in-depth analysis of 12 laws passed during the period of slavery (1776-1863), including the Fugitive Slave Law (1793), the Missouri Compromise (1820), and the Emancipation Proclamation (1863). Part 2, "Postwar Reconstruction," discusses the laws passed from 1865-1875, including the Reconstruction Act (1867) and the Klan Act (1871). Part 3 discusses the Civil Rights era from 1941-1968, with in-depth discussion of the Civil Rights Acts of 1957 and 1960 and the Voting Rights Act (1965). Each law discussed provides notes at the bottom for further research. A bibliography and an index conclude the volume.—**Shannon Graff Hysell**

P

206.   Sitarz, Daniel. **Living Wills Simplified.** Carbondale, Ill., Nova Publishing, 2002. 295p. $22.95pa.; $28.95pa. (w/CD-ROM). ISBN 0-935755-52-7; 0-935755-50-0 (w/CD-ROM).

This guide, written by Daniel Sitarz an attorney and author of several self-help legal guides, is designed for those persons looking to write a legally binding advanced health care directive—more commonly known as a living will. The book begins with a short chapter discussing the nature of living wills and who should consider having one. This chapter also discusses provisions to consider, such as whether one wants to die naturally without life support systems only or without artificially provided food and water as well. Selecting a durable power of attorney for health care and a durable power of attorney for financial affairs is also covered in this first chapter. The remainder of the first chapter covers selecting a designated physician and selecting options concerning organ donation.

The bulk of the book provides samples of the legal forms required by each state for those creating a living will. Each state has its own laws and requirements concerning living wills. Although the forms are in a reproducible format, the publisher also provides a CD-ROM containing the living will and advance health care directive forms for each state in Adobe Acrobat Reader software. This will allow users to create their own living will at a fraction of the cost that it would take hiring a lawyer to draw up the same legal forms. A concluding appendix provides a summary of the laws relating to living wills in each of the 50 states, with information on the specific state law, the state Website, witness requirements, and so on.

The author tries to make clear to users that laws are in a constant state of flux and it is therefore important to check with the state Website to be sure that the information provided here is still accurate. This volume will be most useful in large public libraries.—**Shannon Graff Hysell**

S

207.   Willis, Clyde E. **Student's Guide to Landmark Congressional Laws on the First Amendment.** Westport, Conn., Greenwood Press, 2002. 232p. index. (Student's Guide to Landmark Congressional Laws). $49.95. ISBN 0-313-31416-0.

The massive amount of literature on the First Amendment can be overwhelming to anyone, especially those wanting some direction in beginning research on First Amendment issues as found in congressional statutes. The book opens with a "Timeline of Events" that directly or indirectly contributed to congressional statutes relevant to the First Amendment. The author's introduction offers a brief and clear overview of the First Amendment. Eight chapters focus on different congressional legislative acts that directly affected the First Amendment. Each chapter begins with a general introduction followed by a more specific introduction to each of the statutes included. Typical examples of statutes, and, in parentheses, the chapter title, are the Espionage Act of 1917 (Internal Security), the Draft Card and Mutilation Act of 1965 (Symbolic Speech), the Federal Election Campaign Act of 1971 as Amended (Election Campaign Activities), the Child Online Protection Act of 1998 (Obscenity), the Copyright Act of 1976 (Intellectual Property), the National Labor Relations Act of 1935 (Labor-Management Relations), the National Foundation of the Arts and Humanities Act of 1990 (Federally Funded Programs), and the Religious Freedom Restoration Act of 1993 (Freedom of Religion). The book concludes with two extremely helpful appendixes (a "List of Cited Statutes" and a "List of Cited Cases") and an excellent index. This reference work definitely belongs in high school and college libraries. [R: SLJ, Nov 02, p. 95]—**Michael A. Foley**

C

208.   Zelden, Charles L. **Voting Rights on Trial: A Handbook with Cases, Laws, and Documents.** Santa Barbara, Calif., ABC-CLIO, 2002. 347p. index. (On Trial). $55.00. ISBN 1-57607-794-2.

The subject of voting rights gained fresh importance following the presidential election of 2000. Zelden, a Florida constitutional historian at Nova Southeastern University, is well positioned to analyze how litigation in the courts has shaped this particular U.S. historical controversy. He uses a conversational tone throughout the book, often expressing his opinions. This volume, like all others in the On Trial series, is divided into two parts. Part 1 is 4 well-written chapters of explanatory essays on the history, evolution, cases, and effects of voting rights in the United States, with references at the end of each chapter. Part 2 is selected, excerpted documents supporting part 1. It includes sections from two articles and eight amendments of the U.S. Constitution, sections from five important federal cases, selected key sections of the Voting Rights Act of 1965, and three cases that interpret it (including *Bush v. Gore*).

Students will find the "Key People, Laws, and Concepts" section where short paragraphs explain positions of Supreme Court justices and individual cases as well as terms like *chad* and *vote dilution* handy. The volume ends with a chronology, a table of cases, an annotated bibliography, and an index. Most libraries will find this volume a useful addition to their political science, history, and legal collections.—**Georgia Briscoe**

CRIMINOLOGY AND CRIMINAL JUSTICE

Dictionaries and Encyclopedias

C, P, S

209.   Combs, Cindy C., and Martin Slann. **Encyclopedia of Terrorism.** New York, Facts on File, 2002. 339p. illus. index. (Facts on File Library of World History). $77.00. ISBN 0-8160-4455-4.

Terrorism remains a major preoccupation of Americans. Accordingly, the *Encyclopedia of Terrorism* would seem to be a timely addition to a library's reference shelf, especially if it is up to date. The cover of the present volume features a photograph of the burning World Trade Center towers, following the September 11th attack on them. Final materials for this encyclopedia appear to have been prepared and sent off to the printers in December 2001. Accordingly, quite a few entries address aspects of the September 11th attack, including a 27-page section on "U.S. and International Reactions to September 11, 2001, Day by Day." On the other hand, the aftermath of September 11th, and American responses to it, is an evolving story, and, in this sense, some of the entries become rapidly dated. For many purposes, then, those interested in this story are more likely to turn to the media and the Internet, rather than an encyclopedia.

The authors of this encyclopedia (and they are billed as authors, not editors) have each published books on terrorism. Eleven other contributors are listed. Most of them are colleagues of one of the primary authors at the University of North Carolina at Charlotte. Readers are only provided with their disciplinary or departmental affiliations, and it is unclear whether any of them have special expertise in topics related to terrorism. No bylines (or even author initials) are listed with any of the entries.

This book opens with a brief introductory essay. The authors allude to the conceptual and defining controversies surrounding the term "terrorism." They state that the objective of this encyclopedia is to stress contemporary forms of terrorism, with entries providing a brief description and analysis of the topic at hand. Although they note that the encyclopedia is necessarily selective, they say little about the selection criteria.

Most of the entries in this encyclopedia are quite short, with an emphasis on the descriptive over in-depth analysis. For many of the briefer entries, no bibliographic references are provided; where such bibliographic references are provided they might include a book, several articles, and one or more Websites. Cross-references are also included for some of the entries. In at least some cases, the length of the entry seems to be dictated more by the special interest or knowledge of a contributor, rather than the relative importance of the phenomenon or event. For example, a long entry is included on the somewhat obscure Wilmington, North Carolina Coup and Massacre of 1898 and the entry on animal rights organizations is much longer than the entry on anarchism. Furthermore, the entries on Josef Stalin and Adolf Hitler are quite brief and superficial. At least some of these allocations of space seem to be somewhat arbitrary.

The entries in this encyclopedia seem to fall principally in the following categories: terrorist organizations; terrorist incidents; terrorist modes of operation; forms of response to terrorism; key individuals in the history of terrorism; countries, in relation to their history as sites of terrorism, perpetrators of terrorism, or responders to terrorism; and conventions, accords, and treaties relating to terrorism. This encyclopedia commendably addresses state terrorism—or terrorism carried out on behalf of, or in the name of, states. This major form of terrorism—which by many measures is the most consequential—is often neglected in discussions of terrorism. On the other hand, some questionable entries are included (e.g., the one on Charles Manson).

This encyclopedia closes with appendixes providing some charts and tables relating to aspects of terrorism, a chronological listing of major acts of terrorism from 1941 to 2000, and a chronology of the U.S. and international responses to September 11th through the end of November 2001. A selective bibliography and an index are also included. Altogether, this encyclopedia should certainly be helpful to those seeking some basic, timely information about terrorism, and as a starting point for more substantial research on aspects of terrorism.

—**David O. Friedrichs**

C, P

210.   **Encyclopedia of Crime and Punishment.** David Levinson, ed. Thousand Oaks, Calif., Sage, 2002. 4v. illus. index. $600.00/set. ISBN 0-7619-2258-X.

This four-volume encyclopedia will prove an invaluable addition to any reference collection. There are more than 400 entries, beginning with "Abolitionism" and concluding with "Zero Tolerance Policing." In addition, there is a reader's guide that groups all of the entries into 13 general categories, including "Crimes and Related Behaviors," "Forensics," "Corrections," "Concepts and Theories," and "Special Populations." While focused primarily on the United States, the encyclopedia does not ignore relevant material from other nations. For example, under the general category of "Punishment," readers can find the entry "Alternative Punishments in Sub-Saharan Africa." Under the general category "International," users can find references to China, France, Germany, and Russia as well as references to Buddhism, Christianity, Daoism, and Hinduism. In that same category, there is an entry for "Women and Crime in a Global Perspective."

Each entry concludes with references (if any) to any related entries and recommendations for further reading. For example, under "Whistle-Blowing" the related entries are "Corporate Crime," "Police Corruption," and "Political Corruption." The 4th volume contains four appendixes ("Careers in Criminal Justice," "Web Resources for Criminal Justice," "Professional and Scholarly Associations," and a selected bibliography) followed by an outstanding 80-page index. Each volume concludes with the same 38-page chronology that begins in 1795 B.C.E.— 1750 B.C.E. (the Code of Hammurabi) and concludes in 2002 (the beginning investigations into the Enron scandal). This work is highly recommended without reservation. [R: LJ, 15 May 02, p. 82]—**Michael A. Foley**

C, S

211.   Kushner, Harvey W. **Encyclopedia of Terrorism.** Thousand Oaks, Calif., Sage, 2003. 523p. illus. index. $125.00. ISBN 0-7619-2408-6.

The latest in a genre of reference works begun in 1987 with John Thackrah's *Encyclopedia of Terrorism and Political Violence* (see ARBA 88, entry 701), this well-constructed volume (begun one year prior to September 11, 2001) provides detailed historical and contemporary coverage of a complex and politically timely subject. The author is both a professor of criminal justice at Long Island University specializing in the analysis of terrorism as a criminal phenomenon and a widely heard media commentator for MSNBC, CNN, and Fox News as well as international networks. Of particular value for librarians is the "Reader's Guide," which groups the content articles into 32 topical categories centering on organizations promoting terrorist actions (such as Al Qaeda, Abu Nidal, and

Hezbollah) and specific attacks (such as the events of September 11, 2001 and the earlier World Trade Center bombing of 1993), types of terror activities, and concepts widely used in the literature of terrorism (such as the ideas of *Jihad*). Entries focus on providing both historical background on individuals and organizations and assessing their roles in the overall picture of terrorist activity, with further readings indicated. Four appendixes present the locations of terrorist activity by continent; Websites of journals and reports; media, nongovernmental organizations, and federal and international agencies related to terrorist activity and its suppression; a chronology of terrorist attacks within the United States and on American interests abroad beginning in 1865; and a bibliography. This last is subdivided into overviews; counter-terrorism; primary documents and biography; September 11th; and technical literature on such topics as bomb detection and chemical and biological warfare. The work is indexed by personal, organizational, and geographic names and by subject. The *Encyclopedia of Terrorism* is best suited for high school, college, and university reference collections. [R: LJ, Jan 03, pp. 90-92]—**Robert B. Marks Ridinger**

Directories

C, P

212.   **Bioterrorism and Political Violence Web Resources.** M. Sandra Wood, ed. Binghamton, N.Y., Haworth Press, 2002. 154p. illus. index. $34.95; $19.95pa. ISBN 0-7890-1964-7; 0-7890-1965-5pa.

This guide to World Wide Web resources, a useful background source of materials dealing with bioterrorism and political violence, extends beyond the events of September 11th to provide more general and enduring value. Comprising a set of annotated webliographies compiled with the working reference librarian in mind, this book suits a wide range of library operations. The editor discusses concerns about the volatile nature of Internet addresses by selecting stable and major government, educational, and private sites.

Given the acknowledged problems with proliferating unreliable source material on the Web, this title is a particularly useful tool for the library professional. Coverage includes the origins and definitions of terrorism; biological, nuclear, and chemical resources; disaster preparedness; and selected news sites. Each section includes an explanation of the scope and value of its selected sites. Monochrome screenshots of particularly important sites are also provided. All of the webliographies are clearly written and well explained; the section by Michele Mary Volesko on disaster preparedness for medical libraries supplements its in-depth presentation with a detailed checklist for preparedness activities. While the coverage is selective in the best sense, including materials from outside North America broadens its perspective.

Apart from an editorial slip on page 52 which confuses the president of the Brookings Institution with the President of the United States, very few minor misspellings were noted. Many of the URLs are long and complex, which would justify creating an internal Web page for easy access. Using a random sample of the URLs provided, a return rate of 80 percent was generated (the Scholastic News Service had moved [p. 69]and the Netherlands site of the Organization for the Prohibition of Chemical Weapons was not available [p. 42]). Overall, the utility of this volume as an index to Websites has, therefore, not diminished appreciably with the passage of time. Clearly printed on acid-free paper, with a comprehensive index and a sturdy binding, this volume deserves consideration by any library serving a clientele with interests and concerns relating to this complex and controversial subject area.—**John Howard Oxley**

Handbooks and Yearbooks

C, P

213.   **The American Prison System.** Peter G. Herman, ed. Bronx, N.Y., H. W. Wilson, 2001. 194p. index. (The Reference Shelf, v.73, no.5). $30.00pa. ISBN 0-8242-1002-6.

Herman has edited an interesting collection of diverse print essays (with one exception that is taken from Salon.com) on the prison system that offers a good overview of issues that define, in part, the realities of today's prisons. The book is divided into six primary issue areas. The editor opens each section with a brief introduction, including a brief synopsis of each essay in that section. The short essays (the longest of which is 17 pages) are taken from a variety of print resources, including *Corrections Today, American Psychologist, National Journal, American Behavioral Scientist, The New York Times*, the *Boston Globe*, and *Human Rights*.

Section 1 contains four essays on the transformation of American prisons throughout the twentieth century. Section 2 contains three articles that focus on the philosophical issues associated with punishment (i.e., Why do we punish? How much should we punish? Toward what goals should the prison strive?). Section 3 includes three essays on the economics of the prison system. Section 4 contains four essays on the overrepresentation of minorities as well as the growing population of female inmates. Section 5 contains three essays on prison conditions and realities. Finally, section 6 examines alternatives to imprisonment. Lay readers interested in the current state of affairs in the world of prisons should read these essays. One of the strengths of this collection is that interested lay readers can easily read and understand the essays. There are several very useful bibliographies and a good index. This work is highly recommended, especially for lay audiences.—**Michael A. Foley**

S

214.   Outman, James L., and Elisabeth M. Outman. **Terrorism: Almanac.** Farmington Hills, Mich., U*X*L/Gale, 2003. 235p. illus. index. (U*X*L Terrorism Reference Library). $55.00/vol.; $145.00/set. ISBN 0-7876-6566-5.

S

215.   Outman, James L., and Elisabeth M. Outman. **Terrorism: Biographies.** Farmington Hills, Mich., U*X*L/ Gale, 2003. 235p. illus. index. (U*X*L Terrorism Reference Library). $55.00/vol.; $145.00/set. ISBN 0-7876-6567-3.

S

216.   Outman, James L., and Elisabeth M. Outman. **Terrorism: Primary Sources.** Farmington Hills, Mich., U*X*L/Gale, 2003. 192p. illus. index. (U*X*L Terrorism Reference Library). $55.00/vol.; $145.00/set. ISBN 0-7876-6568-1.

Since the terrorist attacks on the United States on September 11, 2001, there has been a need for more information and history surrounding terrorism both at home and abroad. This need for information extends to children and young adults who are often the most confused and frightened by these acts of violence. This set provides just the type of information that middle school and high school age young adults will be looking for concerning terrorism and its roots.

The set begins with an *Almanac*, which provides nine chapters covering the history and role of terrorism throughout the world. The chapters discuss the legal definition of terrorism, the tactics used, the training of terrorists, political and economic warfare, and state-sponsored terrorism. Sprinkled throughout the text are black-and-white photographs and sidebars with interesting facts and stories concerning terrorism. Each volume in the set provides a timeline of terrorism history beginning with 1793 as well as a glossary for that volume. The *Almanac* volume concludes with an appendix listing and describing some of the terrorist groups operating today, including Colombia's National Liberation Army, Ireland's Irish Republican Army (IRA), and Al Qaeda.

Biographies alphabetically lists 26 notorious terrorist leaders, political figures, and freedom fighters associated with terrorism. Those profiled include Osama bin Laden, Timothy McVeigh, George J. Mitchell, and freedom fighters John Brown and Michael Collins. Each biography includes a black-and-white photograph. The final volume, *Primary Sources*, provides excerpts from speeches and documents concerning terrorism. These are separated into five chapters, including "Philosophy of Terror," which provides excerpts from Charlotte Brontë's *Shirley: A Tale* (1849); "Terrorism and Race in the United States," which includes an article from Claire Safran about a member of the Ku Klux Klan; and "Conflict in the Middle East," which provides an excerpt from Osama bin Laden's "Jihad Against Jews and Crusaders" (1998). Each volume concludes with an index to the entire set.

This resource will be valuable to middle and high school libraries as well as the children's reference departments of public libraries. The information is timely and written at a level that young adult students will be easily able to comprehend.—**Shannon Graff Hysell**

HUMAN RIGHTS

C, P, S

217.   Axelrod, Alan. **Minority Rights in America.** Washington, D.C., CQ Press, 2002. 411p. index. $125.00. ISBN 1-56802-685-4.

Beginning with the assumption that "no subject is more central to the American experience than minority rights" (p. xv), Axelrod has compiled an excellent single-volume reference work covering the entire history of minority rights in the United States. Axelrod defines "minority" as African Americans, Hispanic Americans, Native Americans, Asian Americans, and women; as any additional group defined by the majority as a minority; or as any group that is discriminated against by economically or politically powerful groups.

There are almost 600 entries, ranging in length from a sentence to more than a page, on topics including age discrimination, American Foundation for the Blind, Aryan Nations, The Birth of a Nation, B'nai B'rith, child abuse, Chinese Exclusion Treaty and Act, Cuban refugees, Eugene V. Debs, Medgar Evers, gay rights and the military, Indian wars, the melting pot concept, *Plessy v. Ferguson*, Quakers, Phyllis Schlafly, and Triangle Shirtwaist Fire. All are well written and include clear cross-references within the text. The lists of suggested readings at the end of each entry tend to be fairly brief, but useful. There is a large bibliography at the end of the book. In addition to the entries that make up the bulk of the book, there are 72 important primary documents included as an appendix. These are not indexed, but are referenced within the entries.

There are other reference works that cover similar territory, such as *Civil Rights in the United States* (see ARBA 2001, entry 568) and *The Encyclopedia of Civil Rights in America* (see ARBA 1999, entry 588). Libraries that already own one or both of these will not need to purchase *Minority Rights in America*. Otherwise, it is highly recommended for all academic and public libraries.—**Michael Levine-Clark**

C, P, S

218.   Curry, Lynne. **The Human Body on Trial: A Handbook with Cases, Laws, and Documents.** Santa Barbara, Calif., ABC-CLIO, 2002. 237p. index. (ABC-CLIO's On Trial Series). $55.00. ISBN 1-57607-349-1.

In his classic text *On Liberty*, John Stuart Mill tried to draw a line between individual liberty and legitimate state authority. That line continues to be drawn, especially as it relates to liberty-rights and the control of one's body. Curry's book offers a very clear summation of the conflicts that play out in that debate, along with numerous documents that enable readers to understand more clearly the nature and scope of the issues related to our alleged right to do what we want with our bodies.

The book is divided into two parts. Part 1 focuses on the history of ideas as they relate to the development of the claims of the right to control one's own body. Chapter 1 introduces readers to John Locke's seventeenth-century claim that people have a right to property in their own bodies. From there Curry examines the state's right to regulate individual liberty in the interests of social welfare and the claim that we have a right to privacy, a right nowhere explicitly stated in the Constitution. Chapters 2 and 3 focus on issues such as eugenics, birth control, the right to die, compulsory vaccination, and mandatory sterilization. Part 2 provides a series of documents (mostly constitutional cases) that shaped the constitutional and political debates on liberty-rights relative to the control of one's body. The book concludes with a brief but useful section titled "Key People, Laws, and Concepts," a chronology of important dates from 1868-2002 in the shaping of these debates, an annotated bibliography, and an index. This work is highly recommended, especially for readers in need of an objective review of the history of ideas on the controversial issues relating to the control of one's body.—**Michael A. Foley**

C, S

219.   **Guns in American Society: An Encyclopedia of History, Politics, Cultures, and the Law.** Gregg Lee Carter, ed. Santa Barbara, Calif., ABC-CLIO, 2002. 2v. illus. index. $185.00/set. ISBN 1-57607-268-1.

This two-volume set from ABC-CLIO is an unbiased resource on the controversial issue of gun ownership and gun violence in the United States. In its more than 500 entries the set discusses the latest research in the fields of criminology, law, politics, and sociology as they pertain to guns. The remainder of the entries put gun use in a historical context so that readers can understand how the issue has become so complicated, and how the second amendment's right "to keep and bear arms" is relevant today. Entries include such topics as "Alcohol and Gun Violence," "Accidents, Guns," "Columbine High School Tragedy," and "Genocide and Guns"; such people as James S. Brady, Annie Oakley, and Samuel Colt; and such groups as the National Rifle Association, the Ku

Klux Klan, and the National Council to Control Handguns. Entries also include important court cases in the history of guns and gun control. They typically run several pages in length and many include black-and-white photograph and charts. Each entry provides a list for further reading and many provide cross-references to related topics. The 82 contributors to the volume are listed at the front of the volume with their affiliation and entry titles. The set has four appendixes: a key to federal gun laws, a chart to state gun laws, each state's constitutional right-to-keep-and-bear-arms provisions, and a list of gun-related organizations with contact information. A bibliography and index conclude the volume.—**Shannon Graff Hysell**

INTERNATIONAL LAW

C, P
220.   Ball, Howard. **War Crimes and Justice: A Reference Handbook.** Santa Barbara, Calif., ABC-CLIO, 2002. 259p. index. (Contemporary World Issues). $45.00. ISBN 1-57607-899-X.

Yet another volume in ABC-CLIO's Contemporary World Issues series lands on the desk. *War Crimes and Justice: A Reference Handbook* appears like many of the others. An introductory chapter outlines the issues in this particular contemporary crisis. This is followed by the usual important, if somewhat pedestrian, matters: justice, international laws, major treaties, directory of governmental and nongovernmental agencies, and selected print and nonprint sources.

These volumes are not meant to be monographs by scholars in the field although they are often written by scholars. Each volume contains the usual authoritative essay outlining key and important issues; a chronology of events; various biographies of culprits or heroes and facts, figures, tables, and documents. The cover on the present volume features the scowling face of Slobodan Milosevic and will certainly attract the crowd is seeks by such a display, namely high schools students and first- and second-year college students.

For summary overviews about such topics the ABC-CLIO series is hard to beat, unless it is the Greenwood Series on historical issues. The latter allows its authors more latitude and so students are provided with more critical thinking opportunities. Nevertheless, this volume, along with others in the ABC-CLIO series should be on every library shelf.—**Mark Y. Herring**

11 Library and Information Science and Publishing and Bookselling

LIBRARY AND INFORMATION SCIENCE

Reference Works

Directories

C, P
221.   **American Library Directory 2001-2002.** 54th ed. New Providence, N.J., R. R. Bowker; distr., Medford, N.J., Information Today, 2001. 2v. index. $299.00/set. ISBN 0-8352-4404-0. ISSN 0065-910X.

Now in its 54th edition, the *American Library Directory* is updated annually to reflect changes in library incomes, personnel, expenditures, and automated capabilities. Updates and suggestions for new entries can be submitted via a form provided in volume 1 or at www.bowker.com. Unlike the 53d edition (see ARBA 2001, entry 585), this edition does not cover libraries in Mexico. Following a preface, introductory materials include a sample entry, a table of the number of libraries in the United States and Canada by type, a list of library award recipients for 2000, and a key to symbols and abbreviations.

Volume 1 is devoted to listing libraries in the United States, Puerto Rico, and other regions administered by the United States. The entries are alphabetically organized by state (or region), then by city and institution or library name. All of the entries provide basic contact information (address, telephone and fax numbers, and key personnel) along with an indication of the library's holdings and various other data. Volume 2 contains similar introductory material except that it covers libraries in Canada. This volume also contains entries for networks, consortia, and other cooperative library organizations; library schools and training courses; library systems; libraries for the blind and physically handicapped; libraries serving the deaf and hearing impaired; state and provincial public library agencies; state school library agencies; national interlibrary load code for the United States; and U.S. armed forces libraries overseas. Volume 2 concludes with organization and personnel indexes.

—**Cari Ringelheim**

C, P
222.   **Directory of Library Automation Software, Systems, and Services.** 2002/2003 ed. Pamela R. Cibbarelli, comp. Medford, N.J., Information Today, 2002. 369p. index. $89.00pa. ISBN 1-57387-140-0.

Pamela Cibbarelli, a well-known library consultant, has kept librarians and libraries informed about the library automation software, systems, and services through her directory since 1982. The new edition of the directory includes current and accurate information in the field. The book is divided into five parts. The first part has a listing of software companies arranged alphabetically with full mailing address, telephone and fax numbers, and e-mail address. It also includes information about the programming language, components and applications, system requirements, features, MARC formats and interfaces, and price. Part 2 includes a listing of retrospective conversion services and products. Part 3 lists library automation consultants with their areas of expertise and other services. Part 4 has a listing of database distributors. Part 5 lists conferences and meetings to be held during

2002-2004 in the field of library and information science in Canada, England, and the United States. The directory includes a selected bibliography of library automation periodicals and other recent library automation publications with full bibliographic information. There is a short listing of the Internet resources also. A special feature of the directory is a section entitled "Brief Info," which provides up-to-date information about many library automation products and services that have been discontinued. An index included at the end is also very useful to locate the information. It is certainly a well-prepared directory and is recommended for all types of libraries.

—**Ravindra Nath Sharma**

C, P

223.   **Directory of Special Libraries and Information Centers.** 27th ed. Matthew Miskelly and Chrystal Rozsa, eds. Farmington Hills, Mich., Gale, 2002. 4v. index. $960.00/set. ISBN 0-7876-5636-4. ISSN 0731-633X.

The 27th edition of this useful directory provides information on more than 34,000 subject-specific resource collections. These include collections maintained by government agencies, businesses, newspapers, book publishers, educational institutions, associations, societies, and nonprofit organizations. This edition has expanded international coverage and gives more emphasis to electronic technology, including available electronic access addresses in each entry.

Descriptive entries are arranged in alphabetic order in three volumes or parts. The title page and contents pages actually call the entire set of books "Volume 1" with each book named as a part (parts 1, 2, and 3). Entries contain the name of the library or center, the major subjects of its collection, address, fax, e-mail address, URL, date of foundation, staff size, size of holdings, services, publications, and usually the names of professional staff. Many entries also include notes on automated operations, electronic resources, and other miscellaneous information

Part 3 of the set includes 7 appendixes and a subject index. The appendixes (A through G) are useful for quick access to certain groups of collections and are entitled as follows: "Networks and Consortia"; "Regional and Subregional Libraries for the Blind and Physically Handicapped"; "Patents and Trademark Depository Libraries"; "Regional Government Depository Libraries"; "United Nations Depository Libraries"; "World Bank Depository Libraries"; and "European Community Depository Libraries."

The subject index lists an interesting mix of people, places, and topics. Citations under topics are often arranged geographically by two-character state, territory, and province codes, or by three-character country codes. The subject "American Literature," for example, cites page numbers for the geographic codes CA, BRZ, and TUN. U.S state and Canadian province codes are listed in the front of volume 1, parts 1, 2, and 3. International country codes are listed only in part 3. The numbers cited under each entry refer to entry numbers, not page numbers.

The fourth part of this set of books, "Subject Directory of Special Libraries and Information Centers," is a 425-page list of business, government, and law libraries. It includes military, transportation, and urban/regional planning libraries.

The "Services" section in each entry includes information about whether or not a library is open to the public and if one needs an appointment to use the library. The "Subject" sections describe in detail the kinds of materials one can expect to find in the library. Consultation of this thorough reference work can save researchers wasted trips to libraries that are not public or that require special permission for their use. It can also help researchers focus on the very best libraries for their particular research interests. The addresses and numbers given for each library, plus the additional advantage of finding the names of professional employees at the library is particularly helpful for busy clients who wish to make contact with specific persons or departments. This is a set of books that would be of value in most libraries, both academic and public.—**Dorothy Jones**

C, P

224.   Morris, Leslie R. **Interlibrary Loan Policies Directory.** 7th ed. New York, Neal-Schuman, 2002. 1275p. index. $199.95pa. ISBN 1-55570-423-9.

The *Interlibrary Loan Policies Directory* has long been a vital resource for interlibrary loan (ILL) staff. In 1,275 pages, Morris has compiled information on the ILL policies of over 1,400 libraries in the United States, the Virgin Islands, Puerto Rico, and over 200 foreign libraries. Included in each entry are address and contact information and detailed shipping and loan policies. There are 9 categories new to the 7th edition, including the Internet, OPAC, and ILL policy Web addresses as well as policies regarding electronic delivery of articles, mailing directly to the homes of distance education students, copying of dissertations, and use of ILL Fee Management (IFM).

The most valuable section of the book is the extensive set of 61 indexes. These allow ILL staff to quickly and easily locate libraries that loan any of approximately 25 types of materials; libraries that ship via particular methods; libraries that waive fees for members of particular groups; and libraries that accept particular forms of requests. For this edition, there are six new indexes, covering libraries that loan new books, accept requests via e-mail or Ariel, loan books for more than 29 days, copy dissertations or theses, loan CD-ROMs with books, and loan to U.S. libraries from other countries.

No other tool provides the same detail and depth of information on ILL policies. OCLC's *Name Address Directory* (NAD) comes closest, but is not available to most libraries, and does not provide all of the categories of information included here. For libraries without OCLC access, the *Interlibrary Loan Policies Directory* is an essential tool. For those with access, it is still a very useful resource, especially because of the many indexes.

—**Michael Levine-Clark**

C, P

225. **Subject Directory of Special Libraries and Information Centers.** 27th ed. Matthew Miskelly, ed. Farmington Hills, Mich., Gale, 2002. 3v. index. $945.00/set. ISBN 0-7876-6189-9. ISSN 0731-633X.

As a subject classified-edition of Gale's *Directory of Special Libraries and Information Centers* (27th ed.; see entry 223), this publication provides information on several thousand special libraries and information centers all over the world, with emphasis on the United States and Canada. It consists of three volumes: "Business, Government, and Law Libraries"; "Computers, Engineering, and Science Libraries"; and "Health Sciences Libraries." Volume 1 includes business/finance libraries, law libraries, military libraries, transportation libraries, and urban/regional planning libraries. Volume 2 includes agriculture libraries, biological science libraries, computer science libraries, energy libraries, environmental/conservation libraries, food science libraries, information science libraries, and science and engineering libraries. Volume 3 is devoted entirely to health science libraries.

A typical entry includes entry number, name of the organization, name of library or information center, subject keyword, address, telephone number, head of library or information center, fax number, e-mail, URL, founding date, number of staff, subjects, special collections, holdings, services, electronic resources, publications, special indexes, and professional staff names. There is a master index that provides an alphabetic listing of all libraries and a subject index that classifies the major subject areas of each library. Subject terms in the subject index are arranged geographically within each entry.

The publisher receives no payment for the listing, and the information seems to be objective. The coverage is comprehensive and cross-references are helpful. Large academic and public libraries may wish to purchase the entire set. For special libraries, the volumes can be purchased separately according to their subject interests.

—**Mihoko Hosoi**

Handbooks and Yearbooks

P

226. **The Bowker Annual Library and Book Trade Almanac 2001.** 46th ed. Dave Bogart, ed. New Providence, N.J., R. R. Bowker; distr., Medford, N.J., Information Today, 2001. 861p. index. $199.00. ISBN 0-8352-4385-0. ISSN 0068-0540.

The Bowker Annual Library and Book Trade Almanac has long been considered a standard ready-reference tool. The title has received frequent reviews (44th ed., see ARBA 2000, entry 560; 42d ed., see ARBA 98, entry 576; 41st ed., see ARBA 97, entry 528; 40th ed., see ARBA 96, entry 623; and 39th ed., see ARBA 95, entry 644). Over time, the volume has increased the total pages as well as the price. Two questions need to be answered: is the title still useful and does the contents merit the price? For librarians and publishers, the contents have enduring value from year to year. Where else, in a single volume, can information on legislation, funding, grants, association reports, placement and salaries, library research statistics, best-seller lists, and directories of organizations (to name but a few of the topics covered) be found? Given that the market for this title is somewhat limited to the narrow realm of libraries and publishing houses, readers can understand that it might be priced at a higher level than an equivalent size book for a wider audience. Within the pricing scheme of similar size monographic volumes, the price does not seem inappropriate.

There are four special reports included in the first part of the annual, "Reports from the Field." These reports are designed to highlight certain topics that for the 2001 volume included considerations of electronic publishing, outsourcing, Internet filters used in schools, and electronic journals. The potential uses for this title are many. A beginning librarian can learn which library and information studies programs are accredited by the American Library Association (ALA), learn about scholarships, and read about placements and salaries. State, national, and international library association information is well documented, with the object of the group specified as well as membership, staff, officers, and publications. Major rankings of "Distinguished Books" are presented in the section on "Reference Information." For most of the contributions to this work, the author's name and affiliation are included, with such well-known individuals as Mary Jo Lynch from the ALA Office for Research and Statistics authoring the section titled "Research on Libraries and Librarianship in 2000."

Editor Bogart and consultant Julia C. Blixrud have brought to the reference community another valuable issue of *The Bowker Annual*. This title should be continued in locations already subscribing, and libraries and publishing organizations that do not have access yet should give serious thought to buying this heavily used ready-reference title. It is highly recommended for all library locations and types of book publishers.

—**Graham R. Walden**

C, P, S

227.　**People, Places and Things: A List of Popular Library of Congress Subject Headings with Dewey Numbers.** Dublin, OCLC Forest Press, 2001. 422p. $100.00pa. ISBN 0-910608-69-5.

People, Places and Things provides an alphabetic listing of more than 50,000 Library of Congress subject headings that are paired with Dewey numbers. The work is designed as a companion to *Subject Headings for Children* (see ARBA 96, entry 632), and aims to suit a general audience. Subject heading and Dewey number pairs are identified and extracted from WorldCat, WebDewey, NetFirst, and *Subject Headings for Children*. The subject headings include geographic, personal, and corporate body names, as well as title and topical headings. Topical headings with the subheadings of "Fiction," "Poetry," and "Drama" are excluded. Headings are organized according to American Library Association filing rules; arrangement is alphabetic word by word, and letter by letter within words. Instructions on how to use the book are provided, and include information about the scope and organization of the work. *People, Places and Things* may serve as a teaching tool for school librarians, or as a quick reference guide for public library patrons that want to browse specific subject areas. Since subject headings and Dewey numbers are only current through April 2001, catalogers should consult the most recent version of the Dewey Decimal Classification system when using the book.—**Sharon Ladenson**

PUBLISHING AND BOOKSELLING

Directories

C, P

228.　**American Book Trade Directory 2002-2003.** 48th ed. Medford, N.J., Information Today, 2002. 1809p. $275.00. ISBN 1-57387-136-2. ISSN 0065-759X.

The *American Book Trade Directory* (ABTD) has been published since 1915 and is clearly a standard tool housed either in the reference or in the acquisitions department of all but the smallest libraries. With over 27,000 retail and wholesale booksellers listed, the volume, while not necessarily exhaustive, is certainly comprehensive (the distinction being that entries are based primarily on voluntary responses to mailed questionnaires). A nonscientific review of some entries in multiple states demonstrates that even some very minor establishments have been posted. The information provided per entry is scant, but it is nevertheless what most libraries will be seeking. The following data elements are included: business name, address, telephone number and fax number (where appropriate), Web address, year established, the current owner's start year, square feet, subjects covered, and sidelines and services. An overall category is also assigned, such as general, antiquarian, or computer software.

Coverage is for the United States and Canada, and includes the following major areas: retailers and antiquarians; wholesalers of books and magazines; book trade information (such as auctioneers, appraisers, exporters, importers, and associations); dealers in foreign-language books; types of stores (a subject index by category, such as "German

Language"); and an index to retailers and wholesalers, which provides the city and state for the listed name. (The overall arrangement for the ABTD is alphabetical by state, and then similarly by city name.)

The directory is designed to fill a very specific function. While this information would be easier to access online, the market for the product might be too small to justify the expense associated with such an undertaking. Until an electronic version arises, the paper copy will continue to be needed by librarians and others associated with the book trade. This resource is highly recommended.—**Graham R. Walden**

P

229.   **International Literary Market Place 2002.** Medford, N.J., Information Today, 2001. 1651p. index. $219.00pa. ISBN 1-57387-127-3. ISSN 0074-6827.

One of the major changes to the 2002 edition of *International Literary Market Place* (last reviewed in ARBA 2001, entry 688) is that it is now published by Information Today. Yet, the staff at Bowker seems to still oversee the editing and compilation of the guide—contact information provided in the preface and on the *Literary Market Place* Website are for Bowker. This edition includes 16,763 entries in more than 180 countries. Publishers account for 10,519 of these entries. Overall, the guide's layout follows the same format as in the last couple of editions. Entries are organized under six areas of coverage: "Publishing," "Manufacturing," "Book Trade Information," "Literary Association & Prizes," "Book Trade Calendar," and "Literary Resources." The information in the entries is updated throughout the year via a questionnaire mailed to the entrants or through public resources. If the editors were unable to verify an entry's information, an asterisk is used to indicate that the previous year's data was used. A form is provided at the beginning of the guide for readers to submit revisions or suggestions for new listings. These updates can also be submitted at www.literarymarketplace.com or www.bowker.com.

Following the preface, information on the ISBN system and a list of abbreviations used in the guide are provided. Under the "Publishing" section, entries are organized by country along with general information (e.g., capital city, population, currency). The entries contain basic contact information with an indication of the subjects the publisher is interested in and their ISBN prefixes. A type of publication index and a subject index follow this section. The entries for literary agents, international publishing services, translation agencies and associations, manufacturers, prepress services, book trade organizations, book dealers, literary associations, and more follow the same format as the publisher entries. Various indexes are scattered in between these sections. The last part of the book is the "Industry Yellow Pages," a complete, alphabetic index to the entries with their telephone and fax numbers and e-mail and Website addresses (if applicable).—**Cari Ringelheim**

Indexes

P

230.   Newton, Frances P., comp. **A Checklist of American Imprints 1820-1829: Printers, Publishers, and Booksellers Index, Geographical Index.** Lanham, Md., Scarecrow, 2000. 391p. $85.00. ISBN 0-8108-3924-5. ISSN 0361-7920.

This index rounds out the 1820-1829 annual volumes of *A Checklist of American Imprints*, the monumental guide to American publications of the nineteenth century. Title and author indexes to the set were published previously (see ARBA 74, entry 10, and ARBA 73, entry 11, respectively). The *Printers, Publishers, and Booksellers Index, Geographical Index* is modeled after a similar work the compiler developed for an earlier series, *American Bibliography: A Preliminary Checklist* (see ARBA 84, entry 8), which covers American imprints for the years 1801-1819. The present volume is composed of three parts. A "Printers, Publishers, and Booksellers Index" makes up the bulk of the work. Entries in this section provide individual, corporate, newspaper, and magazine names; city and state of publication; and references to corresponding annual volumes and item numbers. A "Geographical Index" follows the main section, with entries arranged in alphabetic order by city. The final section of the volume lists items that were excluded from the index for various reasons, and provides brief explanations for their omission. The reviewer noted that the table of contents refers the reader to the wrong page number for this section of the book. This oversight is likely to cause few problems, however, as this final section of the book consists of only three pages. Libraries that own the annual *Checklist* volumes for the years 1820-1829 will want to purchase this useful index to the set.—**Janet Dagenais Brown**

12   Military Studies

GENERAL WORKS

Biography

C, P

231.   Hanna, Charles W. **African American Recipients of the Medal of Honor: A Biographical Dictionary, Civil War Through Vietnam War.** Jefferson, N.C., McFarland, 2002. 189p. illus. index. $45.00. ISBN 0-7864-1355-7.

The Congressional Medal of Honor has been bestowed on 3,457 men and one woman since its inception in 1861. In his slim chronologically arranged volume, Medal of Honor Historical Society Secretary Charles W. Hanna details the stories of 88 African Americans who have received the award. Most entries run one or two pages in length and give a brief biography of the recipient, his rank, and reason for his citation; the exact wording of the citation itself is often provided, although not always. Hanna thoughtfully divides his volume by war or engagement, making it relatively easy to discover, for example, who received a medal during the Spanish-American War. Illustrations are few in number, mostly photographs of headstones, with some portraits. Hanna also includes a brief history of the Medal of Honor, and each chapter is preceded by a page or two on the nature of African American involvement in that conflict. Although short, the entries are well written and could easily be understood by high school students. A brief bibliography and index conclude the volume. This work is a fine complement to Elliott Converse's *The Exclusion of Black Soldiers from the Medal of Honor in World War II* (McFarland, 1997), Lee's *Negro Medal of Honor Men* (3d ed.; Dodd, Mead, 1969), and Proft and Demar's comprehensive guide *United States of America's Congressional Medal of Honor Recipients and Their Official Citations* (2d ed.; Highland House, 2000).—**Anthony J. Adam**

Directories

P

232.   Rajtar, Steve, and Frances Elizabeth Franks. **War Monuments, Museums and Library Collections of 20th Century Conflicts: A Directory of United States Sites.** Jefferson, N.C., McFarland, 2002. 328p. index. $75.00. ISBN 0-7864-1231-3.

This one-of-a-kind resource contains more than 3,000 entries (museums, monuments, memorials, and library collections), arranged geographically—first by state and then by cities and towns. Texas has the most by far, with 470 listings over second-place Wisconsin at 266. Primary focus is on the two world wars and the Korean and Vietnam conflicts. Entries for sites typically include address, telephone number, hours, admission charges, and Websites. Narrative descriptions of memorials are generally very good, and often contain interesting background information (e.g., the controversy over the Pancho Villa statue in Tucson, Arizona); descriptions of collections are brief and sketchy. Indexing is limited to the names of sites, with no listing by subject as such. Coverage ranges from major institutions all the way down to single wall plaques and statues honoring individuals. At this level of comprehensiveness the number of omissions—especially of Vietnam War memorials—is troubling.

There are 50 foreign sites included; again, Vietnam conflict-related sites are poorly represented. Nevertheless, although this volume will be of limited use to serious historians, there is no other resource quite like it, as a first-level guide it will be useful to collections serving history buffs. Also, with so many memorials located at military bases, William R. Evinger's *Directory of U.S. Military Bases Worldwide* (3d ed.; see ARBA 99, entry 631) would serve as a useful complementary resource.—**Kenneth W. Berger**

Handbooks and Yearbooks

C
233.   **U.S. War Plans: 1938-1945.** Steven T. Ross, ed. Boulder, Colo., Lynne Rienner Publishers, 2002. 371p. $89.95. ISBN 1-58826-008-9.

The Spanish-American War demonstrated the need for cooperative planning between the U.S. Army and the U.S. Navy. In 1903 the Joint Army and Navy Board was established with four high-ranking officers from each branch participating in the planning activities. The Joint Board functioned until February 1942 when the U.S. Joint Chiefs of Staff was created. Both boards functioned as an advisory panel to the president on global military issues. This volume presents the U.S. War Plans from 1938 to 1945. It is divided into three parts: "Pre-War Plans," "The War in North Africa and Europe," and "The War in The Pacific." One of the largest plans outlined in the book, Operation Neptune, is typical of the information provided. Neptune was a U.S. First Army plan to land 500,000 troops and 70,000 vehicles on the continent of Europe and bring about "the total defeat of Germany." The plan begins with a situation report that outlines the plan goals and supporting forces needed. Next a mission statement is developed, followed by specific operation assignments for each Corp and Division. This is followed by the "Neptune Estimated Available Lift" (troop and vehicle build-up list day by day) and finally the individual vehicle and personnel assignment down to the company (and in some cases team) level. For example, on landing zone "Utah" a Photo Interpretation Team of six men and two vehicles was projected. The Operation Neptune plan became the basis for the U.S. Force invasion of the Normandy beaches on "D Day."

This volume provides interesting insight into pre-war and war planning on the part of the United States. Unfortunately, a number of supporting documents (e.g., charts, maps) referenced in the text were not reproduced within the book. These are mentioned as "Annex" documents, for example, in the Operation Neptune plan. There are no illustrations or index. There is a general table of contents that lists each plan by name. Students of World War II will find in this volume a fascinating chronology of the development of U.S. war strategy during the period 1938-1945.—**Ralph Lee Scott**

NAVY

Chronology

C, P
234.   Sweetman, Jack. **American Naval History: An Illustrated Chronology of the U.S. Navy and Marine Corps, 1775-Present.** 3d ed. Annapolis, Md., Naval Institute Press, 2002. 386p. illus. maps. index. $55.00; $38.95pa. ISBN 1-55750-867-4; 1-55750-430-Xpa.

Chronologies are challenging resources: they are seldom a practical introduction to a subject because they co-mingle multiple unrelated events and make it difficult to follow the development of a specific event. They are not useful to the expert who already knows the background because they rarely address the subject with suffi-cient specificity. In this case, the subject seems too broad to be presented in a chronological outline of this length. The author (formerly of the U.S. Naval Academy) addresses this concern in the preface, explaining how he selected entries, and identifying his intent to "highlight the stages of development" of various events, but it is still difficult to see how one would use the volume effectively.

Longer entries are fascinating, but readers will miss related entries on certain events. The long entry on the suspicious explosion of a turret on the battleship *Iowa* in 1989 provides valuable overview and detail, but one must go to the index and follow subsequent entries before determining that no further entries explain the conclu-sion of later investigations. Skipping from entry to entry, however, certainly does make for interesting reading.

The black-and-white photographs and illustrations are relevant and remarkable. Four indexes provide access to ship names, dates, and general subjects. This is the 3d edition of this chronology (1st ed., 1984; 2d ed., 1991), and coverage begins with the start of the American Revolution and lasts through February 2002, including extensive coverage of the aftermath of September 11, 2001. The volume may find use in academic and public libraries, particularly those that do not own the first two editions.—**Peter H. McCracken**

Dictionaries and Encyclopedias

C, P

235.   **Naval Warfare: An International Encyclopedia.** Spencer C. Tucker, ed., and others. Santa Barbara, Calif., ABC-CLIO, 2002. 3v. illus. maps. index. $295.00/set. ISBN 1-57607-219-3.

This three-volume set is a welcome addition to reference resources in naval and maritime history. As an introduction to many aspects of naval history, it provides an excellent starting point for students and browsers alike. The contents reflect the centrality of World Wars I and II to naval history. Although European and American events or individuals between 1800 and 1950 dominate the text, a wide range of naval history and naval subjects is covered. The volume includes many standard biographies of individuals and of ships, but also has entries on strategy, naval policy, and even a recipe or two (see Burgoo, a sailor's porridge). Every entry contains *see also* and bibliographic references. Entries are written by experts from around the globe, and the editorial board includes some of the most prominent maritime historians in the United States, Canada, and Europe.

Each volume begins with a set of relevant area maps, and instructive battle maps and appropriate illustrations dot the remaining text. A comprehensive review essay on naval history opens the text; it concludes with a lengthy bibliography and an extensive index. Anthony Bruce's single-volume *Encyclopedia of Naval History* (see ARBA 99, entry 639) is much briefer; however, few entries in Bruce do not appear in this title. Entries here are more numerous and more comprehensive, and this title covers the entire range of known maritime history, while Bruce covers the sixteenth century forward. This will be an excellent addition to all reference collections that can afford it.—**Peter H. McCracken**

P

236.   Sasser, Charles W. **Encyclopedia of the Navy SEALS.** New York, Facts on File, 2002. 270p. illus. index. (Facts on File Library of American History). $60.00. ISBN 0-8160-4569-0.

The Bay of Pigs fiasco in Cuba prompted President Kennedy to call for an increase in Special Forces and unconventional warfare units; this served as the spark for the SEALS organization. The U.S. Navy SEALS is a small unit commando force employed in various military operations. Activities include infiltration into enemy territory for purposes of reconnaissance, intelligence gathering, sabotage, rescue of persons, and occasionally kidnapping and assassination. The name is an acronym comprising portions of the words Sea, Air, and Land; the elements in which the force operates. This is a highly professional force whose rigorous basic training eliminates a high percentage of aspirants. Antecedents include divers, frogmen, and underwater demolition teams. The book's preliminaries include acknowledgements and an introduction. The main portion of the text consists of 249 pages of entries ranging from a two-line paragraph to a four-page entry devoted to the SEALS basic training regime. Numerous anecdotal biographical profiles of persons important in SEALS history are included, such as Roy Boehm, Rudy Boesch, Jack Macione, and others. Current Minnesota governor Jesse Ventura was a SEAL and he rates a few lines in the book. There is a two-page, double-column selected bibliography and an index. Charles W. Sasser, the author, served in the U.S. Army Special Forces as a Green Beret for 13 years. He was a combat news correspondent in Vietnam and Central America. He retired from the military after 29 years of service in both the Army and the Navy. He is the author of numerous articles and of the books *Raider* (2002) and *First Seal* (1998), co-authored with Roy Boehm.—**Frank J. Anderson**

WEAPONS AND EQUIPMENT

C, P

237.   **Carrier Aviation Air Power Directory: The World's Carriers and Their Aircraft: 1950-Present.**
Norwalk, Conn., AIRtime Publishing; distr., Stillwater, Minn., Voyageur Press, 2002. 196p. illus. index. $24.95.
ISBN 1-880588-43-9.

Heightened worldwide tensions over terrorism have led national policy-makers to re-examine the world's military balance, an environment dominated by American forces and American industries. No aspect of a nation's military readiness is more important than aircraft carriers, both in number and available carrier aircraft. This reasonably priced and lavishly illustrated reference book provides an excellent overview of world carrier strength, again clearly dominated by the United States. In 14 uneven chapters, the volume covers all aircraft carriers that have been in service for the past 50 years, providing historical, technical, and military details for both ships and individual aircraft. The uneven coverage stems from the fact that 75 pages are devoted to the United States and 35 to Great Britain. Entries for the other 12 nations that employ aircraft carriers are necessarily much briefer—these countries do not have the strong naval air tradition of the United States and United Kingdom. Similar in many ways to Jane's massive military library with titles such as *Jane's Fighting Ships* (see ARBA 97, entry 573) and *Jane's All the World's Aircraft* (see ARBA 99, entry 1575), the volume does include technical references on size, speed, and armaments on both carriers and airplanes. Libraries that own volumes by Jane's Information Group may elect to pass on this selection, but it is ideal for smaller collections that cannot afford the luxury of being a Jane's subscriber.—**Boyd Childress**

C, P, S

238.   Diehl, Sarah J., and James Clay Moltz. **Nuclear Weapons and Nonproliferation: A Reference Handbook.**
Santa Barbara, Calif., ABC-CLIO, 2002. 375p. index. (Contemporary World Issues). $45.00. ISBN 1-57607-361-0.

With the media's focus upon the inspection of Iraqi sites for weapons of mass destruction and North Korea's admission about its ongoing nuclear testing, this excellent up-to-date text should be at the forefront of collection choices. Meticulously organized, this volume is divided into seven sections: "History of Nuclear Weapons and Nonproliferation"; "Issues and Controversies"; "Chronology" (which shows the development of nuclear weapons from 1939 through May 2002); "People and Events"; "Facts and Documents"; "Organizations, Associations, and Governmental Agencies"; and "Selected Print and Nonprint Resources." Each section addresses significant questions, issues, and events and either includes or ends with references and further readings. Among the most chilling documents even today are "The U.S. Military Order to Drop the Atomic Bomb on Japan" and "Some Examples of Radiation Experimentation on Humans." The volume concludes with a glossary of terms and acronyms and a thorough index. Sturdily bound, attractively designed and formatted, and reasonably priced, this text should be a high-priority purchase for high school, academic, and many special libraries.—**Charles R. Andrews**

13 Political Science

GENERAL WORKS

Biography

C

239. **American Political Scientists: A Dictionary.** 2d ed. Glenn H. Utter and Charles Lockhart, eds. Westport, Conn., Greenwood Press, 2002. 516p. index. $99.95. ISBN 0-313-31957-X.

This dictionary provides 2- to 3-page signed articles on 193 major American political scientists, including short bibliographies of their works and, in some cases, of works about them. Scholars were considered to be American if they spent a "substantial portion of their active professional life" in the United States. The editors have not changed the format or approach of the 1993 edition (see ARBA 95, entry 705), but 22 names have been added and 110 of the original 171 articles have been revised. As the preface and forewords to both editions emphasize, the dictionary is intended to describe the contribution of these scholars to the development of political science as a discipline. Thus the articles, consistently well written, emphasize their academic work and in some cases their involvement in practical politics and international affairs. The editors describe the process by which the names were selected for inclusion, beginning with reputation studies and the review of leading journals, and ending with evaluations by former APSA presidents. It is surprising that our political scientists selected were omitted at their own request according to the foreword, since users of the handbook might expect the editors to make these decisions. A list of names by degree-granting institution, a list by subfields of the disciplines, a selected bibliography of sources relating to the discipline, and an index complete the volume. A search using the subject heading "political scientists" will call up resources like *The Routledge Dictionary of Twentieth-Century Political Thinkers* (2d ed.; see ARBA 99, entry 655) and *The A-Z Guide to Modern Social and Political Theorists* (Prentice Hall, 1997). These works, however, are international in scope and concentrate on political theorists rather than academic professionals, so there is only minimal overlap. There is still no other reference work that duplicates the emphasis on professional academic political science provided here, and it is recommended for university libraries where there is an interest.—**V. W. Hill**

C

240. **Who's Who in International Affairs 2003.** 3d ed. Florence, Ky., Europa Publications/Taylor & Francis Group, 2002. 690p. index. $460.00. ISBN 1-85743-156-1. ISSN 0956-7984.

This 3d edition of *Who's Who in International Affairs* provides biographical information on 5,500 people influential in the world of international politics. This reflects a drop in the number of entries in the 2d edition, which provided biographies on more than 7,000 people (2d ed.; see ARBA 99, entry 652). Along with those influential in politics, there are prominent figures in the areas of diplomacy, law, religion, and cultural affairs throughout the world. A handful of writers, journalists, and academics that are influential in foreign policy are also included (e.g., CNN reporter Christine Amanpour). Information provided includes name, birth date, educational and career highlights, publications, and contact information (telephone, address, and e-mail address). Information is gathered by the use of questionnaires and supplementary research from Europa editors. Users can access names by using the index by organization or the index by nationality found at the end of the volume. This work will be useful in university library collections.—**Shannon Graff Hysell**

C

241.   **Worldmark Encyclopedia of the Nations World Leaders 2002.** Susan Bevan Gall, ed. Farmington Hills, Mich., Gale, 2002. 657p. illus. maps. index. $85.00. ISBN 0-7876-6610-6. ISSN 1540-2533.

This book was once issued as volume 6 of the *Worldmark Encyclopedia of the Nations* (10th ed.; see ARBA 2002, entry 85). A total of 193 countries are considered, with roughly 25 percent needing to be updated since the last issuance. Entries are alphabetical by country name, with a photograph of the country leader along with sections on the political and personal background, rise to power, leadership, domestic and foreign policy, and also including a mailing address for each head of government (heads of state are excluded where such a distinction exists). The photographs are black and white and not consistent in style. Photographs for Khatami of Iran and Hussein of Iraq show broadly smiling images, whereas for Blair of the United Kingdom the image is quite the opposite—glum, unsmiling, and tense. There is not a worldwide shortage of photographs of Blair smiling; therefore, the editors should make a choice—either all straight face or all smiling, but not a strange blend of both.

Each entry includes references, ranging from 6 to 22 entries (typically nearer the 6 mark). The intended audience for the volume would seem to be lower-level undergraduates in need of quick background information. The level of depth provided is very rudimentary. Although no other volume combines quite the same approach, there are many other books and sets that have addressed many of the topics covered by the *Nations World Leaders* volume. One element that this book has in its favor is that it is being kept current. The 1999 *Biographical Encyclopedia of 20th-Century World Leaders* (see ARBA 2001, entry 705) is an example of an earlier similar work, with many more black-and-white photographs and which focuses on the lives of the leaders rather than their political positions.

Purchased separately, this volume will add a dimension to the reference collection not easily found in any other single work. There are many resources that contain elements from the book, but no single direct competitor is currently available. Similar in concept, but far smaller in scope, is *Whitaker's Almanack World Heads of Government* (see ARBA 99, entry 651) along with the companion volume *Whitaker's Almanack World Heads of State* (see ARBA 99, entry 650). The *Worldmark* volume is recommended as a quick ready-reference source for students in the first two years of their college careers (including community colleges).—**Graham R. Walden**

Dictionaries and Encyclopedias

C, P

242.   Kurian, George. **Dictionary of World Politics.** Washington, D.C., CQ Press, 2002. 391p. maps. $75.00. ISBN 1-56802-561-0.

More than 2,000 entries are organized in alphabetic order, followed by maps and a bibliography, in this dictionary. Entries cover a wide range of fields: institutions, concepts, ideologies, events, parliamentary procedures, elections, political parties, diplomacy and international relations, territorial divisions, significant places, and biographies. Some terms created during the last decade are included, such as *cabal, cadi,* and *dzong.* Because of its conciseness in format, many other terms are not included, such as international criminal court, United Nations War Crimes Commission, and specialized agencies of the United Nations, of which quite a few do not appear. Nuremberg defense is listed, but no entry of the Nuremberg trial is present. Neither is there an entry of the Tokyo trial.

Republic of China in the entry of "Taiwan" is the official title of its government, not Republic of China *on Taiwan.* In Taiwan, not all functions of the Control Branch (Yuan) are wielded in the Legislative Branch. The government has five branches, namely executive, legislative, judicial, control, and examination. Accordingly, in the entry of "yuan," these should be properly noted. It is hard to make a selection of who should be included. Some prominent political scientists, including Arnold Brecht and Hans Morgenthau, should be given a place. Entries are concise, but, in general, well defined and presented. It is a worthwhile reference book.—**Tze-chung Li**

C

243.   **The Oxford Companion to Politics of the World.** 2d ed. Joel Krieger and others, eds. New York, Oxford University Press, 2001. 1018p. index. $60.00. ISBN 0-19-511739-5.

The 1st edition of *The Oxford Companion to Politics of the World* appeared in 1993 (see ARBA 94, entry 717) to generally favorable reviews. As the editor, Krieger notes that much has changed in the world since the early 1990s and a new edition is much welcomed. Indeed, much in the world has changed, even since the 2d edition went to press. The work consequently contains little on many individuals and entities of central interest in today's world, such as Al Qaeda and the Taliban. Even Hamas lacks its own entry. The work is equipped with an indispensably useful index, where Hamas and the Taliban, but not Al Qaeda, can be found. Useful bibliographies append most of the entries.

This formidable, single-volume work contains 672 articles, written by more than 500 contributors, primarily academics but also a number of practitioners (policy analysts, politicians, and the like). The *Companion* strives to be international in its scope (its contributors come from 40 different countries and each entry is signed), but, perhaps inevitably, it tends to be oriented toward the United States. In addition, the *Companion* includes 23 extended interpretive essays that deal with larger themes, such as democracy, globalization, and modernity. A new feature of the 2d edition is 6 pairs of essays on various critical themes, such as the future of entitlements and sustainable development.

The 2d edition claims that most of the articles from the 1st edition have been revised, but this is clearly not always the case. For instance, no items listed in the bibliography for the entry "Holocaust" are more recent than 1989, despite the large number of important works on the topic that have appeared over the last decade. Similarly, the entry for "Information Society," remarkably, fails to address the 1990s and its most current bibliographic reference dates to 1990. To be fair, many of the essays in the *Companion* have been revised and many of the bibliographies updated.

Some will detect a liberal bent in the *Companion*, despite the claim made on the dust jacket that "varying viewpoints" were deliberately sought out. These varying viewpoints are most clearly in evidence in the six pairs of essays on critical themes. But it is at least coincidental that liberal figures from the past such as Gramcsi, Trotsky, and Hugo Grotius are granted their own entries, while conservative thinkers who arguably have had a more direct impact on recent politics, such as Milton Friedman, Friedrich Hayek, and Ayn Rand, are to be found only in the index and receive only brief mentions in the text.

In spite of, or perhaps because of, these qualities, the *Companion* is generally a good read, very suitable for dipping. But it should be emphasized that the work is self-consciously not an encyclopedia—it is not the best place to go for actual facts. Yet, basic factual information is readily available elsewhere anyway. For brief interpretive essays and analysis on issues of topical importance, the 2d edition of the *Companion* is nearly as important as its predecessor.—**David A. Timko**

C, P

244.   **Political Parties of the World.** 5th ed. Alan J. Day, ed. London, John Harper; distr., Farmington Hills, Mich., Gale, 2002. 604p. index. $180.00. ISBN 0-9536278-7-X.

Any given reference publication of merit will routinely go through several editions whether needed or not. Perpetuation seems to be the theme, so something like *Rock Formations of the World* will undergo multiple revisions despite the fact that igneous and sedimentary really do not change much. This factor is not so with *Political Parties of the World*. When first published nearly a quarter of a century ago, the Soviet Union was a major powerhouse and African countries could be memorized by any seven year old. Today, Russia is fragmented into independent states, while Africa has had fitful attempts at democracy. It is a new world, although perhaps less brave now than then.

The more than 500 entries in this edition not only give readers a sense of the breadth and depth of factions ubiquitously arranged over the globe, but also provide insight as to why easy solutions to political problems will either never hold, or are never attempted. Illegal, guerilla, and terrorist groups are not included, but do appear in a companion volume, *Revolutionary and Dissident Movements* (out of print).

Within each country, political parties are alphabetically listed, typically by the party's English-language version. Under each entry, users will find the party's leadership and a brief history (100-250 words) of that movement. Related parties are listed and cross-references are included. If a Website is maintained its address is provided. After each country, a short historical description is given with minimum statistics (e.g., capital, population). This work is a must-purchase for all but the smallest of collections.—**Mark Y. Herring**

Directories

C, P

245.   **Government Information on the Internet.** 5th ed. Peggy Garvin, ed. Lanham, Md., Bernan Associates, 2002. 990p. index. $75.00pa. ISBN 0-89059-587-9. ISSN 1529-594X.

This newly updated and expanded volume adds to the Bernan Associates series established in 1998 and accompanies the first online edition, which will be launched this year. The editor believes the print edition still offers a service value as well as a historical snapshot of the online government resources. The directory provides access by subject and agency to more than 4,500 government Internet resources. Although the work's primary focus is on the U.S. federal government, there is a chapter on state and local government and another on major foreign governments.

The work is organized under broad chapters (e.g., "Education," "Congress") that are alphabetically arranged. Each chapter briefly introduces the topic and gives a few featured sites. These featured sites are identified as the best starting points for research on the topic. The remaining sites are organized under general subheadings. Each of these site entries is short but includes detailed evaluative information. The entries include alternate URLs, sponsoring agency, and lists online full-text publications. The volume also includes many unique indexes (e.g., URL index, SuDoc Number) and a general master index of subjects, sponsors, and publication titles.

While many libraries may prefer to purchase the online version for the same price, in either format this work provides comprehensive access to a growing body of resources. While there are many Web source books, this one provides unmatched comprehensive access to U.S. government resources. It belongs in all libraries.

—**Paolina Taglienti**

POLITICS AND GOVERNMENT

United States

Biography

C, P

246.   Kane, Joseph Nathan, Janet Podell, and Steven Anzovin. **Facts About the Presidents: A Compilation of Biographical and Historical Information.** 7th ed. Bronx, N.Y., H. W. Wilson, 2001. 721p. index. $95.00. ISBN 0-8242-1007-7.

The 7th edition of *Facts About the Presidents: A Compilation of Biographical and Historical Information* has been updated to include information up to June 2001. The book is divided into two parts. Part 1 includes chronologically listed biographical data on each president. Part 2 lists comparative data. Each presidential biography includes a black-and-white portrait; family information; a biographical sketch of the president's wife; a list of important dates in the president's life; election facts; inauguration particulars; details on the vice president, cabinet, Congress, and the Supreme Court; and key dates in the presidency. Each entry ends with a selection of anecdotes about the president in question. Comparative data in part 2 are divided into two subsections—one relating to the life of the president as an individual, the other to the presidency as an institution. Personal presidential information includes sections on family history, education and career, residences, age and physical characteristics upon taking office, death and burial, commemoratives, and general statistics. Information on the presidency includes entries on elections, conventions, candidates, election returns, inaugural facts, miscellaneous executive office details, and an overview of the presidents and their vice presidents. While this work is not a scholarly source, it should answer the majority of questions an average user might pose. The information provided is a nice mixture of the arcane and the essential, presented in a well-organized way. Suggestions for further reading are provided, although there is not a comprehensive bibliography listed at the end of the text.—**Philip G. Swan**

C

247.   **The Presidents: A Reference History.** 3d ed. Henry F. Graff, ed. New York, Charles Scribner's Sons/Gale Group, 2002. 817p. illus. index. $130.00. ISBN 0-684-31226-3.

In this informative and easy-to-use reference each of the American presidents is individually profiled, with information on their campaigns, foreign and domestic issues, and a bibliography. This title also includes essays on the history of the presidency, on the history of the White House and on First Ladies, and a detailed index. The instructive appendixes include a general bibliography on the presidency, a table of presidential data, and a profile of the Executive Office. The table is especially useful as it provides a quick overview of each president, their elections and appointments, and key events. Students and scholars alike will find this resource useful in conducting research on the American presidents.—**Denise A. Garofalo**

C, P, S

248.   Wilson, Richard L. **American Political Leaders.** New York, Facts on File, 2002. 444p. illus. index. (American Biographies). $65.00. ISBN 0-8160-4536-4.

This collection of more than 250 biographies of American political leaders covers men and women who were elected or appointed to office or have, in some other way, exerted considerable influence in American history. Those chosen for inclusion in this book are frequently mentioned in high school or college textbooks or appear prominently in the news. Biographies range in length from two-thirds of a page to four pages and each entry is accompanied by a short bibliography. Entries are arranged alphabetically. Listings by offices held or sought and by date of birth are included. The index has references to offices, places, political parties, historical events, and cross-references among the entries. The book has a bibliography of other collective biographies and about 60 well-selected photographs.

The aim of the book, to include biographies of prominent individuals in American politics, is achieved. The entries are more substantial than those found in other one-volume collections. The scope differs from most similar collections, which limit their selections by race, gender, or holders of particular offices. The writing style is accessible to the intended audience and the content of the entries would meet the needs of readers seeking more information on the accomplishments and importance of the subject in American politics. As a one-volume collection of biographies, this book is an excellent addition to collections serving general readers, high schools, and undergraduates.—**Jeanne D. Galvin**

Dictionaries and Encyclopedias

S

249.   **Scholastic Encyclopedia of the Presidents and Their Times.** updated ed. By David Rubel. New York, Scholastic, 2001. 232p. illus. maps. index. $18.95. ISBN 0-590-49366-3.

Rubel's *Scholastic Encyclopedia of the Presidents and Their Times* is truly an inexpensive resource for elementary school students. It provides concise information in an easy-to-read format where young readers will enjoy learning about the accomplishments and disappointments of each president, from George Washington to George W. Bush.

Little-known facts are what make this *Encyclopedia* different and interesting. Such as the fact that Herbert Hoover was the first president to have an asteroid named for him, or that Calvin Coolidge had an electric horse installed in his White House bedroom.

Each entry in the *Encyclopedia* includes the president's birth date and place, date of death, party, vice president, family member names, and nickname. Throughout the book certain words are highlighted in red, indicating that the subject is discussed in greater detail in another section of the book. Using the subject index at the end of the book, the reader can then find the page for the most detailed explanations of an entry. Black-and-white photographs of events and people, political cartoons, and artifacts reflecting the period in history as well as maps detailing the growth of the country can be found throughout the book. Rubel's *Encyclopedia* is recommended for the children's section of public libraries and elementary school media centers.—**Vang Vang**

Directories

P

250.   **Congressional Yellow Book: Who's Who in Congress, Including Committees and Key Staff.** Spring 2002 ed. New York, Leadership Directories, 2002. 1315p. index. $342.00pa. (automatic renewal subscription); $360.00pa. (annual subscription). ISSN 0191-1422.

Herein is everything readers always wanted to know about Congress, but just could not bring themselves to ask. The section, "Action on the Hill," a phrase that during certain recent administrations might have caused some to gasp, outline all sorts of new information. It highlights changes that have occurred since the previous edition. These changes range from new members elected in special elections to deaths of congresspersons, changes in committees, resignations, and the upcoming schedule.

As for the bulk of the *Yellow Book*, after its plethora of useful numbers, users will find each entry with the following information: member's name, contact information, photograph, key aides, committee assignments, organizations and state and district offices, and more. Subject, staff, and organization indexes allow access in other ways beyond the obvious. It is hard to imagine a more comprehensive guide to those who lead us by representation. Surely, this government is a government by the people, and such books as this one helpfully remind us of this central, enduring, and, we hope, eternal truth.—**Mark Y. Herring**

P

251.   **Federal Yellow Book: Who's Who in Federal Departments and Agencies.** Spring 2002 ed. New York, Leadership Directories, 2002. 1v. (various paging). index. $342.00pa. (automatic renewal subscription); $360.00pa. (annual subscription). ISSN 0145-6202.

This handy resource, which lists over 39,000 top people along with their titles, addresses, telephone numbers, and related information within the executive branch of the federal government, is 1 of 14 helpful directories available from the publisher. An annual subscription to all 14 directories includes a 5-user license for the Internet and quarterly releases on CD-ROM. While information found in this publication is available from any number of areas, including other reference works and online resources, the value of this reference guide is its comprehensive inclusion of information in a single volume about key people in the executive branch along with its quarterly updates.

Consisting of well over 1,100 pages, the guide is broken down into 4 major sections covering the executive offices of the president and vice president, the executive departments, the independent agencies (which comprise the bulk of this work), and the indexes (which are broken down by subject, organization, and individual names). Several of the valuable features of this publication include "Federal Update" and "User's Guide" sections, which precede the main text. The update outlines new information since the last publication, includes new agency appointees, new offices and commissions added, new senate confirmations, nominations requiring senate confirmations, individuals intended for nomination, presidential appointments, and individuals appointed during congressional recess.

While the cost of the *Federal Yellow Book* is expensive compared to other directories, it remains a valuable compendium of information. As such, public, academic, government, and specialized (e.g., law, corporate) librarians with frequent reference questions requiring contact information in the federal government should be well served by acquiring this work. Librarians might well consider looking into acquiring one or more of the other related 13 companion volumes that quickly provide desired information in a one-stop, convenient resource.

—**James M. Murray**

P

252.   **Government Phone Book USA, 2003.** 11th ed. Detroit, Omnigraphics, 2003. 2v. index. $255.00/set. ISBN 0-7808-0620-4. ISSN 1062-1466.

Seeing a print directory in the era of the World Wide Web usually prompts an automatic reaction of asking why? Why pay so much? Why work with rapidly dated material? However, the vast coverage—federal, state, county, and municipal—of this directory and its easy-to-follow format affirmatively answers these questions. The more than 270,000 listings provide direct telephone and fax numbers as well as postal, e-mail, and Internet addresses. As with earlier editions (10th ed.; see ARBA 2002, entry 732), this expanded 2-volume set is hierarchically arranged. Sections on the federal government are followed by the state, county, and municipal sections. Of great benefit to the user is the inclusion of quick reference listings before the main sections, the state organizational charts, and the variety of useful maps. The detailed state and federal keyword indexes make it all easy to find. Despite the availability of much of this information on the Web, this work is valuable for its easy-to-use, convenient format and the extras it provides.—**Shawn W. Nicholson**

C, P

253.   **The Public Record Research System (PRRS). http://www.publicrecordsources.com.** [Website]. Tempe, Ariz., BRB. $119.00/yr; $39.00/quarterly. Date reviewed: Aug 02.

The *Public Record Research System* (PRRS) from BRB provides all of the information available in *The Sourcebook to Public Record Information* (3d ed.; see ARBA 2002, entry 736) and much more. This source gives information on more than 8,600 state agencies and occupational licensing locations; more than 6,900 courts containing civil, criminal, and probate records; some 500 U.S. District and Bankruptcy courts and 14 Federal Research Centers; and more than 4,265 county agencies. The database gives users the opportunity to search by state, county, or place-name and then they can narrow their search by selecting the specific state agency, state licenses, or federal record center they need. Information for each location includes: address, telephone and fax numbers, Web address, hours of operation, and the chance to print the page or give feedback to the publisher. For the federal records centers it also provides information on indexing and case record information and how to conduct a search by telephone, mail, or in person as well as methods of payment and payment amounts.

Unlike *The Sourcebook to Public Record Information* this work also provides information on more than 4,000 accredited colleges and universities and 2,000 trade schools nationwide. It provides contact information for the offices of records and registration (address, telephone and fax numbers, and Web address), their hours of operation, general information on degrees granted and alumni centers, and information on how to order transcripts (including cost).

The information on this Website can also be found on a semi-annually updated CD-ROM for the same price (see ARBA 2000, entry 624, for a review of the CD-ROM version). At only $119 a year this work is a real bargain considering all of the directory information user's will have access to. It should be considered by both public and research libraries.—**Shannon Graff Hysell**

P

254.   **State Information Directory 2002-2003.** Washington, D.C., CQ Press/Congressional Quarterly, 2002. 641p. index. $100.00. ISBN 1-56802-761-3.

Congressional Quarterly's *State Information Directory* first appeared in 2000, nominally covering the years 2000-2001. The directory seeks to provide basic information on important individuals and agencies in all 50 states and the District of Columbia. Of course, the type of information contained in such a directory quickly becomes dated, and so there is frequent need for a new edition.

The *Directory* includes names and contact information on most major office holders in the states and in the executive, legislative, and judicial branches. Only legislative leaders, such as Speaker of the House, are included. Party affiliations of the listed individuals are noted where applicable. The directory includes both a name index and a "functional" index. The latter is particularly useful, as it allows the user to find a list of all states that have, for instance, a civil rights division. The *Directory* does not contain information on state courts, aside from the state supreme court. Nor does it provide any guidance on local government.

Most of the information contained in the directory is, by definition, public access, and should be available free online. Further, the directly contains only basic contact information—URL, telephone number, mailing and/or street address, and sometimes e-mail address. For more detailed information, the user will have to go to the Web address of the various agencies. The work also provides a hodgepodge of fast facts, such as population figures and an overview of key laws and regulations (such as whether the state has the death penalty). Oddly, not all not the data are the most recent available, specifically population data—1998 estimates are used rather than the more precise results of Census 2000. The *Directory* consists almost exclusively of facts and data; it contains virtually no text, unlike many other Congressional Quarterly publications.

In spite of, or perhaps because of, these limitations, the directory remains a useful compilation for many public, research, and special libraries. There is still something to be said for the utility of pulling all the disparate material on state governments together and making it available in one convenient source. Moreover, the price and relative compactness of the *Directory* compare favorably with one of its most prominent competitors, Omnigraphics' bulky *Government Phone Book USA* (11th ed.; see entry 252).—**David A. Timko**

Handbooks and Yearbooks

C

255.   **Congressional Quarterly's Guide to U.S. Elections.** 4th ed. John L. Moore, Jon P. Preimesberger, and David R. Tarr, eds. Washington, D.C., Congressional Quarterly, 2001. 2v. illus. maps. index. $295.00/set. ISBN 1-56802-603-X.

The appearance of a new edition of *Congressional Quarterly's Guide to U.S. Elections* is a publishing event. The 4th edition will immediately become an indispensable resource for students, scholars, and everyone else interested in the history of electoral politics in the United States. This edition includes a total of more than 1,800 pages in 2 volumes, which represents an increase of well over 200 pages over the 1-volume 3d edition (see ARBA 95, entry 733).

As with former editions, the *Guide* provides electoral data not only for congressional and presidential elections, but also for state gubernatorial elections. One of its many strengths is that it contains electoral results not only from general elections, but also from primaries for presidential, gubernatorial, and senatorial (but not house) races, data that are notoriously difficult to find elsewhere.

The 4th edition updates the previous edition of the *Guide* by including all election returns from 1994 through 2000. It also contains new essays on such topics as electoral campaign financing and the evolution of American elections, which mainly details the electoral fortunes of the Democratic and Republican parties since the era of Franklin Delano Roosevelt. Another chapter entitled "Politics and Issues, 1945-2000" provides a useful, objective synopsis of the course of national politics since World War II.

A particularly helpful feature of the *Guide* is that in most instances the source(s) of the electoral data quoted is given. As was the case with previous editions, sources include the Republican National Committee, the Democratic National Committee, and the Inter-University Consortium for Political and Social Research, and many others. Bibliographies and several very useful indexes (including separate listings of all House, Senate, and gubernatorial candidates) are also included.—**David A. Timko**

C, P

256.   **Presidential Elections, 1789-2000.** Washington, D.C., CQ Press, 2002. 250p. illus. index. $39.95pa. ISBN 1-56802-790-7.

Building on their previous work, Congressional Quarterly offers up-to-date presidential election statistics and analysis. As with earlier reviews (see ARBA 99, entry 682), it is difficult to find areas of presidential elections that are not covered by this book. The highly readable and accessible chronology of presidential elections and the series of analytical articles on topics such as "primaries" and "electoral college" are illuminated with wonderful tables, maps, and figures. Much welcomed is the presentation of vote totals for little-known minor candidates, sometimes even to the fourth candidate. All of the information becomes readily available through the detailed index.

Presidential Elections does not have the corner on the market, as other sources offer very reliable, accessible, and comparable information. Two examples of sources that researchers should also consult are *The Routledge Historical Atlas of Presidential Elections* (see ARBA 2002, entry 750) and the National Archives and Records Administration's Electoral College World Wide Web page located at http://www.archives.gov/federal_register /electoral_college/electoral_college.html. However, *Presidential Elections'* smart analysis and convenient one-volume layout makes it a valuable resource for any level of reader.—**Shawn W. Nicholson**

C, P

257.   **The Tools of Government: A Guide to the New Governance.** Lester M. Salamon, ed. New York, Oxford University Press, 2002. 669p. index. $45.00. ISBN 0-19-513665-9.

The provision of government services has become an increasingly complex activity, both in the United States as well as in the rest of the developed world. The traditional, centralized, bureaucratic state is increasingly an anachronism. Various "third party" agencies, including nonprofits as well as for-profit companies, routinely carry out activities once reserved for the government. The challenge now lies, notes the editor, not so much in reinventing government, but rather in managing a government that has already been reinvented. The editor calls this new paradigm the "new governance," where the emphasis has shifted from the actual program or agency to the tools or techniques used to carry out the program (pp. 8-9).

The work is divided into 22 chapters, each a separate essay on a different "tool" of governance, written by a total of 22 different contributors, in addition to the editor. Representative topics, or tools, covered include vouchers, contracting, regulation, taxes, tort liability, and governmental loans. Most of the essays are written primarily with the federal government in mind, but their implications will be relevant to all levels of government. Each essay is notable for its sober, non-ideological description and analysis. Each contributor duly notes the pros and cons of the application of the "tool" in question, and suggests some possible future directions that the use of this tool might take. The contributors themselves include an impressive list of academics and other public policy experts.

Extensive notes, along with suggested reading lists, accompany each chapter. A detailed bibliography and useful index are also included. In short, *Tools of Government* should quickly become an indispensable resource for all those involved in public administration. No one can afford to neglect this unique work.—**David A. Timko**

C, S

258.   Watson, Cynthia A. **U.S. National Security: A Reference Handbook.** Santa Barbara, Calif., ABC-CLIO, 2002. 357p. index. (Contemporary World Issues). $45.00. ISBN 1-57607-598-2.

National security has received considerable attention in the United States since the September 11, 2001 terrorist attacks and that attention has been augmented by the war against terrorism in Afghanistan and the potential prospect of additional conflict against Iraq. *U.S. National Security: A Reference Handbook*, part of ABC-CLIO's Contemporary World Issues series, is an introductory guide to researching this subject.

Its author, a National War College professor, begins this work with an introduction that includes a definition of national security and how the United States has viewed national security threats from the Cold War to the present. A second chapter briefly reviews past and contemporary U.S. national security policy controversies, such as whether the United States lost China to Communism in 1949, whether antiwar protests restrict U.S. military options in Vietnam, whether China threatens U.S. national security, and how the United States should combat terrorism.

Additional chapters provide a chronology of U.S. national security policy events and actions from 1945 to the present and provide succinct biographical portraits of relevant U.S. and foreign national security policymakers, such as Leonid Brezhnev, George W. Bush, Deng Xiaoping, Saddam Hussein, Henry Kissinger, and Ariel Sharon.

The heart of this work are descriptions of important U.S. national security policy documents with listings of Websites where these resources can be located and the full text of some of these documents. Examples of these documentary resources include Winston Churchill's Iron Curtain speech, the Gulf of Tonkin Resolution, the Shanghai Communique, the Taiwan Relations Act, the 1996 Comprehensive Test Ban Treaty, and President George W. Bush's September 20, 2001 speech to Congress concerning the war on terrorism.

Subsequent chapters describe nongovernmental and government organizations engaged in national security policy research and list the Websites for these entities, which include the International Institute for the Strategic Studies, National Security Archive, Asia Pacific Center for Security Studies, and National Defense University. A final chapter lists and annotates books, journal articles, videos, DVDs, and media organizations covering U.S. national security policy issues.

Watson has produced a helpful introduction to this multifaceted and interdisciplinary subject that should facilitate academic research on national security. There are, regrettably, some errors that could have been caught with more rigorous editing. Former President Clinton's birth date is listed as 1945 instead of 1946 (p. 93), the Institute for National Strategic Studies *Strategic Fora* publication series should be listed as *Strategic Forum* (p. 269), the Bureau of Export Administration is now the Bureau of Industry and Security (p. 279), and the University of Texas-Austin library Website mentioned on page 320 should refer to the University of Texas-El Paso library as being this site's host. These errors do not detract from the high substantive quality of this work and the value it will have for students and other researchers.—**Bert Chapman**

Asian

C

259.   Leifer, Michael. **Dictionary of the Modern Politics of South-East Asia.** 3d ed. New York, Routledge, 2001. 312p. index. $90.00; $29.95pa. ISBN 0-415-23875-7; 0-415-23876-5pa.

This new edition of a useful reference book on the modern politics of South-East Asia has incorporated major political events and changes that have taken place since its two previous editions published in 1995 and 1996. The term "modern" is defined to cover the period after the end of the Pacific War in August 1945.

The first part of the dictionary contains a brief introduction, which is followed by a short description of the current political situations in each of the 10 South-East Asian countries: Brunei, Myanmar (Burma), Cambodia, Indonesia, Laos, Malaysia, Philippines, Singapore, Thailand, and Vietnam. The newly independent state of East Timor is dealt with only as one of the entries in the dictionary.

The main body of the dictionary includes, in alphabetic order, individual entries about significant events, episodes, treaties, political parties and movements, biographies of key political figures, and regional organizations. Attempts were made by the author to provide helpful information, analysis, insight, and commentary on each of these entries. It is very helpful that cross-references to other related entries are given at the end of each country description as well as at the end of each of the entries. A list of "Further Reading" provides selected publications both for the region in general and for each of the countries. The index by country makes it easy for readers to locate entries by each country. Even though this concise dictionary is limited in its coverage, it is a good source for quick reference to a wide range of political topics relating to the countries of South-East Asia up to 2001.—**Hwa-Wei Lee**

European

C

260.   Bugajski, Janusz. **Political Parties of Eastern Europe: A Guide to Politics in the Post-Communist Era.** Armonk, N.Y., M. E. Sharpe, 2002. 1055p. index. $199.95. ISBN 1-56324-676-7.

The collapse of the Soviet bloc during the late 1980s and early 1990s is one of the most phenomenal historical and political developments of the twentieth century or of any century. This collapse resulted in the end of the monolithic political power wielded by the communist party in the former Soviet Union and its Eastern European satellites. The ensuing decade has witnessed a proliferation of political parties in these former totalitarian nationals as they have individually and collectively tried to shed the ossified vestiges of communist rule to develop, with varying degrees of success, more pluralistic political and governmental institutions.

Political Parties of Eastern Europe is an exhaustive and encyclopedic portrait of political party development in the following countries: Belarus, Estonia, Latvia, Lithuania, Poland, the Czech Republic, Slovakia, Hungary, Serbia, Kosova, Montenegro, Bosnia-Herzegovina, Croatia, Slovenia, Albania, Macedonia, Bulgaria, Romania, Moldova, and Ukraine. It begins with an incisive introduction describing the roles played by pluralism and democratization in the political culture of these countries since the collapse of communist rule. This introduction also contains general descriptions of the types of political parties that have emerged in these countries.

The main section of Bugajski's work provides coverage of the political parties and political situation in each of these countries. Entries begin with a national historical overview and emphasize post-communist political developments. These entries proceed to describe the political parties in these countries and include descriptions of their ideological platforms and their relative electoral success or failure. Country entries conclude with the results of recent presidential and parliamentary elections and a bibliography.

Examples of political parties profiled include Belarus' Belarusian Peasant Party, the Latvian Unity Party, the Polish National Front, the Czech Republic's Party of Democratic Socialism, the Association of Germans in Hungary, the Croatian Peasant Party, the Social Democratic Party of Slovenia, and the Albanian Agrarian Party. This exhaustive reference source concludes with a list of abbreviations of East European political party names along with personal and political party names indexes.

This is a superior reference source on Eastern European political parties since the collapse of the Soviet bloc. It provides substantive historical background on these countries and effectively emphasizes the role of regional and economic sectoral parties in shaping the contemporary political development of these countries. Having an analysis of Russian political parties would further strengthen the quality of this work as would listings of Websites these political parties may have. The author may also want to consider a similar work on political parties in other former Soviet republics such as Armenia, Azerbaijan, Kazakhstan, and Uzbekistan. Nevertheless, this will be an essential source for any students and scholar of post-Soviet Eastern European politics and belongs in the collection of any library desirous of maintaining substantive Eastern European reference collections. [R: LJ, 1 Oct 02, p. 81]—**Bert Chapman**

C, P

261.   **The European Union Handbook.** 2d ed. Jackie Gower, ed. Chicago, Fitzroy Dearborn, 2002. 449p. maps. index. $55.00. ISBN 1-57958-223-0.

While this volume contains some typical reference apparatus—statistical tables and select bibliographies—it serves primarily as an introductory text to the European Union (EU) for general readers, students, or practitioners. First published in 1996, this new edition is approximately 100 pages longer, although the basic arrangement remains the same. The *Handbook* consists of 29 essays written by British scholars; each essay contains charts, tables, a bibliography, and sometimes the text of EU documents. The essays are organized into six broad sections: "History," "Politics," "Economics & Policies," "Law & Society," "External Relations," and "The Future." The "External Relations" section is new to this edition—its seven essays deal with world trade issues; security and defense; and relations with the United States, Russia, the Mediterranean, and developing areas. Several useful ready-reference features are appended: a chronology of events, a glossary of terms and acronyms, brief biographical sketches of leading personalities, political representation in EU institutions, and a 13-page general bibliography.

The essays highlight the important changes that have occurred within the EU in the past five years: the introduction of a single currency (the euro), the adoption of the Treaties of Amsterdam and Nice dealing with intergovernmental relations, the adoption of the Charter of Fundamental Rights, decisions toward a single European military force, and the movement toward expansion. The *Handbook* will be a useful addition for most academic libraries, although it may be better suited for the general book stacks. Reference collections should include at least one of the following recent works: *Europe: A Concise Encyclopedia of the European Union from Aachen to Zollverein* (3d ed.; see ARBA 2001, entry 88), the *Encyclopedia of the European Union* (updated ed.; Lynne Rienner, 2000), or *The European Union Encyclopedia and Directory 1999* (3d ed.; see ARBA 2000, entry 94).

—**Thomas A. Karel**

Latin American

C, P

262.   **Encyclopedia of Latin American Politics.** Diana Kapiszewski and Alexander Kazan, eds. Westport, Conn., Oryx Press/Greenwood Publishing Group, 2002. 358p. illus. maps. index. $74.95. ISBN 1-57356-306-4.

Many Americans have misconceptions about Latin American politics. For example, currently all countries in Latin America have democratically elected leaders except for Cuba. Only Mexico, Guatemala, Bolivia, Cuba, and Nicaragua attempted political change by revolution in the twentieth century. In fact, our Latin American neighbors have seldom experienced international conflict in the past 100 years. This collaborative tradition is evident in the appendix that summarizes the numerous political pacts, trade groupings, and international cooperative efforts that are characteristic of the region. The editor profiles the 18 Spanish-speaking republics of Brazil, Haiti, and Puerto Rico. Each country's chapter gives demographics as to governmental structures, population, ethnic groups, religion, literacy rates, infant mortality and life expectancy averages, exchange rates, major exports and imports, Gross Domestic Product, and more. These statistical data are followed by a summary of the nation's history and political development plus entries on key leaders, treaties, and other major events with more emphasis on the twentieth century. Each section ends with a list of the heads of states and the dates they served, a bibliography specific to that country, and a list of electronic resources. It is interesting to note that spurred by the French Revolution, Haiti was the second colony in the Americas to gain independence and that Panama was a province of Colombia until 1902. Appendixes include information on multilateral agreements and wars, U.S. doctrines regarding Latin America, a glossary, and an index. This reference is useful to clarify and raise awareness of the diverse political histories of the countries that make up Latin America and who are now significant players in the global economy. [R: LJ, 15, Sept 02, p. 54]—**Adrienne Antink Bien**

Middle East

C

263.   **The Continuum Political Encyclopedia of the Middle East.** rev. ed. Avraham Sela, ed. New York, Continuum Publishing, 2002. 944p. index. $175.00. ISBN 0-8264-1413-3.

It is not often that current events and publishing intersect nicely to produce a truly remarkable volume. All too often, sound bite mentality dominates and the result is a book about September 11th on the book shelves on September 12th. This does not represent the current tome. Avraham Sela has taken the tiger by the tail and he and his two dozen contributors have tamed it to produce an outstanding reference tool. This is a revision of a volume that appeared only three years ago. But given the events of the September 11th tragedy, the revision is needed. Indeed, very little if anything appeared in the 1999 edition about Bin Laden or al-Qa'ida and the Taliban. Not so this time around.

A volume such as this has every opportunity to fail. But Sela has relied on scholars who are heavy on facts and light on opinions. Clearly, a biased view of the Middle East could erupt in a volume that serves no one and incites many. The entries vary according to the value politically to the region. Some are only a few hundred words, while others exceed 15,000. The Middle East is defined as the region that encompasses the whole of the Arab world, "from Maghreb in North Africa to the Persian Gulf" (preface). It also includes the nominally Arab state, such as Mauritania, Somalia, Eritrea, and Djibouti. Some states, such as Yemen, are treated much less fulsomely as the Palestinian Authority and Israel. Some entries, such as the one on the Arab-Israel conflict and the PLO, are small treatises to themselves.

While the volume covers all the major topics, it is also wonderfully helpful on seminal historical issues such as the Balfour Declaration, Nasserism, Greek Orthodox, FLOSY (Front for the Liberation of South Yemen), and more. Names of people, places, events, and points of pivotal or crucial concern are all included. The end papers of facts about the countries are especially helpful. One would be hard pressed to name a better, more exhaustive treatment of this subject available to day. The *Oxford Encyclopedia of the Modern Islamic World* (see ARBA 96, entry 1477) is so biased as to make it almost worthless. The *Encyclopedia of the Modern Middle East* (see ARBA 97, entry 136) is better, and although much longer (4 volumes), is already out of date. Add to this the signed entries of the present volume (Moshe Efrat, Moshe Gemer, and David Kushner, to name but a few) and the decision makes itself.—**Mark Y. Herring**

IDEOLOGIES

S

264.   **Political Theories for Students.** Matthew Miskelly and Jaime Noce, eds. Farmington Hills, Mich., Gale, 2002. 429p. illus. index. $85.00. ISBN 0-7876-5645-3.

There are 19 major political theories and systems (e.g., anarchism, capitalism, communism, pacifism, populism, utopianism) discussed in *Political Theories for Students*, a volume written by academics and journalists and targeted at high school students, undergraduate college students, and general researchers. A 2-page spread of comparison tables of the 19 theories is introduced to readers, which precedes the detailed and thorough chapter entries for each political theory or system. The comparison tables include categories such as who controls government, who controls production of goods, and historical examples. Each chapter entry includes an overview of the political system, the history of the system, who controls government, how the government is put into power, what roles the people have, who controls production of goods, who controls distribution of goods, major figures, and historical examples. Additionally, significant writings and potential study questions are included in each entry as well as biographical entries (for instance, Aristotle is featured within republicanism). Relevant and current examples of the systems are outlined in the "Theories in Action" section. Other sections included in each entry are analysis and critical response, further readings (for the most part current citations), and an informational sidebar of facts. The work also includes a glossary, a master index, a chronology, and images.—**Leslie R. Homzie**

INTERNATIONAL RELATIONS

C, P

265.   **Encyclopedia of American Foreign Policy.** 2d ed. Alexander DeConde, Richard Dean Burns, Fredrik Logevall, and Louise B. Ketz, eds. New York, Charles Scribner's Sons/Gale Group, 2002. 3v. index. $350.00/set. ISBN 0-684-80657-6.

The editors of this core reference source have understandably determined that with the changes in the world since the 1st edition in 1978 (see ARBA 80, entry 485) that a revised edition is in order. The end of the Cold War, the demise of the Soviet Union, the emergence of the European Union, NAFTA, China as a world power, and the explosion of ethnic conflicts in the Balkans and Near East are a few examples of the ways the world has changed dramatically in recent decades. In response, the new edition of the *Encyclopedia of American Foreign Policy* has been revised to include 48 new essays. The 120 essays in A-to-Z arrangement provide in-depth discussions on the principal figures, movements, events, and ideas in American diplomatic history, from the beginning of the nation to the present day. Some of the subjects covered are obvious choices—Superpower Diplomacy, Treaties, Nationalism, Cold War Origins, and so on. Others, perhaps less predictable, include such topics as African Americans, Gender, Ideology, and Religion. The essay approach provides for in-depth, interpretive coverage by scholars who are experts in their fields. This approach avoids "snippets of information" (p. xv) and the effort to provide a narrative of specific events. The emphasis is on the analysis of key concepts, themes, theories, doctrines, and the placing of events in a broad chronological and historical context. The essays average about 20 pages and end with 1 or 2 page bibliographies. The extensive index provides access to specific terms, concepts, and individuals. There is also a lengthy "Chronology of American Foreign Policy, 1607-2001," which provides the basic facts and dates some users may want from an encyclopedia. A list of contributors, mostly American historians, is provided. Since this three-volume set is scholarly but quite readable, it is suitable for a wide range of users, including faculty, students, government officials, journalists, and the general public. [R: BL, 15 May 02, p. 1628]

—**Henry E. York**

C, P

266.   **Mexico and the United States.** Tarrytown, N.Y., Marshall Cavendish, 2003. 3v. illus. maps. index. $279.95/set. ISBN 0-7614-7402-1.

The introduction to this three-volume set discusses the close relationship between these two nations that now share a 2,000 mile border, especially in the Borderlands area, those states adjacent to both sides of this border. It outlines the political and economic influences, relationships, and disparities between the two countries. The existence, according to the 2000 Census, of 20 million Mexican or Mexican-Americans in the United States is in itself a major factor in this relationship. The focus of this set is specifically on this relationship—how it develops, changes, and influences today Mexico, the United States, and the Mexican Americans now living in the United States. All of the articles are written with this focus in mind and topics not relevant to this relationship are not included.

All of the 430 one- to three-page articles are signed. They begin with a short summary paragraph and end with references to related articles. Most of the articles have one photograph and often a chart or map. The articles are divided into a number of thematic groups: Mexican geography (e.g., Monterrey), American geography (e.g., Florida), history (e.g., Gold Rush, railroads, World War I), economy and environment (e.g., free trade), society and law (e.g., Catholic church, bilingual education, immigration), politics (e.g., Indian policy, land reform, NAFTA), culture (e.g., Chicano art, mariachis), and biographies (e.g., Davy Crockett, Sam Houston, Diego Rivera).

This set serves as a useful encyclopedia on the topic of Mexico and the United States, pulling together for the interested user much diverse information. Given the length of the articles, they can best serve as an introduction or summary of the topics included. Unfortunately, the articles do not end with bibliographies that could lead to further investigation. At the end of the set there is a general bibliography that includes Websites. There are also a number of thematic indexes and an extensive chronology.—**Henry E. York**

PUBLIC POLICY AND ADMINISTRATION

C

267.   **The Blackwell Dictionary of Social Policy.** Pete Alcock, Angus Erskine, and Margaret May, eds. Malden, Mass., Blackwell, 2002. 290p. index. $34.95pa. ISBN 0-631-21847-5.

Designed to accompany the *Student's Companion to Social Policy*, this dictionary serves as an accessible ready-reference to its subject matter. The geographical scope of the volume is almost exclusively British, although there are scattered entries on specifically North American, Western European, and Australian themes. Furthermore, the dictionary deliberately excludes subject areas related to social policy, such as sociology, politics, and social work.

The emphasis throughout tends to be on broad concepts (e.g., discrimination, risk management, social democracy). Specific events, agencies, and laws are generally not to be found, although a number of prominent individuals (mainly politicians and influential scholars and critics) do appear. The intended audience of the dictionary is, primarily, the beginning student. Consequently, the majority of the entries are largely descriptive in nature and brief, many as short as a sentence or two, although some topics deemed by the editors to be more important have been accorded short essays, sometimes as long as two or three pages. All entries, even the longer ones, lack bibliographies. The dictionary does include a detailed index.

There is nothing quite like the *Blackwell Dictionary of Social Policy* currently on the market. Routledge's *Dictionary of Social Welfare* (see ARBA 84, entry 643) comes the closest. It too focuses mainly on British themes. Unlike the Blackwell *Dictionary*, the Routledge dictionary contains bibliographies, but it is now dated and much more costly than the title under review. The Blackwell *Dictionary* is a potentially useful work for undergraduate institutions with public policy or public administration programs that are international in scope.

—**David A. Timko**

14 Psychology and Occultism

GENERAL WORKS

Dictionaries and Encyclopedias

C, P

268.   **Encyclopedia of Psychology. http://www.psychology.org/.** [Website]. Free. Date reviewed: Nov 02.

This site, hosted by the Department of Psychology at Jacksonville State University, has two goals: to provide links to original research findings from respected practitioners in the various fields of psychology, and to provide a "hierarchical" database that links to information on the scientific aspects of psychology. Users can search by 8 categories, which list the number of links they connect to. These include: Career, People and History, Environment Behavior Relationships, Publications, Resources, Organizations, Underlying Reductionistic Machinery (biological factors related to psychology), and Paradigms and Theories. The larger categories, such as Environmental Behavior Relationships with 1,016 links, are broken down into smaller, more manageable categories (e.g., addiction, intelligence, marriage). The Web pages that this site links to are full of information and current research. The host asks for feedback from users for additional sites that should be added or modifications that need to be made. This will be a useful site for those doing research in the field of psychology at the undergraduate and upper-graduate levels.—**Shannon Graff Hysell**

P

269.   **Encyclopedia of Psychotherapy.** Michel Hersen and William Sledge, eds. San Diego, Calif., Academic Press, 2002. 2v. index. $450.00/set. ISBN 0-12-343010-0.

The use of the word "psychotherapy" in a reference title along with a classification as an encyclopedia is highly unusual. Although the term appeared in the late nineteenth century and emerged fully in the twentieth century, a search for encyclopedias of psychotherapy in WorldCat from OCLC retrieves only seven English titles. The volume under review is the sole item clearly described as an "encyclopedia of psychotherapy." Two or three titles use dictionary in their names, and the others presumably have the content if not a title designation. As a result, the volumes reviewed here claim the attention of all psychology reference librarians as well as the students, researchers, and clinicians in the field. Attention should also be given to the four-volume *Comprehensive Handbook of Psychotherapy* (see ARBA 2003, entry 766), which provides additional recent coverage that might also be considered encyclopedic. At the same time, it should be noted that psychotherapy, the use of psychological rather than physical measures, is a term associated with or implied in the use of many terms, including psychology practices, mental health care, treatment plans, psychiatric disorder management, clinical psychology, and others. ARBA has published numerous reviews of encyclopedias, handbooks, and dictionaries covering these terms in recent decades.

Without a doubt, there is a tremendous confluence of authority, research, and breadth of coverage in this encyclopedia. Hersen, Sledge, four associate editors, and a strong editorial advisory board have compiled and edited "a comprehensive reference to extant knowledge in the field" (p. xvii). As expected, the articles are arranged alphabetically, but the nature of the title would not be obvious since some describe a treatment, some refer to the patient treated, some are theoretical, and so on. Entries range from relatively short (2 to 3 pages) to lengthy (15 or more pages), and many include a glossary, description of treatment, case illustration, theoretical basis, applications and exclusions, empirical studies, summary, and further reading (e.g., "Competing Response Training").

Some articles, however, do not lend themselves to this approach; for example, "Behavior Therapy: Historical Perspective and Overview" includes a glossary, brief history, conceptual foundations, science and practice, and then a summary and further readings, or "Self-Help Groups" that covers an overview and history, a description of how self-help groups work, effectiveness, and the future. Still others, such as the entry on "Flooding," include brief commentaries on theoretical bases and empirical support. All include a glossary, a summary, *see also* references, and bibliographic citations. A few articles also have tables to display information, but there are no illustrations.

The contributors and their affiliations are identified in volume 2 just before a detailed subject index. The volumes are well designed and printed but given the breadth of the subject, coverage is inevitably weaker in some areas than others—and the motivation and organization of the articles varies from instructional to general informational to specialized purposes. [R: LJ, 15 Oct 02, p. 62]—**Laurel Grotzinger**

C, P

270. **The Gale Encyclopedia of Mental Disorders.** Ellen Thackery and Madeline Harris, eds. Farmington Hills, Mich., Gale, 2003. 2v. illus. index. $250.00/set. ISBN 0-7876-5768-9.

Some 30 million people visit physicians and 2 million spend time in hospitals every year due to mental disorders. Many people visit a library to learn more about them. *The Gale Encyclopedia of Mental Disorders* provides a good overview of mental illness, psychotherapy, and other treatments. Medical writers, pharmacists, and mental health professionals wrote and edited the 400 signed, alphabetic entries in the set.

The entries cover disorders (anorexia nervosa, schizophrenia), diagnostic procedures and techniques (magnetic resonance imaging, Kaufman Short Neurological Assessment Procedure), therapies (behavior modification, electroconvulsive therapy), medicines and herbs (Paroxetine, St. Johns Wort), and related topics (advance directives, neurotransmitters). Entries for disorders include a definition, description, cause and symptoms, demographics, diagnosis, treatments, prognosis, and prevention. Those for medications contain the definition, purpose, description, recommended dosage, precautions, side effects, and interactions. Entries for herbs and supplements have a leaf icon next to the heading. All entries have a resource list of print and electronic sources and organizations to contact. Some 100 black-and-white photographs and charts illustrate the text. A color photograph gallery repeated in both volumes has enhanced versions of some of the photographs. There are ample cross-references, making it easy to locate drugs, which are entered by generic name. Boxes with definitions of key terms help readers understand the material. A full glossary is at the end of volume 2. Users will find a symptom list here also, which demonstrates patterns that are linked to various disorders.

Although there is some overlap with *The Gale Encyclopedia of Medicine* (2d ed.; see ARBA 2003, entry 1437), *The Gale Encyclopedia of Mental Disorders* offers more detailed coverage of psychiatric disorders and their treatments. The articles are more accessible than those in a medical textbook or the DSM-IV-TR, but they still require a fairly high level of literacy. This is an excellent resource for public, academic, and consumer health libraries.

—**Barbara M. Bibel**

C, P

271. **Internet Mental Health. http://www.mentalhealth.com/.** [Website]. Free. Date reviewed: Sept 02.

Internet Mental Health was designed by Canadian psychiatrist Phillip Long to make much-needed mental health information available to those in the profession, mental health patients and their families, support groups, and students. The site provides information on disorders, such as schizophrenia, anxiety disorders, alcohol dependence, and many more. Each disorder is given an American description, a European description, a general description of how it can be treated, recent research and important past research, and downloadable pamphlets from mental health organizations and agencies (e.g., American Psychiatric Association). Users can also research common psychiatric medications on this site. Each medication description provides information on pharmacology, indications and counterindications, adverse effects, dosage and overdosage, and precautions to take when on the drug.

Users are provided with additional resources to consult (e.g., articles, books, booklets, news, newsletters, and stories of recovery) through the "Magazine" and "Research" links. The site also provides links to related Internet sites, generally those of official agencies and organizations (e.g., Anxiety Disorders Association of America). A list of one to three asterisks following the site indicates the sites popularity. Diagnosis programs are available by linking to Dr. Long's related site, MyTherapy.com, for a fee.

The information provided here is lengthy and authoritative. While written in easy-to-understand language, it will still be best understood by those with some upper-level education. This will be a useful place for those researching mental health disorders to begin their research.—**Shannon Graff Hysell**

Directories

C, P

272. **The Complete Mental Health Directory, 2002: A Comprehensive Source Book for Individuals and Professionals.** 3d ed. Lakeville, Conn., Sedgwick Press/Grey House Publishing, 2002. 687p. index. $190.00; $165.00pa. ISBN 1-930956-07-X; 1-930956-06-1pa.

C, P

273. **The Complete Mental Health Directory. http://www.greyhouse.com.** [Website]. Millerton, N.Y., Grey House Publishing. $215.00/year subscription; $300.00 (w/purchase of print directory). Date reviewed: May 02.

This directory, available both online and as a book, is invaluable for health professionals and people researching a particular mental health disorder. The directory covers 24 broad categories of mental disorders with particular disorders described in each. For example, the section on impulse control disorders includes kleptomania, pyromania, pathological gambling, and so on. After a brief description, associations, agencies, books, Websites, support groups, and hotlines are then listed for these disorders. Information on addresses, telephone numbers, prices, and the people in charge is very complete.

This resource could be used a number of ways. A health professional could use it to enrich his or her own knowledge, to help a patient, or as a referral tool for advising patients. Library professionals could use it as a selection tool for books and a research tool for Websites in the health field. Finally, high school and college students will find it very helpful for writing papers in psychology.—**Carol D. Henry**

P

274. Grohol, John M. **The Insider's Guide to Mental Health Resources Online.** 2002/03 ed. New York, Guilford, 2002. 309p. index. $21.95pa. ISBN 1-57230-754-4.

Now in its 4th edition, this guide for professionals is also invaluable for students and others with a strong interest in mental health. It describes hundreds of online mental health resources, including Websites, databases, and search tools, as well as communication vehicles like chat rooms, newsgroups, and listservs. Changes from the 2000/01 edition (see ARBA 2001, entry 767) include coverage of more than 40 new resources, updated reviews and critical ratings of sites from previous editions, and current URL and e-mail addresses. There continues to be an accompanying Website that provides ongoing updates to the current edition.

Grohol is a psychologist whose vast experience includes co-founding the search guide *Mental Health Net*, building the mental health center at *drkoop.com*, and creating *Psych Central* (his own highly regarded Website located at http://psychcentral.com). His selection of key resources and lesser-known sites gives the book its "insider" quality, while clear writing and good organization make the large amount of information understandable. The author's method of evaluating Websites is fully explained and includes a four-star rating system.

The book is arranged into three parts. The first is an orientation to the basic features of the online world, such as the Web, search engines, and search strategies. The second covers specific topics of interest, including finding treatment information online, networking with other professionals, and finding and downloading psychology-related software. The third part features online resources for patient education and self help. Four appendixes comprise a glossary of terms, resources for further reading, ways to get online, and basics of creating a Website. A general index and an index of Websites are also included. This book serves Internet novices and old timers equally well and is highly recommended for all libraries.—**Madeleine Nash**

Handbooks and Yearbooks

P

275.   **Depression Sourcebook.** Karen Bellenir, ed. Detroit, Omnigraphics, 2002. 580p. index. (Health Reference Series). $78.00. ISBN 0-7808-0611-5.

This newest addition to the Health Reference Series displays the high quality and usefulness of the other titles in the long-standing Omnigraphics effort. This volume, following the series' standard format, contains reprints of government documents, with additional documents from other organizations, publications, and individuals. The articles, targeted for consumer health, contain information about all types of depression in different groups of people.

The first three sections cover the causes of depression, how depression affects the individual suffering from it, and the various treatments currently in use. Written in an easy-to-understand style and covering all facets of the subject, the book offers much valuable information in a readable style. For example, the question "How does depression differ from occasional sadness?", is answered clearly and succinctly in three paragraphs (p. 209). While not an in-depth description of the two states and their differences, it serves the purpose for which it is intended.

Covered in the latter part of the book are common health problems that are often accompanied by depression, such as diabetes or heart disease. Another section covers suicide, with a following one dealing with current research. Each chapter closes with a listing of resources for more information on the particular facet of depression covered in the preceding pages. The final section of the book boasts a complete glossary and five different listings of sources of more information and help. An index completes this comprehensive coverage of depressions geared to the average consumer. This volume is recommended for purchase.—**Nancy P. Reed**

C

276.   **Handbook of the Psychology of Women and Gender.** Rhoda K. Unger, ed. New York, John Wiley, 2001. 556p. index. $75.00. ISBN 0-471-33332-8.

Women and gender studies have been in the research mainstream and the university curriculum for decades. A current, comprehensive research handbook on the psychology of women is long overdue. Rhoda K. Unger, distinguished in women studies and psychology, has compiled such a resource. *Handbook of the Psychology of Women and Gender* provides a review of the research in 27 thought provoking articles. The only comparable work is Denmark and Paludi's *Psychology of Women: A Handbook of Issues and Theories* (Greenwood Press, 1993). Unger's handbook provides a needed update and expands on this work. It will be an essential source for graduate students, faculty, and professionals, as it will be for undergraduates involved in capstone-level research. Many of the articles provide a deep level of analysis that scholars will find interesting and valuable but will likely be challenging for students. Five sections organize the chapters by categories: theoretical/methodological issues, developmental issues, social roles and social systems, physical and mental health, and institutions/power. The specific areas covered within these broad divisions are comprehensive, addressing issues and content areas of research on women and gender. Subsequent editions could provide chapters on women and the workplace and careers. While workplace issues are addressed in a number of articles, particularly Gilbert and Rader's article on work, family, and life, it is such a major aspect of a woman's life that it justifies greater focus. Likewise, a discussion of gender and the schools would warrant a chapter, if not more. Neither is there a specific discussion of female participation, or lack of, in male-marketed sports (e.g., skateboarding, snowboarding). Articles such as Kite's on changing gender roles and Good and Sherrod's article on the psychology of men certainly provide ideas that would help one speculate on the issue.

The volume and quality of analysis far outweigh any omissions, however, and simply provide content for future handbooks. An added bonus to this resource is that many of the chapters are written in a way that provokes ideas and questions in the reader's mind. This makes for interesting reading, an excellent tool for teaching, and an incubator for research ideas. Such qualities are not found in many handbooks. There is an index and a comprehensive list of references. Unger's handbook should be a part of any academic library or larger public library collection.—**Lorraine Evans**

P, S

277.   **Psychology.** Bethel, Conn., Grolier Educational, 2002. 6v. illus. index. $379.00/set. ISBN 0-7172-5662-6.

Psychology is a six-volume set produced by Grolier Educational that explores the various components found within the field of psychology. Geared for a high school level and above researcher, the articles included contain concise information, with a multitude of photographs, charts, and illustrations that supplement the text. The publisher has incorporated a color-coded box system that highlights important information for the reader, such as key points for a chapter summary, key theories, works or dates related to the topic covered, experimental work that fostered theory development, or in-depth studies by field researchers in that particular area of psychology.

Broken into six main categories, starting with the history of psychology, each volume has its own focus, such as developmental or social psychology. Chapters such as "Mental Disorders" (found in volume 6, "Abnormal Psychology") investigate subtopics of the main subject. All have a cross-reference box titled "Connections," which provide links to related topics in other chapters. Conveniently located in each volume is both an identical glossary, which provides the psychological definition of terms used in the chapters, and an alphabetically arranged keyword set index. Another opportunity to provide further research is a section titled "Resources Section," which contains three types of resources (print sources, Websites for that subject category, and quotation information for that volume). Ease of use, quality of each volume, good binding, bright colors, and easily read fonts all contribute in recommending this as a worthwhile basic reference set in psychology for all libraries, and as a necessary acquisition for those libraries serving high school students and above.—**Marianne B. Eimer**

C

278.   Roeckelein, Jon E. **Psychology of Humor: A Reference Guide and Annotated Bibliography.** Westport, Conn., Greenwood Press, 2002. 579p. index. $119.95. ISBN 0-313-31577-9.

The discipline of psychology has long considered humor a trivial topic for systematic inquiry and largely neglected it, according to the author, a psychology professor at Mesa Community College and author of *The Dictionary of Theories, Laws, and Concepts in Psychology* (Greenwood Publishing Group, 1998). Searching PsycINFO, the premier database for psychology, Roeckelein found, however, that there has been a dramatic increase in such studies over time, with more than 2,500 being conducted since 1970. This increase, and his discovery that no major works, reviews, or bibliographies have appeared for two decades, led the author to write what he calls a "21st century state-of-the-art appreciation of the psychology of humor" (p. 4). Students, professionals, and others with a strong interest in psychology will find his effort hugely successful.

The book explores the origins and evolution of the concept of humor in psychology from ancient to modern times. Its experimental/empirical approach includes comprehensive discussion of methodological issues that concern psychologists who conduct scientific investigations. Its six chapters contain more than 3,000 citations and references relating to history, theories (psychological, nonpsychological, and philosophical), and definitions of the concept of humor. Each of the first five ends with its own list of sources, while the sixth chapter is a separate, wide-ranging, and well-annotated bibliography of more than 380 humor studies in psychology from 1970 to 2001. The work concludes with thorough name and subject indexes. It is highly recommended for academic libraries, especially those with programs in psychology and related disciplines.—**Madeleine Nash**

OCCULTISM

P

279.   Buckland, Raymond. **Buckland's Complete Book of Witchcraft.** rev. ed. Saint Paul, Minn., Llewellyn, 2002. 346p. illus. index. $17.95pa. ISBN 0-87542-050-8.

Raymond Buckland is a prolific writer in the areas of the occult and New Age spirituality. This revised edition of his introduction to witchcraft and magical practices is a good place to start for those with little or no experience with this topic and are interested in the subject. In a workbook-type format, Buckland presents the kernels of a mass of subject information that would take the reading of a hundred other books to truly understand. The 15 lessons that conveniently divide the book introduce users to the strands of this subject without overwhelming the reader with unnecessary or confusing details.

Each lesson is comprised of text, questions on the text, and suggested readings to expand one's knowledge of the specific topic covered in the chapter. The back of the book has descriptions of various sects of witchcraft, the answers to the questions asked in each section, and examples of music that can be used in the rituals. There is a small bibliography at the end. Throughout the book are small illustrations of the subject matter and diagrams to aid in everything from how to raise a "cone of power" to the construction of the magical altar.

While the book advertises itself as an introduction to the subject and does accomplish this task, it is limited to discussing all things occult in the light of Gardnerian and Bucklandian witchcraft. This narrow view keeps the book from truly introducing its readers to the wonder of the subject. It is of note that 10 of the 15 lessons refer the novice to readings in books by either Buckland or to Gerald Gardner. The bibliography contains current titles and few citations of real historical content are listed.—**Kennith Slagle**

C, P

280.   **Encyclopedia of Occultism & Parapsychology: A Compendium of Information on the Occult Sciences, Magic, Demonology, Superstitions, Spiritism ....** 5th ed. J. Gordon Melton, ed. Farmington Hills, Mich., Gale, 2001. 2v. index. $360.00/set. ISBN 0-8103-8570-8.

The editor of the *Encyclopedia of Occultism & Parapsychology* is J. Gordon Melton. Melton is a renowned scholar in the fields of American religion and the occult and any book edited by him is likely to be of scholarly quality. Likewise, one hopes that any book reaching 5th edition status has had any errors edited out.

The *Encyclopedia* is a massive work—two large, heavy volumes. It is suggested that the next edition take pity on carpal tunnel sufferers and publish the work in several smaller volumes. The 1st edition compiled two previous works into one—the *Encyclopedia of Occultism* by Lewis Spence published in 1920 and the 1934 volume by Nandor Fodor titled the *Encyclopedia of Psychic Science*. Editor Leslie Shepard later added new articles and updated those of Spence and Fodor.

The breadth of subject matter is extraordinary. It includes all of paranormal phenomena, such as clairvoyance, telepathy, psychokinesis, spiritual healing, and more. It covers ghosts, demonology, alchemy, divination in all its myriad forms, alternative religions (including Wicca and Druidism), medieval witchcraft, ceremonial magic, yoga, psychic development, prayer, mysticism, UFOs, Bigfoot, and the Loch Ness monster. People and organizations involved in all of the above are covered. Many of the articles include a list of sources. Articles range from a sentence to several pages in length. It would be useful for the articles that came from Spence or Fodor to be marked as such, but it may be that those have been updated so much as to make the original article something almost new.

The introduction includes the definition of "occult" used, as well as the background of the work, the evolution of occultism and the New Age Movement, the need for a new edition, and the format of entries. An address is included to which users may send comments. The second volume, besides articles from M-Z, contains an index of Internet resources, a general bibliography that is over 100 pages in length, and an extensive general index. The Internet resources are a particularly welcome feature, despite the fact that Internet addresses change so often. For those libraries needing only one reference book on the occult, this is a good candidate. The *Encyclopedia of Occultism & Parapsychology* is highly recommended.—**Mary A. Axford**

P

281.   Lewis, James R. **The Encyclopedia of Cults, Sects, and New Religions.** 2d ed. Buffalo, N.Y., Prometheus Books, 2002. 951p. illus. index. $180.00. ISBN 1-57392-888-7.

This book, now in its 2d edition, has been greatly expanded and enlarged from the 1st edition. It includes a comprehensive index and larger bibliography; select references at the end of each entry; cross-references; Website addresses (where appropriate); and new entries on more than 50 groups, 100 topics, and on religious traditions and movements. There are few current reference resources that document the fringe, obscure, bizarre, and even sinister religious groups that are practicing around the world today. More than 1,000 diverse religious groups and movements have entries in this updated edition. There are entries on well-known groups such as the Branch Davidians and Heaven's Gate, to obscure groups like the Nudist Christian Church of the Blessed Virgin Mary. *The Encyclopedia of Cults, Sects, and New Religions* is a very well-constructed reference work in an area of knowledge that has few sources.—**Bradford Lee Eden**

15 Recreation and Sports

GENERAL WORKS

Biography

C, P, S

282.   Edelson, Paula. **A to Z of American Women in Sports.** New York, Facts on File, 2002. 278p. illus. index. (Facts on File Library of American History). $44.00. ISBN 0-8160-4565-8.

The latest in the Facts on File Library of American History series, this book documents the contributions of women to sports in American society, primarily during the twentieth century. The author clearly defines her criteria for inclusion in her opening note, and follows this with an excellent introductory essay. The alphabetically arranged entries are focused on the sports and competitive aspect of each woman's biography, with only brief notes on personal matters. Each entry ends with a "Further Reading" list, which contains references to more in-depth articles, books, and Web pages on each individual. Entries are presented from a wide selection of sports, some rarely associated with women, such as boxing, wrestling, shooting, automobile racing, and bowling. A list of recommended sources on American women in sports, a standard index, and two uniquely helpful indexes in which entries are organized by sport and by year of birth close the book. This work is highly recommended for public libraries, high school libraries, and community college and undergraduate libraries. [R: LJ, 1 Oct 02, p. 81]
—Lynn M. McMain

Dictionaries and Encyclopedias

P

283.   **Canada: Our Century in Sport 1900-2000.** Markham, Ont., Fitzhenry & Whiteside, 2002. 592p. illus. index. $60.00. ISBN 1-55041-636-7.

Although most people would automatically think hockey when sports in Canada are mentioned, Canadians have a rich heritage and history of other sports as well, including football, baseball, basketball, track and field, swimming, golf, skating, skiing, and many more. In an elaborately illustrated volume, former Director of Education for the Canadian Olympic Association, Dave Best, puts the nation's best sporting foot forward, presenting Canada's top athletes and sports moments in a worthy patriotic collection. What the book lacks in organization—the chapters appear in no logical order—it makes up for in breadth of sports. Not only are Lord Stanley's Cup and football's Grey Cup included, Canada's Olympic participation is thoroughly documented (both the winter and summer games). Names from the Sports Hall of Fame introduce the volume and succeeding chapters focus on an assortment of Canadian champions and championship events. Best draws freely from the archives of Maclean's to document first-hand accounts of media coverage, including a fully illustrated record. The usual names are here, including track's Donovan Bailey, hockey's Wayne Gretzky, and baseball's Joe Carter, but so are hundreds of other Canadians who contributed to the national sports legend. The first book and initial effort in Canada, this volume is a handsome, reasonably priced anthology of sports in Canada. The title's Website can be found at http://www.ourcenturyinsport.com.—**Boyd Childress**

C, P

284.   **Quick Reference Dictionary for Athletic Training.** Julie N. Bernler, ed. Thorofare, N.J., Slack, 2002. 352p. illus. $24.00pa. ISBN 1-55642-461-2.

Of the hundred of books devoted to athletic training, most consist of guides, programs, assessments, and textbooks. There is also a wide range of topics considered, such as sports injuries, endurance training, weight management, and strength conditioning. Very few of these books, however, are designed as reference tools. One title available, similar to the one under consideration, is Marcia K. Anderson's *Quick Reference Guide for Sports Injury Management* (Williams & Wilkins, 1998), while another, Donald Dean MacChia's *Weight Training in Sports: A Reference Guide* (see ARBA 86, entry 783), is out of print.

This brings us to Bernler's new *Quick Reference Dictionary for Athletic Training.* Although this book is intended as a dictionary for clinicians and students, with more than 2,100 definitions to terms relating to athletic training, less than half the book actually serves as a dictionary. The majority of the book contains 22 appendixes that cover many additional aspects of athletic training, mostly in sports physiology. Much of this information is enhanced with charts, tables, diagrams, and photographs. There are also appendixes for acronyms, abbreviations, symbols, and special tests. Appendixes 17-22 provide quick access to pertinent National Athletic Trainer's Association (NATA) membership. These include a code of ethics, membership policies and privileges, standards of professional practice, and state licensure boards. The book also includes a short bibliography.

If this is a particular weakness in one's reference collection, due perhaps to a paucity of material in this subject area, this reviewer can think of no better way to start or add to a reference collection in athletic training than to purchase this compact but highly informative reference book.—**Richard Slapsys**

Handbooks and Yearbooks

P, S

285.   Craig, Steve. **Sports and Games of the Ancients.** Westport, Conn., Greenwood Press, 2002. 271p. illus. index. (Sports and Games Through History). $49.95. ISBN 0-313-31600-7.

This is the first volume in Greenwood Press's Sports and Games Through History series. It has two primary goals: to provide a comprehensive, worldwide view of sports, play, and games of the ancients and to make suggestions for modern play. The author, the winner of the New Hampshire Sports Writer of the Year award, identifies sports and games that were popular at least 1,500 years ago. He defines "sports" as activities that are rule governed, determine a victor, have social or religious meaning, and are used as preparation for some greater concern to the community. "Play" includes activities that did not require an audience and were not associated with important cultural events. "Games" are either board games or dice games. Some activities, such as the gladiatorial contests of the Roman Empire and several animal-related sports, were purposefully omitted.

The entries are divided into seven regions of the world, and each section starts with an introduction, followed by the subcategories "Sports," "Play," and "Games." Each entry describes the history, purpose, equipment, rules, and suggestions for modern play. In addition to the source list under each entry, there is a separate comprehensive bibliography and index.

This book is valuable in that it covers lesser-known sports and suggests applications for modern play. Some sports are addressed in multiple sections, and the differences that are reflective of their culture and similarities are described thoroughly. Photographs and diagrams illustrate how the games and sports were played, and geographical coverage is well balanced. Libraries that emphasize sports or physical education may want to offer this publication. [R: LJ, 1 Nov 02, p. 78]—**Mihoko Hosoi**

P, S

286.   Wilkins, Sally. **Sports and Games of Medieval Cultures.** Westport, Conn., Greenwood Press, 2002. 325p. illus. index. (Sports and Games Though History). $49.95. ISBN 0-313-31711-9.

Recreational activities are important in every society. In *Sports and Games of Medieval Cultures*, Wilkins discusses the recreational activities of people from all areas of the globe between the fall of Rome and the rise of printing. She answers such questions as: Where did sports and games come from? How did societies share ideas and contribute toward forming the games that we play today?

This work has many strengths. The work's individual consideration of each continent merits praise. In addition, each section is subdivided by game and play (sports). The activities' descriptions vary in length, but have detailed summaries. Where possible, Wilkins includes how to adapt methods of playing modern games to their medieval equivalents. The path that a game took in being introduced to various cultures also receives attention here, especially when the modern descendant(s) came from a common ancestor. Where she needs to make a geographical distinction, the author does so, especially where specific societal groups are concerned.

There are a few areas in which the book is lacking. First, what were Wilkins' sources? She might have included a list of further reading for the user's benefit. Also, the work suffers from the author's imposition of the Western medieval dates upon the rest of the world. Not every society's medieval period can be dated between 476 and 1476. Given the rest of her organization and planning throughout the book, this oversight is unfortunate.

Despite these issues, this work will provide a useful reference for medieval social activities. This work is recommended for public, school, and academic libraries.—**David J. Duncan**

BASEBALL

Biography

P

287. Skipper, John C. **A Biographical Dictionary of Major League Baseball Managers.** Jefferson, N.C., McFarland, 2003. 370p. index. $45.00. ISBN 0-7864-1021-3.

Skipper, the author of this biographical dictionary and onetime general manager of a minor league baseball team, has pulled together the biographies of more than 600 major league baseball managers and interim managers from the past 125 years. Much of his research consisted of personal interviews with the managers and anecdotes from owners, coaches, and players. After a short introduction the book lists each manager in alphabetic order. Skipper provides information on the manager's birth and death date (if applicable), team(s) managed and the years managed, a one- to two-paragraph description of their career and popularity among players and fans, win-loss records, and standings. The author has chosen to leave out data that could not be confirmed. Three appendixes are included, which provide information on those managers who managed the most and fewest games, those with the most wins or highest winning percentage, and a chronological roster of managers (arranged first by National and American leagues and then by team). A bibliography and an index conclude the volume.

—**Shannon Graff Hysell**

Handbooks and Yearbooks

P

288. **Official Baseball Rules.** 2002 ed. St. Louis, Mo., Sporting News Publishing, 2002. 103p. index. $6.95pa. ISBN 0-89204-671-6.

Like everything else about this book, its title is informative and concise. *Official Baseball Rules* is indeed the code of rules written by the Professional Baseball Official Playing Rules Committee to govern the playing of baseball games by professional teams. For this reason, managers, coaches, players, and umpires at all levels of the sport refer to it to resolve disputes. This book is concise in both format and style. At 6 ½ inches high and 5 inches wide, with only 103 pages, it is truly pocket-sized. The text of the code is presented with the bare minimum of introductory material. However, the prefatory material is important because it highlights any changes that were adopted and explains that notes that interpret or elaborate on the basic rules (and thus have the same effect as the rules) are incorporated directly into the text at the appropriate places. These notes are printed in italic type to distinguish them from the actual rules. Both the rules and notes are clearly written enough to be easily understood by the average player and fan. In addition, the "Definition of Terms" division of the code provides a useful and comprehensive glossary of terms commonly used throughout the sport.

The code consists of 10 divisions: "Objectives of the Game," "The Playing Field," "Equipment," "Definition of Terms," "Game Preliminaries," "Starting and Ending the Game," "Putting the Ball in Play," "Dead Ball and Live Ball (in Play)," "The Batter," "The Runner," "The Pitcher," "The Umpire," and "The Official Scorer."

Each division is arranged by numbered, but untitled, subdivisions (1.01, 1.02, and so on). The longest division, "The Official Scorer" (25 pages), does provide a small, but quite useful, index at the beginning. In addition, a brief (less than two full pages), but useful and fairly adequate, index of the entire code is provided at the end of the book. However, access to rules in future editions could be enhanced by providing an appropriate outline (by subdivision number) at either the beginning of the volume or the beginning of each division.

The 2002 edition is intended for use during the 2002 season, and the page preceding the text clearly states that no changes to the code have been adopted for the 2002 season. Indeed, the title page states that the code was last recodified, amended, and adopted by the Committee in January 1996. Because no changes have been adopted since 1996, slightly older editions of this title still contain the correct information. However, the reasonable price of this edition, coupled with baseball's popularity throughout the United States, makes it a highly recommended purchase for public libraries and any other library that collects baseball materials.—**Karen Selden**

P

289.   **STATS Player Profiles 2002.** Morton Grove, Ill., STATS Publishing, 2001. 532p. $19.95pa. ISBN 1-884064-94-9.

Although most baseball statistics books offer interesting facts about players, few provide the statistical information that managers and players actually use. *STATS Player Profiles* is an exception because it shows how hitters and pitchers performed in different environments (e.g., home versus away, grass versus turf, day versus night) and in different situations (e.g., runners in scoring position). In addition, users learn that hitters who faced Seattle reliever Jeff Nelson with two strikes hit a paltry .073 in 2001, Ichiro Suzuki hit .442 when swinging on the first pitch, and few hitters came close to Jose Vidro's .471 average when the game was both close and late (i.e., seventh inning or later). Statistical breakdowns for each month of the baseball season highlight slow starters, the most consistent players, and those positions where fatigue becomes evident late in the year. Fans can make striking discoveries by comparing the statistics for 2001 with the five-year (or less) totals for each player. For instance, Bret Boone hit .444 against left-handed pitching in 2001 compared to only .286 over the past 5 years.

STATS Player Profiles also provides measures of each team's performance in 2001. For example, the Giants hit better as a team on the road than at their home park, whereas the ERA of the World Series champion Diamondbacks was a dismal 5.09 in April. Leader boards include the top 10 players in numerous statistical categories for 2001 and the last 5 years. This volume fills a niche and is perfect for armchair managers.—**Ken Middleton**

BASKETBALL

C, P

290.   **Blue Ribbon College Basketball Yearbook.** 2001-2002 ed. Chris Dortch, ed. Herndon, Va., Brassey's, 2001. 384p. $21.95pa. ISBN 1-57488-396-8.

For the college basketball fan—either a casual or dedicated follower of the game—the *Blue Ribbon College Basketball Yearbook* is the ultimate source. Covering all 318 Division I teams, more than 30 writers provide in-depth overviews of each school. The top 40 teams are profiled in even greater depth in the opening section, with summaries of each program and coach, starters and subs not returning, returning and projected starters, all reserves, and new players (transfers and freshmen), as well as a schedule, record, and the RPI data for the last five years, and other team and school information in brief. Editors pose questions about the team and then turn to answers. An analysis of the team includes grades (A, B, or C) for the frontcourt, backcourt, bench, and intangibles.

The information is the latest as of the publication date and the analyses are accurate and generally on target. Beyond the top 40, teams are divided by conference, and although coverage beyond the top teams is not as thorough, the evaluations are not token treatment. Each conference editor (or editors) also provides a synopsis of the conference including projected order of finish.

The only criticism is what *Blue Ribbon*'s top 40 looked like before the season. Eight made the NIT and five more failed to qualify for any post-season play. The 2002 final 4 teams were ranked 4, 8, 16, and 24. In the SEC (Southeastern Conference), Georgia (SEC East co-champs) was picked last, yet made the NCAA tournament. Arkansas (SEC West 4th place) was picked in the top 40 and to win the West, but fell below .500, did not make the post-season, and lost its head coach before the season ended. These remarks do not detract from what is simply the best college basketball source available—in print or on the Internet.—**Boyd Childress**

P

291.　*The Sporting News* **Official NBA Guide.** 2002-2003 ed. Craig Carter and Rob Reheuser, eds. St. Louis, Mo., Sporting News Publishing, 2003. 748p. illus. index. $16.95pa. ISBN 0-89204-680-5.

P

292.　*The Sporting News* **Official NBA Register.** 2002-2003 ed. David Walton and John Gardella, eds. St. Louis, Mo., Sporting News Publishing, 2002. 471p. illus. $16.95pa. ISBN 0-89204-682-1.

Sporting News Publishing offers some of the best print volumes of sports statistics available, and these two volumes are no exception. Covering the 2001-2002 NBA season, the two volumes together offer complete information on both the players and teams. The *Guide*'s focus is on the team statistics. It begins by listing the current roster of the 2002-2003 season for each team in alphabetic order. It also includes information on the team's schedule, a review of their 2001-2002 season results, team leaders, and season highlights. This volume also offers 2001-2002 season reviews, with play-off results, all-star game results, and award winners. The history of the NBA is included as well as records, year-by-year reviews, and the official rules of the NBA.

The *Register* looks specifically at the players. It begins with listing individual players' statistics, including personal information, transactions and career notes, collegiate record, and NBA regular-season record. A black-and-white photograph of each player is presented. This volume also features individual career highlights, a list of promising newcomers, all-time great players, and all-time great coaches. The work concludes with a list of the NBA statistical leaders.—**Shannon Graff Hysell**

FOOTBALL

P

293.　*The Sporting News* **Pro Football Guide.** 2002 ed. Craig Carter, ed. St. Louis, Mo., Sporting News Publishing, 2002. 439p. $16.95pa. ISBN 0-89204-674-0.

P

294.　*The Sporting News* **Pro Football Register.** 2002 ed. Jeff Paur and David Walton, eds. St. Louis, Mo., Sporting News Publishing, 2002. 493p. $16.95pa. ISBN 0-89204-673-2.

The *Pro Football Register* and the *Pro Football Guide*, both put out by the Sporting News Publishing, combine to form a perfect compendium for those interested in the National Football League. The *Register* focuses solely on players and coaches for the 2002 season. Both veteran players and 2002 draft picks are included. Players are listed alphabetically and the information on each includes their date of birth, their high school and college, and a history of transactions. Additional information varies from player to player, with some entries listing "Playing Experience" and others listing "Single Game Highs" or "Championship Game Experience." These seemingly arbitrary categories are interesting to stumble upon, but the lack of consistency from player to player is somewhat frustrating for purposes of comparison. The *Guide* reviews the 2001 season, including statistics, and looks ahead to the 2002 season on a team-by-team basis. Also included is a short but thorough history of the league that covers year-by-year standings, league records, statistical leaders, first-round draft choices, and a team-by-team history. Filled with the statistical minutia one would expect of such books, there are some odd bits of miscellaneous information, including the flagship radio station of each team and the seating arrangements of every stadium, that make them pleasurable to browse through even for the casual fan. Of the two, the *Guide* would probably be the more essential purchase for most libraries, while the *Register* would most interest users participating in fantasy leagues.—**Philip G. Swan**

HIKING

P

295.　**OneDayHikes.com. http://www.onedayhikes.com/.** [Website]. Free. Date reviewed: Sept 02.

This guide to hiking trails covers trails found all over the world. The goal is to cover only those trails that will take only one day to hike—beyond this criterion they range from a simple two-hour hike on a well-paved path to a full eight-hour hike on rugged terrain. The hiking trails are accessed by going first to the country to be explored, and then to the region or state within that country. For each country some general information is given, including population, area in square miles, official language, and natural world heritage sites (10 are listed for the United States, including Yosemite and the Grand Canyon). As the user scrolls down they will find the list of hiking trails organized by state or region. For each trail the following information is included: a thorough description (several paragraphs long), location and directions on how to get there, where the trailhead is located, the length in miles and kilometers, elevation change, number of hours it will typically take to complete the hike, features (e.g., rivers, lakes, wildlife), nearby accommodations, and any additional advice. Also noted are nearby hiking trails that can be consulted. Each description gives the user access to a printer-friendly format. The site also features news stories and travel features, reviews of hiking guides (written by voluntary reviewers), links to several related Websites, and the ability to recommend a hiking trail to be included.

The descriptions of trails on this Website are thorough and provide good directions to trailheads. Unfortunately, no maps are provided. This does not, however, detract from the value of the site. This will be a useful resource for libraries that serve the general public.—**Shannon Graff Hysell**

P

296.   Rajtar, Steve. **Historic Hiking Trails: A Directory of over 900 Routes with Awards Available to Hikers.** Jefferson, N.C., McFarland, 2002. 163p. index. $45.00pa. ISBN 0-7864-1196-1.

Hiking a trail used by pioneers or a battleground from the Civil War can make history meaningful and fun, as well as provide healthy exercise. This directory lists approximately 900 such trails. Many are sponsored by local organizations, often Boy Scout troops or historical clubs, which promote the trail by selling a patch or other award souvenir.

Basic information for each trail is listed alphabetically by state in two paragraphs. Each trail entry provides the location, theme (e.g., history, nature, recreation), sponsor (with name, address, telephone number, and Website), length (in miles and whether the trail is straight or a loop), route (usually beginning and ending points), terrain, awards (most often a patch with a price), and whether users are required to register or not. The author recommends that hikers contact the trail sponsor for details and current information before embarking for the trailhead.

Coverage is uneven. The author's home state of Florida has 170 trails and Illinois has 61; however, Montana, Wyoming, and New Hampshire have no trails listed. Washington has only one trail listed and Colorado has three trails listed but the popular Colorado Trail is not included. California has 13 trails plus a list of about 60 "Other California Hiking Awards" mostly for Boy Scouts. There are 20 "Interstate Trails" listed, such as the Appalachian Trail and the Pacific Crest Trail. The book is well indexed. This book will be popular with public libraries, especially those in states that are well represented in the book or where scouting is active.—**Georgia Briscoe**

HOCKEY

P

297.   *The Sporting News* **Hockey Guide.** 2002-2003 ed. Craig Carter, ed. St. Louis, Mo., Sporting News Publishing, 2002. 420p. index. $16.95pa. ISBN 0-89204-679-1.

P

298.   *The Sporting News* **Hockey Register.** 2002-2003 ed. David Walton and Jeff Paur, eds. St. Louis, Mo., Sporting News Publishing, 2002. 464p. $16.95pa. ISBN 0-89204-678-3.

The Sporting News Hockey Guide and *The Sporting News Hockey Register* offer a lot of statistical information that will be valuable in a reference collection. The *Guide* begins with an alphabetic listing of the 2002-2003 teams, which provides information on draft choices, the training camp roster, individual statistics, goal tending statistics, and final results. It then lists the final standings of the 2001-2002 season. The second half of the volume is dedicated to providing historical data for the National Hockey League, including Stanley Cup champions, year-by-year standings, award winners, and milestones. The NHL, minor leagues, major junior leagues, and college hockey are all discussed here.

The *Register* looks closely at the players that played in the 2001-2002 season of the NHL as well as the top prospects signed with NHL teams in 2002. For each player the following information is provided: personal information, transactions and career notes, honors, and regular season and play-off statistics. The work concludes with a list of head coaches and statistics of leaders by specific categories (e.g., scoring, goals by rookies, assists, power-play assists).

These volumes are very well organized and offer a lot of information. These volumes are recommended for libraries needing statistical information on the NHL and its players.—**Shannon Graff Hysell**

SKIING

P

299.   **Skiing USA: The Top 31 U.S. Resorts for Skiers and Snowboarders.** 4th ed. Emmanuelle Morgen, ed. New York, Fodor's Travel Publications/Random House, 2003. 386p. $18.95pa. ISBN 1-4000-1230-9.

This new edition of *Skiing USA* updates the previous editions with accurate information for alpine skiers and snowboarders thinking about or planning to take a ski vacation to a destination ski resort in the United States. The 31 resorts covered include 3 in California; 10 in Colorado; 1 each for Idaho, Montana, New Hampshire, New Mexico, New York, and Wyoming; 2 in Maine; and 5 each in Utah and Vermont. Important omissions are Breckenridge, Colorado; Mt. Bachelor, Oregon; and Kirkwood, California. The other major destination resorts are included. Each resort listing includes detailed advice on ski and snowboard runs broken down for beginner, intermediate, and expert skiers; recommendations for lodging (expensive, moderate, inexpensive); dining; and nightlife and entertainment. This information is quite insightful for such a general, large-scale guide. Alternative activities, including snowmobiling, Nordic skiing, sleigh rides, tubing, and shopping, are included for each resort. Travel information, including information on how to get there by plane, car, train, and bus; important telephone numbers and Website addresses; and important statistics (e.g., base and summit elevations, vertical drop, number of runs and longest run, number of lifts and hourly capacity, lift ticket price, snowmaking, resort terrain mix of beginner/intermediate/advanced), are provided. *Skiing USA* is recommended for major metropolitan public libraries and for travel collections in academic libraries.—**Thomas K. Fry**

16 Sociology

AGING

P
300.   **Encyclopedia of Aging.** David J. Ekerdt, ed. New York, Macmillan Reference USA/Gale Group, 2002. 4v. illus. index. $495.00/set. ISBN 0-02-865472-2.

Interest in the problems of aging has increased considerably in the past several years not only because people are living longer but because older people themselves and their families want a better quality of life than was available to past generations. Also, research into the health, economic, and social issues of aging continues to be extensive, and seniors and those working with them want to avail themselves of this new knowledge. The goal of this 4-volume encyclopedia was not only to make available this new knowledge but also to provide information about basic concepts of aging to a broader audience, particularly students, so that they can better understand the progression of their own lives and those of their loved ones. The editor points out in his preface that while some scholarship on aging tends to be limited mainly to biological and physical processes and their effects on aging, this work includes also contributions from the social sciences, fine arts, religion, law, and engineering.

Three lists precede the articles, which comprise the main part of the encyclopedia: an alphabetic list of the articles and their authors, a list of authors with the institutions they represent and the articles they have contributed, and an outline of the contents. The outline is a systematic list of some 38 broad topics, such as the genetics of aging, psychological theories, and relationships, which the editors intended to be helpful for those developing courses, pursuing research, or those simply wishing to browse in an orderly fashion. These topics, with their many subtopics, are listed in an order that is familiar to specialists in the field of aging, but in this context is meant to present an overview of the field for the student or nonspecialist wanting to pursue a particular topic through many interrelated articles.

The encyclopedia contains over 400 alphabetically arranged articles covering all aspects of aging from the perspective of many different fields, including biology, sociology, literature, and ethics. All articles are signed by the author and are followed by references to related articles. Additionally, each article contains a bibliography of scholarly books and articles, ranging from 2 to 35 items, but with few references to Internet sources. There is no separate bibliography at the end of the four volumes. There is, however, a detailed index, which shows page numbers not only for the articles and all of the subheadings, but also indicates whether there are tables, figures, or photographs.

The articles, informative and exceptionally well written, are enhanced by the excellent drawings, which are especially useful for health-related articles, and valuable charts and figures, which clearly indicate sources and dates. The few black-and-white photographs are interesting but add little to the information in the text. Some quality photographs, perhaps in color, would be a welcome addition. Other additions that should be considered are related to authors and subject content. The eight members of the editorial board are listed with their degrees, titles, and institutions, whereas the authors of the articles have only the institution designated and sometimes not even that. It would seem that the added information would give a better assurance of the qualifications of authors. A name with only a university added, for example, gives no indication whether the writer is a professor with years of experience or a graduate student. Another more serious omission is the lack of substantial information in the field of alternative or complementary medicine—a field that many elderly are turning to for various reasons, frequently because of the rising cost of medical care and prescription drugs. There is no entry in the index for the words "alternative" or "complementary" except for a *see* reference to "Herbal Therapy," as if that were the only form of alternative medicine. Under "Herbal Therapy," further reference is made to articles on "Drugs," "Evidence-based Medicine," and "Vitamins." It would be useful to have a more complete coverage of this field by some of the medical doctors or other recognized specialists who are actually practicing and doing research in alternative medicine.

In spite of these limitations, however, the encyclopedia overall is comprehensive, up to date, and well worth the cost. Although it might have limited use for high school students because of the reading level and content of many articles, which would seem to require some college study, for educated seniors and all those working with the aging it should be an excellent source. It should be helpful for those doing research in related fields, such as economics, who wish to become familiar with recent scholarly research in the field of aging. [R: LJ, 1 Nov 02, p. 78]—**Lucille Whalen**

P

301.   **Older Americans Information Directory, 2002/03.** 4th ed. Millerton, N.Y., Grey House Publishing, 2002. 1126p. index. $165.00 (print edition); $215.00 (online database); $300.00 (print and online editions). ISBN 1-930956-65-7.

P

302.   **Older Americans Information Directory. http://www.greyhouse.com.** [Website]. Millerton, N.Y., Grey House Publishing. $165.00 (print edition); $215.00 (online database); $300.00 (print and online editions). Date reviewed: Dec 02.

This large, paperbound book, with an online database also available, now contains more than 12,000 listings. The resources listed "address physical, biological, psychological, social, political and economic aspects of aging."

It is fairly user-friendly, with clear indexing and reasonable (not large) print size. While it claims to be a comprehensive source, the section on assisted living facilities lists only one facility in all of Colorado, while the Denver phonebook lists over 100 in the Denver area alone. No explanation or inclusion criteria are given.

—**Anthony Gottlieb**

P

303.   **The Resource Directory for Older People. http://www.aoa.dhhs.gov/directory/.** [Website]. Bethesda, Md., National Institute on Aging, and Washington, D.C., Administration on Aging. Free. Date reviewed: Sept 02.

The Resource Directory for Older People is a collaborative effort of the National Institute on Aging and the Administration on Aging—two well-respected authorities on aging and the elderly. The site is designed to be of use to the elderly and their families, librarians, health care providers, and social service providers. It provides directory-type information on organizations and agencies that provide services specifically for the elderly. Typical information includes: name of the organization, telephone and fax numbers, e-mail and Website addresses, and a brief description of the goals of the organization. The site is searchable by browsing the alphabetical table of contents for the site one wants to research or by the subject index (for those who do not know the specific name of the organization). Both ways of finding information are convenient. For those needing to print out pages of the directory (or apparently the entire directory) there is a downloadable PDF file available in Adobe Acrobat. Two appendixes are provided: a list of state agencies on aging and list of state long-term care ombudsman programs (both from the Administration on Aging's Website).

This site provides a wealth of information for both elderly people and their families. Public libraries and health care libraries providing information for the general public will find this site extremely useful.

—**Shannon Graff Hysell**

DISABLED

P

304.   **The Complete Directory for People with Disabilities, 2003: A Comprehensive Source Book for Individuals and Professionals.** 11th ed. Millerton, N.Y., Sedgwick Press/Grey House Publishing, 2002. 1139p. index. $165.00pa. (print edition); $215.00 (online database); $300.00 (both print and online database). ISBN 1-930956-69-X.

P

305.   **The Complete Directory for People with Disabilities. http://www.greyhouse.com.** [Website]. Millerton, N.Y., Grey House Publishing. $165.00pa. (print edition); $215.00 (online database); $300.00 (both print and online database). Date reviewed: Dec 02.

   The Complete Directory for People with Disabilities, now entering its second decade, has emerged as a vital tool for locating resources and services for people with physical and mental disabilities. The 11th edition has 9,867 entries, an increase of 131 from the previous edition (see ARBA 2002, entry 845). Although the entire directory has been updated, the editors have made a practice of beefing up particular sections for each new edition; for the 11th, they have concentrated on rehabilitation facilities and living centers, thoroughly revising those sections and adding a new chapter on "Sub-Acute Facilities."

   There are 27 chapters, directing users toward resources (assistive devices, clothing, computers, print and electronic media, and toys); activities (arts and entertainment, camps, conferences and shows, education, exchange programs, sports, and travel); facilities (living centers, libraries, and rehabilitation facilities); and services (associations and organizations, consultants, education, foundations, government agencies, law, support groups, veteran services, and vocational and employment programs). Most of these chapters are subdivided by categories or geography.

   There are multiple access points for each entry. A detailed table of contents allows for quick access to subchapters, and three indexes (disability and subject, entry and company, and geographical) provide more specific access to the directory.

   The directory is also available in an online version. It provides the same information as the book version but with the convenience of having the information in database format. The information is searchable by keyword, resource type, and state.

   The most directly comparable work, *Resources for People with Disabilities: A National Directory* (see ARBA 2002, entry 848), is not updated as often (the first two editions were published three years apart), and is not as well indexed. Libraries considering purchase of either should go with *The Complete Directory for People with Disabilities*.—**Michael Levine-Clark**

FAMILY, MARRIAGE, AND DIVORCE

C, P

306.   Hawes, Joseph M., and Elizabeth F. Shores. **The Family in America: An Encyclopedia.** Santa Barbara, Calif., ABC-CLIO, 2001. 2v. illus. index. (The American Family). $185.00/set. ISBN 1-57607-232-0.

   What could be more ubiquitous to the human condition than the family? It crosses all cultures and time frames. It is impacted by our social and political institutions, yet it also influences these same institutions. The enormous body of literature on the topic demonstrates an interdisciplinary interest and a vibrant area of research. *The Family in America* provides a topical overview of issues with a wide and popular appeal. Transformation in the structure and life of the American family, as seen through a historical perspective, is a common theme in this two-volume encyclopedia on the American family. The authors note the tremendous variety of family types and discusses the societal forces that have fundamentally transformed family life. These transformations and features that define the family are discussed in a historical and cultural context.

Major issues of current concern, such as homosexuality, parental involvement in schools, and stepparenting are addressed, along with enduring icons such as the family vacation. If your library has the *Encyclopedia of Marriage and the Family* edited by David Levinson (see ARBA 96, entry 863) there is some overlap, as would be expected, but the unique topics and the historical focus in Hawes's work would make this a worthwhile addition. *The Family in America* is written for a broader audience and does not have the scholarly depth of Levinson's encyclopedia. It would be appropriate for high school students, undergraduates, and the general public. The entries are well written, clear, and interesting. There are more than 180 articles and each contains cross-references and a bibliography.—**Lorraine Evans**

C, P

307.   Turner, Jeffrey Scott. **Families in America: A Reference Handbook.** Santa Barbara, Calif., ABC-CLIO, 2002. 351p. index. (Contemporary World Issues). $45.00. ISBN 1-57607-628-8.

A new addition to ABC-CLIO's Contemporary World Issues series, Jeffrey Scott Turner's *Families in America* provides a comprehensive overview of the diverse modern-day family in one compact package. The arrangement of *Families in America* follows the standard format of the series.

Appropriate for a variety of audiences, general readers and scholars alike will benefit from the authoritative introductory essays at the beginning of the first three chapters. These chapters address a wide range of topics and trends, and include discussions from historical, multicultural, and international perspectives. General statistics and current research findings are also presented. The remaining chapters do not include essays, but include a forum in which specific information is presented. Reference lists are included at the close of each chapter. Readers will find these, coupled with the extensive directory of organizations and annotated bibliographies of print and nonprint resources (videos, Websites, and search engines), most beneficial.

Chapter 6 presents facts and statistics in graphic formats that are easy to read and analyze. Chapter 8, the annotated bibliography for print resources, is subdivided into two sections: books and research journals. In addition to annotations, chapter 9 also includes timesaving purchase and contact information for the educational videotapes. A detailed table of contents, complete subject index, and glossary make this unique reference tool simple to navigate and a pleasure to use. This handbook is highly recommended for public and all levels of academic libraries.

—**Leanne M. VandeCreek**

GAY AND
LESBIAN STUDIES

C, P

308.   Rosario, Vernon A. **Homosexuality and Science: A Guide to the Debates.** Santa Barbara, Calif., ABC-CLIO, 2002. 323p. illus. index. (Controversies in Science). $85.00. ISBN 1-57607-281-9.

The author, who is a practicing psychiatrist at the University of California, Los Angeles, holds both medical degrees and a Ph.D. from the Department of the History of Science at Harvard University. With this book, he has written a scholarly but highly readable history of the relationship in Western culture (principally American) between various branches of science and the study of homosexuality. In nine chronologically arranged chapters, this topic is covered from Victorian times to the year 2000. Coverage includes significant theories, studies, treatments, controversies, and established truths that have been promulgated during this period.

Homosexuality is broadly defined to include such related areas as bisexuality, masturbation, and transgenderism. Although the material emphasizes psychiatric studies, biomedical topics are covered as well as other social sciences like sociology. The wealth of included background historical information is also amazing. For example, the chapter on developments during the 1960s includes material on the emergence of aversion and group therapies as well as material on the formation of the lesbian organization the Daughters of Bilitis and the Stonewall riots of 1969. Each chapter is illustrated with several photographs and contains five or six sidebars that elaborate on material covered in the chapters. For example, in the last chapter, on current concerns, there are sidebars on gay teenage suicide and the problems related to coming out. The approach is objective and each study or publication covered is succinctly summarized and given an in-text footnote. Each chapter ends with complete citations for each of these references plus a chatty annotated listing of further readings. Appended material includes a collection of 14 pertinent documents, a 4-page chronology of important events, a glossary of terms with clear definitions, and a 22-page general bibliography of both books and periodical articles. Lastly, there is a thorough index that includes references to the main text and the appended documents. This worthy addition to the Controversies in Science series will be useful in both public and academic libraries in either the reference or circulating collections. [R: SLJ, Nov 02, p. 105]—**John T. Gillespie**

PHILANTHROPY

P

309.   **Annual Register of Grant Support, 2002: A Directory of Funding Sources.** 35th ed. Medford, N.J., Information Today, 2001. 1469p. index. $229.00. ISBN 1-57387-126-5. ISSN 0066-4049.

This essential resource, now in its 35th year, is a crucial tool for finding grant support from private foundations, corporations, government sources, and federated organizations. The 2002 edition lists 3,501 sources, many of which grant multiple awards annually. Of these, close to 100 are new entries and about the same amount are programs renamed since the last edition.

Information Today has taken over the publication of this title from R. R. Bowker, but the content and format remain the same. The book is broadly arranged by discipline, with programs alphabetically listed in each section. The helpful introductory material, including a guide to proposal writing, is the same as in previous editions. The indexing—by subject, organization and program, geography, and personnel—is the same as under R. R. Bowker as well.

Entries, too, follow the same familiar format, providing contact information, fields of interest for each program, financial figures, data on the numbers of previous applicants and grants, and details on how to apply. Where a single organization supports multiple programs, all are listed with separate application instructions for each. The *Annual Register of Grant Support* is recommended for all libraries.—**Michael Levine-Clark**

P

310.   Dumouchel, J. Robert. **Government Assistance Almanac, 2002-2003.** 16th ed. Detroit, Omnigraphics, 2002. 952p. index. $225.00. ISBN 0-7808-0580-1. ISSN 0883-8690.

Government publications are usually not noted for their brevity, readability, or organization. Many reference works exist because of the author's ability to condense, organize, and add value to the labyrinth of information contained in government publications. Omnigraphics' *Government Assistance Almanac* is an example of this segment of reference materials. The author attempts to provide information on all federal domestic assistance programs and to help users trying to obtain assistance from these programs. This is the 16th edition of the work, which is ample evidence of the continued usefulness of the *Almanac* to those seeking federal grant support. The strength of the volume is its ability to reduce the entries of the Catalog of Federal Domestic Assistance to the essential reference information. This makes the *Almanac* a valuable desk reference; something the unwieldy Catalog could never be. The *Almanac* offers enhancements to the information supplied in the Catalog. One example is a convenient telephone book of contacts organized by assistance program number. Another enhancement beyond the contents of the Catalog is the table of funding levels, which presents the expenditures by programs for the prior four years. Also included in this section are tables showing the 50 largest and smallest federal domestic assistance programs. An additional enhancement is the abbreviations list, which is not available in the Catalog, even though many abbreviated terms appear in entries. The real strength of the *Almanac* is the thorough master index. To identify all available aid for programs for the aged in the online Catalog requires the use of the five separate terms; the *Almanac* uses just one—"aging and the aged"—which is cross-referenced from other keywords such as "elderly" or "senior citizen." The *Government Assistance Almanac* is a shining example of the value that thoughtful authors can add to the wealth of information available from the federal government.—**Lynne M. Fox**

P

311.   Miner, Jeremy T., and Lynn E. Miner. **Funding Sources for Children and Youth Programs 2002.** Westport, Conn., Oryx Press/Greenwood Publishing Group, 2002. 339p. index. $37.95pa. ISBN 1-57356-541-5.

Jeremy T. Miner, president of the grant consulting firm Miner and Associates, Inc., and Lynn E. Miner, associate dean of the graduate school and director of research and sponsored programs at Marquette University, wrote *Funding Sources for Children and Youth Programs 2002.* It lists sponsors of funding from foundations, corporations, government agencies, and other organizations for a total of more than 1,600 entries. The instructions about who to contact for different kinds of information and how to write a grant proposal are well written and contain detailed, practical advice. The foundations' Websites and head organizations, which they list separately, should have been included under each entry of foundation grant program. The separate lists cause the reader to continually flip back and forth through the book for each entry. The subject index should have the grant programs under each subject heading listed by state of geographic interest. The lists of grant programs under each subject heading become so long they are meaningless without indicating the geographic limitations. The reader would need to read each grant program in a long list to weed out the many programs that do not apply due to the geographic limitations. Finally, there is a listing of programs by state with national and regional programs included under each state. Even though this book includes federal government programs and some grants to individuals, the number of entries is very limited, and limited even more so by geographic limitations. A better title to add to a library's collection is The Foundation Center's book titled the *National Guide to Funding for Children, Youth, and Families* (3d ed.; see ARBA 97, entry 698), which lists more than 5,130 entries (not including federal programs).—**Peggy D. Odom**

SUBSTANCE ABUSE

P, S

312.   **Drug Information for Teens: Health Tips About the Physical and Mental Effects of Substance Abuse.** Karen Bellenir, ed. Detroit, Omnigraphics, 2002. 452p. index. (Teen Health Series). $58.00. ISBN 0-7808-0444-9.

Although teen substance or drug abuse fluctuates over time and with different drugs, the overall pattern of abuse is alarming. The physical, mental, emotional, and behavioral effects of hallucinogens, inhalants, tobacco, ecstasy, cocaine, steroids, and others can be substantial. This handbook, written for a teenage audience, provides information on the causes, effects, and preventive measures related to drug and substance abuse among teens. Overall, there are 57 chapters grouped into 8 sections or parts: understanding substance abuse; alcohol; tobacco; other abused drugs; other drug-related health concerns; treatment; drug statistics and policy controversies; and resources for help and additional information.

The chapters in section 1 explain many of the common physiological effects of various drugs, patterns of addiction, effects on the brain, and the influence of peer pressure. There is even a self-diagnostic quiz on one's knowledge of drugs. Sections 2 through 4 address alcohol, tobacco, and a range of other common drugs and substances that are abused. The section on related health concerns deals with such topics as teen suicide, AIDS, rape, youth violence, and other problems that are drug-influenced. There are an additional number of chapters dealing with treatment, statistics, and policy controversies. All chapters are excerpted or adapted from other sources, which are cited. Chapters also include definitions of "weird words" (i.e., technical terms), things to remember, quick tips, and important facts. A final section of the book provides directory information on state and national organizations that provide additional information or assistance. There are also suggestions for further reading, as well as a combined subject/name/title index.

Except for the chapter on the physiology of the brain, the chapters are quick to make a connection to their teenage reading audience. The prose is straightforward and the book lends itself to spot reading. It should be useful both for practical information and for research, and it is suitable for public and school libraries.—**Stephen H. Aby**

C, P, S

313.   **Drugs, Alcohol, and Tobacco: Learning About Addictive Behavior.** Rosalyn Carson-DeWitt, ed. New York, Macmillan Reference USA/Gale Group, 2003. 3v. illus. index. $275.00/set. ISBN 0-02-865756-X.

Presenting the interconnectivity of addictive behavior and society, the editor of this work has included the historical background and social impacts of addictive substances and behavior along with encyclopedic definitions of terms in entries. Composed of both current topics, such as "binge drinking" or "terrorism and drugs," and revisions of authoritative articles such as "cocaine" or "cocaine treatment" originally published in the 2d edition of the *Encyclopedia of Drugs, Alcohol, and Addictive Behavior* (see ARBA 2002, entry 868), the content is easily understood by the general reader, middle school level and above.

Alphabetically arranged, lengthier entries include sidebar comments describing such information as connotations of terms found there, or the explanation of a graph used to present statistical information for that subject. These articles offer cross-references to other articles within the set for further research. However, it would have been beneficial for such topics as "Gangs and Drugs" or "Gender and Substance Abuse" to immediately include references at the end of the entry to encourage additional research. Color photographs and illustrations, good quality paper, eye-catching fonts, and attractive binding of the set ensure that this will be a viable reference tool for several years.

Special features for each volume include a table of contents, a glossary of terms used, an "Organizations of Interest" section (which provides addresses, telephone numbers, and Websites), and subject bibliographies for main topic areas only. Volumes 1 and 2 have their own indexes, with volume 3 providing the cumulative index. This set is recommended as a suitable purchase for libraries needing an entry-level treatment of this topic.

—**Marianne B. Eimer**

C, S

314.   **Drugs and Controlled Substances: Information for Students.** Stacey L. Blachford and Kristine Krapp, eds. Farmington Hills, Mich., Gale, 2003. 495p. illus. index. $99.00. ISBN 0-7876-6264-X.

Learning about drugs and controlled substances is useful for maintaining health. It is also a common assignment for middle school and high school students. Finding accessible, current, objective material can be a challenge. *Drugs and Controlled Substances: Information for Students* is a good place to start. The contributors are physicians and medical or science writers. The entries cover legal addictive drugs, illegal drugs, other controlled substances, and commonly abused prescription and over-the-counter drugs. The 50 signed alphabetic entries contain the official and street names of the drugs; the pharmacological class; the chemical composition; ingestion method; therapeutic use; usage trends; mental and physiological effects; interactions with other substances; treatment and rehabilitation information; and the personal, social, and legal consequences of use. All entries begin with an overview and end with a resource list of books, articles, and Websites. Definitions of key terms appear in boxes. Sidebars offer additional information such as myths, current news, and historical data. Black-and-white photographs and charts illustrate the text. A chronology from 5000 B.C.E. to 2002 provides a brief history of substance use and abuse in various cultures. A photograph gallery of commonly used and abused prescription drugs, a glossary, an appendix with the text of the Controlled Substances Act, and variant name and general indexes complete the work.

Drugs and Controlled Substances: Information for Students is very useful because it covers a wide range of substances, including diuretics, herbs, diet pills, and steroids, in addition to the usual narcotics and psychedelics. The information is current, objective, and accessible to young adults and adults reading at the high-school level. Students doing reports will get a great deal of information here, but they may want to consult other resources such as *Uppers, Downers, All Arounders* (CNS Publications, 2000) for more background. Patrons who need basic information about drugs will be satisfied with this source. It is an excellent addition to school, public, and consumer health library collections.—**Barbara M. Bibel**

YOUTH AND
CHILD DEVELOPMENT

C, P

315.   Reef, Catherine. **Childhood in America.** New York, Facts on File, 2002. 408p. illus. index. (Eyewitness History). $75.00. ISBN 0-8160-4438-4.

Children's impact on American society is much greater than is often appreciated. Through hundreds of first-hand accounts, many reprints of photographs, and other primary documents (e.g., Massachusetts Compulsory School Law of 1850), Reef offers an extremely accessible and readable survey of American history as seen through the point of view of children.

Childhood in America is arranged around rough time periods. The chapters cover an extensive time frame (1619-2001) and are often presented around themes of national crisis (e.g., the Civil War). Each chapter provides a brief yet cogent introductory essay, a chronology of events, and eyewitness testimonies or first-hand accounts. It is these first-hand accounts that make the work stand out. Although a work about the point-of-view of children, many of the first-hand accounts are drawn from memoirs of adults. This aspect is both expected and acceptable. To round out the volume, a set of short biographies is included. To the benefit of the general reader, the text does not get bogged down by an endless number of notes. Instead, the author has chosen to place all citation information in a lengthy bibliography so that full exploration of the first-hand accounts may be explored, if desired.

The breadth, covering nearly 400 years, comes at the expense of depth on any given topical area. However, through its ability to conveniently present a wonderful array of personal accounts, this work holds broad appeal and easily carves out a niche. It is a wonderful work that fits nicely within the eyewitness history series.

—**Shawn W. Nicholson**

17 Statistics, Demography, and Urban Studies

DEMOGRAPHY

C, P

316.   **American Men: Who They Are & How They Live.** By the New Strategist Editors. Ithaca, N.Y., New Strategist, 2002. 387p. index. $89.95; $169.90/set. ISBN 1-885070-44-6.

C, P

317.   **American Women: Who They Are & How They Live.** 2d ed. By the New Strategist Editors. Ithaca, N.Y., New Strategist, 2002. 413p. index. $89.95; $169.90/set. ISBN 1-885070-42-X.

Demographics from the 2000 Census, the 2000 General Social Survey, the 2000 Consumer Expenditure Survey, and the 1998 Survey of Consumer Finances are compiled into meaningful statistics in this two-volume set. The 1st edition of *American Women: Who They Are and How They Live* (see ARBA 98, entry 247) set the pattern repeated in this 2d edition and the new companion volume *American Men.* Including the normal statistical coverage of health, education, income, labor, population, and spending habits, *American Women* and *American Men* also cover attitudes on political and social issues, living arrangements, and wealth. New to this edition of *American Women*, a chapter profiles the businesses owned by women and a bibliography leads the patron to additional sources. A section titled "For More Information" lists telephone numbers, Websites, names of experts for specific subjects, and e-mail addresses when available.

All the demographic information represented in the set is for the United States; however, the State Data Centers and Business and Industry Data Centers contact information is included in the "For More Information" list. Quick access to market data is provided in easily comprehendible tables and charts. The set is thoroughly indexed and includes a detailed table of contents, a list of tables, a list of charts, and a glossary. These two volumes are highly recommended for academic and public libraries supporting a business collection.—**Ladyjane Hickey**

P

318.   **AmeriStat. http://www.ameristat.org/.** [Website]. Washington, D.C., Public Reference Bureau. Free. Date reviewed: Nov 02.

This site, developed by the Public Reference Bureau, brings together demographic information and statistics in both textual and graphic form from the 2000 U.S. Census. The format of this site will save users time when searching for population information because it pools together the information from a wide range of sources. It also provides links to related Websites for those seeking additional information. *AmeriStat* can be used to show historical and population trends in the U.S. population from 1970 to the present day. It is updated on a regular basis to be as current as possible.

Users can search the site by 14 topics, including children, education, labor/employment, fertility, foreign-born, income/poverty, marriage/family, migration, mortality, older population, political arithmetic, estimates/projections, race/ethnicity, and the 2000 U.S. Census. After clicking on the topic of interest the reader is taken to a page of specific demographic results. For example, when researching marriage/family the site pulled up information on the increase in the number of single-father households, variations of the traditional family, and information on where the baby-boomers are residing. The site uses maps and charts as visual guides and each articles offers links to related files and related sites.—**Shannon Graff Hysell**

STATISTICS

P

319.   Hovey, Kendra A., and Harold A. Hovey. **CQ's State Fact Finder 2002.** Washington, D.C., Congressional Quarterly, 2002. 418p. index. $44.95pa. ISBN 1-56802-731-1.

This volume is the 8th annual edition of *CQ's State Fact Finder*. While preserving the structure of the previous editions, it provides new data for more than 90 percent of the statistics covered. Thus, using previous editions of the work can help identify changing trends. For the 2002 edition a new section of statistics on technology has been added, providing coverage of this rapidly changing sector of the economy.

Although this is a work of statistics, *CQ's State Fact Finder* differs from most standard statistical compilations. It provides coverage of data not found in other sources, such as the *Statistical Abstract of the United States* (Hoover's, 2002). The editors do not rely solely on published governmental sources for the statistics they include, but seek out unpublished data and data from nongovernmental organizations. The presentation of the data also differs from other sources. For each specific subject, the states are listed alphabetically in one chart and then in rank order in a second chart. The heart of the book is the subject rankings. Charts are divided into the following categories: population, economies, geography, government, federal impacts, taxes, revenues and finances, education, health, crime and law enforcement, transportation, welfare, and technology. Within each category, various topics are presented, yielding a total of 248 different charts and rankings. In addition to standard statistics such as population, income, and tax revenues, charts on topics such as the number of registered boats, the average cost per kilowatt hour, state government bond ratings, proportion of sentence served, and state government Website ratings are given. For each chart, a brief discussion is given that includes the source of the data and often a Web address so that the user can find additional information.

The volume also includes a section entitled "Finding Information Users Want to Know," which guides users in answering questions about using the data to determine where to live, where to locate or expand a business, and how public policy is being affected by changing trends. A composite listing of the state rankings is given by state in a special section. The index, while sparse, does provide adequate access to the data.

For libraries that seek to provide state level data to their customers, this is a worthwhile publication. Many of the statistics can be found elsewhere, but this volume pulls together a wide variety of data in a convenient and easy-to-use format.—**Gregory A. Crawford**

URBAN STUDIES

C, P

320.   **America's Top-Rated Cities, 2002: A Statistical Handbook.** 9th ed. Lakeville, Conn., Grey House Publishing, 2002. 4v. $195.00pa./set; $59.95pa./vol. ISBN 1-930956-44-4.

Where someone chooses to live may be based on the heart, but *America's Top-Rated Cities* provides plenty of statistics to guide the analytical thinkers among readers. The 9th edition contains statistics and descriptive information on 100 cities. The format is largely unchanged from previous editions, but inclusion of 20 additional cities and data from the 2000 census is new. While much of the data are from current sources, there are also 1990 census data reported—so readers should check the cited sources carefully. Cities are selected based on a number of criteria, rankings from trade and popular magazines, the *Places Rated Almanac* (millennium ed.; see ARBA 2001, entry 889), and the subjective decisions of the editors.

The organization is clear and easy to follow. Four volumes divide the cities by Southern, Western, Central, and Eastern regions. Each volume contains chapters for 25 cities presented in alphabetic order. The city chapters are organized into three sections, background about the city, rankings, and statistical tables. The statistical tables are further divided by "Business Environment" and "Living Environment." The rankings section consists of excerpts from a wide variety of publications. Here, readers can see where a city has been ranked based on specific criteria (best place for singles, healthiest cities, and so on). Since these entries are only excerpts, it would be advisable to consult the original source. It would be interesting to place these data in a table so that readers could quickly compare the selected cities on these criteria. One real strength to this set is the wide range of information provided in a concise and well-organized format. A valuable tool for any library, *America's-Top Rated Cities* meets the quick reference needs of both the business community and general public.—**Lorraine Evans**

C, P

321. **America's Top-Rated Smaller Cities, 2002/03: A Statistical Profile.** 4th ed. Lakeville, Conn., Grey House Publishing, 2002. 1072p. $160.00pa. ISBN 1-930956-67-3.

Although less than two years have passed since the previous edition of this work (see ARBA 2001, entry 888), there have been significant changes to the content. First, all of the 60 cities profiled are brand new—there are no repeats from earlier editions. Second, the criteria for selection have been altered in important ways. Formerly, a "smaller city" had to be either the primary or secondary city within a Metropolitan Statistical Area (MSA). That requirement has been dropped, and the editors have instead focused on four key statistical measures: population growth, income, crime rate, and unemployment rate. The size of the cities chosen remains the same; the population must fall between 25,000 and 99,000.

The format of the book is similar to that of previous editions. Each city profile is 15 to 17 pages in length and contains background information, rankings (derived from a variety of books, periodicals, and reports), and statistical tables (divided into "business" and "living" categories). Seven new tables have been added to this edition: housing permits, home ownership rates, tax audit rates, bankruptcy rates, 2000 presidential election results, superfund sites, and watershed health. There are two new appendixes: an index that matches the city with county location; and a section of comparative statistics for the 60 cities. Among the statistical tables, some of the more interesting (and unusual) include data on cultural institutions, the library system, AM and FM radio stations, a "roadway congestion index," and a range of "maximum pollutant concentrations." Because of the new criteria, many of the cities in this edition will be unfamiliar to most readers (e.g., Ballwin, Missouri; Cary, North Carolina; Friendswood, Texas). However, a few well-known places have been selected (White Plains, New York; Folsom, California; Dublin, Ohio; and Westport, Connecticut).

This compilation continues to provide useful information for business research and is a very popular job-hunting resource. It is highly recommended for public and academic libraries.—**Thomas A. Karel**

P

322. **Sperling's BestPlaces. http://www.bestplaces.net.** [Website]. By Bert Sperling. Free. Date reviewed: Oct 02.

For those looking to move or thinking about retiring in a new location, this resource from Bert Sperling of Fast Forward, Inc. will provide valuable information on 3,000 U.S. cities. The site makes it easy to compare two cities in areas of cost of living, housing costs, crime, education, economy, health care, and climate. Also provided is a tool that enables the user to put in two cities and find out how much they will have to make in order to maintain or enhance their standard of living. It shows where each city falls in comparison to national standards in the areas listed above. For those looking for a place to retire or looking to make a fresh start in a new city, there is a quiz called "Find Your Best Place to Live," which takes into account one's personal preferences regarding climate, population, cost of living, education, and entertainment. Special features include statistics on schools throughout the United States, crime rates throughout the United States, and climate profiles for 2,000 countries worldwide. This is not only an interesting site to browse, it will also be extremely useful as a ready-reference tool at the reference desk of public libraries.—**Shannon Graff Hysell**

18 Women's Studies

BIBLIOGRAPHY

C, P

323.   **Early Modern Women Database. http://www.lib.umd.edu/ETC/LOCAL/emw/emw.php3.** [Website]. Free. Date reviewed: Sept 02.

This free resource, provided by the Arts and Humanities Team of librarians at University of Maryland libraries, features links to sites on the World Wide Web that will further aid in the study of women in early modern America and Europe. All of the selected sites feature information on women from 1500 to 1800. Most of the sites this database links to are free but when a subscription is required it is noted.

Users can search the site by keyword or by title, subject (e.g., art and architecture, science and technology), type (e.g., journal literature, reference sources), time period, language, or geographic area. An advanced search is available for those wanting to narrow their search down to specific topics. The sites that this database links to include bibliographic databases, full-text resources, images, and sound recordings. Some examples are: *Index to Early American Periodicals*, *Grove Dictionary of Art*, and the *Centre for Reformation and Renaissance Studies* from the University of Toronto. This is a worthwhile site for academic librarians to consult or recommend to patrons seeking information on this topic.—**Shannon Graff Hysell**

BIOGRAPHY

P, S

324.   Duncan, Joyce. **Ahead of Their Time: A Biographical Dictionary of Risk-Taking Women.** Westport, Conn., Greenwood Press, 2002. 312p. illus. index. $55.00. ISBN 0-313-31660-0.

The author, who teaches service-learning courses in English and the humanities at East Tennessee University, has identified 75 women from the mid-19th century to the present whom she believes broke "traditional bounds and ventured into unchartered territory" (p. ix). Among the pioneers are the expected (e.g., Amelia Earhart, Margaret Mead, Rachel Carson) and the lesser-known (e.g., mountaineer Gertrude Beham, entomologist Evelyn Cheesman, cosmonaut Valentina Tereshkova Nikolayev). Most of these risk-taking women are from the United States and England. Fifty-four of the alphabetically arranged entries are two to four pages long; the rest, in an appendix, are given a paragraph or two each. About one-half contain black-and-white photographs. In a book such as this one, it is unfortunate the author did not include a picture of every woman. Each biography concludes with a very brief list of books and magazine articles.

Two appendixes divide the women by category (anthropologists, explorers, humanitarians, oceanographers, and so on) and by nationality, while a useful subject index provides additional access. Although most of this information is available elsewhere, this is a handy text for its target audience, which is mainly high school students who can use it to identify unusual women and as a jumping-off point for further research. [R: C&RL News, May 02, p. 375]—**Hope Yelich**

C, P, S

325.   Windsor, Laura Lynn. **Women in Medicine: An Encyclopedia.** Santa Barbara, Calif., ABC-CLIO, 2002. 259p. illus. index. $85.00. ISBN 1-57607-392-0.

Windsor, a health sciences reference librarian at Ohio University, profiles more than 250 physicians, nurses, and medical researchers in this attractive volume. Although women from the United States and Western Europe make up the majority of the entries, the author also covers women who were the first physicians in such countries as China, the Philippines, and Uruguay. Biographical entries range in length from a short paragraph, to several pages for well-known individuals (e.g., Elizabeth Blackwell). Using a straightforward writing style, Windsor emphasizes the accomplishments and personal qualities of these women much more than the specific acts of discrimination that many of them faced. Nevertheless, "Barriers to Success" and "Women of Color in Medicine" are among the insightful topical entries, which also include "Mission Work," "Public Health and Women," and "Wars and Epidemics." Each entry concludes with a list of references for further study. The excellent index is particularly helpful for finding coverage of individuals from specific countries and regions.

Windsor omits a significant number of noteworthy women in medicine, such as pioneer neonatologist Ethel Collins Dunham, bacteriologist and physician Ruth May Tunnicliff, gynecologist Elizabeth Hurdon, and Australian pediatrician Kate Campbell. Still, the author has successfully condensed into a single volume information that had been scattered in such sources as *American National Biography* (see ARBA 2001, entry 17), *Women in World History: A Biographical Encyclopedia* (see ARBA 2000, entry 793), *Biographical Dictionary of Women in Science* (see ARBA 2001, entry 897), and *Dictionary of American Medical Biography* (see ARBA 85, entry 1535). In addition, she provides entries about numerous women who are not covered in readily available sources. *Women in Medicine* will be a valuable addition to high school, academic, and public libraries.—**Ken Middleton**

DICTIONARIES AND ENCYCLOPEDIAS

C

326.   **Historical and Multicultural Encyclopedia of Women's Reproductive Rights in the United States.** Judith A. Baer, ed. Westport, Conn., Greenwood Press, 2002. 238p. index. $79.00. ISBN 0-313-30644-3.

Historical and Multicultural Encyclopedia of Women's Reproductive Rights in the United States is a single volume primarily containing entries about court cases, history of birth control methods, descriptions of organizations, and key reproductive rights concepts. Baer, a prolific scholar on women and the law, assembles entries on an often controversial topic in an attempt to both educate and challenge the reader. Baer's encyclopedia is well put together. While a broad range of topics are discussed in regards to women's reproductive rights, Baer does a good job of keeping them focused and useful for the researcher. Forms of reproduction are defined (e.g., abortion, sterilization, medication), key court cases are introduced, and organizations representing pro-choice and pro-life positions are profiled.

As with most resources, Baer also attempts to be inclusive, and entries are devoted to women of color and reproductive rights. There are nine entries concerning African American women included, and four entries concerning Native American women are included. A future edition may want to broaden the definition of diversity and specifically include entries on Latina and Asian American women. While the index includes entries on rural women, no entry parallels that of African American or Native American women.

Access to other entries in the volume is done with ease. The index is accurate and useful. Related readings in the volume are listed at the end of each entry, and full citations are provided for further references. A biographical entry is included for Margaret Sanger, pioneer of the birth control movement. The encyclopedia is recommended for all college and university libraries.—**Courtney L. Young**

C, P, S

327.   Kuhlman, Erika. **A to Z of Women in World History.** New York, Facts on File, 2002. 452p. illus. index. (A to Z of Women). $49.50. ISBN 0-8160-4334-5.

In this one-volume encyclopedia of women's history, Kuhlman presents snapshots of various women throughout the ages. Crossing many centuries and many countries, stories of courageous women are brought forth. Many are well known, but many more are not. Yet all of the women demonstrate uniqueness in their lives and are important to a new understanding of history. With 260 biographies, Kuhlman provides details of each woman's life and her contributions as well as additional references to other works about the individual in each entry. As she states in her introduction, "*A to Z of Women in World History* is an attempt to reveal not only the distinction of the women it covers but also the ingenious ways in which women skirted the numerous barriers society placed in their paths" (p. viii). This she does in a lively and engaging manner.

Arranged alphabetically within fields of accomplishment (journalists, performers, scholars, and so on), Kuhlman also provides appendixes that list each woman by country of birth and year of birth, as well as an extensive index that provides subject searching. More than 30 photographs of various women are included. This volume is very well organized and easy to navigate. *A to Z of Women in World History* will be an excellent introductory volume for high schools, community colleges, and public libraries.—**Deborah L. Nicholl**

HANDBOOKS AND YEARBOOKS

C, P

328.   Plowden, Martha Ward. **Famous Firsts of Black Women.** 2d ed. Illustrated by Ronald Jones. Gretna, La., Pelican Publishing, 2002. 171p. illus. $18.95pa. ISBN 1-56554-197-9.

Plowden uses "famous firsts" as a clever hook to get middle school students interested in reading about the achievements of African American women. For instance, the first sentence in the profile of Shirley Chisholm states that she was the first African American woman elected to Congress. Plowden then provides a good overview of Chisholm's political career. In a similar fashion, the author highlights the achievements of other women in such fields as poetry, film, law, opera, education, and sports.

In this 2d edition, Plowden adds biographical profiles of Coretta Scott King and Oprah Winfrey to the 20 found in the 1st edition (see ARBA 95, entry 908). Although this work is serviceable and inexpensive, eight of the entries are so short that they provide little more than a brief summary of the achievements and awards that the individual received. In addition, Plowden has not edited the profiles from the 1st edition to reflect changes in our knowledge of these women. Therefore, Wilma Rudolph's death is not noted, and the latest information that Plowden provides about several women who are still living is from the 1980s. The bibliography is similarly outdated and does not list Websites. A comparable work, Tonya Bolden's *And Not Afraid to Dare: The Stories of Ten African American Women* (Scholastic, 1998), covers fewer women but provides better overall profiles.

—**Ken Middleton**

Part III
HUMANITIES

19 Humanities in General

HUMANITIES IN GENERAL

C, P

329. Miner, Jeremy T., and Lynn E. Miner. **Directory of Grants in the Humanities 2002/2003.** 16th ed. Westport, Conn., Oryx Press/Greenwood Publishing Group, 2002. 600p. index. $84.95pa. ISBN 1-57356-567-9.

The contents of this book are available in a number of electronic formats. The humanities volume is but one of seven directories included in the GRANTS database, which is available on the Web as *GrantSelect* (also available through Dialog as well as Knowledge Data Systems, and as a CD-ROM product with monthly updates through Dialog). In each of these electronic environments the grant information being searched will be more accessible and more readily identifiable than through the paper volume. In grant research inadequate information (unless the searcher is working with a known entity) is more likely to be the nature of the effort. When individual keywords or partial names of people or organizations are involved, the true benefits of electronic searching are displayed (and conversely, the serious limitations of paper indexes are experienced). While the 16th edition of the print version has tried to provide indexing (subject, sponsoring organizations, program type, and geographic), the limitations of such paper efforts are very apparent. Given the nature of the information compiled for this directory, the first choice would certainly have to be one of the electronic modes. In the absence of that possibility, the print directory provides the next best option for access to the specialized world of grants in the humanities and related areas.

The print volume has a short, useful introduction, followed by a clear "how to use" section. A 16-page list of Websites found in the directory is included. A "Guide to Proposal Planning and Writing" caps the introductory material. The key information provided for each annotated grant entry includes a paragraph description, followed by the grant requirements and restrictions, grant amounts, contact information, dates, and street and Internet addresses. In some cases descriptions of sample awards are provided. Overall, the arrangement is alphabetical by grant name. Overall, the indexing pages take about a quarter of the pages in this directory.

Interestingly, the price for the printed volume has remained virtually unchanged for the last decade. During that time collection managers have seen the costs associated with most continuations as anything but stagnant. There are of course many alternative products on the market, but these tend to either have broader coverage than just the humanities or they may have a more specialized focus, such as The Foundation Center's *Foundation Grants to Individuals*. In summary, for locations where the electronic modes are unavailable, this volume continues to offer a valuable service at a remarkably reasonable price.—**Graham R. Walden**

20 Communication and Mass Media

GENERAL WORKS

C, P
330. **Working Press of the Nation 2002.** 52d ed. New Providence, N.J., R. R. Bowker, 2001. 3v. index. $475.00/set; $259.00/vol. ISBN 0-8352-4407-5. ISSN 0084-1323.

According to the publisher, this annual directory is primarily designed for media personnel, market analysts, and mailing list compilers. This 3-volume media source, however, contains much useful information for reference librarians in public, academic, and special libraries. (See ARBA 2001, entry 921, for a review of the 51st edition.)

The 1st volume contains almost 8,000 entries on newspapers, feature syndicates, and news and photo services. Most of the 16 sections are arranged by publishing frequency (daily and weekly) and by topic (religious, ethnic, and foreign-language newspapers). An alphabetic title index provides easy access to these sections. Each newspaper entry includes, among many other items, U.S. mail, e-mail, and Web addresses; telephone and fax numbers; subscription rates; circulation; bureau locations and contacts; and year established. Some especially useful features found here but not in some other media directories include time and day of deadline, management and editorial personnel, name and address of the owner (individual or corporate), and supplemental and special editions.

Volume 2 ("Magazine and Newsletter Directory") and volume 3 ("TV and Radio Directory") contain similar information and are also accessibly organized with large, easy-to-read fonts. The "Magazine and Newsletter Directory" contains short and useful descriptions of the publications and the readership, while the "TV and Radio Directory" indicates the numbers of the potential market served. Included in both volumes are a subject index to types of programming, hours of air time, network affiliation, and the call number frequency. Probably the most noticeable drawback occurs in the 1st volume. Only a small number of foreign-language and ethnic newspapers are listed and these entries do not adequately reflect the tremendous increase in the number of these publications in recent years. Nevertheless, this work still provides much important and useful information, which is easily accessible.

—**Donald Altschiller**

AUTHORSHIP

General Works

P
331. **The Writer's Handbook 2003.** Elfrieda Abbe, ed. New York, Watson-Guptill, 2002. 1055p. index. $29.95pa. ISBN 0-87116-196-6.

A few years back, *Library Journal* touted *The Writer's Handbook* as the best resource a beginning writer could have. Now in its 67th edition, we find that time has not diluted this work's importance. Completely updated and revised, the latest edition provides more than 1,000 pages of essential information, how-to advice, and important market lists that every writer needs.

The first one-third of this year's volume contains over 50 highly readable articles, interviews, and practical advice from writers such as Elmore Leonard, Ursula K. Le Guin, Evan Hunter, Sue Grafton, and many others. These articles are grouped into broad categories, such as "The Professional Basics," "The Craft of Writing," "Professional Development," and "Ideas & Inspiration." Topically, they cover the gamut from the "Art of Beginnings" to "Writing a Series."

The remainder of the book consists of current book and magazine markets that buy articles and book manuscripts. The 3,300 detailed entries cover what each one publishes, a brief description of their requirements, Websites, and how to contact them with queries and submissions. *The Writer's Handbook* also includes over 300 additional listings for agents, writer's organizations, literary prize competitions, writer's conferences, writer's colonies, and more.

Traditionally, *The Writer's Handbook* competes neck-and-neck with the better-known *Writer's Market* (2002 ed.; see ARBA 2002, entries 930 and 931). While coverage of the markets and resources is about the same, *The Writer's Handbook* wins hands down with its support of the neophyte writer. [R: LJ, Dec 02, p. 112]

—**Steven J. Schmidt**

Style Manuals

P

332.   **The Oxford Guide to Style.** By R. M. Ritter. New York, Oxford University Press, 2002. 623p. index. $25.00. ISBN 0-19-869175-0.

This vibrant revision by Ritter treats readers to an instructive, meticulous, and scholarly examination of all the elements involved in preparing a manuscript for publication. The volume is well organized and offers clear procedures and explanations. The text is well written and user friendly. The book begins with a revealing preface about Horace Hart, the original author and printer of *Hart's Rules* from which this book is based. The introduction also explains why this particular edition differs from the preceding ones, the purpose of the examples, and why the different fonts are used.

The book is organized into 16 topic-based chapters. Each chapter contains 6 to 13 headings and various subheadings. The illustrations support the purpose for which they are intended and the book concludes with 15 pages of index. The indexed entries appear in word-by-word alphabetic order. The text gives extensive details on how to express the writing fundamentals. Copious explanations and examples are given, which take into consideration their use by nonspecialist typesetters, proofreaders, writers, and editors. Definitions with multiple meanings (e.g., billion, bomb), foreign quotations, lists, mathematical symbols, and phonetic abbreviations are also given special treatment. In addition, there is a subheading on electronic data. Four pages are dedicated to showing how electronic documents from several fields should be cited.

The book will be useful for those involved in the writing field. Both national and international writers and publishers will find it a great source. High school and college students, in particular, will appreciate the infinite attention to detail, the focus on various writing concepts, the consideration given to different text categories, and the startling clarity and authoritative stance on the writing genre as a whole. It should be noted that Ritter also authored *The Oxford Dictionary for Writers and Editors* (2d ed.; see ARBA 2001, entry 937), which complements *The Oxford Guide to Style* very well.—**Alice A. Robinson**

NEWSPAPERS AND MAGAZINES

C, P

333.   **Fulltext Sources Online, July 2002.** Donald T. Hawkins, Mary B. Glose, Lara E. Fletcher, and Suzanne D. Bromberg, eds. Medford, N.J., Information Today, 2002. 1506p. index. $129.50pa. ISBN 1-57387-151-6. ISSN 1040-8258.

C, P

334.   **Fulltext Sources Online Edition. http://www.fso-online.com/.** [Website]. Donald T. Hawkins, Mary B. Glose, Lara E. Fletcher, and Suzanne D. Bromberg, eds. Medford, N.J., Information Today. $249.00 (single users); $1,995.00 (unlimited users). Date reviewed: Nov 02.

Fulltext Sources Online (FSO) provides useful information for researchers, reference librarians, and collection development librarians. The current volume lists 17,467 titles of newsletters, newspapers, newswires, periodicals, and radio and television transcripts available electronically in full text from various aggregators and on the Web. Updated twice a year, the text covers information from 26 aggregators, including FirstSearch,

LEXIS-NEXIS, and Ovid. Titles from EBSCOhost, InfoTrac, ProQuest, and WilsonWeb are included, although the text does not specify individual databases for these products. The current issue also includes Factiva as a new aggregator; titles from Dow Jones Interactive and Reuters Business Briefing are listed separately. The content and organization of this work are comparable to those of previous volumes (see ARBA 2002, entry 944; ARBA 2000, entry 39; and ARBA 98, entry 51). A significant change is that FSO no longer indicates whether aggregator coverage of individual titles is selected or comprehensive.

The main section provides an alphabetic listing of publication titles. FSO entries typically include the ISSN of the publication; a list of aggregators that provide full-text access; delay between the print and online availability; dates of coverage and frequency of updates; and the amount of time material remains in an updated file. Selected entries include additional information about the publication, such as title changes. In some cases, the language of the publication (if other than English), and/or its geographic focus, is specified. If the publication is available on the Web, the uniform resource locator (URL) is included. Web publications are also listed in a separate section, along with their respective URLs and back issue information. Subscribers to FSO have access to the "Private Zone" Website, which provides links to the Web publications listed in the text. FSO also includes subject, geographic, and language indexes, and contact information for vendors.

This resource is also available online for a subscription. The site is searchable by title or by subject. Users can also search those titles that have archives available on the Internet. This resource, whether in print or electronic format, is recommended for academic and large public libraries.—**Sharon Ladenson**

RADIO, AUDIO, AND VIDEO

P

335.   **A V Market Place 2001: The Complete Business Directory of Products and Services for the Audio/Video Industry.** 29th ed. New Providence, N.J., R. R. Bowker; distr., Medford, N.J., Information Today, 2001. 1693p. index. $189.00pa. ISBN 0-8352-4363-X. ISSN 1044-0445.

This 29th edition attempts to be a one-stop guide to the audio/video industry, which is defined to include audio, audiovisual, computer systems, film, video, and programming. It lists more than 7,400 companies, including full contact information, which is updated via questionnaires sent to each entrant in the last edition and to potential new listees. Other new entries were found through researching the field.

The volume is organized with a product and service index followed by the product and service listings. The listings provide the company name and are organized by state. Once users have identified the company, they need to look in the next section, "AV Product and Service Providers," which alphabetically lists the companies. There is also a calendar of events and information about film and television commissions, awards and festivals, and periodicals and reference books relevant to the trade. A final yellow pages section includes a company index and a personnel index. Like any print directory of this type, there are some out-of-date entries, but it is a comprehensive source to the industry and one that is well organized and well researched.—**Joshua Cohen**

21 Decorative Arts

COLLECTING

General Works

P

336. McAlpine, Alistair, and Cathy Giangrande. **The Essential Guide to Collectibles: A Source Book of Public Collections in Europe and the U.S.A.** New York, Penguin Books, 2001. 640p. illus. index. $29.95. ISBN 0-670-03032-5.

It is important that one take note of the subtitle of this work as it is a source for identifying museums and special collections consisting of collectibles. This reference is not a price guide nor does it identify individual items within a collection. And these collections contain more than merely collectibles, since many also have collections of items that may be considered to be objects of fine art or valuable antiques. The authors point out that in recent decades there has been a tremendous increase in the number of museums worldwide; therefore, all museums could not be included. The reference is well organized by categories, which include chapters on antiquities and ethnography, books and manuscripts, memorabilia, decorative arts, military collections (including miniatures), the natural world, science and technology, sports memorabilia, textiles, transport (including carriages and automobiles), and unique and curious collections (including erotic art). The book is well indexed by subject and also by museum name. Full color illustrations highlight items in some of the museums. This work should be a part of museum in-house library collections, and available for public use in academic libraries and in the fine arts departments of larger public libraries.—**Louis G. Zelenka**

Antiques

P

337. Maloney, David J., Jr. **Maloney's Antiques & Collectibles Resource Directory.** 6th ed. Iola, Wis., Krause Publications, 2001. 950p. index. $32.95pa. ISBN 0-87349-340-0.

Maloney, an experienced certified property appraiser, has compiled the latest edition of the "bible" of the collecting world, now with more than 23,000 entries—up from 18,000 in the last edition published in 1999 (5th ed.; see ARBA 2000, entry 832). Listings are free, thus the impressive size of the book. Potential users include attic-combers and garage-sale enthusiasts hoping to sell or value their finds, collectors seeking additional information or replacement parts, used and antique dealers who need to contact an expert, and anyone else generally interested in the aesthetic and economic appreciation of material culture. Several hundred classified listings (e.g., Covered Bridges, Sports Collectibles) are alphabetically arranged, with entry types such as collectors, dealers, experts, Internet resources, museums/libraries, periodicals, and manufacturers. Entries have contact name, address, telephone, e-mail, and Website information along with a description with further details.

The book is fun to browse, given the incredible range of categories, from the expected (paintings, cookbooks, and militaria) to the more unusual (créches, lottery tickets, funeral items, and bubble blowers). Many headings also have subclassifications by manufacturer or style. For example, under "Ceramics (American)," after some general entries for dealers, there are a number of specific listings (e.g. "Bennington," "George Ohr," and "Southern Folk Pottery"). The cross-referencing is very helpful. For example, "Textiles" has a note to see also "Clothing and Accessories," "Feed & Grain Bags," "Looms," "Repair/Restoration/Conservation," and much more. There is an excellent topical and brand name index. Appendixes arrange appraisers, auction services, and repair firms by zip code, but also include international and Internet entries. There are similar, if less comprehensive, directories, and some of these contacts can be found online. But this directory is so easy to use, and half of the listings do not have Websites. It will be popular in any public or academic library that puts it on the reference shelf. It is highly recommended.—**Deborah V. Rollins**

P

338.   Miller, Judith. **Antiques Price Guide 2003.** New York, DK Publishing, 2002. 752p. illus. index. $35.00. ISBN 0-7894-8940-6.

Judith Miller was from 1979 until 1988 the co-author, with Martin Miller, of *Miller's International Antiques Price Guide.* Miller, who began collection when she was in college at Edinburgh University, is now a leading expert on collecting antiques. She is the author of more than 80 books on collecting. Miller has a regular BBC and Discovery Channel program on antiques. This volume boasts of being "the best full-color guide to over 8,500 antiques." Each page of the volume is full of 11 to 12 color illustrations of antiques. The volume is divided into major subject groupings: Porcelain and Pottery, Oriental, Furniture, Glass, Metal Ware, Clocks, Jewelry, Textiles, Toys and Dolls, Antiquities, Tribal Art, Architectural Antiques, Decorative Arts, Modern Classics, Marine Antiques, Miniatures, and American Paintings. The work starts with two half-page essays: "How To Use this Book" and "Using the Internet." The "Using the Internet" essay is odd in that it mentions neither Websites or eBay, and consists of general information about bidding on the Web. Each illustrated antique has a code letter, which corresponds to the name of the dealer or auction house that sold the item. There is an index to these individuals called the "Key to Illustrations." Ten of the seventy-two individuals listed are from outside the United Kingdom. Some individuals are listed with only the notation "Mob" followed by a number. This appears to be a mobile telephone number, although that is not immediately apparent to the reader. A few dealers have taken out full-page advertisements in the book, so there is an index of advertisers as well as a directory of auctioneers and antique specialists (most of whom are in the United States). There is also a glossary that defines terms such as *Wax Doll*, *gadroon*, *finial*, *cultured pearl*, and *chassis*. There is a fairly comprehensive index to the illustrations, although not all items are indexed. The sword on page 478 and the lantern on page 637, for example, failed to make it into the index. The pretty Mission Style tall case clock on the dust jacket and book cover is not in the book either. Some items, such as radios, are left out of the book entirely.

The illustrations are well done and convey well the item described. No other antique guidebook is as lavishly and comprehensively illustrated as this one. There are over 700 pages of illustrations on heavy paper stock, which may over time place a strain on the binding. Most general reference collections will want to own this major antique reference work.—**Ralph Lee Scott**

P

339.   **Prices 4 Antiques. http://www.prices4antiques.com.** [Website]. Dayton, Ohio, Prices 4 Antiques. Price varies. Date reviewed: May 02.

For the public library serving clientele looking for detailed price information from recent auctions on antiques, collectibles, and fine art, this database will be a good start to finding the answers in a timely manner. This Website's mission is not to sell antiques or endorse products, but rather to provide collectors access to accurate information on the worth of their collectibles, much like television's popular *Antique Roadshow*. The sponsors of this site travel to auctions across the country recording the most current prices that collectibles and antiques are selling for.

The Website offers users two options: they can search the database looking for price information from past auctions or look for price and inventory information from upcoming auctions. When searching the prices of collectibles from past auctions users can search item by category, type, origin, keyword, and year of origination. When a search is recovered, the user is given a detailed description of the item, the pre-sale estimated price, information about the auction (date, price the item sold for, the auction house's contact information, and a brief description of the auction). The information provided for items for sale at upcoming auctions includes: the complete description of the items for sale, an estimated price, the date of the auction, a photograph of the item, and information on how to contact the auction house to make an absentee bid or arrange for telephone bidding. At the bottom of the page is a list of the upcoming auctions currently listed.

This database is easy to search or browse and provides a lot of options in the search categories with which to narrow ones search. Public libraries that cater to clientele requesting information on collectibles, antiques, and fine art will find this site extremely useful.—**Shannon Graff Hysell**

Books

P

340. Ahearn, Allen, and Patricia Ahearn. **Collected Books: The Guide to Values.** 2002 ed. New York, G. P. Putnam's Sons/Penguin Books, 2001. 788p. $75.00. ISBN 0-399-14781-0.

This is the most comprehensive and useful one-volume published price guide to collectable English-language books of the past 200 years. The authors have been involved in the rare book trade for over four decades and are well known as the proprietors of Quill & Brush, a supplier of collectable nineteenth and twentieth century fiction. With some 20,000 items arranged alphabetically by author, this 2002 edition is strongest in the areas of literature and history, and frequently provides helpful pointers on identifying first editions and first issues. Those, however, building comprehensive collection of the works of a specific author and those focused on a particular historical time or topic, such as the American Civil War, will have to consult the catalogs or Websites of specialty dealers as will collectors in the domains of the natural and social sciences. Although there are several other one-volume price guides, such as *Bookman's Price Index* (see ARBA 2000, entry 836) they are simply compilations of dealers' catalogs and are either more expensive or less detailed and informative than this work. Currently, dealers and collectors are frequently using the Internet sites of the Advanced Book Exchange (www.abe.com) and Bookfinder (www.bookfinder.com) to determine the current market value of collected books. With over 20 million items, these Websites are certainly very comprehensive and current. However, using these Websites can be quite time consuming as one has to sort through myriad copies of a specific book in various condition and often the truly rare books are not listed at all. Serious collectors have always consulted with and relied on the seasoned judgment of experienced rare book dealers. This work allows them to do this quickly and conveniently.

—**Joseph Cataio**

Firearms

P

341. Walter, John. **The Greenhill Dictionary of Guns and Gunmakers: From Colt's First Patent to the Present Day, 1836-2001.** Mechanicsburg, Pa., Stackpole Books, 2001. 576p. illus. $59.95. ISBN 1-85367-392-7.

This ready-reference volume by a major authority in the firearms field limits itself to small arms both military and civilian, together with designers, inventors, ammunition, trademarks, terms, and monograms. It does not cover cannon or grenade launchers, nor does it concern itself with "non-guns" (e.g., projectile weapons like crossbows and slings).

The introduction admirably outlines the scope and limitations of the work, which intends to inform about both gunpowder and pneumatic weapons of all nations, ranging from low-power weapons used at the turn of the nineteenth century for indoor recreational shooting to the latest military machine guns. Some 10,000 entries explore subjects as obscure as Chinese industrial marks and as well known as Winchester rifles. All major manufacturers, weapons, and concepts have extended descriptive sidebars with monochrome illustrations, and these entries are supported by critical bibliographic notes. The book is extensively cross-referenced, allowing rapid retrieval of related facts and concepts, this is of particular significance where some entries have dozens of definitions.

While coverage is comprehensive, it is not exhaustive; for example, there is no definition given for the "bullpup" rifle configuration, and while other rare weapons are covered, the Dardick pistol and its associated "tround" are absent. The occasional error was noted, the most severe being the truncation of the entry on page

11. On page 13, "Sprnngfield" should read "Springfield," on page 139 the cross-reference for "Damascus finish" is blind, and on page 324 part of a sentence has been dropped. A major error of fact appears on page 302, where the Lebel rifle is stated to have a box magazine, when in fact it had a tube magazine.

These blemishes are minor indeed when compared to the scope and authority of the overall work. Crisply printed on high-quality paper in a sturdy binding, this book deserves consideration from any library serving a clientele interested in military or civilian weapons, firearms history, or related collecting aspects.—**John Howard Oxley**

Quilts

P
342.   Aug, Bobbie, Sharon Newman, and Gerald Roy. **Vintage Quilts: Identifying Collecting, Dating, Preserving & Valuing.** Paducah, Ky., Collector Books, 2002. 221p. illus. $24.95. ISBN 1-57432-285-0.

It is safe to say that the majority of quilt collectors pursue their hobby for love, not money. And as the authors point out, the only sure value of an item is established between a buyer and a seller—in other words, what the market will bear. Nevertheless, even hobbyists occasionally need to establish the value of a treasured quilt for insurance purposes or for tax purposes when one is donated to a museum or other charity. This book establishes, by numerous examples, guidelines for assigning such a value.

The three authors are all experts in the field of quilt history and collecting. Aug and Newman are also quilters, while Roy is a gallery owner with a fine arts background. They have produced a colorful, easy-to-use picture guide to all varieties and ages of American quilts. Quilts are arranged in 16 sections by type, including such categories as Amish quilts, appliqué, and crazy quilts. There are also sections on quilt tops and on quilt blocks. Within each section, actual quilts are pictured one to three to a page, with information on size, age, origin, and condition. Each is then assigned a price range; for example, $1,000.00 - $1,200.00 for an 1890 Amish crib quilt in excellent condition. Readers need only find a quilt that most resembles theirs in type, age, and condition to get an estimate of its value.

In a short introductory chapter, the authors also discuss types of collections—ones limited by color, by pattern and style, or by age. They also give hints on displaying, storing, and protecting quilts in a collection.
—**Carol L. Noll**

CRAFTS

P
343.   Bednar, Nancy, and JoAnn Pugh-Gannon. **Encyclopedia of Sewing Machine Techniques.** New York, Sterling Publishing, 2001. 336p. illus. index. $24.95pa. ISBN 0-8069-6365-4.

Written by two sewing professionals, this reference covers most techniques that sewing machines can accomplish. From seasoned sewers to beginners, all readers will find instructions and advice on a variety of ways to do bias binding, buttonholes, gathering, hemming with seven finishes, and appliquéing with different stitches. For each technique, color pictures; machine setups; and guidance on fabrics, stitching, needles, threads, tension, and the presser foot are provided. The entire book is also thoroughly indexed for easy accessibility.

To take projects from ordinary to exceptional, sewers can try *ruching* or gathering through the middle of a strip of ribbon or fabric, mitering corners, or *smyra* embroidery where stitched loops are clipped and then fluffed up for a pretty three-dimensional effect. Sterling's use of high-quality, heavy paper and durable binding will ensure a lasting, useful manual. Although public libraries may want to buy this work for their reference collections, the nicely photographed, comprehensive resource really belongs in the personal collections of crafters and sewers.
—**Susan C. Awe**

FASHION AND COSTUME

C, P

344.   **Contemporary Fashion.** 2d ed. Taryn Benbow-Pfalzgraf, ed. Farmington Hills, Mich., St. James Press/ Gale Group, 2002. 743p. illus. index. $170.00. ISBN 1-55862-348-5.

The 2d edition of *Contemporary Fashion* is a wonderful reference book full of information and critical essays on the many facets of the fashion world. Each entry is listed alphabetically and includes a biography or history, in the case of a company. There are high-quality black-and-white photographs and sketches throughout the book that will prove to be an enjoyable reading experience for both readers and researchers. More important, Website addresses are provided when possible.

The strengths of this edition of *Contemporary Fashion*, like its predecessor, are its international coverage, the credentials of its contributors, and the amount of information provided such as citations to other sources. It is recommended for the reference collection of any university library.—**Vang Vang**

22 Fine Arts

GENERAL WORKS

Biography

C, P

345. **Contemporary Artists.** 5th ed. Sara Pendergast and Tom Pendergast, eds. Farmington Hills, Mich., St. James Press/Gale Group, 2002. 2v. illus. index. (Contemporary Arts Series). $250.00/set. ISBN 1-55862-407-4.

Perhaps the most obvious change to the latest edition of this standard art reference title is that it is now a two-volume set. In terms of content, updates have been made but the presentation of information is the same as in previous editions (see ARBA 97, entry 795, and ARBA 90, entry 948). A glance at the nationality index will inform readers that the majority of artists included in this work are American, but a significant number of artists from other nations are represented. In total, nearly 850 prominent artists (those who have exhibited works in major galleries or museums) are listed. The emphasis is on living artists, but a few major artists who died prior to 1990 are included. Alphabetic entries provide biographical information (e.g., nationality, education, address), individual and select group exhibitions, collections in which the artist's work is contained, publications by or about the individual, a critical essay or essays, and occasionally a statement by the artist. The essays highlight the artist's achievements and offer insight into their work. A few black-and-white images accompany the text; some are of the artists but most are representative samples of their artwork. As a reference tool, this publication remains a classic, indispensable part of every art library's collection and is highly recommended.—**Terrie L. Wilson**

P

346. **St. James Guide to Hispanic Artists: Profiles of Latino and Latin American Artists.** Thomas Riggs, ed. Farmington Hills, Mich., St. James Press/Gale Group, 2002. 682p. illus. index. $185.00. ISBN 1-55862-470-8.

As another impressive addition to the list of St. James publications on artists, this reference work profiles 375 artists from North, Central, and South America and the Spanish-speaking nations of the Caribbean. The geographical and cultural parameters of the guide are outlined in the preface; artists from wide-ranging backgrounds are brought together because of strong cultural, linguistic, and historical ties. In addition, terms such as Latino, Hispanic, and Latin American are defined and their usage explained. Twentieth-century visual artists, working in every conceivable medium, are discussed. North and Central American artists comprise the majority of entrants. Male and female artists appear to receive equitable treatment. A typical entry for an artist contains the following: name, medium or media, birth and death dates, education, career history, awards, agents and address (for living artists), individual and group exhibitions, collections, publications by or about the artist, and an essay.

Written by a variety of contributors, the essays focus on biographical information and summarize the artist's achievements. Despite the large number of contributors, the writing is consistently clear and concise. Illustrations are in black-and-white only and do not accompany every entry. A bibliography and indexes for nationality, medium, and illustrations are included. Also, background information on advisors and contributors is provided. It will be difficult to find a more comprehensive and thorough starting point for research on artists in this category. This work is an essential purchase for academic and larger public libraries and for libraries with collections focusing on Latino culture.—**Terrie L. Wilson**

C, P

347.   **Who's Who in American Art 2001-2002.** 24th ed. New Providence, N.J., Marquis Who's Who/Reed Reference Publishing, 2001. 1525p. index. $275.00. ISBN 0-8379-6302-8.

This edition of *Who's Who in American Art* provides biographical information for more than 11,100 artists (or those influential in the field of art)—3,000 of which are new to this edition. As stated, this volume provides information on artists as well as critics, curators, administrators, historians, collectors, conservators, and dealers of art. Information has been gathered through questionnaires sent to the biographees, so the depth of information provided varies. The most complete biographies include full name, date and place of birth, education and training, exhibitions, museums holding their work, professional positions, media in which they work, their dealers and representatives, awards, and contact information. A geographical index and an index by professional classification (with more than 50 categories) will help users find what they are researching. A final index lists biographees from previous volumes who died between 1953 and 2000. This work will be useful in academic libraries and larger public libraries.—**Shannon Graff Hysell**

Catalogs and Collections

C, S

348.   **Greek Art from Prehistoric to Classical: A Resource for Educators.** [CD-ROM]. By the Metropolitan Museum of Art. New Haven, Conn., Yale University Press, 2000. Minimum system requirements (Windows): Pentium processor. CD-ROM drive. 16MB RAM. 640x480 monitor with thousands of colors. Minimum system requirements (Macintosh): PowerPC processor. CD-ROM drive. 16MB RAM. 640x480 monitor with thousands of colors. $69.95.

Greek Art from Prehistoric to Classical is an interesting electronic collaboration between the Metropolitan Museum of Art and Yale University Press. Weaving together images of stunning artwork with teaching materials, the project creates an impressive work that will visually capture the interest of students while teaching them about the development of Greek art through the ages.

The program runs well on both Windows and Macintosh equipment with few or no problems encountered. The CD-ROM is a bit odd for today's insert and play needs; it does not have a start program to automatically start an introductory screen of some sort when the CD-ROM is inserted into the drive. The user needs to insert the disk then browse through it to find the appropriate starting place. Images are well lit and fully centered for easy viewing, and many of the images are somewhat monochromatic. Useful and interesting lesson plans and a discussion guide that stimulate student interaction with the works and Greek art are included on the disk. This is an extremely useful addition, especially for those instructors that may not have extensive experience with the history of Greek art themselves. Several themes of interest to students appear as jumping off points for discussion (e.g., animals, humans).

This work will find use in elementary through high school classroom settings, school libraries, and academic libraries supporting teacher education programs. It is reasonably priced with system requirements that are low enough to allow the CD-ROM to be run by most machines in use today. [R: LJ, Jan 02, p. 167]

—**Gregory Curtis**

Dictionaries and Encyclopedias

C, P

349.   **Art History Resources on the Web. http://witcombe.sbc.edu/ARTHLinks.html.** [Website]. Free. Date reviewed: Sept 02.

This Web resource is maintained by Christopher L. C. E. Witcombe, Professor of Art History at Sweet Briar College in Virginia. It has been online since 1995, and has won numerous awards. The home page of this resource presents the table of contents in two ways to the user: as a chronological index listing that runs on the left and right sides of the home page, and as a chronological table that sits in the middle of the home page. This resource on art history is very thorough, presenting online resources from prehistoric times all the way up to the present. Witcombe prominently displays the date the site was last updated at the top of each resource page, and this information indicates that he is constantly revising and maintaining this resource. The major subdivisions include: "Prehistoric Art," "Ancient Egypt & Near East," "Ancient Greece & Rome," "Middle Ages," "15th Century," "16th Century," "17th Century," "18th Century," "19th Century," "20th Century," "21st Century," "Prints & Photographs," "Asia," "Africa," "The Americas & Oceania," "Museums & Galleries," "Research Resources," and "Various & Miscellaneous." There are numerous subheadings and resources underneath these major subdivisions. This is an essential resource for anyone wanting information in the areas of art, art history, art resources, and art museums.—**Bradford Lee Eden**

C, P

350. **The Penguin Concise Dictionary of Art History.** By Nancy Frazier. New York, Penguin Books, 2000. 774p. index. $20.00pa. ISBN 0-14-051420-1.

The Penguin Concise Dictionary of Art History is a good second source for beginning students of art of the last 500 years in Europe and the United States. Literate ancient periods are perfunctorily summarized, and literate pre-Columbian and Oriental are neglected. Pre-literate arts are only mentioned as sources of later styles. Frazier, a clear and erudite former *Newsweek* writer and MA in art history, prefers the current social science perspective of societal and diffusionist explanations—not amazing emergences of genius nor universal archetype theories. The result is that history and theory are presented with a slant that, since it is explicit, is agreeable enough. The index and bibliography are helpful. It is too bad that footnotes are not part of a dictionary's expectations. Frazier has added succinct quotes at the beginning of many entries. She writes out the plots of myths, sensitively describes some specific pieces and styles, and traces the influence of some art types through their succeeding centuries. These give an intense air of valuable literacy to the effort. There are no pictures and the sites where the originals of these precious contributions to history are not reported.—**Elizabeth L. Anderson**

Directories

P

351. **Hislop's Official International Price Guide to Fine Art.** Duncan Hislop, ed. New York, Three Rivers Press/Crown Publishing Group, 2002. 933p. $20.00pa. ISBN 0-609-80874-5. ISSN 1537-5889.

Hislop's Official International Price Guide to Fine Art is usually published as a very large, two-volume set that has, in the past, sold for more than $200.00. This new paperback edition is now available for $20.00, and is well worth the price, even if it is printed as a cheap paperback with less information and much smaller print. The 2002 version provides essential information for anyone who is buying or selling art and wishes to get an indication of prices covering the past three years of international auction sales of original art. (This edition provides summarized prices for fine art and sculpture that sold at public auction during 2000.) More than 25,000 artists are represented in the guide. The editor points out that this work is considered so reliable that it is a reference guide for the IRS, estate planners, dealers, and auction houses throughout the world. There is a companion CD-ROM available entitled "The Art Sales Index," which provides much more information and lists each lot sold for each artist. The latest 2000/2001 edition of "The Art Sales Index" provides information for more than 140,000 works.

Each entry contains the artist's name, the number of works sold, total value of works sold, lowest price, media price, and highest price. In addition, the dates of birth and death, nationality, and some additional information are sometimes included. All information is provided by the auction houses, and prices listed are the gavel prices (excluding additional fees and charges). Also, the introductory material provides a basic education on art pricing and is well worth reading. This work is highly recommended for all larger public and academic libraries where patrons may be interested in art prices. It is also recommended as an individual purchase for anyone interested in the world of art collecting. At $20.00 the work is sure to find a large audience.—**Robert L. Wick**

Handbooks and Yearbooks

C, P

352.   Cumming, Robert. **ART: A Field Guide.** New York, Alfred A. Knopf/Random House, 2001. 480p. illus. index. $27.50pa. ISBN 0-375-41312-X.

There are many guides and handbooks available today covering the subject of art reference. Reference works dealing with artist biographies, dictionaries of art terms, guides to museum collections, and values of art works are too numerous to be mentioned here. The latest addition to this repertoire is Robert Cumming's *ART: A Field Guide*. Cumming packs a lot of information into a fairly slim volume, intending to enlighten the average art enthusiast as to his personal observations about a variety of artists. In addition, Cumming offers information on how many of the artists' works sold at auction from 1999 to 2000, with figures on lowest and highest prices achieved. The main section of the book consists of alphabetic entries for more than 770 artists who are broken down into 5 categories: all time greats, old masters, modern masters, national heroes, and contemporary stars. There are also 700 full color illustrations throughout this section and a number of symbols are used to help interpret the information.

The next section consists of a discussion of subjects and stories used in western art (mainly religious and mythological), and includes an extensive visual vocabulary of codes and symbols that artists have used. There are extensive cross-references used throughout this section. The third section is a glossary of art terms for which the author has specifically given short, concise definitions. The work ends with a section for art on the Internet, a list of illustrations, and a general index.

At first glance, this book looks a little confusing, but the author does a fine job of explaining his methodology in the introduction. This work is recommended mainly on the basis of the current auction information, but the author's personal observations on the artists could also serve as a nice complement to the more concrete information one might find in typical entries from a work such as *The Grove Dictionary of Art* (see ARBA 2002, entry 993, for a review of the online version). [R: LJ, 1 Nov 01, p. 82; SLJ, April 02, p. 186]—**Richard Slapsys**

C, P

353.   Honour, Hugh, and John Fleming. **The Visual Arts: A History.** 6th ed. New York, Harry N. Abrams, 2002. 960p. illus. index. $85.00. ISBN 0-8109-3593-7.

Now in its 6th edition, *The Visual Arts: A History* represents nearly all types of art and provides an exploratory history of the evolution of art. Hugh Honour is considered a leading art historian and has authored many books on the subject of art history, and John Fleming, who died in 2001, authored several art history reference titles. This work focuses on explaining the history of art rather than providing critical analysis of the art.

The work is arranged chronologically beginning with the artwork of early civilizations and ending with new forms of twenty-first century art, such as video art and installation art. Included within are descriptions of sculpture, painting, mosaic, photography, textiles, pottery, and enamels, and how the artists used them to define their historical time period. The work is divided into five parts, each containing several chapters: "Foundations of Art," "Art and the World Religions," "Sacred and Secular Art," "The Making of the Modern World," and "Twentieth-Century Art." The authors often focus on the influence of religion and culture in the progression of art history. The 1,400 illustrations, maps, time charts, and architectural plans serve to enhance the text. A glossary, list of further reading, list of picture credits, and an index conclude the volume.

This work will be useful for undergraduates of art history as well as the layperson with an interest in art. This will be a valuable addition to public and academic libraries.—**Shannon Graff Hysell**

Indexes

C, P

354.   **Index to Artistic Biography: Second Supplement.** Patricia Pate Havlice, comp. Lanham, Md., Scarecrow, 2002. 2v. $195.00/set. ISBN 0-8108-4062-6.

The *Index to Artistic Biography* was first published in 1973 and quickly became a standard reference source for biographical information in the fine arts. A *First Supplement* was published in 1981 (see ARBA 83, entry 832), which increased the sources in which biographical information could be found. With the publishing of this *Second Supplement* the work is brought up to date. The primary index and the supplements are standalone sources in that they may be used separately to find artists' names and sources for biographical information. Artists are sometimes listed in more than one volume in order to add additional biographical information as it becomes available. The *Second Supplement* includes more than 130 sources not published in the original volume or the *First Supplement*. The compiler points out in his preface to the *Second Supplement* that he "was struck by the number of biographical works devoted to the work of female artists" (p. v) now available. Most of the works are in English, but a few French and Spanish titles are included. Some information is included that is not strictly biographical for minor and lesser-known artists in order to provide some material on these individuals.

The format has remained consistent throughout the three volumes. While the coverage is worldwide, the majority of artists listed are from Europe and the United States.

This work is highly recommended for academic and public libraries already owning the first two volumes of this set, and would even make a logical purchase as a standalone volume. As mentioned, it has become a standard reference source for biographical information on artists. [R: Choice, June 02, p. 1738]—**Robert L. Wick**

23 Language and Linguistics

GENERAL WORKS

Dictionaries and Encyclopedias

C, P

355.   **The Oxford Dictionary of Word Histories.** Glynnis Chantrell, ed. New York, Oxford University Press, 2002. 560p. $25.00. ISBN 0-19-863121-9.

The etymologies in standard dictionaries are usually curt, factual, and minimally informative, conveying little except to those with some knowledge of the history of the language and linguistics. The entries here either condense information in the *Oxford English Dictionary* or make it fuller for clarity, typically adding explanations of origin and supplying reasons for changes in meaning and in form. Chantrell intelligently selects from the bulky information in the OED about the word "water" to tell us that it comes from an Indo-European root shared by Russian voda, Latin unda, and Greek hudor, a piece of information that stays in the user's mind by reason of its simplicity. She is particularly good at indicating links that are not obvious between words, as between "charade" and "charlatan." She is not always consistent in that, however, overlooking some clear links: is not "leak" related to German *Loch*? And is not "cheek" related to Russian *shcheka*?

Chantrell's love of words is obvious, and it gives a human touch, even a charm, to the book, a quality that dictionaries do not normally have. She assumes an educated audience that has some knowledge of European languages without being trained linguists, and so writes only a brief history of the English language. She does not explain linguistic phenomena like assimilation or Ausdehnung; when she uses a term like "metathesis," she immediately defines it. Her list of entries is of course selective, but much less arbitrary than one might expect; the entries are extremely well chosen.—**John B. Beston**

Handbooks and Yearbooks

C, P

356.   **The Cambridge Grammar of the English Language.** By Rodney Huddleston and Geoffrey K. Pullum. New York, Cambridge University Press, 2002. 1842p. index. $150.00. ISBN 0-521-43146-8.

Given the bulk and quality of this new English grammar, its publication must be considered a major event. It comes only 17 years after the publication of *A Comprehensive Grammar of the English Language* (Longman, 1985). The newer book is as bulky as the older one; including the indexes, the 2002 book has 1,842 pages and the 1985 one has 1,779 pages. An important point, however, is that one of the books does not make the other superfluous. On the contrary, a serious student of English will have to use both of them. The reason for this consists in the fact that the older publication uses a structure that is closer to the usual sequence of chapters in other grammars. Also, the treatment and discussions are concerned in the first line with the description of grammatical sentences and their components as opposed to ungrammatical ones. The work under review, however, is more concerned with the logical reasons for some phenomena, with the illocutionary force of various speech acts and their realization in various constructions, and so on. Not that the older work has not included that as well. On the contrary, after all, a modern grammar cannot be written without it; but, in this title, the reader gets the whole panoply of the new notions and modern terms, even with occasional etymologies of the (yet) unusual Greek, Latin, or Graecoid terms.

The 2 authors of the new book, and their 10 colleagues who provide shorter passages in the grammar, all live in territories where English is the majority language of most native speakers, including Australia and New Zealand. While this aspect adds to the scope of the subjects treated, it is standard English that is the center of attention. This work will certainly be published in new editions and printings and some minor errors should be taken care of at that time. Many frequently hear the reproach that modern grammatical research since the second half of the preceding century is quite fragmented and that only single phenomena, even only single sentences, are studied. One of the achievements of these grammars, taken either singly or as a pair, is that they prove an exhaustive treatment of a language to be possible provided that readers are not too single-mindedly doctrinaire. [R: LJ, 1 Sept 02, p. 166]—**L. Zgusta**

C, S

357.   **Grammar Smart: A Guide to Perfect Usage.** 2d ed. New York, Princeton Review/Random House, 2001. 222p. index. (Smart Guides). $12.00pa. ISBN 0-375-76215-9.

Grammar Smart: A Guide to Perfect Usage is written for "people who can't stand grammar" but who must also take standardized tests (such as the SAT and ACT), which call for a working knowledge of grammar. As with the courses offered by the Princeton Review, the aim of this book is to present exactly what students need to know in a way that is "smart, efficient, and fun."

Like standard grammar texts, *Grammar Smart: A Guide to Perfect Usage* begins with a review of the parts of speech. Unlike most such books, however, the exercises provided in leading the student to identify the parts of speech in question are "hip" and entertaining. In a discussion of tense, for example, the future is called "the Star Trek" tense, and many of the sentences offered as examples are humorous. Also included in *Grammar Smart: A Guide to Perfect Usage* are chapters and exercises on the sentence, problems in writing sentences, and punctuation and usage. The latter chapter, "Easy Ways to Look Bad," features problems like the lie/lay distinction, the difference between their/there and infer/imply, and common mispronunciations and their cure. Another chapter deals with the kinds of questions likely to be on specific tests. The final chapter, "The World Series," provides a mini-examination of the points covered in the text.

Grammar Smart: A Guide to Perfect Usage is a valuable study tool that should be made available not only to test-takers but to anyone who wants to brush up on grammar without being bored.—**Kay O. Cornelius**

ENGLISH-LANGUAGE DICTIONARIES

General Usage

C, S

358.   **American English Study Dictionary.** P. H. Collin, B. Kipfer, R. Martinez, and H. Spradling, eds. London, Peter Collin; distr., Chicago, Independent Publishers Group, 2002. 710p. $12.95pa. ISBN 1-901659-69-0.

This American dictionary, published Peter Collin a London-based publisher, is designed with intermediate level English students in mind. It provides definitions of 18,000 of the most commonly used words in American English. What makes this dictionary especially useful for students is the fact that each term is given at least one illustrative example. For example, the term *game* has seven illustrative sentences in its definition, including one for the term used as a sport, the term used for wild animals, and the term used as an adjective ("ready and willing"). Along with these illustrative sentences the work provides a pronunciation guide for each word as well as a 1-4 number based on the frequency the word appears in speech and examinations. This small dictionary will not replace the larger, more-established dictionaries such as those from Merriam-Webster or Oxford University Press, but it will serve as a useful ready-reference in high school and undergraduate libraries or on the desks of undergraduate students.—**Shannon Graff Hysell**

C, P

359.   **The American Heritage Dictionary for Learners of English.** rev. ed. New York, Houghton Mifflin, 2002. 999p. $24.00. ISBN 0-618-24951-6.

Designed as a ready resource for learners of English as a second language, this dictionary will also be useful to native English speakers. The dictionary includes more than 40,000 words and phrases, drawn mainly from books, magazines, and encyclopedias used by students. Special attention has been given to include new words in the fields of business, medicine, science, and technology. Words are listed alphabetically in bold type with syllables noted by bullets. An easy-to-master pronunciation system is used with the key to the system being given at the bottom of each left-hand page. Simple, clear definitions are presented, with the most common definition given first. Short sample sentences use the word to provide contextual information. The dictionary also includes entries on prefixes, suffixes, and abbreviations. In addition, word building notes, usage notes, and illustrations are given to increase the efficacy of the work.

This work is designed for regular use and features clear, dark print and a sturdy binding. Although general dictionaries are often used for ESL instruction, this resource is specifically designed to assist the ESL student in correctly learning the various meanings of words by giving short, clear definitions and good examples of their use in sentences. The inexpensive price makes it a worthwhile purchase, especially for libraries that support ESL classes. Purchasing additional copies for circulation would be a boon to students. [R: LJ, 1 Feb 03, p. 72]

—**Gregory A. Crawford**

C, P

360.   **Oxford Advanced Learner's CD-ROM Dictionary.** [CD-ROM]. Cincinnati, Ohio, Encomium Publications, 2000. Minimum system requirements: IBM or compatible PC. 24-speed CD-ROM drive. Windows 95, Windows 98, Windows NT, or Windows 2000. 32MB RAM. 30MB hard disk space. SVGA monitor (600x800 screen resolution). Optional SoundBlaster sound card, headphones, speakers, and microphone. Mouse. $49.95. ISBN 0-19-436795-9.

The *Oxford Advanced Learner's Dictionary* has long been a standard tool for advanced students of English. With more than 80,000 references, it defines a much larger set of terms than most ESL (English as a second language) dictionaries. However, because it uses a vocabulary of only 3,500 words to define those terms, it should not overwhelm students.

The CD-ROM version of this dictionary consists of the contents of the print edition (presumably the 6th edition) plus over 4,500 new definitions and several interactive features specific to the CD-ROM. The main portion of the dictionary is a browseable and searchable A-Z section, allowing users to locate definitions, examples of usage, and idioms. Audio clips are available for all entries, permitting students to listen to correct pronunciations and to practice and hear their own pronunciation of terms. For some entries, video clips or still images can be accessed as well, letting users get visual definitions of the terms. Exercises and games allow users to practice what they have learned. Unfortunately, because the dictionary uses British English, the exercises and games can often be confusing in an American context. A somewhat unclear "3-D Search" section that provides displays of words linked to related terms seems unnecessary.

The CD-ROM is easy to install. Although it requires Adobe Acrobat and Microsoft Media Player, these will automatically load from the CD-ROM. It is possible to install the CD-ROM so that the dictionary can be used directly from a word processor. It is also possible to install at three levels, allowing some or all of the features to be loaded directly on the hard drive. The dictionary appears to work equally well at all three levels. Libraries that serve ESL students will want to purchase this dictionary. Although the print version will be adequate for most, the CD-ROM version does provide added interactive functionality at a reasonable price. [R: LJ, 1 Feb 02, p. 144]—**Michael Levine-Clark**

C, P

361.   **The Oxford Desk Dictionary and Thesaurus.** 2d American ed. Elizabeth J. Jewell, ed. New York, Oxford University Press, 2002. 1008p. $17.95. ISBN 0-19-515934-9.

First published in 1997, *The Oxford Desk Dictionary and Thesaurus* is described by the publishers as a "bestseller," with more than 200,000 copies in print. The 2d edition has been updated with new words, which include *9/11*, *burka*, *cargo pant*, and *tankini*. Its content is based on the 1,800-page *Oxford Dictionary and Thesaurus* (American ed.; see ARBA 98, entry 994). While some 800 pages smaller, the volume is hardly a comfortable weight for a backpack, as the publisher suggests.

A one-volume reference that serves a dual purpose is appealing. Both meanings and related words are given within the same entry. In a comparison of the word "cold" with the entry in a dedicated thesaurus, the one-volume work lists fewer synonyms and no antonyms, and the print is much smaller. However, most writers will find that *The Oxford Desk Dictionary and Thesaurus* meets their needs for a one-stop desk reference.

In addition to the dictionary and thesaurus entries, a special reference section offers information about a variety of topics ranging from standard weights and measures and chemical elements to U.S. Presidents, area codes, and international time zones. Especially valuable is the updated section on countries of the world. However, it is unlikely that the "Dictionary Games" page will see much use.

For the office or individual whose desk space is limited, *The Oxford Desk Dictionary and Thesaurus* is a useful choice. More serious writers, or those who prefer larger print, may find that the two-in-one approach is not for them. [R: LJ, 1 Nov 02, p. 80]—**Kay O. Cornelius**

Juvenile

S

362.   **The McGraw-Hill Children's Dictionary.** Columbus, Ohio, McGraw-Hill Children's Publishing, 2003. 830p. illus. maps. index. $24.95. ISBN 1-57768-298-X.

S

363.   **The McGraw-Hill Children's Thesaurus.** By the Wordsmyth Collaboratory. Columbus, Ohio, McGraw-Hill Children's Publishing, 2003. 294p. illus. $19.95. ISBN 1-57768-296-3.

The colorful cover of *The McGraw-Hill Children's Dictionary* claims it is "The Only Dictionary Your Child Will Ever Need!" With 830 entry pages and 97 more "reference" pages, this volume may seem at times to contain almost too much information. Many of the illustrations are in full color and useful. Others, like that of a girl standing with her hand to her head beside the entry for the word "misunderstanding," are less useful. Double-page spreads on subjects such as "Musical Instruments" and "The Solar System" are impressive, as are the word histories and a color-coded system to relate a word to 10 areas, ranging from the human body and communication to economy and government and law. Younger children may be overwhelmed by *The McGraw-Hill Children's Dictionary*, but this volume would be a great addition for those from the fourth grade up.

A companion volume, *The McGraw-Hill Children's Thesaurus*, claims to be "the only thesaurus your child will ever need." Its aim is "to help the young reader build a vocabulary that is expressive, versatile, and precise." Many entry words have been keyed to the same topics used in the companion dictionary. This volume contains fewer illustrations, but most are well chosen. Full-page spreads on words like "dogs," "insects," and "trees" encourage the user to employ specific, rather than generic, terms. With or without its *Dictionary*, *The McGraw-Hill Children's Thesaurus* will be a valuable addition to the upper elementary classroom, library, or any place where children write or do homework.—**Kay O. Cornelius**

Terms and Phrases

C, P

364.   **Brewer's Dictionary of Modern Phrase and Fable.** Adrian Room, comp. Cassell, London; distr., New York, Sterling Publishing, 2002. 774p. $39.95pa. ISBN 0-304-35871-1.

Like its forerunners that also bear the "Brewer's" imprimatur, this work consists of a single A-Z listing of about 8,000 defined entries that are names of persons, places, expressions, things, and ideas that are based in fact or fiction, and that largely define the cultural trappings and traditions most familiar to today's British and American citizenry. Specifically, Room focuses upon items that gained or regained appreciable cultural prominence during the twentieth century.

This resource is essentially an updating of *Brewer's Dictionary of Twentieth Century Phrase & Fable*, edited by David Pickering (see ARBA 93, entry 1294), itself a descendent of generations of the venerable *Brewer's Dictionary of Phrase & Fable*. Further, the volume at hand updates its hardcover predecessor. Death dates for George Harrison and Ken Kesey are included here, as are entries for such 2001 films as *Bridget Jones's Diary* and *Tomb Raider*. In several entries, the terrorist attacks of September 11, 2001 are covered as well. While most entries consist of fewer than 100 words, some extend to twice or thrice this length (e.g., Vietnam, Bandit Country, Peter Pan, Lawrence of Arabia). In addition, 28 so-called "list entries" are lengthier yet (e.g., political correctness, medical abbreviations, string quartets). A significant number of foreign-language entry words and phrases are contained, as well. However, this book has a decided British slant in its selection and definition of entries. "Ants in one's pants" is accompanied by an aside informing the reader that "pants" means "trousers." Such skewing is evident in other instances as well. For instance, despite their formidable influence, it is arguable whether the Beatles and their music merit the 30 or so entries accorded them. The entry for the television game show *Price Is Right* states that the series aired only during the mid-1980s, without noting that the U.S. counterpart debuted in 1956, and has continued into the new millennium. On the other hand, Room accommodates interests from both sides of the Atlantic with his "Dennis the Menace" entry, which provides information on the two distinct cartoon characters created in 1951 by British cartoonist David Law and in the U.S. by Hank Ketcham.

This compendium is particularly strong in its inclusion of entries of acronyms, names of obscure and semi-obscure personalities, and nicknames. Entries have not been devoted to such influential persons as Frank Sinatra, Billy Graham, Bob Dylan, H. G. Wells, Walt Disney, Fred Astaire, Gore Vidal, or Stephen King. It is sometimes only through serendipity that biographical information may be discovered in this book. For example, consult "Ol' Blue Eyes" or "Scooby Do" for information on Frank Sinatra or see "Blairism" for information on Tony Blair. Users may also be put off by the tabloid tone of many entries. Room's proclivity for chatty editorializing can become annoying. Do we need to know that he considers the Beatles' "All You Need Is Love" to be an "undistinguished" song, or that he believes Hillary Clinton to be a "long-suffering" wife?

Unfortunately, in their degree of factuality, entries are occasionally incomplete, uneven, misleading, disputable, or incorrect. Why include sayings from Sam Goldwyn and Arthur Mizner, but not from Yogi Berra, Mae West, or Dorothy Parker? Why include one of London's airports (Heathrow) but exclude the other (Gatwick)? The entry on the film *Fail-Safe* fails to mention the award-winning film or book adaptation. Surprising omissions include marijuana, pot, joint, and acid; computer, microchip, and hacker; VCR and DVD; Stephen Spielberg, Bill Gates, and Jack Kilby (microchip inventor); O. J. Simpson; Philo T. Farnsworth (television inventor); Ted Bundy, the Zodiac Killer, and John Wayne Gacy; "right to die," euthanasia, and Karen Ann Quinlin; Osbert Sitwell; slinky; cloning; drive-by shooting; "go postal" (although "go ballistic" is included). Weaknesses and gaffes in this volume's format, layout, and copyediting crop up on occasion as well. Page numbers have been placed all but out of sight by the binding's crease. The name of Beavis' cohort is variously spelled "Butthead" (p. 12) and "Butt-head" (p. 13). A spurious hyphen interrupts "paint-ing" (p. 25). Under Beatles, the reference to the Fab Four's first motion picture includes the unaccountable italicizing of a letter. For its breadth of coverage, this dictionary is of value to public and academic libraries. However, it should be used with some caution in light of its aforementioned shortcomings. [R: BL, 1 Oct 01, p. 346]—**Jeffrey E. Long**

C, P

365.   **Facts on File Dictionary of Foreign Words and Phrases.** By Martin H. Manser. David H. Pickering, ed. New York, Facts on File, 2002. 432p. index. (Facts on File Library of Language and Literature). $45.00. ISBN 0-8160-4458-9.

This book is a must for writers, editors, students, and language lovers. It is also an irresistible resource for browsers and the curious. Even the most adept and well-read persons will occasionally need to look up the correct usage of foreign phrases, and this volume provides easy access to the ones most commonly used. It includes entries from all fields of endeavor, such as music, law, cuisine and philosophy, and entries that originated in a number of foreign languages, including Latin. It also provides pronunciation guides, along with concise quotations that help illustrate usage. Here users can check on the correct spelling of *je ne sais quoi*, the etymology of *denim* (French, meaning "from *Nimes*"), the meaning of *apparatchik*, the correct usages of *fiancé* and *fiancée*, the translation of *quo vadis* (where are you going), and the correct spelling of *eisteddfod* (Welsh festival of the arts). Apart from the professional user, curious browsers will find hours of enjoyment perusing more than 4,000 cleanly laid out terms and expressions from around the world. [R: LJ, 15 May 02, p. 86]—**Koraljka Lockhart**

C, P

366.   **The Facts on File Dictionary of Proverbs: Meanings and Origins of More Than 1,500 Popular Sayings.** By Martin H. Manser. Rosalind Fergusson, ed. New York, Facts on File, 2002. 440p. (Facts on File Library of Language and Literature). $45.00. ISBN 0-8160-4607-7.

This is a basic collection of general, English-language proverbs arranged alphabetically by the first word of the saying. Each proverb is defined in simple, modern English. An example of usage is usually given, either in a made-up sentence that reinforces the meaning or with a quote from the published literature. Sometimes the entry includes information on the first known published use of the proverb, although no sources for the information are given and there is no claim that the author has used anything but secondary resources for this information. When appropriate, alternate versions of the proverb or citations of proverbs that offer either the same or opposite piece of wisdom also appear.

Cross-referencing is provided within the alphabetic sequence between versions of a saying as well as from forms used less frequently to better-known versions. In addition, two indexes are provided, one by theme and one by keyword. The terms in the former are quite broad and probably less useful than the detailed and specific terminology of the 112-page keyword index.

This collection is useful for checking the wording of a proverb or reading a succinct description of its meaning. If, however, one requires a more scholarly approach to information on the history, development, or background of a proverb, larger collections or even another small dictionary of proverbs, such as the *Concise Oxford Dictionary of Proverbs* (Oxford University Press, 1998), would be preferable. A very readable, easy-to-use collection of proverbs, this book will be useful either at home or in most types of libraries. [R: LJ, Jan 03, p. 92]—**Florence W. Jones**

Thesauri

C, P, S

367.   **The American Heritage Thesaurus for Learners of English.** Joyce LeBaron and Susannah LeBaron, comps. New York, Houghton Mifflin, 2002. 326p. $18.00. ISBN 0-618-12990-1.

Similar to its companion, *The American Heritage Dictionary for Learners of English* (see entry 359), this thesaurus attempts to help ESL students build their English vocabulary. To do this, each synonym for a word includes a brief definition and a sample sentence, greatly increasing the understanding of the differences and similarities between the synonyms. The two appendixes provide direction on the correct use of irregular English verbs and on the idiomatic use of prepositions.

The thesaurus is designed for frequent use and features clear, easy-to-read print and sturdy binding. Although other thesauri are often effectively used for ESL instruction, this particular resource has been specifically designed to assist students in correctly learning the various meanings of the synonyms by giving short, clear definitions and good examples of their use in sentences. The inexpensive price will make this a worthwhile purchase, especially for libraries that support ESL classes. Students will definitely appreciate additional copies being purchased for circulation. [R: LJ, 1 Feb 03, p. 72]—**Gregory A. Crawford**

NON-ENGLISH-LANGUAGE DICTIONARIES

Hebrew

C, P

368.   Zilkha, Avraham. **Modern English-Hebrew Dictionary.** New Haven, Conn., Yale University Press, 2002. 457p. (Yale Language Series). $55.00; $19.00pa. ISBN 0-300-09004-8; 0-300-09005-6pa.

The author wrote this dictionary to address a common problem in most bilingual dictionaries—translating words that have multiple meanings in a way that enables the user to make a distinction between them. As an example of the need for this dictionary, if a student had an assignment to translate "I am traveling home for the spring break" from English into Hebrew, he might accidentally write "I am traveling homeward on the path of the broken metal spring" in Hebrew. Zilkha's dictionary quickly shows the student that, while the word for bedspring or metal coil is *kafitz*, the season is *aviv*. This attractive volume should be quite user-friendly for English-speaking students who will find it handy for Hebrew courses and trips to Israel.—**Anthony Gottlieb**

Spanish

C

369.   Langenscheidt's New College Spanish Dictionary: Spanish-English, English-Spanish. Ambler, Pa., Langenscheidt Publishers, 2002. 1062p. $32.95; $34.95 (thumb-index edition). ISBN 1-58573-245-1.

Among the crowded field of bilingual Spanish/English dictionaries Langenscheidt's updated college edition offers little to distinguish itself from the competition. Like similar titles, it has the usual guides to pronunciation; grammar reviews; and charts of irregular verbs, numerals, and weights and measures. Its supplementary material also includes a well-organized, easy-to-follow user's guide and an outline of the differences between British and U.S. English orthography. Although the text appears in small print and a tight format (three columns per page), it has a clear, dark typeface that makes it reader-friendly.

Of special interest are new translations based on contemporary usage, as in the entry for the word *surf*. Following the traditional meaning of *espuma (de las olas)*, *oleaje*, and the sports term *hacer surf, practicar con tabla hawaiana*, one also finds an equivalent of more recent vintage: *navegar* (referring to the Internet). Many neologisms and words currently in vogue are included, but there are some curious omissions. For instance, listings appear for *camcorder* (*videocámara*), *telemarketing* (*telemarketing, marketing telefónico*), *anthrax* (*ántrax*), and the new European currency *euro*, but there is no entry for *audiobook* or for *sonogram*.

One drawback is the lack of reciprocity between the two sections. This is especially true in the case of acronyms where, for example, UN appears in the English/Spanish listings, but ONU is absent from the Spanish/English section. The inclusion of NATO, OAS, and OPEC and the corresponding omission of OTAN, OEA, OPEP further illustrate this annoying defect. Also, there are instances where a Spanish equivalent for an English term has no listing of its own; such is the case with the word *chayote* (*squash*). A related example is the absence of the word *máquina* from the equivalents given for *car*. This is problematic because in the Spanish listings *car* does appear as one of the meanings of *máquina*. This imbalanced coverage of the two languages is nowhere more evident than in the way the work is divided. Whereas most dual-language dictionaries devote roughly 50 percent of the volume to each language, in this one there are less than 400 pages in the Spanish/English section but almost 650 pages in the English/Spanish portion.

With regard to size (125,000 references), scope (emphasis on the spoken and written language of today, including coverage of Latin American variants of Spanish), and price, the title under review is comparable to *Cassell's Spanish Dictionary* and the *American Heritage Spanish Dictionary* (2d ed.; see ARBA 2002, entry 1040). Despite this dictionary's shortcomings, it has much to offer. As a language reference tool it provides reliable and extensive coverage, and it should prove to be a valuable guidebook for any serious student of Spanish or English.
—**Melvin S. Arrington Jr.**

C, P

370.   The University of Chicago Spanish Dictionary: Spanish-English, English-Spanish. David Pharies, ed. Chicago, University of Chicago Press, 2002. 300p. $27.50; $11.00pa. ISBN 0-226-66688-3; 0-226-66689-1pa.

This new edition of a well-known, concise Spanish-English/English-Spanish dictionary has been substantially revised, updated, and expanded since the last edition 15 years ago (see ARBA 88, entry 1107). It includes 80,000 entries, divided into two sections, each with a list of abbreviations, guide to pronunciation, and notes on grammar. The brief definitions include pronunciation (English), grammatical category, and illustrative phrases. There is no systematic attempt to distinguish regional usage, in English or in Spanish. The dictionary is well organized and easy to read, using two columns and boldface for the headword and phrases. There is a short preface and helpful introduction (both in Spanish and English) on how to use the dictionary. It clearly describes the order of entries, spelling, omissions, and structure of entries. The dictionary is aimed for the American learner of Spanish and the Spanish-speaking learner of American English, at any level of fluency. It aims to provide a core, up-to-date vocabulary, one that is concise yet comprehensive enough to satisfy both beginners and advanced speakers. Its scope is broad, including new terms in science, technology, medicine, business, politics, and popular culture. Among abridged Spanish-English/English-Spanish dictionaries, this new edition of a classic, authoritative work provides a useful tool for a large and growing audience in the United States as well as in other parts of the Spanish-speaking world. It is an important addition to reference collections, particularly in high school, community college, and public libraries.—**Susan J. Freiband**

24 Literature

GENERAL WORKS

Bio-bibliography

C, S

371. Galens, David, ed. **Literary Movements for Students: Presenting Analysis, Context, and Criticism on Literary Movements.** Farmington Hills, Mich., Gale, 2002. 398p. illus. index. $125.00/set. ISBN 0-7876-6517-7.

Gale's series of books "for students," whose ever-expanding volumes already cover the standard genres, adds yet another set. The 28 lengthy entries—14 in each volume—treat movements such as humanism, Renaissance literature, magic realism, or existentialism in a consistent scheme, which consists of a brief description or history of the subject, representative authors and works, typical themes, and styles. Other features include a movement's variations, its historical context, and an overview of criticism, plus one or more critical essays, the latter occasionally overly academic for the intended audience. Bibliographic sources are listed, as are suggestions for further reading. Meant to appeal to a younger audience are sidebars, which include "What Do I Study Next?," "Topics for Further Study," and "Media Adaptations," as well as a liberal sprinkling of attractive illustrations.

Volume 1 treats pre-twentieth-century movements, while the twentieth century and beyond are found in volume 2. Rather than listing the movements in typical chronological order, the movements are listed alphabetically. Contributors of the signed entries are identified in a separate list as various writers, students, and scholars. Each volume ends with a glossary of literary terms, an author/title index, a national/ethnicity index, and a subject/theme index. Unfortunately, the indexes are by no means comprehensive. Numerous themes listed in the main section are not found in the subject/theme index, even though the introduction assures us they will be there in boldface (for example, Dreams and Visions is not listed for the Romanticism entry). Also, many authors and works mentioned in the larger entries do not appear in author/title index.

High school teachers and students and college undergraduates will find these volumes useful. They offer a one-stop introduction to literary history and themes. The steep price, however, may make its purchase debatable.
—**Willa Schmidt**

Handbooks and Yearbooks

C, P

372. **Great American Writers: Twentieth Century.** R. Baird Shuman, ed. Tarrytown, N.Y., Marshall Cavendish, 2002. 13v. illus. index. $459.95/set. ISBN 0-7614-7240-1.

This 13-volume set from Marshall Cavendish introduces students to notable U.S. and Canadian writers. While some of the writers included were born in the nineteenth century, all of the writers included in this set published their works during the twentieth century. Overall, this set covers trendsetters that broke away from the genteel writing of the nineteenth century—such as Jack London, Upton Sinclair, and Gertrude Stein—along with groundbreaking authors throughout the twentieth century, including F. Scott Fitzgerald, John Steinbeck, Toni Morrison, and Margaret Atwood. Playwrights, such as Eugene O'Neill, Arthur Miller, and Tennessee Williams are also covered.

The alphabetic entries begin with a summary of the vital facts about the author (i.e., birth and death dates and writing genres) and a paragraph about the writer's significance in American literature followed by four main sections. "The Writer's Life" discusses important events in the writer's life and "The Writer's Work" focuses on the writer's literary contributions, including issues they addressed, recurrent themes, and character development. The "Reader's Guide to Major Works" section provides essays on a selection of the writer's most notable and representative works. This section also includes lists of sources for further study. The last section, "Other Works," briefly summarizes the writer's other works not covered in the previous section. The entries then conclude with an additional list of resources, including books, Websites, and videos.

Color photographs and illustrations are present throughout the volumes. Each volume contains a volume-specific index and volume 13 contains a comprehensive index for the entire set. This volume also includes a glossary; a list of Noble Prize winners in literature; a list of Pulitzer Prize winners; a further reading list; a guide to the writers by genre; and additional indexes by literary works, visual arts, visual artists, films, literary characters, and geographical locations. At nearly $460, this set is recommended for larger middle school, high school, and college libraries and smaller libraries that can afford it. It is a good introductory resource to many of the writers that are commonly studied in today's curriculum. [R: SLJ, Nov 02, p. 106]—**Cari Ringelheim**

CHILDREN'S AND YOUNG ADULT LITERATURE

Bibliography

P, S

373.   Ansell, Janis, and Pam Spencer Holley. **What Do Children Read Next?/What Do Young Adults Read Next? Volume 4.** Farmington Hills, Mich., Gale, 2002. 2v. index. $199.00/set. ISBN 0-7876-4799-3. ISSN 1525-3740.

This two-volume readers' advisory tool is designed to help guide young readers to the appropriate books for their interests. Each volume contains 1,100 titles with easy access provided by 11 indexes: award, time period, geographic, subject, character name, character description, age, page count, illustrator, author, and title. Entries are arranged alphabetically by author, and each entry, in addition to the information reflected in the various indexes, includes a brief plot summary, citations to reviews, other books by the same author, and other books similar in style or theme. Titles for inclusion were selected based on their currency, reader appeal, and literary merit. Books in the children's volume were selected from those published during 1999-2000, while the volume aimed at young adults includes both recent and classic titles. Each volume begins with an introduction that provides an overview of issues related to reading for children and for young adults.

With more than 1,000 entries per volume and 11 ways of accessing those entries, these volumes seem to be the answer to a prayer for busy school or public librarians. Since titles included span the range of readers from "reluctant" to "avid," these reference books are useful for the full range of young patrons. Here is a quick way to answer that question so frequently encountered by librarians, "What should I read next?" The plot summaries are clear and well written and provide a good overview of the book, and the added bonus of review citations make these volumes useful for ordering and for preparing that "wish list" for unexpected windfalls.—**Constance A. Mellon**

S

374.   **Children's Literature Comprehensive Database. http://www.childrenslit.com.** [Website]. Bethesda, Md., CLCD Company LLC. $249.95/year (for 1st subscription); $200.00/year (for 2d subscription); $150.00/year (for 3d subscription); $100.00/year (for 4th and subsequent subscriptions). Date reviewed: Mar 02.

The *Children's Literature Comprehensive Database* (CLCD) is an extensive resource to 600,000 MARC records and more than 70,000 reviews of children's books. Recently, the publisher has begun incorporating information on prizes and awards that the books have won. For example, users can access data on the 2002 winners of the Pura Belpré, Batchelder, Caldecott, Coretta Scott King, Newbery, Michael L. Printz, and Robert F. Sibert Awards. With the database being updated on a monthly basis, subscribers will have up-to-date access to the most recent reviews of children's books, including recent American Library Association award winners.

User's can search for and access the reviews and MARC records in several different ways. Naturally, a basic word search function is provided. But users can refine their searches to locate words or phrases within entry titles for fiction or nonfiction (or both) works and for works from one or more genres (atlases, biography, dictionaries, encyclopedias, folklore, horror, poetry, sports, fantasy, historical fiction, mystery, and science fiction). Word qualifiers can also be used to help narrow search fields. For example, the database can search for singular and plural forms, word variants, the exact word or phrase, all of the words, or any of the words. Further, users can designate specific fields to be searched: "Author," "Title," "Subject," "ISBN," "Annotation," "Review," or "Reviewer." A full text search capability is also available along with other qualifiers, such as age group, language, author/illustrator, publisher, and publication date. Works in English, Spanish, French, German, Russian, Italian, Chinese, Japanese, and Vietnamese are included.

The "CATSearch" feature allows users to browse for words or phrases within a specific category: "Author (Last Name First)," "Reviewer (First Name First)," "Subject," "LC Classification," "Dewey Classification," and "Text Words." From the search results list users can select one or more items to view. The items selected can be saved to a separate list and viewed when the user chooses. Users can also choose a specific number of records to be viewed at a time and they can sort them by year of publication, author, title, language, or Dewey or LC classification in ascending or descending order. Selected items can be downloaded in brief, full, or MARC format and custom reports can be created in HTML (Hypertext Markup Language) or text format. Entries contain cataloging data; a list of awards, honors, or prizes won with links to other winner's entries; and a link to view the book's MARC record. This database is extremely useful for elementary teachers and librarians and public librarians who work with juvenile collections. Navigating the database is fairly straightforward, but may be confusing to users with not much experience with the Internet or computers.—**Cari Ringelheim**

S

375.   Raum, Elizabeth. **Every Day a Holiday: Celebrating Children's Literature Throughout the Year.** Lanham, Md., Scarecrow, 2001. 278p. index. (School Library Media Series, no.21). $32.50pa. ISBN 0-8108-4043-X.

Elementary teachers and librarians in search of ways to celebrate the usual (e.g., Memorial Day) and the unusual (e.g., Monopoly Invented) will welcome this resource. In fact, there is cause to celebrate nearly every day of the year—with quality children's book to serve as the focus. Each entry includes the following: a brief description of the holiday; one or more featured picture books; additional books, when appropriate; and suggested activities. Most of the books have been published since 1990. The balance includes classics or long-time favorites. The brief activities are somewhat predictable, such as making popcorn during National Popcorn Poppin' Month. However, a seasoned teacher or librarian will easily expand upon these as time and energy allow. A few key holidays were omitted, such as Labor Day and Halloween. Presumably, books are not always available for some holidays, such as Labor Day. However, there is an abundance of books for Halloween and the user might have appreciated a different take on how to observe the holiday. The bibliographies are useful. The subject index provides users an opportunity to look for topics or to determine opportunities, such as whether their state has a special celebration in the book. An index of the holidays would have enhanced the usability of the book. Every school or public library will find this an invaluable resource.—**Suzanne I. Barchers**

Bio-bibliography

P, S

376.   Helbig, Alethea K., and Agnes Regan Perkins. **Dictionary of American Children's Fiction, 1995-1999: Books of Recognized Merit.** Westport, Conn., Greenwood Press, 2002. 614p. index. $95.00. ISBN 0-313-30389-4.

Written by teachers of literature with over 30 years of experience, this book on literature for children and young adults, the third in a series of five-year updates, provides an overview of the highlights of the time period covered. Only recognized children's and young adult fiction of 5,000 or more words by 20th-century American authors selected from lists of award-winners or special citation lists for the years covered are included. While most of the writers in this volume appear for the first time, some have been included in previous editions or at least have written books during a different time period. This volume contains more entries than the previous volume (see ARBA 97, entry 938).

The book begins with the awards and citations lists from which the included works were chosen. An alphabetic arrangement of authors, titles, characters, and such miscellaneous items as settings of special significance and elements that need further explanation make up the dictionary, or main body, of the work. Title entries provide bibliographic data, genre, period, setting, plot, character data, and critical evaluation of each work. Length varies, reflecting plot detail. Author entries provide place and date of birth and death, educational background, contribution to children's literature, other publishing history, and awards won. A critical judgment of the author's style and facts that affect his or her writing are also presented. Characters are listed by the name most often used, with cross-references to other names. Names appear first name first. Listings explain the roles of characters that are not fully covered by the plot.

Entries are intended to supplement each other. An asterisk following an entry indicates that there is at least one other entry that provides additional information. An appendix that follows the main body of the work groups the books listed by the awards they have won. In addition to providing more access points for entries, the detailed index is a useful tool for locating books by subject and theme. Other recent reference books on children's literature lack the depth of this one. It is recognized as a valuable literary and sociological reference tool. Academic libraries that support children's and young adult literature or teacher education as well as school and public libraries should have this work and others in the series. [R: BR, May/June 02, p. 69]—**Lois Gilmer**

S

377.   **TeachingBooks.net. http://www.teachingbooks.net.** [Website]. Madison, Wis., TeachingBooks.net LLC. Free. Date reviewed: Jan 03.

TeachingBooks.net is just the sort of sight that children's librarians, school librarians, and elementary teachers dream about. This site brings information about the most popular children's authors of the day into both classrooms and libraries. The site was founded with the idea that those using children's books to teach will get more out the book if they know more about the author/illustrator. To do this the site gives users access to teacher's guides, video files, and activity ideas for each author listed. Users can access an author by using the search engine provided or by browsing the list (currently 12 pages long). Authors are listed in a chart that lists their name, featured title, subject of the title, grade level, status, and source of information. The source of information varies from *TeachingBooks.net*'s own interviews, to NPR audio clips, to the author's personal Website, and more. The site allows users to learn more about children's authors by watching videos (through Quick Time or Media Player), access discussion guides, listen to audio interviews, and even ask the author questions through e-mail links. By providing links to so many authors, activity guides, and interviews, the site will save teachers and librarians time in their research and will inevitably provide them with more creative teaching ideas. For those interested in specific authors, the site offers "Eye-on-the-Web" customized e-mails, which allows *TeachingBooks.net* to inform the user when new information is added on their authors of interest. The majority of the site is free but in order to access the site users must fill out a short registration form. This site is highly recommended for children's librarians, school librarians, and elementary educators.—**Shannon Graff Hysell**

Dictionaries and Encyclopedias

P, S

378.   **The Essential Guide to Children's Books and Their Creators.** Anita Silvey, ed. New York, Houghton Mifflin, 2002. 542p. index. $28.00; $17.00pa. ISBN 0-618-19083-X; 0-618-19082-1pa.

The Essential Guide to Children's Books and Their Creators is an updated, more selective version of Anita Silvey's 1995 work, *Children's Books and Their Creators* (see ARBA 97, entry 939). It contains 475 alphabetically arranged entries consisting primarily of biographies of authors and illustrators. Silvey selected 375 entries from the 1995 text and updated them for this volume. One hundred new entries were added, including J. K. Rowling and Lemony Snicket. Although Silvey emphasizes contemporary American works, this volume is intended to represent the "canon of children's books, which continue to be read in the twenty-first century."

Following the introduction, Silvey offers a basic, helpful reading list of about 300 of the finest works for children. These works are divided into basic age and topical categories, including board books, counting books, poetry, middle-grade fiction, and African American literature. The biographical entries, typically about a page in length, include the author's birth and death dates, genre, common themes, significant or representative titles, and a critical assessment. Thirty nonbiographical essays review issues and genres and historical topics, such as African American children's books, biographies, design and typography, information books, and mysteries. An index is provided as well as cross-references within the articles. The critical essays are very informative but are hard to find, both in the book and in the index. A separate section or at least separate indexing would help. It is necessary to peruse the index to determine the number and range of essays included. For example, "Information Books" appears only as a reference under "Nonfiction" in the text, not in the index. In "Voices of the Creators," 30 authors and illustrators discuss their careers and works.

The intended audience includes parents, teachers, children, and anyone with an interest in children's and young adult books. Librarians will want to keep the old edition so as not to lose content. *The Essential Guide to Children's Books and Their Creators* is significantly more selective with 258 fewer pages than Silvey's 1995 volume. This affordable single-volume book is recommended for libraries of all types as well as teachers, parents, and children interested in choosing a good book to read or satisfying their curiosity about a favorite author. [R: LJ, 1 Oct 02, p. 81]—**Arlene McFarlin Weismantel**

Handbooks and Yearbooks

P, S
379.   Lesesne, Teri S., and Rosemary Chance, for the Young Adult Library Services Association. **Hit List for Young Adults 2: Frequently Challenged Books.** Chicago, American Library Association, 2002. 62p. $25.00pa. ISBN 0-8389-0835-7.

If there is one book that every public and school librarian should have in their professional collection it is this work. *Hit List for Young Adults 2* is a concise, yet thorough, document that provides strategies for the practicing librarian to deal with censorship challenges to materials in their collection. This work also includes a critique of 20 of the most challenged young adult books by such authors as Judy Blume, J. D. Salinger, Robert Cormier, S. E. Hinton, and others. Following each critique is a bibliography of recommended articles, book reviews, and a list of awards and prizes that these challenged books have received. Especially helpful is an extensive appendix of resources germane to combating censorship activities. Resources that recommend challenged books, selected books dealing with intellectual freedom, Internet sites and guides highlighting intellectual freedom, and tips for dealing with censorship and selection are just a few of the areas librarians can draw from when confronted with a censorship issue. Appendix G, entitled "How to Write a Book Rationale," is extremely useful in assisting librarians with creating their own responses to censorship. As alluded to in this section, a carefully crafted rationale serves many purposes. The most important of these is to gather together, in a single document, materials that are indispensable in the event of a challenge. In short, librarians no longer have to feel alone when or if they are presented with censorship controversy. This book is highly recommended not only for school and public libraries, but is a must have for all librarians and library school students preparing for a career in librarianship.—**Patrick Hall**

FICTION

General Works

Bibliography

P
380.   Pearl, Nancy. **Now Read This II: A Guide to Mainstream Fiction, 1990-2001.** Westport, Conn., Libraries Unlimited/Greenwood Publishing Group, 2002. 300p. index. (Genreflecting Advisory Series). $55.00. ISBN 1-56308-867-3.

Oprah's recent pronouncement to the contrary, the world of contemporary fiction is alive and well. In *Now Read This II*, a companion to *Now Read This* that treated the period of 1978-1998 (see ARBA 2000, entry 977), Pearl offers a guide to literary (as opposed to genre) novels of the last decade. Once again, she uses the "appeals approach" to organize her book: each of the more than 500 novels selected is categorized by its strongest appeal (setting, story, characters, or language).

Books are alphabetized by the author's name. Publisher, year published, and page count are given. Each entry consists of a one-sentence plot summary followed by the subjects of the novel (e.g., family relationships, small-town life, Korean Americans, or World War II) and a "Now Try" section featuring other contemporary novels with similar subjects. Award-winning books and those suitable for book groups are indicated. Appendix A gives pointers on creating a dynamic book club. Appendix B describes the various book awards represented in the guide. Appendix C lists those books that may also appeal to readers of genre fiction, such as romance, historical, mystery, and fantasy. There are two author/title indexes (one for the present book and one for its companion) with boldface type indicating main entries and italic type indicating novels listed in the "Now Try" section. Finally, a subject index provides further access to the novels included.

Now Read This and *Now Read This II* are excellent guides to some of the finest works in contemporary fiction that will be especially useful to librarians and teachers. Perhaps Pearl will next turn her sights to short story collections. [R: LJ, 1 May 02, p. 141]—**Lori D. Kranz**

Handbooks and Yearbooks

P

381.   Barron, Neil, and others. **What Do I Read Next? A Reader's Guide to Current Genre Fiction, 2002. Volume 1.** Farmington Hills, Mich., Gale, 2002. 679p. index. $135.00. ISBN 0-7876-5294-6.

This volume of *What Do I Read Next?* concentrates on genre fiction, which the authors consider to include mystery, romance, westerns, fantasy, horror, science fiction, inspirational, and popular fiction titles. The last category is hardly comprehensive, but this volume alone contains 1,214 entries for titles published in 2001 and early 2002.

This splendid reference book needs to be viewed in three contexts: the print series of which it is a part, the online version of this and other Gale publications, and NoveList. The other volumes in the print series are *What Do Children Read Next?/What Do Young Adults Read Next?* Volume 4 (see entry 373), *What Do I Read Next?: Multicultural Literature* (see ARBA 2000, entry 975), *What Historical Novel Do I Read Next?* (see ARBA 99, entry 1034), and *What Inspirational Literature Do I Read Next?* (see ARBA 2001, entry 1060). Each title in the series serves as a powerful readers' advisory tool by providing for each book the story type, series, subjects, major characters, time period, locale, plot summaries (in one paragraph), other books by the same author, and other books the reader might like. Another strength of the series can be found in the extensive indexes—by series, time period, geography, genre, subject, character name, character description (e.g., abuse victim, activist, actor), author, and title.

The second context is the online version produced by Gale, incorporating all of the titles in the series into *What Do I Read Next?* The speed and sheer convenience of working online make this series a natural for computer-based searching, but at this point in the development of these databases the online version cannot compete with the depth and complexity of the printed indexes. Nor does it include the excellent essays that precede each chapter in the print version.

The third context is NoveList, a first-rate online database with its own set of strengths, against which this series needs to be compared according to the needs and reader characteristics of the purchasing library. Indeed, given the considerable cost of each of these resources, both in print and online, librarians with limited budgets will face difficult choices between and among such an embarrassment of riches. Certainly, the print edition of *What Do I Read Next?* is worth considering. In addition to its virtues of content, it succeeds as a book. It is attractively bound, well laid out, and a pleasure to read.—**Edwin S. Gleaves**

Crime and Mystery

P

382.   **The Mammoth Encyclopedia of Modern Crime Fiction.** Mike Ashley, comp. New York, Carroll & Graf, 2002. 780p. $12.95pa. ISBN 0-7867-1006-3.

Modern crime is defined by the author as being produced since World War II and involving the "breaking and enforcement of the law." Within this definition are included many themes: private eye or detective; the police detective; amateurs (including medical sleuths, art theft, and stage and screen); legal thrillers; historical mysteries; gangsters and villains; thrillers, suspense, and noir; fun and games; and the traditional. Excluded are espionage or spy fiction, supernatural thrillers, and the suspense or general mystery. Also, the compiler excludes books that use stereotypes of various cultures. A preface and introduction clarifies the author's definitions and provides a historical overview of the genre.

The main body of the volume consists of two alphabetically organized sections: "Books and Authors" and "Television Series and Major Films." "Books and Authors" covers approximately 500 authors and over 10,000 books and is arranged by the author's most common form of name with cross-references to pen names and variants. Each entry begins with a short biography including birth and death dates, followed by a bibliography of their writings, awards, Websites, biographies of the author, similar writers, and final facts (which includes interesting notes or trivia). "Television Series and Major Films" contains over 300 entries arranged by title. The entries were selected on influence and popularity or originality and relation to modern crime fiction. Classic and golden age characters are not included. Each entry includes year of release, country of origin, length in minutes, number of episodes in the series, producers and directors, writers of the screenplay, and leading actors. Appendix 1 lists 20 awards in the field with the purpose of the award, when and where presented, and a list of the winners given in each entry. Appendix 2 provides the reader with 14 current magazines and 10 Websites for further information or reading. Magazine information includes country of publication, beginning publication date, current publisher and editor, publication cycle, subscription address, and Website (if available). The index refers to main characters and series with reference to their author or film/television series in the appropriate section. The compiler provides a bibliography of resources used in the compilation of the book. It is an inexpensive and valuable resource for enthusiasts of crime fiction as well as librarians building collections on this genre. [R: LJ, 15 June 02, pp. 56-58]—**Elaine Ezell**

Horror

P

383.   **Supernatural Fiction Writers: Contemporary Fantasy and Horror.** Richard Bleiler, ed. New York, Charles Scribner's Sons/Gale Group, 2003. 2v. index. $240.00/set. ISBN 0-684-31250-6.

The 2d edition of the Scribner Writers Series 1986 edition contains new essays for well over 100 writers. The editor of the 2d edition of *Science Fiction Writers*, Richard Bleiler, is also the editor of this 2-volume reference work. The essays are written for the high school and undergraduate student, nonspecialists, and as a resource for teachers needing background on writers they have not taught or studied before. Since the entire spectrum of a writer's career is covered, this is also an excellent resource for public libraries.

Each essay has a selected bibliography of primary works, a selected biographical and critical bibliography listing articles and books, any interviews, and a list of book reviews. Newer writers, such as Patrick McGrath, Steve Erickson, and Scott Bradfield, are included with well-known science fiction writers, such as Ursula K. Le Guin, Anne McCaffrey, and Ray Bradbury. Overall, these two volumes provide in-depth coverage of the authors researched, and are good starting points for information on the science fiction, fantasy, and horror authors that are profiled.
—**Bradford Lee Eden**

Short Stories

C, P

384.   Smith, Patrick A. **Thematic Guide to Popular Short Stories.** Westport, Conn., Greenwood Press, 2002. 318p. index. $44.95. ISBN 0-313-31897-2.

This book will help teachers, librarians, students, and general readers choose among 450 international short stories. Arranged alphabetically by author, each entry includes a detailed summary of the story's plot followed by a much briefer critical interpretation. Included are many very well-known stories by classic writers, such as "A Good Man is Hard to Find" by Flannery O'Connor and "The Cask of Amontillado" by Edgar Allan Poe, as well as lesser-known stories and writers, such as Colby Radowsky's "Amanda and the Wounded Birds" and Sui Sin Far's "In the Land of the Free." A bibliography of anthologies in which these stories appear follows the main entries. There are also indexes by author, title, and themes.

Users needing a more comprehensive index to international short stories in anthologies should consult the various volumes of *Short Story Index* (H. W. Wilson). Readers wanting a critical overview of many of the best short fiction writers in the nineteenth and twentieth centuries should turn to *The Reference Guide to Short Fiction* (see ARBA 95, entry 1167) or various volumes of the *Dictionary of Literary Biography* focusing on short story writers. Smith's book differs from the *Short Story Index* because of its much more detailed plot summaries, but it does not provide the extensive critical evaluations of *The Reference Guide to Short Fiction* or the even more in-depth discussions in the *Dictionary of Literary Biography*.

Since a number of novellas (or quite long short stories), like Melville's "Billy Budd" and Henry James's "Daisy Miller" are included, this book would be more accurately entitled a guide to popular short fiction rather than to short stories. Readers should use the index of themes with caution: many of the themes are so broad (e.g., identity, illusion v. reality, grief, coming of age) as not to offer much guidance to the reader. Aside from these caveats, this book is a useful, selective, one-volume guide for readers needing help selecting some of the best short fiction.—**David Isaacson**

NATIONAL LITERATURE

American Literature

General Works

Bio-bibliography

C, S

385.   **American Writers Classics. Volume 1.** Jay Parini, ed. New York, Charles Scribner's Sons/Gale Group, 2003. 388p. index. $130.00. ISBN 0-684-31248-4. ISSN 1541-4507.

Academic libraries have long been familiar with the Scribner Writer Series, which offer biographical and bibliographic information on well-known and often-studied American authors. This new series, edited by Jay Parini (editor of the formerly mentioned series), looks closely at specific works written by many of the same authors featured in the Scribner Writer Series. The first volume of *American Writers Classics* offer in-depth analysis and critical attention to such classics as *The Catcher in the Rye*, *The Adventures of Huckleberry Finn*, *The Scarlet Letter*, *A Streetcar Named Desire*, *Lolita*, and *Beloved*, along with 14 others. Each essay runs about 20 pages in length and begins with information about the author, a background to the work, discussion of the work's basic elements (e.g., imagery, character development, stylistic strategy), an analysis of the critical reception of the work (both then and now), and bibliographic lists of primary and secondary sources for further study. The essays are written by scholars in the literature field, which are listed with their accomplishments in the "List of Contributors" at the beginning of the volume.

This source will be useful to high school and undergraduate students needing background information on these popular authors and their works. The well-written essays will provide them with a good starting point for further research. This set may be most worthwhile for teachers and professors teaching these works in their classroom as they provide substantial topics for discussion. This set is recommended for high school and undergraduate library collections.—**Shannon Graff Hysell**

Biography

C, P, S

386.   **African American Writers.** 2d ed. Valerie Smith, ed. New York, Charles Scribner's Sons/Gale Group, 2001. 2v. illus. index. (The Scribner Writers Series). $240.00/set. ISBN 0-684-80638-X.

The 2 volumes of *African American Writers* comprise the 2d edition of a work first published in 1 volume in 1991 (see ARBA 92, entry 1156). The 2d edition contains 55 essays, 52 of which are bio-critical, and 21 of which are new to these volumes. All essays are lengthy and signed; many are written by the top scholars in the field. Researchers will find such names as Thadious M. Davis, Henry Louis Gates, and Arnold Rampersad among the contributors. Each essay concludes with a lengthy bibliography of primary and secondary sources, and the set concludes with a lengthy index.

The 2d edition of *African American Writers* is excellent, but it is not perfect. On a trivial level, only the first volume has a table of contents. Equally seriously, the ideas of balance and criticism are almost absent from the pages of this set, and many of the essays are no more than extended appreciations—panegyrics rather than assessments. Indeed, so glowing are virtually all the essays that it comes almost as a surprise to read a blunt "she lied" in Cheryl Wall's discussion of Zora Neale Hurston's life. Finally, for all that it is an excellent set, it is also a set that concentrates on an established canon rather than attempting to expand and redefine the canon, and nowhere is this more evident than in the presentation of the writers known for their genre work. Octavia Butler, Samuel R. Delany, and Chester Himes—all safe choices—are discussed, but Clarence Cooper, Veronica Johns, Ernest Tidyman, Frank Yerby, and such relatively new voices as Walter Mosley are not accorded mention, although their accomplishments are perhaps greater than some of the writers profiled.

The 2d edition of the *African American Writers* set belongs in all public, high school, and academic libraries. One nevertheless hopes for a 3d edition.—**Richard Bleiler**

Dictionaries and Encyclopedias

C, P

387.   **Reader's Encyclopedia of American Literature.** 2d ed. George Perkins, Barbara Perkins, and Phillip Leininger, eds. New York, HarperCollins, 2002. 1126p. $49.95. ISBN 0-06-019815-X.

The editors of this encyclopedia aim to continue the primacy of *Benet's Reader's Encyclopedia of American Literature* (see ARBA 92, entry 1155), last updated in 1991, by revising that well-respected reference work to reflect the changes affecting American literature at the start of the twenty-first century. They have succeeded for the most part—it is certainly comprehensive. The scope, while emphasizing U.S. literature, also encompasses Canadian, Latin American, and Caribbean literature. The entries, by nearly 130 contributors, cover authors and critics, book and periodical titles, historical and fictional characters, literary genres and movements, and relevant historical events (e.g., the Vietnam War) and documents.

Langer theme essays include "History of American Literature," a 22-page entry ranging from European exploration to the end of the twentieth century. Most of the longer entries include suggested biographical and critical works for further reading. The literatures of most ethnic groups—Asian American, Native American, African American, and Jewish American—are given due consideration, but there are gaps. Gay and lesbian literature is not represented, nor is there mention of Arab literature or culture. There are ample cross-references but no index. Nevertheless, all that the *Encyclopedia* includes and its remarkably affordable price make it a highly recommended ready-reference tool for all libraries, including personal libraries.—**Helene Androski**

British Literature

General Works

Chronology

C, P

388.   **The Oxford Chronology of English Literature.** Michael Cox, ed. New York, Oxford University Press, 2002. 2v. index. $195.00/set. ISBN 0-19-860026-7.

Who can forget Vaughan's marvelous lines about eternity: "I saw Eternity the other night,/ Like a great ring of pure and endless light,/ All calm, as it was bright;/ And round beneath it, Time in hours, days, years,/ Driv'n by the spheres/ Like a vast shadow mov'd; in which the world/ And all her train were hurl'd." Time has always held sway over the minds of men and women because it is, as Tennyson so aptly put it, "a fury slinging flame." One supposes it is this powerful image of time like some maniac ransacking our years that causes us to mark it well and often.

Chronologies, by and large, are a nuisance, until you need them. When you have to have them, nothing else will do. The current volumes serve that capacity nicely. Once published as the *Annals of English Literature*, *The Oxford Chronology of English Literature* brings together the literature of more than 500 years (1474-2000). The volume covers only British authors published in Britain with a few exceptions. The 30,000 works by 4,000 authors will provide readers with quick access to when things were published, a trail of publishing record, and a plethora of trivia answers just waiting the right questions.

It does not compare with massive bibliographic records, such as the *English Short Title Catalogue*, who's content is nearly 10 times as large. But that is not the intent. The intent is to provide snapshots of significant works of records, when they were published, and some brief but notable facts about each. The volume is arranged alphabetically by year. The second volume is an author and title index as well as an index to translated authors. [R: LJ, 15 Oct 02, p. 62]—**Mark Y. Herring**

Canadian Literature

C, P

389.　**Encyclopedia of Literature in Canada.** William H. New, ed. Toronto, University of Toronto Press, 2002. 1347p. index. $75.00. ISBN 0-8020-0761-9.

An ambitious attempt to provide a broad perspective on the totality of Canadian literary heritage, this one-volume reference provides an impressive compilation of wide-ranging information. Utilizing a very broad definition of "literature in Canada," the emphasis is a general consideration of Canadian identity in literary expression and production. Organized alphabetically, entries are in bold typeface with cross-references (sometimes extensive) in small capitals. Although not all entries conclude with suggestions for further reading, they are a valuable additional resource. The main entries vary considerably with references to individuals focusing on general biographical information, cultural influences, and the scope of works. Other entries describe or define genre, movements, or terminology. Some are primarily data lists; for example, the extensive 31-page entry for "Awards and Literary Prizes." Still others are more discursive, providing connections between elements affecting the Canadian literary landscape.

Following the entries, there is a short chronology beginning with the year 11,000 B.C.E. and ending in 1999. Divided into two columns, "Milestones" and "Communications and Culture," its utility is marginal, as the inclusions seem wholly arbitrary. For 1532-1533 Francisco Pizarro's conquest of the Incas is noted; however, there is no entry for Sir Humphrey Gilbert's 1593 English claim for Newfoundland and surrounding waters, although this is arguably more pertinent to the development of the Canadian cultural milieu.

Three indexes conclude the volume. The first is an alphabetic list of contributors with entries noted. A second index of authors enumerates all page references to the name with primary references bolded. A final supplementary index brings together a disparate alphabetic list of terms and names mentioned in the text but without a separate entry.

This encyclopedia will be a significant reference resource, providing a comprehensive overview of literature in Canada. It does suffer somewhat in the unevenness of the entries, both in length and breadth. This may be due in part to the difficulties inherent in such a broad interpretation of Canadian literature. While there is some superfluous inclusion of literary terminology easily accessible in standard literary dictionaries, those terms with cultural relevance to Canada are the primary focus. For research, study, or enjoyment, this volume is recommended.

　　　　　　　　　　　　　　　　　　　　　　　　　　　—**Virginia S. Fischer**

POETRY

Biography

C, P

390.　**Contemporary American Women Poets: An A-to-Z Guide.** Catherine Cucinella, ed. Westport, Conn., Greenwood Press, 2002. 402p. index. $94.95. ISBN 0-313-31783-6.

According to the preface, this guide provides bio-bibliographical information concerning 74 "American women poets who published a significant part of their work from 1946 to the present" (p. xi). While many are familiar, such as Maya Angelou, Amy Clampitt, Rita Dove, Maxine Kumin, Mary Oliver, and Sylvia Plath, others, such as Natasha Sajé, Beatriz Badikian, or Ruth Stone, may be less so. Diversity is striven for. Black, Hispanic, American Indian, and Asian American writers are represented, as are lesbians and feminists and those with an immigrant viewpoint. Each signed entry includes a brief biography, discussion of major works and themes, a summary of critical reception, and a bibliography of the poet's works, plus secondary literature and reviews. A list of contributors reveals entry writers to be mostly professors and graduate students at various North American universities. The two-page name/subject index is too scant to be very useful.

A similarly oriented work edited by Pamela L. Shelton, *Contemporary Women Poets* (St. James Press, 1998), contains 250 writers (mostly American), 52 of which are also found in the present volume. Information provided is similar, although the newer volume tends toward essay instead of list format and offers better coverage of critical sources. Unfortunately, it does not provide sample verses to illustrate its points, a nice feature of the earlier compilation. Those owning the Shelton volume may consider passing on this one, but libraries that can afford it will want both; new writers do appear here and overlapping ones are updated.—**Willa Schmidt**

Dictionaries and Encyclopedias

C

391. Burns, Allan. **Thematic Guide to American Poetry.** Westport, Conn., Greenwood Press, 2002. 309p. index. $54.95. ISBN 0-313-31462-4.

It is often said by knowing pundits that poetry, for all practical purposes, is dead. It entered the twentieth century in robust health but by the 1950s began to show evidences of malaise. Following the devastating sequella known as the sixties, poetry went from life-support to a vegetative state. American poetry was said to be the same, only worse. Given the fact that we have not seen a major poet in this country in the last 50 years, there may be some truth to the canard. If, as Robert Frost once said, that poetry is "a way of taking life by the throat" it would appear life won the stranglehold.

Allan Burns, however, believes otherwise. So strong is his faith in Calliope, and not just poetry but American poetry, that he has assembled this handy thematic guide. Drawing upon the works of nearly 90 poets and 250 poems, Burns is able to guide the unwary through the arabesque of themes, ideas, concepts, and more. Using 21 recurring themes, readers are presented with discussions on art and beauty, freedom and slavery, love and sex, life and death, loss, war, and more.

The volume is a good mix of various kinds of poetry but one will find far more pre-1950s material than not. This is only to the good. While it is customary to include a poet like Ginsberg in such a collection, Ginsberg coruscations are merely that: roman-candle like, then darkness.

In addition to the 21 themes, there are also biographical sketches of the poets whose works have been used. Students, specialists, and educators alike will find much in this volume to recommend it. The college-age will welcome its unraveling of poetic mysteries they may heretofore have been unable to fathom.

—**Mark Y. Herring**

S

392. Schwedt, Rachel, and Janice DeLong. **Young Adult Poetry: A Survey and Theme Guide.** Westport, Conn., Greenwood Press, 2002. 192p. index. $49.95. ISBN 0-313-31336-9.

Young Adult Poetry: A Survey and Theme Guide is intended to help teachers, librarians, and parents in the selection of poetry for 12- to 18-year-olds. The work is comprised of 2 principle sections: an annotated bibliography of 198 poetry anthologies and a thematic index to over 6,000 individual poems.

Approximately one-half of this work is devoted to the annotated bibliography of poetry anthologies. Entries are listed alphabetically by author or editor, and then by title. Each entry is numbered and the indexes refer to this numbering scheme. Works include both single- and multi-authored volumes, and vary from those focusing on a single theme to those with a variety of themes. The poetry included in these anthologies ranges from ancient to contemporary. All poetry included is either written in English or translated into English. The dates of publication span more than 50 years, although most of the works were published in the 1990s. The majority of volumes referenced are currently in print, although content is not limited to in-print works. Anthologies were chosen based on a survey of classroom teachers and consultation of standard reference books and periodicals. Nearly

400 volumes were examined before 198 were chosen. The principle criteria were a variety of themes, ease of interpretation, creative use of language, interests of students, and usefulness in the classroom. Recommended grade levels are provided, and the authors were sensitive in including poetry appropriate for both struggling and gifted readers.

The other major section of this work is the "Thematic Guide to Poems," which covers nearly 6,000 individual poems. Poems are categorized under approximately 200 headings, such as "African-American heritage," "daydreams," "deafness," "depression," "football," "Hispanic heritage," "love, crushes," "parents," "rejection," "rural life," and "urban life." This thematic guide can be very useful to those attempting to identify a poem by broad topic.

Other indexes in *Young Adult Poetry* include: an "Index of Writers with Book Titles," containing entries for both authors and editors or compilers; an "Index of Book Titles"; and an "Index of Illustrators." The final index is a catchall titled the "Index of Other Significant Items," which includes authors of poems included in larger anthologies and geographic locations. The "Index of Other Significant Items" also lists headings that might have been included in the thematic guide, such as AIDS and Ojibwe Indians. Using so many different indexes is cumbersome.

Young Adult Poetry is authored by Rachel Schwedt, Director of the Curriculum Library, and Janice DeLong, a faculty member who teaches children's literature, both from Liberty University. Although Liberty University is a Christian institution, the authors do not shy away from including controversial poems, authors, or topics. The *Complete Collected Poems of Maya Angelou* is included in the annotated bibliography, for example. While there are no headings for "sex" or "virginity," headings for "abusive relationships," "divorce," and "suicide" are included. This work is a useful resource for both teachers choosing poetry for young adults and librarians developing poetry collections. [R: VOYA, Oct 02, p. 323]—**Arlene McFarlin Weismantel**

25 Music

GENERAL WORKS

Biography

P, S

393. Earls, Irene. **Young Musicians in World History.** Westport, Conn., Greenwood Press, 2002. 139p. index. $44.95. ISBN 0-313-31442-X.

Author Irene Earls selected 13 musicians who mastered their instruments while they were very young to feature in this volume. The child prodigies include Louis Armstrong, J. S. Bach, Beethoven, Pablo Casais, Sarah Chang, Ray Charles, Charlotte Church, Bob Dylan, John Lennon, Midori, Mozart, Paganini, and Isaac Stern. The author states: "The goal was to provide role models who came from different types of backgrounds and different periods in history. Many were selected because they had to rise above adversity in order to achieve. All became publicly successful before the age of twenty-five." The volume should be of interest to young musicians and teachers. One hopes that the book will make apparent to the young student the difficulties of obtaining success at an early age and the great determination involved in mastering an instrument. The volume includes bibliographies, illustrations, a glossary, and a general index. *Young Musicians in World History* is especially recommended for the juvenile section of general libraries and for music department libraries.—**Robert Palmieri**

Dictionaries and Encyclopedias

C, P

394. **The Oxford Companion to Music.** Alison Latham, ed. New York, Oxford University Press, 2002. 1434p. index. $60.00. ISBN 0-19-866212-2.

No edition statement appears with this work, even though a note states that this volume was first published 2002—so a little explanation is in order. Percy A. Scholes wrote the 1st edition, published in 1938, in one volume. The 10th edition appeared in 1970 (see ARBA 71, entry 1236) with John Owen Ward as editor, but was still predominantly the work of Scholes. *The New Oxford Companion to Music*, in two volumes, came in 1983 (see ARBA 84, entry 889); Denis Arnold was general editor, and a team of scholars prepared the signed entries. Nineteen years have transpired between that work and the current one, which reverts to the original title and one-volume format while still being the work of numerous individuals. All of this information is elaborated in the preface; however, a summary publication history would help and the absence of an edition statement is lamentable.

Most of the entries are dictionary length while others are encyclopedic. Users will find numerous biographies, accounts of individual musical works, translations of foreign terms, as well as topical articles with bibliographies. The entry for "Opera," set off on a gray-shaded background, is 27 pages long. The work is extensively self-referenced using asterisks within articles. In the back of the volume is a 35-page "Select Index of People" who do not have their own entries. There is also a list of contributors with a key to their initials, some of whom have a brief biography following (it is frustrating that not all of them do).

The scope of the volume is focused on Western art music. A British orientation is evidenced in the entry for "Copyright" that has sections headed "International Perspective" and "Essentials of UK Copyright Law," but not one on U.S. law. Some entries have references to longer articles. The low countries and Latin America are treated as a unit. Some entries are quite obscure, such as "*Eis*" (German for E sharp, a note rarely used). This title can serve as a handy, quick reference tool, but may duplicate other materials in collections. The preface refers readers to the 29-volume *New Grove Dictionary of Music and Musicians* (see ARBA 2002, entry 1139, for a review of the online edition) for further, more specialized articles. Other notable titles from this publisher include *The Oxford Dictionary of Music* (2d ed.; see ARBA 96, entry 1270), which is similar in scope and arrangement. [R: LJ, 15 June 02, p. 58; AG, Nov 02, pp. 72-74; SLJ, Nov 02, p. 102]—**Ian Fairclough**

MUSICAL FORMS

Classical

P

395.   Brown, A. Peter. **The Symphonic Repertoire, Volume II. The First Golden Age of the Viennese Symphony: Haydn, Mozart, Beethoven, and Schubert.** Bloomington, Ind., Indiana University Press, 2002. 716p. illus. index. (The Symphonic Reptertoire, v.2). $75.00. ISBN 0-235-33487-X.

Brown's premise is that the symphony needs a work on par with Donald Jay Grout's *A Short History of Opera* (Columbia University Press, 1988), using a single author's continuity. The last scholarly effort in this regard was that of Swiss musicologist Karl Nef in his *Geschichte der Sinfonie und Suite* (Breitkopf & Härtel, 1921). *The First Golden Age of the Viennese Symphony* represents the first published volume of the five-volume work.

Vienna's first golden age was from approximately 1760 to 1825. Over 175 symphonies are analyzed: Franz Joseph Haydn (1732-1809) composed over 100, Wolfgang Amadeus Mozart (1756-1791) created 41, Ludwig van Beethoven (1770-1827) and Franz Schubert (1797-1828) each composed 9 each. Many of these composers' symphonies became established in the repertoire and provided a standard against which every other symphony would be measured. Although only Schubert was born in Vienna, the city influenced the life and music of all four. The scope is slightly broader than symphony and includes a brief essay on Beethoven's *Wellington's Victory*.

Brown incorporates elements of symposium papers, college-level texts, and program notes. His writing is more detailed than most textbooks or program notes. He includes several quotes from the composers and their contemporaries, for which he provides English translations only; those seeking the original German texts may find them in research collections. The author creates numerous tables, concert schedules, and each composer's symphonies chronologically. Several plates accompany the volume, including illustrations, photographs, facsimiles, and autographs.

Symphonies of Haydn are identified according to the sequence developed by Eusebius Mandyczewski in *J. Haydn Werke* (Breitkopf & Härtel, 1907-1933); Brown adds his own chronological sequence in parentheses. He then provides specific analyses of most of these symphonies. He also relates the symphonies to other works of that composer or others, such as the similarities and developments from Schubert's string quartets into his symphonies.

Concluding each major chapter is a bibliographic overview, in which the author presents an analysis of bibliographic history, illustrates how scholars authenticated the music, and identifies sources for further research (such as the Center for Beethoven Studies). Near the conclusion of the volume is a lengthy bibliography with complete citations. The indexes are well constructed. The first index names composers, performers, places, institutions, and titles by composers other than the four examined. Those wishing to compare particular movements of different symphonies will find it useful. Labels include finale, first movement, scherzo, second movement, and slow movement. One can find false recapitulations in the works of Beethoven, Haydn, and Schubert. The "Index of Works" includes all compositions by the four composers discussed laid out in a readily accessible format. Only the multiple numeration systems, particularly for Haydn, may elude the reader new to this genre of research.

—**Ralph Hartsock**

C, P

396. Hall, Charles J. **Chronology of Western Classical Music.** New York, Routledge, 2002. 2v. index. $225.00/set. ISBN 0-415-93878-3.

This exceptionally detailed directory provides abstracted information on music for the years 1751 through 2000, with each year having nine subject areas: births, deaths, debuts, new positions, prizes and honors, biographical highlights, cultural beginnings, musical literature, and musical compositions (each of these subdivided as appropriate). The coverage for the year begins with general historical events and those related to art and literature. In 1780, as an example, India's Second Mysore War is reported, along with the death of Maria Theresa and the birth of Ingres. Among the births of musicians for that year are tenor Louis Nourrit and violinist Franz Clement, the death of organist Ludwig Krebs and the debut in Florence of soprano Nancy Storace. Antonio Lolli became Kapellmeister in St. Petersburg (following gambling debts) and Haydn entered the Modena Philharmonic Society. Oslo's Dramatiske Selskab was founded and Lefébure published his solfège manual. The two symphonies of Saint-Georges were published, along with Mozart's symphony K. 338 and Boccherini's two sets of six quintets (opus 30 and 31).

This resource will certainly be of value to those seeking a cultural or historical identity for a given year, while others will welcome the two indexes duplicated in each volume. In the first index reference is made from the composer to specific works, while the second index sends the reader to the year in question with respect to names, institutions, ensembles, cities, and journal titles. This was a major undertaking, but all one knows of the methodology is that *Baker's Biographical Dictionary of Musicians* (centennial ed.; see ARBA 2002, entry 1134) and *The New Grove Dictionary of Music* (see ARBA 2002, entry 1139, for a review of the online edition) ended any discrepancies. [R: LJ, 15 Nov 02, pp. 60-62]—**Dominique-René de Lerma**

Operatic

P

397. Lewsey, Jonathan. **Who's Who in Verdi.** Brookfield, Vt., Ashgate Publishing, 2001. 560p. $44.95pa. ISBN 1-85928-441-8.

Many books have been written about Verdi's operas. Most examine them both dramatically and musically, but tend to emphasize musical analysis with many musical examples presented in score format. This approach puts off those who do not read music, but who are, nevertheless, looking for a detailed examination of Verdi's great operas that goes beyond mere plot synopsis. Lewsey is interested only in the plots and characters, which removes it from direct comparison with the other books about this composer's works. The nonmusician looking for a key to these operas will be well served by the author's approach.

Entries are alphabetic by opera title or character name. It is, therefore, possible and profitable to read about the opera *Otello* and individually about the characters Otello, Iago, Desdemona, and Emilia in separate entries. This format permits detailed information about characterization and psychological and motivational elements that a straightforward plot summation would not bother to explore. Verdi, the composer, was a master of responding musically to subplots and subtleties of character, which is what makes his operas so satisfying. His operas are not free of improbable plots and unlikely dramatic confrontations, but he was a man of the theater and made opera's conventions seem unimportant by his handling of them and by the power of his music that transcended them. He was also a product of his time, a period of great unrest for Italy and of the Catholic Church, which had an impact on daily life there. Censorship problems had to be faced and overcome with great cleverness. Lewsey is not afraid to confront the issues that made Verdi operas what they are. He admits that many of the psychological factors are subjective and is willing to promote debate.

A glossary gives a structural breakdown of each opera (scene-by-scene), setting up the dramatic situation and listing the musical numbers (with Italian and English titles) that follow. One appendix lists the six operas Verdi revised for Paris and their requirement of ballets for the third acts. This information about the Verdi ballets is especially useful and not easy to locate, especially in such a concise format. A discography by opera lists most recordings in enough detail to be useful. The glossary is alphabetically arranged. The appendixes and discography chronologically list the same operas in order of composition. [R: Choice, May 02, p. 1558]

—**George Louis Mayer**

Popular

General Works

Biography

S

398.   Knight, Judson. McNeill, Allison, ed. **Parents Aren't Supposed to Like It: Rock & Other Pop Musicians of Today, Volumes 4-6.** Farmington Hills, Mich., U*X*L/Gale, 2002. 3v. illus. index. $115.00/set. ISBN 0-7876-5387-X.

Volumes 4, 5, and 6 of *Parents Aren't Supposed to Like It* have changed format from the first three volumes (U*X*L/Gale, 1998). While the title of the work has remained the same, the entries are now alphabetically arranged instead of being organized by musical genre. But the entries are still categorized by genre in the table of contents in the front of each volume. The premise of the work is that most popular music sounded like "noise" to parents in the early days, but that the genres (e.g., rock, rap) often provide an insight to our culture. Each volume begins with an in-depth overview of the particular genre that provides a basic explanation of what that particular music is trying to communicate. The first three volumes covered popular musicians performing and recording in the 1990s. More than 150 biographical entries were included. The present set of volumes continues this process by covering bands and artists relevant to the later 1990s and early 2000s. Previously covered musicians and bands are updated with new entries, and many more have been added. Each volume begins with a "Musical Genre Overview" that provides a background to the particular style being covered.

The entries generally cover several pages and include a history of the performer or group, photographs (which are usually provocative in some manner), lists of awards and hit songs, and a selected discography. In the case of well-known groups or individuals, the entry includes a bibliography listing items for further reading. The histories are amazingly candid. Some list arrests of individuals and other trouble with the police. The discussions of lyrics can be used by parents, or other listeners, to determine the appropriateness of the music for younger listeners. The entry for Bone Thugs-n-Harmony points out that "the five youths supported themselves by selling crack cocaine [and that later one of the members] had been arrested for assault four years . . . before he was a star" (v.4, pp. 45-46]. This type of information is generally not available in other sources where the intent is simply to sell recordings. The series is recommended for both young adults and parents. It is not recommended for younger children. The work should be considered for junior high, high school, and public libraries.—**Robert L. Wick**

Dictionaries and Encyclopedias

C, P

399.   Hischak, Thomas S. **The Tin Pan Alley Song Encyclopedia.** Westport, Conn., Greenwood Press, 2002. 530p. index. $74.95. ISBN 0-313-31992-8.

This work primarily includes songs that came into popularity by way of vaudeville, sheet music, piano rolls, concerts, records, or through nightclub performances as opposed to musical theater and films. The songs date from the pre-Civil War period through the end of the 1950s. Tin Pan Alley refers to the music publishing industry located in New York City, not any particular location. It reflects a concept of composers, lyricists, publishers, and song pluggers with the end product being primarily printed sheet music. All over America these songs were played in homes for family entertainment. The author explains that as the parlor piano faded away so also did Tin Pan Alley eventually cease to exit. Other factors contributing to the death of Tin Pan Alley were the shift in emphasis from the song to the performer, and, in some vague way, the advent of rock and roll.

The work is a companion book to the previously published *The American Musical Theatre Song Encyclopedia* (see ARBA 96, entry 1416) and *The American Musical Film Song Encyclopedia* (see ARBA 2000, entry 1159). Songs are arranged alphabetically by title. Each entry includes the year the song became a hit, along with a highly readable short paragraph usually mentioning the composers, the singers who made the song popular, the bands that played the hit, and some of the more popular recordings. There is a refreshing use of adjectives, such as when a song is described as a "plucky song," "a perennial favorite," "a gentle ballad," "an entrancing ballad," "a mindless little novelty number," or "a jumping song of sweet revenge." (This latter refers to "Goody-Goody" by Johnny Mercer and Matty Malneck.) Final chapters include ASCAP's Hit Parade of the top 16 songs, the National

Endowment for the Arts top 20 songs and Alternate Song Titles (e.g., "Remember" vs. "You Forgot To Remember"), and a thorough index to the book. This reference is highly recommended for music historians, social historians, and public library fine arts and media departments, high schools, and academic and special libraries. [R: LJ, 1 Feb 03, pp. 76-78]—**Louis G. Zelenka**

Jazz

C, P

400. Oliphant, Dave. **The Early Swing Era, 1930 to 1941.** Westport, Conn., Greenwood Press, 2002. 464p. index. $99.95. ISBN 0-313-30535-8.

The last few years have seen a large number of publications in the area of jazz history. In addition, attention has been paid to specific types and eras of jazz. Any book that tackles the Swing Era of the 1930s and 1940s will have to face stiff comparison to Gunther Schuller's highly acclaimed study *The Swing Era: The Development of Jazz, 1930-1945* (Oxford University Press, 1991), which is the second volume of his monumental *The History of Jazz*. Dave Oliphant has now also attempted to cover approximately the same period (1930-1941), this time as a reference volume.

Although most of the book is in narrative form, Oliphant arranges five of the six chapters by type of band: "Name Black Bands," "Name White Bands," "Other Black Bands," "Other White Bands," and "Small Swing Groups." All entries in each chapter begin with the bandleader's name, and range from Fletcher Henderson to Harry James. The first chapter discusses precursors to and birth of big band swing. Each chapter has extensive notes to references, and the debt Oliphant owes Schuller is quite evident as *The Swing Era* appears quite frequently in the notes section. After chapter 6, there is an A-Z section of short biographical entries for other big band leaders not mentioned in the main text, and other artists connected with swing bands. The book ends with a short bibliography and a general index.

While each entry discusses major hit tunes for each band, there is no separate section for a discography. With this in mind, Oliphant's book would nicely complement such discographies as Steve Knopper's *MusicHound Swing! The Essential Album Guide* (Schirmer Books, 2000). This book is certainly a worthwhile acquisition for any music reference collection. This reviewer would only quibble with the high price of a single-volume text, and the use of "early" in the title, since Oliphant covers most to he Swing Era period, which essentially came to an end around 1947.—**Richard Slapsys**

C, P

401. Shipton, Alyn. **Jazz Makers: Vanguards of Sound.** New York, Oxford University Press, 2002. 263p. illus. index. (Oxford Profiles). $39.95. ISBN 0-19-512689-0.

This latest volume in the Oxford Profiles series continues the series' mission of introducing young adult readers to a new field. It has been prepared by a major contributor to the field, Alyn Shipton, and appears to be adapted from his 2001 work, *A New History of Jazz* (Continuum, 2002). However, *Jazz Makers* is more concerned with giving the reader "a good idea of how the sound of Jazz developed" (p. 7).

The slim volume is organized into parts by periods, which include brief chapters on over 50 of the more important innovators. Each chapter includes a discography, further reading section, and a list of Websites for interested readers who want to continue learning. Each part also includes an introduction and a conclusion of other notable musicians. Shipton's aim is to present the figures in jazz who have influenced the development of the genre. The flow from period to period and style to style shows the progression of the music clearly.

Although it is targeted for a young adult audience, the work will also appeal to adults who are new to the art form. The lives of some of these musicians may be a bit colorful for the very young (e.g., Morton's early life as pimp is mentioned in passing). The work is interesting, accessible, and is worth the purchase for its "Essential Listening" appendix alone. It belongs in all school and public libraries.—**Paolina Taglienti**

Sacred

P

402.   Powell, Mark Allan. **Encyclopedia of Contemporary Christian Music.** Peabody, Mass., Hendrickson, 2002. 1088p. index. $29.95pa. (w/CD-ROM). ISBN 1-56563-679-1.

This hefty paperback's author, a faculty member of Ohio's Trinity Lutheran Seminary, adopts a rather informal style as he surveys almost 2,000 individuals and ensembles that have recorded Christian music in the past 30 years. The entries include a discography (album title, label names, and release dates are provided), memberships of the groups, biographical sketches, subjective evaluations, "chart hits," and awards. Websites are included and, in fact, updates are projected. The front matter surveys the history, while the volume concludes with a glossary, contents list, and a CD-ROM of the entire work (needing 15MB of free space). No other undertaking in this area is known to exist, and the vast coverage appears to be quite comprehensive. This reference offers a large perspective on its subject, and the entries—while of scholarly value—are refreshingly chatty. This is an impressive endeavor. [R: LJ, 1 Nov 02, p. 82]—**Dominique-René de Lerma**

26 Mythology, Folklore, and Popular Culture

FOLKLORE

P

403.   **The Penguin Dictionary of American Folklore.** By Alan Axelrod and Harry Oster, with Walton Rawls. New York, Penguin Books, 2000. 527p. illus. $18.00pa. ISBN 0-14-100240-9.

In the preface to this book, the authors state some of the problems associated with constructing a dictionary of American folklore. Since the precise meaning of "folklore" in current definition is vague and given different meanings within different groups, the authors quite clearly indicate that this work includes subjects that they believe will be of most interest to people interested in folklore. A short discussion of general folklore, popular culture, and American folklore follows as a prelude to the contents of the book. More than 750 entries and 225 photographs and line drawings are included. The audience for this book, as defined by the authors, includes students of American art and American studies programs, folklorists, those interested in ethnic history and culture and popular culture, as well as students of American history in general. There are entries on folklore from different regions (Appalachian), groups (Native American), and occupations (lumberjack folklore); scholars and collectors of folklore (Alan Lomax); and singers and their songs (Joan Baez), to name a few. While far from comprehensive, this book is well constructed and contains much useful information. It is as comprehensive as possible on the subjects that it does present.—**Bradford Lee Eden**

P

404.   Seal, Graham. **Encyclopedia of Folk Heroes.** Santa Barbara, Calif., ABC-CLIO, 2001. 347p. illus. index. $75.00. ISBN 1-57607-216-9.

The introduction to this book is an impressive discussion of the current thought and definition of folk heroes in culture and history. This particular encyclopedia is an alphabetic arrangement by surname of major folk heroes throughout history. Each entry points to related entries in the encyclopedia, and includes a short reference and further reading section. Major gods, mythological characters, and heroes of literary epics are not included, since relatively few of them appear in folklore. Popular icons and sports stars are not included as well, since they generally do not persist beyond two generations. Religious heroes and saints are only lightly touched upon, given that they are too numerous and highly localized in their popularity. Two thematic indexes, one for heroic types and one for country/culture, are included, as well as a chronology of folk heroes. The author uses the introduction of the book to discuss some of the qualities, interpretations, and meanings of folk heroes and heroines in culture. A general bibliography and index are provided as well. [R: LJ, 1 Feb 02, p. 86; SLJ, May 02, pp. 98-99; BL, 15 May 02, p. 1630; Choice, May 02, p. 1560]—**Bradford Lee Eden**

MYTHOLOGY

P, S

405.   **The Greenhaven Encyclopedia of Greek and Roman Mythology.** By Don Nardo. San Diego, Calif., Greenhaven Press/Gale, 2002. 304p. illus. index. (The Greenhaven Encyclopedia of . . . Series). $74.95. ISBN 0-7377-0719-4.

Classical myths have become so interwoven into today's culture, society, and literature that the average person cannot be expected to recognize and identify all the gods, heroes, and events of these stories without assistance. *The Greenhaven Encyclopedia of Greek and Roman Mythology* is that aid. Topics in the encyclopedia are divided into chapters, each covering a major aspect of the myths. For example, a chapter is devoted exclusively to the gods (listed in alphabetic order), one to human characters, another on monsters, and so on. There are a total of six chapters with a table of contents and an index. A chapter on the myth tellers and their works, like Homer and his *Iliad*, is also included. *The Greenhaven Encyclopedia of Greek and Roman Mythology* is a bonus to any library's reference collection. Its entries are easy to read, informative, and well cross-referenced. [R: BR, Sept/Oct 02, p. 75]—**Vang Vang**

P

406.   Sax, Boria. **The Mythical Zoo: An Encyclopedia of Animals in World Myth, Legend, & Literature.** Santa Barbara, Calif., ABC-CLIO, 2001. 298p. illus. index. $85.00. ISBN 1-57607-612-1.

The Mythical Zoo: An Encyclopedia of Animals in World Myth, Legend, & Literature is a handy reference book that will be useful to just about anyone from storywriters to television producers, newspaper editors, or just plain interested readers. Anyone checking some background information or some last minute facts will find this book a must. More than a simple compendium of animal facts, *The Mythical Zoo* also shows how much animals and their symbolism are intertwined with human life and thought processes.

Classification of the animal kingdom became central to the scientific studies of Swedish naturalist Carolus Linnaeus and others in the nineteenth century as they sought to establish the order of the living world. More recent scientific projects, such as the Human Genome Project, have revealed amazing insights into human genetic makeup that will inevitably filter out to and shape the common person's view of life on earth. In this encyclopedia of the animals of myth, legend, and literature, the author reminds us that contemporary genetic theory is apt to view animals less as individuals or representatives of species than as repositories of hereditary information. He reminds readers that in their rush to run down exciting new roads, they should not forget what they once learned in the past. To define an animal strictly in terms of biology is too narrow, too technical, and too restrictive he argues, suggesting instead that we define each sort of animal as a tradition. This process involves inclusiveness—genetics in relation to other values, like ideas, practices, and the events that make up human culture. Since time immemorial, humans have held customs, beliefs, and traditions that intimately entwine with the animal kingdom: metaphorical animals, demonic animals, satirical animals, and even political animals. In short, animals are a vast part of human heritage that cannot be ignored.

The Mythical Zoo emphasizes depth over breadth in conveying ideas supporting the treatment of animals in myth, legend, and other aspects of human culture. It presents a contextualized, rounded sense of a given animal instead of dishing up disconnected bits of information. For this aspect, the reader will be grateful. [R: Choice, Mar 02, p. 1212]—**Arthur Gribben**

POPULAR CULTURE

Dictionaries and Encyclopedias

C, P

407.   **The Greenwood Guide to American Popular Culture.** M. Thomas Inge and Dennis Hall, eds. Westport, Conn., Greenwood Press, 2002. 4v. illus. index. $399.95/set. ISBN 0-313-30878-0.

This four-volume study of popular culture is fascinating for the serious student or scholar of popular culture in the twentieth century. The essays include photographs, illustrations, chronological timelines, and cross-indexing. The most important features include the reference tools, bibliographies, histories, critical studies, and journals in each field. Everything from catalogs to comics to television to sports, radio, computers, and more are carefully researched and reported. The topics are selective but much is gained in the thorough study of the topics covered rather than snippets on too many unresearched items. This set of volumes is valuable for the general reader and curious student as well as the trained scholar in each field. This set is a recommended purchase for all libraries.

—**Linda L. Lam-Easton**

P, S

408.   Miller, Anistatia R., and Jared M. Brown. **More On This Day in History.** Paramus, N.J., Prentice Hall, 2002. 411p. illus. index. $18.00pa. ISBN 0-7352-0233-8.

More On This Day in History offers a follow-up to *On This Day in History*, written in 1997 by Miller and Brown (see ARBA 2000, entry 1136). The authors, in the introduction, provide an overview to the guide: "[this is a] compendium of more than 8,000 important national and international incidents, anniversaries, holidays, and other observances" (p. iii). Additionally in the introduction, they proffer that they hope readers will refer to *More On This Day in History* as an access point to locate quotes and trivia for papers and presentations.

Between 2 and 11 entries are provided for each day of the year, including a listing of an event and a brief summary. The majority of the entries occurred in the twentieth century, however, some are from the nineteenth century and a sampling are from the late eighteenth century. Most days of the year include a well-known personality's birth date; one oddity, however, is an illustration in the plates of Confucius with a caption making note of his September 28, 551 B.C.E. birthday. The majority of the entries highlighted fall into the categories of political events, legal landmarks, entertainment highlights, and sporting news.

Some examples of the chosen events are October 27, 1904 when New York City's subway opened; October 2, 1950 when Charles Schultz's *Peanuts* was first published; January 2, 1974 when President Nixon made 55 mph the national maximum highway speed; and August 1, 1981 when MTV began broadcasting on cable television. *More On This day in History* includes the tragedy from September 11, 2001. The authors acknowledge the use of the Internet in finding out dates of events, and encourage its use to search for interesting topics (perhaps as a way to follow-up on the entries). The work includes photographs, an index, and cross-references.—**Leslie R. Homzie**

27 Performing Arts

GENERAL WORKS

Biography

P

409. Sonneborn, Liz. **A to Z of American Women in the Performing Arts.** New York, Facts on File, 2002. 264p. illus. index. (Facts on File Library of American History). $44.00. ISBN 0-8160-4398-1.

This reference work provides short biographical and bibliographic information on 150 American women whose talent has entertained audiences worldwide. The author defines "women in the performing arts" fairly narrowly, focusing on performers rather than talents working behind the scenes. The term "American" is used much more loosely, including foreign-born women such as Claudette Colbert, Ingrid Bergman, and Elizabeth Taylor, given their influence on American culture (although Sofia Loren was not included). Younger women performers were also not included, although the author seems to have made the decision to include Jodie Foster and Julia Roberts.

Overall, the author states her reasons for inclusion and exclusion of important American women in the performing arts in her introduction. The book is alphabetically arranged. An index of entries by area of activity and an index by year of birth accompany a general index. A short bibliography of recommended sources on American women in the performing arts is included as well. This book is a quick and selective guide to information on this subject area, with entries determined by the author's personal and professional judgment. [R: LJ, 1 Mar 02, pp. 88-90; Choice, May 02, p. 1554]—**Bradford Lee Eden**

Directories

C, P

410. Catron, Louis E. **Theatre Sources Dot Com: A Complete Guide to Online Theatre and Dance Resources.** Westport, Conn., Heinemann, 2001. 215p. $18.95pa. ISBN 0-325-00382-3.

Knowledge is power in the realm of theater and dance as well as in the outside world. This book will help users obtain immediate access to that knowledge. The author provides a guide to more than 750 Websites that provide information on theater and dance resources. The author begins this work with an overview of computer systems, the Internet, the World Wide Web, search engines, and so on. His easy-to-understand presentation is a refresher course for the computer literate and a demystification for the novice Internet user. The book also guides the readers on how to reach these information sources in a step-by-step manner. The author presents and describes sites for playwrights, directing, choreography, dramaturgy, theater and dance research, acting, stage combat, mime, improvisation, dance, technical theater (e.g., design, costume, makeup, scenery, lighting, sound, properties), theater and dance management, job opportunities, and copyright law. Each citation provides the site name, address, and a detailed description of the site's capabilities. Some sites are tagged as especially useful by an "Author's Choice" notation. This book is a must for every academic or practitioner involved with theater and dance. Most importantly, it is user-friendly. [R: LJ, Dec 01, p. 103]—**Charles Neuringer**

DANCE

P

411.   Cavalli, Harriet. **Dance and Music: A Guide to Dance Accompaniment for Musicians and Dance Teachers.** Gainesville, Fla., University Press of Florida, 2001. 425p. index. $29.95pa. ISBN 0-8130-1887-0.

Many of us adore the full ballet, with orchestra, but what occurs prior to these public performances depends on rehearsal pianists. "Music must move a dancer emotionally, literally, and figuratively. It must give the dancer a reason to dance" (p. 1). In a volume first published in German as *Tanz und Musik* (1998), Cavalli endeavors to encourage more musicians to explore dance accompaniment, to offer suggestions to those already in the profession, to provide musical assistance to dance teachers, and to promote productive communication between dance teachers and accompanists. Cavalli outlines the essential elements of dance (rhythm, meter, tempo, harmony), and various forms of dance music (e.g., tango, march, bolero, minuet, gavotte). In a segment for dance teachers, she addresses such issues as learning to count correctly and the execution of combinations. The author elucidates terms succinctly and sufficiently for nonmusicians. To explain syncopation (p. 5) she amplifies a basic reference source, indicating that syncopation accents a weak instead of a strong beat. She suggests listening to a tango or a rag to understand syncopation. Cavalli also explains the difference between rhythm and melody so that it is quite comprehendible by dancers not well versed in musical notation.

The chapter for accompanists includes etiquette and tools of the accompanist's trade (e.g., repertoire, an overview of various leveled dance classes). She then discusses facets of behind the scenes work and relations between the choreographer, conductor, accompanist, and photographer. She presents a detailed analysis of the musical examples with counting structures for dances.

Cavalli concludes with nearly 180 pages of piano music to accompany dancers. These examples illustrate specific genres used in dance, such as mazurka, sarabande, and minuet. They contain her choreographic notations below each staff of the piano music to which these apply. Links back to the primary textual commentary provide easy navigation. While the book is laid out well for library use, the musical examples (pages 219-400) would serve pianists better by being laid flat. Cavalli is the pianist for Martin Schläepfer's Ballet Mainz at the Mainz State Theater in Germany. All those involved with the production and performance of dance will benefit from this book.—**Ralph Hartsock**

FILM, TELEVISION, AND VIDEO

Biography

P

412.   Slide, Anthony. **Silent Players: A Biographical and Autobiographical Study of 100 Silent Film Actors and Actresses.** Lexington, Ky., University Press of Kentucky, 2002. 439p. illus. index. $40.00. ISBN 0-8131-2249-X.

Anthony Slide has used a personal approach, via interviews and remembrances, to provide insightful portraits of the lives and careers of 100 of the silent screen's best and brightest. The result is a wide spectrum of actors and actresses that have been personally chosen by the author. The volume is intended to serve both as a reference work that includes new information and as a lively and interesting study of players from America's silent films.

Most entries are arranged individually, except for a section entitled "The Legends," which contains portraits of five who have achieved legendary status (Chaney, Chaplin, Garbo, Keaton, and Valentino). Biographical citations are included, as are black-and-white photographs and bibliographies for further research. An index assists in locating players who do not have separate entries.

Slide's approach, focusing on talented and vibrant personalities, differentiates this work from others chronicling the silent film era. As such, it supplements our knowledge of an important time in the history of American movies. [R: LJ, 1 Sept 02, pp. 166-168]—**Anita Zutis**

C, P

413.   Thomson, David. **The New Biographical Dictionary of Film.** 4th ed. New York, Alfred A. Knopf/Random House, 2002. 963p. $35.00. ISBN 0-375-41128-3.

Although its title calls it "new," this volume is actually a 4th edition of the author's well-known *Biographical Dictionary of Film.* Besides adding "new" to the title, David Thomson has added 300 new entries to the collection of more than 1,300 entries as well as revised many of the existing entries. Thomson, a recognized scholar of and writer about film, wrote every entry, which range in size from a hundred words to several thousand. Entries are organized alphabetically and provide the biographee's real and stage names, vital dates, place of birth, and filmography. The narrative section of the entry is part biographical and part Thomson's reflections on the biographee's career and achievements. While the scope is worldwide, most entries are of American and English actors. Actors, directors, producers, and writers are all included, although actors predominate. Those included range from Antonio Banderas to Veronica Lake to Debra Winger and from John Ford to Akira Kurasowa to Lina Wertmuller. There is no index or cross-referencing. Thomson's book is a personal one. His assessments are witty and insightful, but a bit short of standard biographical detail. There are, however, other places to look for that. While his choices are interesting and comprehensive, one must wonder why he includes Gillian Anderson but not David Duchovny, or Quentin Tarantino but not Robert Rodriguez. Eddie Murphy and Bill Murray make the list but Dan Ackroyd, John Belushi, John Candy, and Chevy Chase do not. All in all, this is a great film book that libraries and film buffs should consider a must-purchase. [R: LJ, 1 Oct 02, p. 84]—**Ronald H. Fritze**

C, P

414.   Tibbetts, John C., and James M. Welsh. **The Encyclopedia of Filmmakers.** New York, Facts on File, 2002. 2v. illus. index. $125.00/set. ISBN 0-8160-4384-1.

Reference books that concentrate on film directors or, at least, contain substantial material dealing with film directors are common. A new and up-to-date encyclopedia that consists of thoughtful and scholarly entries on film directors, however, is always welcome and *The Encyclopedia of Filmmakers* is such a book. The editors, Tibbetts and Welsh, are accomplished scholars of film who have assembled a team of 50 expert contributors to write the more than 350 entries on the various directors. Their choice of directors is judicious and comprehensive and ranges from the beginning of the film industry until the present. The selected directors come from all over the world, although Americans dominate, and represent the myriad types of directors from independents to the superstars and from the world of the blockbuster to makers of documentaries. Patriarchs of film, such as D. W. Griffith and Sergei Eisenstein, can be found along with such current giants as Steven Spielberg and James Cameron. Others included range from such predictable choices as Akira Kurasowa and Werner Herzog to John Carpenter and John Sayles.

The individual entries are well written and researched, trace the directors' careers as well as their significance, and tend to be significantly longer than are usually found in standard works of film reference. Each entry is signed by the contributor and includes a list of references for further reading. The two-volume set concludes with a detailed general index. This excellent work will prove useful to anyone interested in film studies and film history. [R: LJ, 1 June 02, p. 134; LJ, 1 June 02, p. 134]—**Ronald H. Fritze**

Dictionaries and Encyclopedias

P

415.   Lackmann, Ron. **The Encyclopedia of American Television: Broadcast Programming Post World War II to 2000.** New York, Facts on File, 2003. 528p. illus. index. $75.00. ISBN 0-8160-4554-2.

This survey encyclopedia covers popular broadcast television shows and specials from 1945 to 2000. Standard appendixes of yearly top-rated programs and annual Emmy awards are included, along with a thorough index. The one-page bibliography is inadequate.

The majority of entries are for programs and actors. Each program entry includes a description of the show, times the show aired, complete cast listings and notable guest stars, and the occasional interesting fact. Biographical entries include dates of birth and death, along with the actor's television credits. Any significant acting work done outside of television is also mentioned. All entries are enhanced with excellent cross-references to related shows and actors.

Coverage of special television events and programs is also included, but is not extensive. While the author includes his criteria for selection, there are few surprises in the actors and programs selected for inclusion. The photographs are almost exclusively from the author's collection and are not always adequately captioned.

In comparison with two other significant one-volume encyclopedias of television history, the coverage of programs in *The Encyclopedia of American Television* is not as extensive or thorough as *Total Television* (4th ed.; see ARBA 97, entry 1132), nor does it include executive biographies and entries on television technologies as does *Les Brown's Encyclopedia of Television*. However, within its own limits *The Encyclopedia of American Television* is well written and easy to access. While not a necessary purchase for libraries with solid collections on television history, this encyclopedia may be considered an adequate addition for libraries that do not own other reference works on television programming history.—**Mark van Lummel**

Directories

P

416.   **Hollywood Creative Directory, Winter/Spring 2003.** 47th ed. Hollywood, Calif., iFilm Publishing, 2003. 424p. index. $59.95pa. ISBN 1-92893-622-9.

Calling itself "the phone book to Hollywood," the widely consulted *Hollywood Creative Directory* is a mainstay in the entertainment business, frequently consulted by industry professionals trying to contact production companies, studios, networks, and the key people who run them. So authoritative is this directory, that in 1992 when the Internal Revenue Service was investigating tax abuse in the entertainment industry, they purchased a copy to use as a guide for their operations.

The bulk of the volume is an alphabetic directory of more than 2,000 companies and staff, which for each lists address, telephone, fax, e-mail, Website, names and positions of top executives, and a brief outline of the company's activities, which can include specialties (e.g., made-for-television movies), what projects they have under development or in production or post-production, and what projects they have completed. Extensive indexing provides excellent access to this material. More than 10,000 names are listed in the name index, and there are cross-reference indexes by state, by type (e.g., animation, documentaries), and by deal (which specifies which companies have some kind of production arrangement with which studios and networks).

While this is the 47th edition of this highly esteemed sourcebook, its favorable reputation has been achieved in fewer years than those assuming annual editions would expect. It has been around in various incarnations, with variant titles, for the past 16 years, usually published 3 times per year with successive edition numbers. A challenger appeared in the mid-1990s, the Carronade Group's *Multimedia Directory* (see ARBA 97, entry 1363), similar in format in scope, but it appears to have ceased publication.

Online subscriptions to the database from which this directory is generated are also available for $199.95 per year, allowing unlimited access with no per search charges. The database is updated weekly. Further information is available at their website (http://www.hcdonline.com). This resource is essential for libraries serving companies in the entertainment industry and a possible purchase for academic cinema and television libraries serving a clientele active in show business.—**Richard W. Grefrath**

Filmography

P

417.   Tracey, Grant. **Filmography of American History.** Westport, Conn., Greenwood Press, 2002. 336p. index. $55.00. ISBN 0-313-31300-8.

Using films in the teaching of a history class has long achieved respectability as a methodology—but with any methodology, instructors need guidance. Grant Tracey wrote *Filmography of American History* to provide guidance for high school and college teachers. More than 200 films are described, with information on directors, cast, years of production, distributors, running times, and ratings. A detailed summary describes the plot or contents of each film and concludes with a list of further readings. Most of the films listed are works of fiction that were first released theatrically but there are also made-for-television movies and documentaries (e.g., *Eyes on the Prize* and Ken Burns' *The Civil War*). One innovative touch has two closely related films jointed into a "Double Bill" and describes them together (i.e., *Dr. Strangelove* and *Fail Safe*).

The films are organized into 14 roughly chronological chapters. All of Antebellum American history is contained in the first brief chapter, which inexplicably leaves out *Northwest Passage* and *The Alamo*. After World War II, the six remaining chapters, which comprise half of the book, become more thematic, including "Postwar Alienation and Despair, 1946-1962" and "Watergate, Political Cynicism, and Home, 1972-Present." Each chapter concludes with a list of other films for further viewing. The volume also provides appendixes listing multicultural films and women-centered films, along with a general index and a title index. Tracey's volume provides a nice-up-to-date guide that complements Michael Pitts' *Hollywood and American History* (McFarland, 1984). Some readers may find Tracey's commentaries to be a bit left of center. His comments on *Executive Decision* (undoubtedly made pre-September 11, 2001) sound more than a little hollow after the fact. [R: LJ, 1 April 02, p. 96; BR, Sept/Oct 02, p. 79]—**Ronald H. Fritze**

Handbooks and Yearbooks

C, P

418.   **Magill's Cinema Annual 2002: A Survey of the Films of 2001.** 21st ed. Christine Tomassini, ed. Farmington Hills, Mich., Gale, 2002. 663p. index. $120.00. ISBN 1-55862-458-9. ISSN 0739-2141.

Since first appearing in 1982, this annual publication of film reviews and credits information has become a reference staple in most public and academic libraries. Initially published by Salem Press and similar in format to their famed *Masterplots* series, Gale assumed publishing duties with the 1995 volume (see ARBA 97, entry 1131). Gale introduced a glitzier format featuring graphics, black-and-white photographs, and sidebars with background facts and quotations from the movies under discussion. More importantly, the reviews (now done by Gale's VideoHound team of entertainment industry writers) were more entertainingly written than their predecessors.

Although the photographs and sidebars have been dropped from the 2002 annual, the format remains nearly unchanged from recent years. A brief essay presenting an overview of the films of 2001 prefaces the main section of the annual, which is an alphabetically arranged title list of 300 film entries. Each entry includes the movie's tagline (promotional catch phrases), year-end domestic box office gross, a signed review and comments on the film's reception, cast/production credits, a bibliography of reviews from major newspapers and industry trade papers, memorable dialogue quotes, a trivia section, and awards and nominations. Reviews average about two pages in length and strive to be both entertaining and analytical. In addition to numerous specialized indexes (directors, screenwriters, editors, cinematographers, performers, and subject), the annual also features an obituaries section and a selected list of film books published in 2001. This is a popular film review source best suited for public libraries and the college and university undergraduate population.—**David K. Frasier**

Videography

P

419.   Wiener, Tom. **The Off-Hollywood Film Guide: The Definitive Guide to Independent and Foreign Films on Video and DVD.** New York, Random House, 2002. 535p. index. $16.95pa. ISBN 0-8129-9207-5.

With this resource, Wiener has provided an excellent guide to movies that are generally far from the Hollywood mainstream. While some of the movies examined, like *Amelie* (France/Germany, 2001) and *The Full Monty* (United Kingdom, 1997) did quite well in major cinema release, the majority of the films described were found only in America's art houses and can often be difficult to locate for rental or purchase. Wiener provides short yet complete synopses of each of the hundreds of movies covered in the book, and lists year and country of release, format, genre, rating, and run time as well. The films he considers essential are clearly marked, and his picks cover a broad spectrum of genres, time periods, and styles. One of the unique features of the book is a listing of films that go well with each listed film, for the fan who wants to plan for a perfect double feature.

The book is well indexed, including genre and subgenre (using a handy classification system developed by the author), director, major actors, and country. He also provides a list of films available on DVD as of the writing of the book. Its wealth of information and ease of reading make this book an excellent addition to the reference collection of public libraries with a large film department and diverse audience. Academic libraries with a film studies department may also find it useful. This unique and excellent resource comes highly recommended. [R: LJ, 1 June 02, p. 136]—**Mark T. Bay**

THEATER

Chronology

C, P

420.   Norton, Richard C. **A Chronology of American Musical Theater.** New York, Oxford University Press, 2002. 3v. illus. index. $395.00/set. ISBN 0-19-508888-3.

Theatrical producer Norton presents here a monumental work. It encompasses in three volumes a year-by-year record of the Broadway musical stage from 1850 to 2001. (An introductory chapter features selected productions from 1750 to 1850, "included because of their importance to future theatre.") The shows are listed in chapters for each theatrical season, running from June 1 through May 31. Each show is given a serial number beginning with its year of production. For example, for its original production *Carousel* has the entry number 1945.05, indicating it was the fifth musical in the calendar year 1945. It is included in the chapter for the 1944-45 season, because it opened on April 19, 1945. Revivals of *Carousel* on Broadway have their own numbers, with some referencing back to the original production. For each entry the following information is given: title, composer and librettist, other principals involved in the production, opening date, theater, length of run, cast members (principals in capital letters), a list of scenes, and a list of musical numbers. No plot summaries are given, nor is there information on sound recordings.

The third volume includes three indexes—shows, songs, and selected individuals. Under each index entry the reader is referred to an entry number only (not a page). The indexes are not particularly easy to use. There are no markers at the page edge to set off each index, nor are running heads in somewhat larger type given on each page to assist scanning. Similarly, there are no running heads on text pages either—only the season (e.g., 1944-1945 season). One must scan the pages for the appropriate entry number (happily given in bold typeface). One must also take care that a show with an entry number beginning with 1945 can be listed either in the 1944-1945 season chapter or the following one for 1945-1946. Thus, one consults the indexes, knowing it will not be a speedy operation.

Immersing oneself in these volumes, one becomes quickly aware that this is an invaluable source for research on theatrical history. The chapter for each season begins with a full-page illustration of a musical of that time. The amount of research taken to compile this work is awe-inspiring.

Norton's work is a big brother to Gerald Bordman's *American Musical Theater: A Chronicle* (3d ed.; see ARBA 2002, entry 1242). Norton has worked closely with Bordman and acknowledges his debt. Indeed, because of its compact size and ease of use, Bordman's work can serve as a guide to the more comprehensive volumes. Norton complements Kurt Gänzl's *The Encyclopedia of Musical Theatre* (2d ed.; see ARBA 2002, entry 1243), which employs a single alphabetic arrangement for shows, composers, performers, and so on. (Gänzl has an international tone in that he also covers Britain and several nations on the European continent.) The song index itself, with approximately 41,500 entries, calls for comparison with Ken Bloom's *American Song: The Complete Musical Theatre Companion* (see ARBA 2002, entry 1171, and ARBA 97, entry 1077).

Norton is very liberal in what to include as a musical, not only book shows, but reviews, and one-person shows. He also includes some works that include music incidentally (e.g., Coward's *Tonight at Eight-Thirty*, 1936.29) and operas that were produced on Broadway. He includes operettas and musicals presented by New York City Opera but excludes similar works (e.g., *The Merry Widow*) if done at the Metropolitan Opera.

A major lack in Norton's volumes is no consideration of the off-Broadway stage. Thus, unless an off-Broadway show transferred to Broadway, it is excluded. For the student of American musicals there is no border between Broadway and off-Broadway, and Norton should include these works in a new edition. Norton acknowledges these gaps and notes in his preface: "Next edition—perhaps."

Even with this reservation, Norton's work is a major achievement and merits a place on the reference shelves of all comprehensive performing arts collections. [R: LJ, 1 Nov 02, p. 76]—**Richard D. Johnson**

Directories

C, P

421.   **Internet Broadway Database. http://www.ibdb.com.** [Website]. New York, League of American Theatres and Producers. Free. Date reviewed: Oct 02.

Created by the research department of the League of American Theatres and Producers, this database provides information on Broadway Theater dating from the 1700s to the present. It serves as a comprehensive history for those in the performing arts, journalists, and Broadway enthusiasts. Most of the information available here was entered in according to the playbill available on the opening night of the performance as well as newspaper and magazine articles, theater textbooks, and the archives of the League. Users can conduct a basic search by entering a keyword and searching by "Show," "People/Organization," "Theatre," or "Season." A more advanced search is available, which allows the user to enter such information as show type, number of performances, opening and closing dates, or character name. The site provides the following information for each play: opening/closing dates; number of performances; category of performance (e.g., musical, drama, comedy); the setting; information about the theater; information about the author, choreographer, and production staff; performers and understudies; and replacement or transfer information.

This is an easy site to use and provides a lot of useful information in one place. Journalists writing on theater will find it especially useful for research, as will avid fans of Broadway Theater.—**Shannon Graff Hysell**

28 Philosophy and Religion

PHILOSOPHY

C
422.   Edgar, Andrew, and Peter Sedgwick. **Cultural Theory: The Key Thinkers.** New York, Routledge, 2002. 288p. index. $65.00; $17.95pa. ISBN 0-415-23280-5; 0-415-23281-3pa.

Complementing *Key Concepts in Cultural Theory* (see ARBA 2001, entry 1260), by the same editors and publisher, this volume focuses on the individual thinkers prominent in the field of "cultural theory" as it understands itself today as well as those who represent its most influential historical antecedents, reaching back to Plato and Aristotle. Jacket blurbs identify these thinkers as "the literary critics, sociologists, artists, philosophers and writers who have shaped contemporary culture and society, and the way in which we view them." Under this description, cultural studies would seem to be a generic discipline encompassing all perspectives on and approaches to its subject matter. But that is hardly the case. For a more (although not fully) adequate characterization of the field that intimates its more specific methodological proclivities and sociopolitical leanings, readers will need to consult the introduction to the earlier volume. That will shed some light on what connects the somewhat disparate group of thinkers included here, ranging from Matthew Arnold and Luce Irigaray to Max Weber and Jacques Derrida, and, as importantly, what might exclude others, such as John Locke, Friedrich von Hayek, T. S. Eliot, or Ayn Rand, whose respective influences on contemporary society and culture or "the way we [others of us] understand them" are, while different, no less pervasive than those of, say, Emmanuel Levinas, Walter Benjamin, or Julia Kristeva. That understood, this joins the *Key Concepts* volume as a useful guide to a significant realm of recent and contemporary thought. Like its older sibling, it offers articles that are reasonably clear and self-contained, although marred by occasional lapses into obscure terminology or dense exposition likely to baffle the uninitiated. Its biographical entries are supplemented by a brief glossary of key concepts, a 38-page bibliography of primary and secondary sources, and an adequate index.—**Hans E. Bynagle**

RELIGION

General Works

Biography

C, P
423.   Hall, Timothy L. **American Religious Leaders.** New York, Facts on File, 2003. 430p. illus. index. (American Biographies). $65.00. ISBN 0-8160-4534-8.

Facts on File has always done a good job of publishing handy, quick reference books, and this newest edition carries on the tradition. For those unfamiliar with Facts on File books, these editions are not comprehensive encyclopedias or in-depth reference books. They are easily accessible, first sources for people who simply want a starting place to begin their studies. *American Religious Leaders* contains short (one-page in length) yet informative articles on more than 270 religious leaders, including non-Americans. The author and the editors of the

American Biographies series have kept the emphasis on the life facts of the individuals and left out any editorializing. Each article ends with a listing of suggested articles and books for further reading. The organization of the book is alphabetic, with entries listed from A to Z, which makes a table of contents unnecessary. Most helpful are the included glossary of religious terminology, an excellent bibliography and recommended sources that invite the reader to investigate any area that peaks their interest, and a listing of entries by religious affiliation and by birth date. A comprehensive index is also included. This is a perfect source for fast, basic information for anyone who wishes a two-minute reading synopsis on an American religious leader. It should be within arms reach of any reference librarian working an information desk or a telephone.—**Glenn Masuchika**

Dictionaries and Encyclopedias

P
424.   Day, Peter. **A Dictionary of Religious Orders.** New York, Continuum Publishing, 2001. 453p. $49.95. ISBN 0-86012-314-6.

Christian men and women have lived in ordered faith communities almost from the beginning. From St. Antony's monks in the fourth century to the Taizé Community in the twentieth, religious orders have played a prominent role in shaping Christian faith and practice. This 1-volume dictionary examines 1,450 Catholic, Anglican, and Protestant religious orders (both male and female, current and defunct), as well as secular chivalric orders with religious roots. Each entry provides the current headquarters of the order, its date of founding, the name of its founder, and the original habit. A brief history follows, along with an account of the contemporary ministries of the order. The work concludes with a glossary, a list of abbreviations, the alternate names for each order and the corresponding entry for each, and a summary list of the orders contained in the work. The latter serves no useful purpose and easily could have been eliminated.

Day, author of *The Liturgical Dictionary of Eastern Christianity* (see ARBA 95, entry 1467), notes that this work is a dictionary, not a directory; so while each order's "location" (i.e., city and nation) is provided, no street address is given. Of more concern is the inclusion of several ancient entries for which almost no information is available, yet neglecting to include many contemporary non-Catholic orders (e.g., the Lutheran Benedictine communities in Sweden). Given Roman Catholic dominance in the religious world, however, the work is recommended for theological libraries and public libraries with substantive religion collections.

—**Christopher Brennan**

P, S
425.   **The Usborne Internet-Linked Encyclopedia of World Religions.** By Susan Meredith and Clare Hickman. Tulsa, Okla., EDC Publishing, 2001. 127p. illus. index. $19.95. ISBN 0-7945-0182-6.

The Usborne Internet-Linked Encyclopedia of World Religions explains the major world religions as well as several ancient Western belief systems. It is intended for late elementary to middle school-aged children but even adults will find it useful. Several pages are devoted to each religion, with lots of beautiful photographs and illustrations to support the text. The entries are written with the juvenile audience in mind, but adults and college students could use the resource for quick overviews of the history and beliefs of each religion covered. The coverage of the work seems balanced, with no preference of place or language given to particular types of religions. The work begins with some ground rules of Internet safety for children, and moves on to an overview explaining for younger readers what religion is and is not before examining specific religions.

While this encyclopedia stands alone as a great resource, as an added bonus the publisher has a Website where links for more in-depth information on each topic are listed and kept up-to-date. Each section of the encyclopedia points users to appropriate sections of the publisher's Website. The book is well indexed, and contains a map and timeline of world religions in an appendix. This is a great reference resource for public library children's collections, school libraries, and academic libraries with collections of juvenile materials.—**Mark T. Bay**

Handbooks and Yearbooks

P, S

426.   Breuilly, Elizabeth, Joanne O'Brien, and Martin Palmer. **Festivals of the World: The Illustrated Guide to Celebrations, Customs, Events and Holidays.** New York, Checkmark Books/Facts on File, 2002. 160p. illus. index. $29.95. ISBN 0-8160-4481-3.

This companion volume to *Religions of the World* (see ARBA 98, entry 1348) uses liturgical calendars of the world's religions to introduce students to the major (and some minor) religious festivals. The yearly cycle of feasts and festivals is used to illustrate how these events celebrate the historical events of each faith.

Festivals of the World's major religions covered—Judaism, Christianity, Muslim, Hinduism, and Buddhism—are presented in extensive entries. Other traditions covered include festivals of the Sikhs, Taoists, Zoroastrians, and Shintos. Baha'i, Jain, and Rastafarian celebrations are covered to a lesser degree.

Entries for each religion begin with a summary of its origin, history, religious practices, sacred texts, and customs. Major festivals and their significance to the faith are explained in depth. The background of each event is told through stories and legends from sacred texts that put the festival in context of the religion's history and beliefs. The liturgical calendar for each is a major feature of each entry. The calendars are depicted cyclically and each festival is briefly described on the same page, making the calendar page a useful quick reference guide. Color photographs, illustrations, and sidebars catch the eye of the reader and serve to supplement the clearly written text. For example, the Passover entry contains a full-page color spread of the elements of the Seder plate; the Hajj rites are outlined in detail, as are some Christian symbols. There are also recipes for traditional dishes such as latkes and kiribat. A glossary, bibliography (print and Websites), and an index complete the book.

Some of the information presented here is covered in less depth in *Religions of the World*. Certainly, books on specific religions will offer similar information but this is a bright, attractive book that offers visual appeal and just the right amount of information for students researching religious festivals.—**Marlene M. Kuhl**

Bible Studies

Dictionaries and Encyclopedias

C, P

427.   **The Oxford Essential Guide to People & Places of the Bible.** New York, Berkley Books/Penguin Books, 2001. 374p. index. $6.99pa. ISBN 0-425-18067-0.

The Bible is the bedrock of Judaism and Christianity. Traditional and critical interpretation illustrate its centrality in molding and shaping world culture in general and western civilization in particular. Here, an international and cross-denominational team of 125 leading biblical scholars contribute 280 articles about key people (individuals and groups) and places whose accounts are the matrix around which the biblical saga is told. The familiar and the not-so-familiar from the Hebrew Bible, the Apocrypha, and the New Testament are discussed in articles of unequal length. Pages are two columns and most contributions are a page; notable exceptions are the entries on Moses (3 pages), the Kingdom of Judah (5 pages), and Jesus (13 pages). The *Guide* is linked to the *Oxford Companion to the Bible* (see ARBA 94, entry 1545) and the nondogmatic entries, for the most part, discuss biblical items by citing archaeological, historical, theological, and contemporary data. There is bound to be restrictive (e.g., "Who is a Jew?") and controversial opinions drawn (e.g., Jesus "was more interested in what God was doing through him than in what he was in himself"). The work is fully cross-referenced and includes a select bibliography and subject index; however, there are no maps as mentioned in the introduction. Informative and useful, this is a valuable guide to biblical studies.—**Zev Garber**

Handbooks and Yearbooks

C, P

428.   **The Oxford Illustrated History of the Bible.** John Rogerson, ed. New York, Oxford University Press, 2001. 395p. illus. index. $40.00. ISBN 0-19-860118-2.

John Rogerson's *The Oxford Illustrated History of the Bible* provides historical, literary, and religious scholars with a single-volume collection of academic pieces written by top-notch authors in their respective fields.

The work is well organized and topically arranged by "The Making of the Bible" (two sections), followed by "The Study and Use of the Bible" and "Contemporary Interpretations." In addition, the contributors detail key aspects of the Apocrypha and describe how it fits into the biblical tradition. Another strength is the analysis of how the Bible fits into and how it has affected societal development in both the eastern and western worlds, across religious faiths, and within different periods. In terms of the latter, the late antique, medieval, reformation, early modern, and the modern eras are treated separately. Rogerson and his fellow contributors also look at the effects of feminist scholarship as well as the forms of liberation theology taking root in separate areas of the world. Finally, the bibliography is arranged by subject and provides excellent suggestions for further reading.

The work does have two notable weaknesses. First, as Rogerson himself admits, there should be more coverage of biblical studies through the humanities, particularly in regard to art and music (p. xv). Secondly, a section on Islam and the interconnectivity between the Bible and Qur'an would have strengthened the quality of this work.

The Oxford Illustrated History of the Bible is a fine reference for the beginning scholar and expert alike. It is highly recommended for public, college, and university libraries. [R: LJ, 15 Oct 01, p. 68; RUSQ, Fall 01, pp. 81-82]—**David J. Duncan**

P

429.   Worth, Roland H., Jr. **Biblical Studies on the Internet: A Resource Guide.** Jefferson, N.C., McFarland, 2002. 316p. index. $35.00pa. ISBN 0-7864-1327-1.

This book is a compilation of Internet resources on biblical studies currently available for use online or to be downloaded to one's personal computer. More than 3,300 Websites are cited on a range of topics, from English-language Bible translations to Bible translations in over 57 languages, English and non-English commentaries on books of the Bible, ancient-language texts and resource materials, and devotional studies, as well as translations and guides to writings of the early church. The book is designed for the average computer and Internet user. The author provides only brief commentary throughout the work; it is apparent that there are many Websites and downloadable items available in the area of biblical studies, and the author illustrates this variety in his presentation of the table of contents. Some interesting areas where information is provided include biblical maps, apocryphal literature, ancient gentile writings, orthodox and heretical church-related authors, and ancient biblical city Websites. The book is meant to be informational and current; the lack of commentary and critical appraisal of the Websites contributes to the objectivity of the information. The author has provided the size of downloadable files where appropriate, in order to appraise users of file size and space considerations. [R: LJ, 15 May 02, p. 88]
—**Bradford Lee Eden**

Buddhism

C, P

430.   Baroni, Helen J. **The Illustrated Encyclopedia of Zen Buddhism.** New York, Rosen Publishing, 2002. 426p. illus. index. $119.95; $89.95 (school libraries). ISBN 0-8239-2240-5.

The Illustrated Encyclopedia of Zen Buddhism is a first-class reference for the practitioner, neophyte, or student of Zen Buddhism. As befitting a Zen tome, it introduces the reader to Zen Buddhism as a religion and as an artistic, philosophical, and spiritual practice. It is written in a clear and accessible style.

Baroni "includes over 1,700 in-depth entries in an A-Z format. Each entry provides information on the beliefs, practices, and history of Zen Buddhism as well as the significant movements, organizations, and personalities that are part of this culture and religion" (editors notes). The five-page introduction includes a brief history of Zen in both the traditional and the historical accounts. It also includes brief comments on Zen teachings, Zen practice, and the Zen monastery and encyclopedia entries. There follows a short "How to Use This Book" and a "Contents by Subject" guide that simplifies searching for specific subject entries. Additionally, the entries are heavily cross-referenced. Black-and-white photographs illustrate the many aspects of Zen Buddhist culture and religion. Finally, there is a bibliography and an index.

The author is a well-trained and educated professor of religion with excellent credentials. This reference is recommended for all types of libraries, particularly those with courses in religion.—**Nadine Salmons**

Christianity

Biography

P

431. **Great Popes Throughout History: An Encyclopedia.** Frank J. Coppa, ed. Westport, Conn., Greenwood Press, 2002. 2v. illus. index. $125.00/set. ISBN 0-313-29533-6.

This two-volume encyclopedia by historian and noted author Frank J. Coppa of St. John's University is a fine contribution to the study of the papacy, specifically the more influential popes, from Peter to John Paul II. Not every pope is included in this work, only those that "played crucial roles in both the institution of the papacy and in European and world events."

Great Popes uses a chronological format, with selected "significant" popes having entries written by contributors who are experts in their specific area. Individual entries average several pages in length and a useful chronology of all popes and a good index helps make it user-friendly. It is divided into five sections: "The Early Papacy," "The Medieval Papacy," "The Renaissance and Reformation Papacy," "The Early Modern Papacy," and "The Modern Papacy." Each includes an introduction that provides the historical perspective of the popes of that section. A general bibliographic note concludes each section. An example of a typical entry is Patrick Granfield's entry on John XXIII. It is eight pages in length, including a two-page selected bibliography and a photograph. The first three pages are dedicated to his life before being elected pope in 1958. The next main point deals with the Second Vatican Council. It concludes with the author's three-page explanation of detailing the contributions and impact of John XXIII.

This work is informative, readable, and a nice contribution to the study of the papacy. It is a solid resource, especially for the price. *Great Popes Throughout History* is recommended for all libraries. [R: LJ, Dec 02, p. 106]
—**Scott R. DiMarco**

Dictionaries and Encyclopedias

C, P

432. Barrett, David B., George T. Kurian, and Todd M. Johnson. **World Christian Encyclopedia: A Comparative Survey of Churches and Religions in the Modern World.** 2d ed. New York, Oxford University Press, 2001. 2v. illus. maps. index. $295.00/set. ISBN 0-19-507963-9.

A perfect example of a misnamed resource, this encyclopedia will be of little use to those seeking an explanation of the teachings of Christianity or its historical development. Instead, it is a rich compilation of demographic data about the state of Christianity around the world. A revision of the 1981 original (see ARBA 84, entry 986, for a review), the *World Christian Encyclopedia* draws on the statistical compilations of each denomination. Through the 15 parts of this 2-volume work, the reader is provided with a country-by-country analysis of Christian and non-Christian religious life, religious analyses of various ethnic groups (including evangelization efforts among them), demographic data concerning various linguistic groups, and so forth. Drawing on historical data and present trends, the authors also interpolate the likely state of the faith by 2025.

The compilation of data is impressive but overwhelming. The authors' explanations often succumb to jargon and rely heavily on neologisms (e.g., *ethnosphere*, *autoglossonym*) when simpler language would suffice. The statistical summaries are often incomprehensible without recourse to other parts scattered across both volumes, making the work difficult to use. Also, greater attention to proofreading would have been helpful. For example, it is said that Great Britain is subdivided into 64 provinces. In fact, the British do not use provincial language.

The nation is subdivided into counties, districts, and regions. Even so, the work is recommended for theological libraries, larger public libraries, and academic libraries with sizeable collections in statistics, sociology, demography, or religious studies.—**Christopher Brennan**

P

433.   Water, Mark, comp. **The New Encyclopedia of Christian Martyrs.** Grand Rapids, Mich., Baker Book House, 2001. 956p. index. $29.99. ISBN 0-8010-1225-2.

This encyclopedia is a compilation of writings on martyrs from the Old Testament to the twenty-first century. The excerpts are arranged chronologically, the exceptions being the account of Christ's crucifixion that begins the book and the final chapter on martyrs from the seventeenth to the twenty-first centuries, which is arranged geographically.

The compiler of *The New Encyclopedia of Christian Quotations* (Baker Books, 2001), Water clearly states in his introduction the aim of this work is to both inform and to exhort his audience to a fuller Christian life. The introduction clarifies what types of literature and accounts he finds acceptable or unacceptable for inclusion, and he acknowledges his heavy use of the writings of John Foxe. Commendably, he also discusses the criticism and shortcomings of Foxe's works and includes additional sources to balance Foxe's accounts.

The definition of martyrs used is sufficiently broad to include Protestant, Catholic, Orthodox, and other Christian sects. Modern martyrs include Bonhoffer, Romero, Martin Luther King, Jr., and Cassie Bernall, one of the students tragically shot at Columbine High School in 1999.

There are seven parts, each with a separate table of contents citing the martyrs discussed in the section and the author whose account is used. Each part also includes brief but interesting excerpts of Christian writings at the end. Throughout the work Water adds helpful comments to provide historical context to the account. The bibliography and index are adequate.

One need not share Water's convictions to derive benefit from this encyclopedia, but those who have questions concerning the historical authenticity of some of the excerpted accounts will find those questions neither raised nor answered in this work. Scholars and graduate students will want to work with the original sources, but for those unfamiliar with primary and historical texts recounting Christian martyrdom, this encyclopedia is a good place to begin their study. [R: LJ, 1 Mar 02, p. 90; Choice, Mar 02, p. 1210]—**Mark van Lummel**

Hinduism

C, P, S

434.   Sullivan, Bruce M. **The A to Z of Hinduism.** Lanham, Md., Scarecrow, 2001. 257p. $24.95pa. ISBN 0-8108-4070-7.

Written by a professor of religious studies and of Asian studies, this is an erudite, subject-specific dictionary with a fine introductory essay. The 18-page introduction is both scholarly and accessible. Hinduism has "the longest history of any of the world's major religions. Multiple streams of tradition have merged to create Hinduism" (p. 1). Hinduism is therefore difficult to define, and so complex that scholars disagree on whether it is one religion with many sects, or several religions with historical and theological commonalities. The sociological and political influence of Hinduism in Indian culture is ubiquitous and its historical place from the Vedic Period to the present is well sketched in the introduction. For the novice student of Hinduism or of comparative religions, the introduction may serve as an impetus for the profitable use of the dictionary.

The dictionary entries are well designed so that, unlike many other dictionaries, its pages entice the eye. The headings of every entry are in large print accented with typographical ornaments. Definitions are clear and complete with almost encyclopedic detail. Entries include the names of movements, theological terms, sects, religious leaders, military leaders, saints, gods, sacred writings, festivals, places, and words that describe almost every possible aspect of Hinduism.

A pronunciation guide at the beginning of the book lists symbols used throughout. It is followed by a chronology summarizing major movements, events, people, and literature of Hinduism by century. A useful memory tool for the general reader, the author describes the chronology as "helpful but entirely artificial" (p. 4) because old cultural patterns persist long after new ones predominate. This is a well-written, well-designed book that is wonderfully suited for the student, scholar, or casual reader interested in the many facets of Hinduism.—**Dorothy Jones**

Islam

Atlases

C, P

435.   Freeman-Grenville, G. S. P., and Stuart Christopher Munro-Hay. **Historical Atlas of Islam.** New York, Continuum Publishing, 2002. 414p. illus. maps. index. $50.00. ISBN 0-8264-1417-6.

The purpose of this atlas is to present a pictorial representation of the history and expansion of Islam. Starting before the birth of Mohammed, the book is divided by historical period and then geographically. The text is readable and coverage of significant events in the history of Islam is thorough.

Maps depict the physical terrain, political boundaries, populations, trade routes, and many other aspects of the expansion of Islam. However, the book is not limited to maps, but also includes many photographs of significant people and places in the history of Islam. The book is further enriched by illustrations from manuscripts and photographs of works of art and artifacts. The index is well done and includes personal and place names and historical references. The glossary of relevant historical terms and frequently used Arabic terms is most helpful. The authors defend the absence of a bibliography by asserting that excellent bibliographies can be found in their widely held earlier works: *Historical Atlas of the Middle East* (see ARBA 94, entry 460), *The New Atlas of African History* (see ARBA 92, entry 85), and *The Oxford Encyclopedia of the Modern Islamic World* (see ARBA 96, entry 1477).

This book supercedes earlier atlases of Islam in that it is richer in both content and illustrations. Furthermore, it covers the history and geography of Islam up to 2002, while the classics were published 20 or more years ago. This book is recommended for all collections.—**Jeanne D. Galvin**

Dictionaries and Encyclopedias

P

436.   Glassé, Cyril. **New Encyclopedia of Islam: Revised Edition of the** *Concise Encyclopedia of Islam.* Walnut Creek, Calif., Alta Mira Press, 2001. 534p. illus. maps. $89.95. ISBN 0-7591-0189-2.

The *New Encyclopedia of Islam* is a wealth of accurate and complete information about Islam and its many facets. Improving on the *Concise Encyclopedia of Islam* (see ARBA 91, entry 1448), this work updates the previous volume; adds important concepts left out of the previous volume; and provides clear and concise entries specifically written for users unfamiliar with Islamic faith, philosophy, and history. The important figures in the development of the religion as well as some of the important, yet minor players, are given their due, and the sometimes puzzling (to non-Muslims) concepts of the faith are laid out in an easy-to-understand yet scholarly manner. Scattered throughout the work are impressive colored plates to illustrate the text, and the maps at the back of the book are well done, allowing a user to place the people and events defined by the encyclopedia in proper geographic perspective. The map of the *hajj*, showing Mecca and all the stops a pilgrim makes while traveling there, is particularly useful to non-Muslims. Finally, a chronology of Muslim history helps the user to put the events into perspective with the history of the rest of the world. An extensive bibliography finishes off the work, giving users possible sources for further inquiry.

This reference work is highly recommended for all types and sizes of libraries. There are simply no other sources of comparable quality, especially in one volume and at a reasonable price. Curiosity about the Islamic faith is at an all-time high in the Western world, and any library staff wanting a good source for answering questions in a balanced and fair manner should have the *New Encyclopedia of Islam* close at hand. It comes very highly recommended for all libraries. [R: Choice, June 02, p. 1738]—**Mark T. Bay**

Judaism

C, P

437.   **The New Encyclopedia of Judaism.** Geoffrey Wigoder, Fred Skolnik, and Shmuel Himelstein, eds. New York, New York University Press, 2002. 856p. illus. index. $99.95. ISBN 0-8147-9388-6.

Following the greatly applauded 1st edition, a 1989 American Libraries Association Outstanding Reference Book (see ARBA 91, entry 1449), this 2d edition contains 250 new articles beyond the original 1,000 and updated information to reflect current issues and developments in the religious life of all the major branches of Judaism. As before, there is an emphasis on liturgy, and the influence women have had, from ancient times to the feminist movement. Biographical entries have been expanded to cover later rabbinical authorities; biblical, Hasidic, academic, and popular figures; and more of the Talmudic sages. Other fortified areas include biblical and Second Temple history, the Apocrypha and Pseudepigrapha, and Zionism.

Since the work is intended for both laypeople and students, and for non-Jews as well as Jews, cross-referencing of Hebrew words to English facilitate its use. A new feature of this volume aimed at the goal of accessibility is an annotated bibliography of basic works on Judaism for the general reader. Further, related articles are noted by capital letters within each entry. Completing the user's tools is a key to abbreviations, a glossary, and rules of transliteration. Numerous sidebars of useful information add interest and helpful tips for further study.

Editorially speaking, the qualifications of the compilers and the 80 writers are impressive. The late Geoffrey Wigoder's previous credits include chief editor of the multivolume *Encyclopaedia Judaica*, and more recently, a comprehensive work on the Holocaust. The contributors represent an international authority of Reform, Conservative, and Orthodox Jewry. Even taken alone, the more than 300 black-and-white and color illustrations tell a fascinating story of Jewish history and customs and folk traditions. They do much to augment the written material at an emotional and artistic level.

This work offers a thorough, one-volume reference for Jews and those interested in the Jewish religion and way of life. With continued Middle East conflict, many people are questioning the beliefs and history of Islam and Judaism that underlie the struggle. This book should be available in libraries to aid the public in this quest. [R: LJ, 1 Sept 02, p. 168]—**Janet J. Kosky**

Part IV
SCIENCE
AND
TECHNOLOGY

29 Science and Technology in General

BIOGRAPHY

C

438. **The Cambridge Dictionary of Scientists.** 2d ed. By David Millar, Ian Millar, John Millar, and Margaret Millar. New York, Cambridge University Press, 2002. 428p. illus. index. $50.00; $20.00pa. ISBN 0-521-80602-X; 0-521-00062-9pa.

The Cambridge Dictionary of Scientists is in its 2d edition and has been revised, expanded, and updated. The value of the resource has been expanded both in the content and visual aids. It was updated to reflect new relevant data since 1996. The present edition offers 1,500 biographical profiles of scientists starting 550 B.C.E. from 40 countries. It was expanded with 157 new entries, including 70 entries on pioneer women whose achievements laid the foundation for others pursuing a career in the sciences. In the preface the authors indicate the central objective of the *Dictionary* is to "survey the sciences through the lives of the men and women whose efforts have shaped modern science." Although it can be argued that rather than "survey the sciences," a dictionary, as a type of information resource, offers an easy and quick access point to the core data in a condensed form. For a survey of sciences and realization of the development in particular a reader probably will not read a dictionary front to back. It is useful that the profiles are associated with their scientific contributions. The effects, theories, laws, chemical reactions, and diseases are described shortly and often illustrated schematically. The coverage extends to the fields of biology, chemistry, physics, mathematics, technology, space, and medicine. The portraits of many scientists (about 150) have been inserted in the 2d edition, thus enhancing the image and the overall quality of the book. In addition to people profiles, 38 panels give a brief overview on some selected topics of historical importance or current interest. Six new and two slightly changed from the previous edition panels are "Global Warming," "Pheromones," "Periodic table of the chemical elements," "Long-range communications," "The History of the heat engine," "The Internet and international scientific collaboration," "The Different forms of Carbon" (instead of the former "The three forms of carbon"), and "A strange biochemical: Nitric Oxide" (instead of "NO - molecule of the year 1992") highlighting the 1998 Nobel Prize shared by three American pharmacologists for their discovery that nitric oxide can transmit signals in the cardiovascular system. Also included are an updated compilation of the Nobel Prize winners (1901-2001) and a list of winners (1936-1998) of the Fields Medal (the mathematician's equivalent of the Nobel Prize).

The *Dictionary* is well designed stating the objective for a survey. The subject panels are related to the personal profiles. Scattered throughout, the volume panels are easily recognized in frame boxes. A list of panels is given separately following the table of contents. The index indicates the words linked to the panels in italics. Many illustrative figures are inserted into the text. Symbols and conventions are mentioned in the preface. All biographical entries are organized alphabetically and are about 200 words in length.

It can be concluded that the present *Dictionary* is an authoritative source of information. The initial foundation of *The Cambridge Dictionary of Scientists* was the authors' *Chambers Concise Dictionary of Scientists* (see ARBA 91, entry 1460) now out of print. The sources of information are mentioned in the preface: *The Dictionary of Scientific Biography* (a 14-volume set with supplements), autobiographical writing by scientists, Nobel Prize lectures, and personal interviews. Based on a collaborative work of four family members it is the latest writing project among many others successfully published by an "author team" (over 90 research papers and 5 books).

The Cambridge Dictionary of Scientists will be a perfect addition to public, school, and small college libraries or anyone interested in quick but brief access to massive information on the life and work of researchers, whose achievements from the beginning to present day make science. The resource will be a valuable reference world-wide. The success of the *Dictionary* can be indicated by a number of holdings—the 1st edition (1996) is listed in 900 library catalogs (both public and academic) and the 2d edition in 40 catalogs already (WorldCat, September 2002). Also, it is valuable to mention that the list of different "dictionaries of scientists" is extensive (dozens of titles published just within the last two years), so that the market is saturated (and competitive) to serve a range of needs. Some of those titles include *The Biographical Dictionary of Women in Science: Pioneering Lives from Ancient Times to the Mid-20th Century* (see ARBA 2001, entry 897); *The Biographical Dictionary of Scientists* (see ARBA 2002, entry 1302); *Concise Dictionary of Scientific Biography* (2d ed.; see ARBA 2001, entry 1307); *Notable Scientists from 1900 to the Present* (see ARBA 2002, entry 1304); and *The Nobel Scientists: A Biographical Encyclopedia* (see entry 439).—**Svetlana Korolev**

C

439.   Kurian, George Thomas. **The Nobel Scientists: A Biographical Encyclopedia.** Buffalo, N.Y., Prometheus Books, 2002. 420p. index. $75.00. ISBN 1-57392-927-1.

George Thomas Kurian has put together a tribute to Nobel scientists to commemorate 100 years of Nobel prizes (1901-2000). The book contains profiles of 466 laureates in 3 sections: "Chemistry," "Physics," and "Physiology or Medicine." The names of the award winners are listed chronologically within each discipline or section. Each laureate is profiled individually, even if he or she achieved the honor with others for the same body of work. There are no descriptions of the career paths or trials and errors of these successful scientists, just a basic summary of their education and a paragraph describing the crucial work that led to the highest, most prestigious award a scientist may receive.

The profiles consist of the year the prize was awarded, the birth date and date of death (if applicable), nationality, education, main career locations, other awards received, the citation used when the prize was bestowed (e.g., "In recognition of the extraordinary services he has rendered by his work on sugar and purine synthesis."—Emil Hermann Fischer, 1902, Chemistry), a summary of the laureate's work, highlighted publications, and a bibliography.

In addition to the easy-to-use table of contents that lists the names of the scientists, their fields of endeavor, and the pages where their profiles can be found, the book contains three indexes to facilitate finding the laureate of choice. The first is a six-page index of names and corresponding pages; the second is a nine-page index of laureates by nation; and the third is an eight-page index by scientific work. Many of the entries use terminology that require familiarity with basic to intermediate scientific vocabulary. In several cases the work of a collaborating scientist is described using the same language and some of the same sentences in the "Life Work" paragraphs that were used for the other collaborators. Perhaps the author could have chosen more individual characteristics or descriptors (where possible) to differentiate the work of the collaborators to a greater degree.

This reference book will be a good resource for quick look-ups about major scientific contributors of the twentieth century. It is recommended for public libraries as well as community college and undergraduate academic libraries.—**Laura J. Bender**

C, P, S

440.   **Portraits of Great American Scientists.** Leon M. Lederman and Judith Scheppler, eds. Buffalo, N.Y., Prometheus Books, 2001. 305p. illus. $28.00. ISBN 1-57392-932-8.

Between the introduction and the epilogue of this creative book are 15 biographies of scientists whose specialties range from cultural anthropology to physics. Lederman, the author of the introduction and the epilogue, is the resident scholar for the Great Minds Program at the Illinois Mathematics and Science Academy (IMSA), located in Aurora, Illinois. He won the Nobel Prize in Physics in 1988, and is the inspiration behind this collec-tion of biographies. The mission of IMSA is to offer challenging educational opportunities to students, grades 10-12, with talents in mathematics and science (they also take courses in the arts and humanities) and to provide an educational laboratory to design and test innovative programs, projects, and methods that can be shared with others in the field of education. This book is one such project.

The authors of the biographies are students of IMSA who answered an invitation sent by Lederman to participate in the writing of this volume. Scheppler, coordinator of IMSA's Inquiry Program, helped compile the original list of potential candidates for the biographies and edited the final collection for publication. The students embarked on extensive research to narrow down the original list of 100 names to 1 per participant, or 15 names. Between 1999 and 2001 the students interviewed their chosen scientists, sent many follow-up questions via e-mail, and learned much about the nuts and bolts of the scientific enterprise.

Readers of this book cannot help but get caught up in the students' voyages of discovery. In the midst of growing concern about declining test scores and declining scientific and cultural literacy among Americans, these biographies rekindle hope for the intellectual future. The personal stories of the scientists (those of Sally Ride in astronautics, George Smoot in astrophysics, and Paul Sereno in paleontology, just to same a few) are fascinating in themselves. But the students' perspectives and emphases shine through and point to the exciting success of independent inquiry as a learning process. The students immersed themselves in contexts similar to those they will find in their professional lives.

This book is a powerful introduction to the challenges and joys of doing science. Although written by high school students, the writing is compelling and the information appropriate for teachers and laypersons interested in science. It is recommended for high school, public, and undergraduate academic reference collections.—**Laura J. Bender**

DICTIONARIES AND ENCYCLOPEDIAS

S

441.   **The American Heritage Student Science Dictionary.** New York, Houghton Mifflin, 2002. 376p. illus. $18.00. ISBN 0-618-18919-X.

The 376 pages of alphabetic entries featured in this volume include information about pronunciation, irregular plurals, closely related words, and cross-references and chemical formulas. Entries are complemented by 425 color photographs and drawings. Supporting tables and charts include a timeline of computing, geologic time, measurement, organic compounds, a periodic table, rocks, the solar system, and taxonomy. There are 21 biography sidebars that support 300 biographical entries of major men and women in science. Front matter includes a table of contents; a list of special entries; a preface; an excellent, diagrammatic explanation of the elements found within the dictionary; and a pronunciation guide. End matter consists of a listing of picture credits.

There are several features that make this volume user-friendly and increase the utility of this dictionary beyond that of most simple-definition dictionaries. The 12 "A Closer Look" text boxes (side bars) explain broader concepts, such as the greenhouse effect or photosynthesis. There are 105 "Did You Know" text boxes provided to expand information about concepts and processes, such as acid rain, the big bang, or transcription. The 31 "Usage" text boxes explain how similar words are incorporated into language, such as bacteria and bacterium or the differences between fruits and vegetables. There are 19 "World History" text boxes that expand upon the definition to include its interaction with people, cultures, and events. More than 300 entries address the men and women of science. In addition, there are 21 "Biography" text boxes providing greater detail about the lives and efforts of those individuals generally recognized as the scientific "greats." In some instances, significant additional information is provided to expand upon the basic definition, such as the supporting data for "organic compounds."

This is a comprehensive, affordable reference volume that would be useful to students in upper-elementary grades and above or as a general household, nontechnical science dictionary. It does not affect its usage, but the separation of expanded entries into variously named text boxes may be confusing to some readers. It may be difficult to understand why photosynthesis is listed as "A Closer Look" while plate tectonics is "Did You Know."

—**Craig A. Munsart**

C, P

442.   Burns, William E. **Scientific Revolution: An Encyclopedia.** Santa Barbara, Calif., ABC-CLIO, 2001. 387p. illus. index. $85.00. ISBN 0-87436-875-8.

Drawing on recent changes in the ways scholars view the rise of modern science, Burns has produced an attractive reference work that discusses the personalities, ideas, and instruments that comprised this era. The author focuses on the period from the late fifteenth to the early eighteenth centuries, providing articles on both the traditional subjects of the history of science as well as related issues, such as music, religion, and the occult sciences. All of the obvious scientific figures and fields are included, as well as a number of lesser-known topics. The book is aimed at the general reader, and the nontechnical writing style suits high school age and older readers.

Entries average half a page to a page in length, although notable subjects receive several pages of discussion. Each entry ends with a number of cross-references to related articles and a small bibliography. The bibliographic references typically include both classic and recent publications. Quality black-and-white reproductions of illustrations from books published during this era are judiciously sprinkled throughout the volume. A minimal list of pertinent Websites (all seemingly stable), a brief chronology, and a nicely detailed index conclude this work.

This title was published at about the same time as Wilbur Applebaum's *Encyclopedia of the Scientific Revolution* (see ARBA 2001, entry 1313). Both are well executed, and there is substantial overlap, but Applebaum's work includes the work of many authoritative contributors (rather than just one author) and has both more and longer articles. The work by Burns, however, has an edge in readability and cost and will be a solid addition to many collections. [R: LJ, 15 Sept 01, pp. 68-69; Choice, Mar 02, p. 1212]—**Christopher W. Nolan**

C, P

443.   **Encyclopedia of Science and Technology.** James Trefil, ed. New York, Routledge, 2001. 554p. illus. $50.00. ISBN 0-415-93724-8.

Although the scope of the *Encyclopedia of Science and Technology* is not unique, the resource is unique. The editor indicates that the encyclopedia is a popular form of information resource that is best suited for the kind of learning to which the modern reader has become accustomed and which approximates how learning actually is done: in small interconnected bits of information. In regards to an information resource, it is mentioned that a new encyclopedia is written based on a modern standard for a science reference. This book invites a reader for an interesting journey starting with an entry of "Absolute Zero" through the most important sights with the "travel" assistance offered in the "How To Use this Book" section. Toward the end readers will gain an attitude regarding science implications and the realization of personal responsibility to be a part of the ongoing discussion.

This 1-volume encyclopedia consists of about 1,000 entries, which are concise but of longer length than those found in some other related titles. Each article distills a subject's main aspects—either theoretical or practical—with insights on disputes and the excitement of scientific discovery. A brief one-sentence definition prefaces each concept. Many fascinating features are included in the text. The "Critical Path" feature appears above and below each entry. In the form of the words "First see" and "Next see" it is possible to follow the thread of the discipline back to its more fundamental concept (the article above the title) and forward to the subject's more developed state (the article below the title). A "Signpost Box" feature is placed at the end of many entries, where other relevant titles with some annotations are included. Thus a unique cross-referencing system enables the user to gather as much information as possible on a particular subject by tracing relationships across concepts and time. Sidebars are inserted in many entries to highlight observations of striking phenomena, interesting historical anecdotes of discovery, or reports on the cutting edge of current research. A brief list for further readings on some subjects is given in the margins. Special emphasis is placed on illustrations. The text is enriched with 750 vivid and excellent full-color photographs, drawing, and diagrams. The article titles are color-coded: blue for physical science and mathematics, green for life science and medicine, and red for technology. The index mirrors the color scheme of the headings, thus intending to constitute a table of contents for the encyclopedia.

The *Encyclopedia of Science and Technology* is an authoritative source of information. General editor James Trefil is a professor of physics at George Mason University and is one of the founders of modern quark theory. Consulting editor Harold Morowitz is a biophysicist and professor of biology at George Mason University, who has published widely on popular topics in science. Together they have edited a high-quality dictionary that is informative, engaging, and enjoyable. It will be useful for the academic and general reader. This volume is highly recommended for school, college, and public libraries as well as for family collections. Updated and expanded material in this encyclopedia will be made available in both print and online versions. [R: LJ, Dec 01, p. 106; SLJ, Feb 02, p. 92]—**Svetlana Korolev**

P, S

444.   Sachs, Jessica Snyder. **The Encyclopedia of Inventions.** Danbury, Conn., Franklin Watts, 2001. 192p. illus. index. $29.95. ISBN 0-531-11711-1.

This single volume includes alphabetic entries to more than 200 inventions, many illustrated with photographs or drawings to show what they do. Within the entries, words written in small capitals refer the reader to other articles addressing the same topic. Pages follow a two-column format and entries vary in length from a few sentences to multiple pages. Contained in the volume are 12 articles of broad subject interest such as "Agriculture" and "Power Generation." Profiles are provided for six inventors and are placed in the book near their respective subjects. Throughout the book, inventions are placed within a temporal framework. Eleven one-page articles (sidebars) provide an overview of events and inventions in a given year, from 250,000 B.C.E. to 1995. A three-page chronology at the back of the book shows the date of an invention with corresponding events in world history. The index lists inventions, inventors, articles, and illustrations.

The strength of this book is its presentation of many inventions as an evolution of ideas and process in a single, useful volume. Many of the inventions listed can be credited to a single individual. Others (like soap or concrete) have merely evolved though common usage. Still others are wrongly credited to an individual who improved or refined a preexisting device. Their contribution was significant nonetheless, but it is erroneous to credit James Watt with the invention of the steam engine when his important contribution was to dramatically improve the efficiency and power of the existing steam engine developed by Thomas Newcomen. Other inventions involved a continuum of refinements, developments, and combinations of other newly invented engineering components.

There are many publications showing how inventions work, containing detailed biographies of dozens of inventors, or merely listing who invented what and when. The attempt of this work is not to create the world's most comprehensive publication of inventors and inventions. Instead, this work is a useful, user-friendly single volume about inventions that would be useful in both the home and school library, serving virtually all grade levels and adults. [R: BR, Nov/Dec 01, p. 82]—**Craig A. Munsart**

HANDBOOKS AND YEARBOOKS

S

445.   Bazler, Judith A. **More Science Projects for All Students.** New York, Facts on File, 2002. 1v. (various paging). illus. index. (Facts on File Science Library). $166.50 looseleaf w/binder. ISBN 0-8160-4518-6.

This work is an updated and expanded volume of *Science Projects for All Students* (see ARBA 99, entry 1326). This edition retains the same goal as the first: to present modified "traditional science experiments so that all students could conduct them in the same way" (p. 1). Basically, these experiments were designed so that students with physical or learning disabilities can perform the experiments with few or no problems. The type is large (for those with visual impairments), the instructions are easy to follow (for those with learning disabilities), and the objects used to conduct the experiments are large and sturdy (for those with physical disabilities).

The book begins with an introduction and reproducible safety instructions. It then goes on to list experiments by specific areas of science: earth sciences, weather, space sciences, life sciences, and physical sciences. The author has made the instructions easy to follow and uses illustrations to make them even more clear. Each experiment ends with a list of observations and a reference to the list of "Our Findings" located at the back of the volume. Appendixes include a list of related literature, hints, and experiment adaptations; a guide for teaching students with disabilities; and a guide to experiments, skills, and a glossary.

This work is highly recommended for elementary and middle school libraries. The work is also available online from the publisher (see ARBA 2002, entry 1338, for a review). [R: SLJ, Nov 02, p. 95]
—**Shannon Graff Hysell**

S

446.   **Science Activities.** Danbury, Conn., Grolier, 2002. 10v. illus. index. $365.00/set. ISBN 0-7172-5608-1.

Each of the 10 volumes in this set addresses a different subject of science: "Electricity and Magnetism," "Everyday Chemistry," "Force and Motion," "Heat and Energy," "Inside Matter," "Light and Color," "Our Environment," "Sound and Hearing," "Using Materials," and "Weather and Climate." The volumes have a table of contents, a two-page introduction of its subject, and a half-page "Good Science Guide" describing the processes of science, such as documentation, repeatability, and data analysis. These processes are often grouped under the controversial heading, "The Scientific Method." Each of the 10, 64-page volumes contains a 2-page glossary of terms from only that volume and a 1-page (superficial) index for the entire set. The volumes are well illustrated by diagrams and color photographs. Units of measurement are given in both English and SI (metric) units. Historical connections are frequently made. In volume 6, "Light and Color," the 300-year-old debate about the nature of light is chronicled and the historical development of telescopes and cameras is discussed. The first photograph (an eight-hour exposure through a pinhole camera) is also reproduced.

As indicated by the title of the series, the core of each volume is a group of 10 activities reflecting the subject of the volume. The text surrounding each activity reinforces and enhances the subject of the activity. For instance, the activity "Wind Direction" (in volume 10) is preceded by two pages of text describing what causes wind and global wind systems. The activity itself is "Making a Weather Vane." The activity is succeeded by a "Follow Up" section to the weather vane and an "Analysis" section of prevailing global wind patterns. The activities are illustrated by sequential photographs of a student completing each step.

The vast majority of supplies for the activities are readily available materials, but obtaining some unique items (such as polarizing filters, four-foot-long balsa wood, a collection of glass or plastic lenses, foot squares of Plexiglas, swanee whistles, and methylated spirits) could cause frustration. The publisher describes the activities as innovative, but several (such as making a pinhole camera, heating water with food, testing for starch with iodine, or building an electromagnet by coiling copper wire around a nail) are much less innovative than others.

This series could be very useful as a reference in an elementary or middle school media collection. Students looking for a class or science fair project could gain both project ideas and background knowledge. While the content is good, at a time of tightening education budgets, the price might provide a reason for pause to carefully consider its value. [R: SLJ, Nov 02, pp. 105-106]—**Craig A. Munsart**

INDEXES

P, S

447.   **Science Experiments Index for Young People.** Mary Anne Pilger, comp. 3d ed. Westport, Conn., Libraries Unlimited/Greenwood Publishing Group, 2002. 294p. $65.00. ISBN 1-56308-899-1.

This book is essentially an updated edition of this very popular and useful title (see ARBA 97, entry 1244, for a review of the 2d edition). The current edition indexes 526 additional elementary and intermediate science titles whose copyrights range from 1989 to 2000 with the majority from the recent period of 1995 to 2000. The experiments range from the simple and easy to more complex and involved ones. The *Index* meets its intended purpose of providing a guide to children locating experiments and projects or just wanting to explore and find answers to science ideas. It also provides a quick and convenient resource to librarians, teachers, and parents who are seeking experiments, demonstrations, projects, and activities.

An alphabetic list of the subject headings used is given at the front of the book. The body consists of the entries indexed by subject with a brief description of the experiment, the book number, and the page number within the book. The body is followed by two sections: a list of the books indexed arranged by assigned book number and a list of the books indexed arranged by author. Many cross-references are provided. The arrangement of the book and the formatting of the text on the page make it very easy to use. Those who purchased the previous edition will also want this one. It is highly recommended for school, public, and academic libraries. Science teachers will also find it to be a valuable resource.—**Elaine Ezell**

30 Agricultural Sciences

FOOD SCIENCES AND TECHNOLOGY

Dictionaries and Encyclopedias

P

448.   **Encyclopedia of Food and Culture.** Solomon H. Katz and William Woys Weaver, eds. New York, Charles Scribner's Sons/Gale Group, 2003. 3v. illus. maps. index. (Scribner Library of Daily Life). $395.00/set. ISBN 0-684-80568-5.

Since food is a necessity, it plays an integral role in all aspects of life and culture. The *Encyclopedia of Food and Culture* explorers this relationship with 600 alphabetic signed entries by an international group of scholars and food specialists. The interdisciplinary approach examines the significance of food from diverse points of view; historians, anthropologists, archaeologists, folklorists, economists, and food critics have contributed to this encyclopedia.

The entries cover specific foods (chili peppers, soup); preparation methods (baking, roasting); distribution (farmers' markets, retailing of food); storage (packaging and canning, pantry and larder); and nutrition and health (vitamins, obesity). There are also articles about various cultures and cuisines, religions, food as a symbol, and writing about food. Readers will find everything from aphrodisiacs to "icon foods" (bagels, peanut butter) to the evolution of the chef de cuisine here. The contributors examine feasts, festivals and fasts, hunger, and how Betty Crocker's image has changed with the times as well as food as a weapon of war. They include biographies of people, such as Epicurus, Clarence Birsdeye, Louis Pasteur, and Julia Child. All articles have bibliographies. Many have sidebars with interesting facts, such as one about Halloween in the article on candy and confections. Many color and black-and-white illustrations enliven the text. An appendix offers the revised Dietary and Reference Intakes from the National Academy of Sciences and a systematic outline of the contents as well as a list of contributors.

A unique approach, accessible language, and fascinating content that covers gender and food and Rabelais's vivid food imagery as well as cannibalism, the noodle in Asia, and food in the Bible make The *Encyclopedia of Food and Culture* an outstanding resource for high school, academic, and large public libraries. Users will learn and be entertained in the process.—**Barbara M. Bibel**

P

449.   **Epicurious Food Dictionary. http://www.epicurious.com/run/fooddictionary/home.** [Website]. Free. Date reviewed: Oct 02.

Packed with more than 4,000 food terms, the *Epicurious Food Dictionary* is an amazingly comprehensive Website of everything one wants or needs to know about culinary terms, cooking techniques, and ingredients, plus recipes. This site is based on *The New Food Lover's Companion* by Sharon Tyler Herbst (Barron's Educational, 2001). Users can type in a word or phrase in the search box or even just a few letters to find definitions of ingredients, cooking utensils, sauces, and names like *semifreddo, pfeffernuesse, bagoong, banana chile, Peking duck,* and *physalis.* Foreign cooking phrases and dishes like *pain perdu, petite marmite, toad-in-the-hole,* and *bagna cauda* can also be found. Definitions often include a link to recipes using it. Users can browse the alphabet by letter to locate new and interesting ingredients and recipes. Cocktails, beers, and wines, such as Harvey Wallbanger, bock beer, sidecar, Manhattan, and sangria are also identified and linked to recipes.

The search engine is sometimes problematic and often quite slow. If "hazelnuts" is searched, no matches are located. Search "hazelnut" and an entry is found. If a user searches "basic pesto," no matches result. "Pesto," on the other hand, is easily found and defined. Links are available to practical "Reference Guides" like the "Herb and Spice Chart," "Metric Conversion," "Common Measurements and Equivalents," and "Temperature Equivalents" also taken from *The New Food Lover's Companion*. Well-written, accurate, and uniquely comprehensive, this ultimate and indispensable kitchen reference source will be used in special and public libraries as well as by every cook.

—**Susan C. Awe**

P

450.   **New Sotheby's Wine Encyclopedia.** 3d ed. By Tom Stevenson. New York, DK Publishing, 2001. 600p. illus. maps. index. $50.00. ISBN 0-7894-8039-5.

The 3d edition of this well-respected volume is both visually appealing and full of current information for the avid wine collector. Stevenson describes within this bulky volume 4,000 appellations and wine styles from almost 2,000 producers. Not simply a guide to great wines, Stevenson begins the volume with guidelines on wine tasting, assessing wines, factors that affect taste and quality, a guide to vineyard soils, a step-by-step process of how wine is made, and a glossary of grape varieties. Within these chapters are various illustrations, photographs, and maps that further explain the text.

The bulk of the book is arranged geographically into chapters (i.e., France, Germany, Italy, Spain and Portugal, the rest of Europe, North and South Africa, North and South America, and Australia and New Zealand). A typical chapter provides a background on the history of winemaking in the country, instructions on how to read a wine label from that country, and statistics (e.g., a breakdown of wine production, export numbers). The book then goes on to list the winemaking regions, listing information on grape varieties used, climate of the region, and methods of cultivation unique to that area. For each region several wineries are listed with a short description and a one- to three-star rating. Symbols are also given that note if the winery produces a wine at an exceptional value, wines that are inconsistent, or wines that are underperformers. The author provides an abundant use of illustrations and maps throughout the volume and several sidebars can be found throughout chapters noting special features of that region. Each regional description concludes with a list of the author's favorites.

The work concludes with tips on serving wine, presenting wine and food together, a guide to good vintages, a glossary of technical terms, and an index. There are several similar reference works on wine and winemaking on the market, including the *Larousse Encyclopedia of Wine* (see ARBA 2002, entry 1349) and *The Oxford Companion to the Wines of North America* (see ARBA 2001, entry 1329). This work is a good choice for current information for public libraries.—**Shannon Graff Hysell**

Handbooks and Yearbooks

P

451.   Roberts, Cynthia A. **The Food Safety Information Handbook.** Westport, Conn., Oryx Press/Greenwood Publishing Group, 2001. 312p. index. $52.50. ISBN 1-57356-305-6.

There is so much to appreciate in this book that it is difficult to know where to begin. From the helpful list of acronyms following the preface, to the glossary and index at the back of the book, this is a useful resource. The book has two major divisions: an overview of food safety and resources in food safety. The highly organized chapters in the food safety overview each begin with a summary and end with a well-documented sources cited list. One particularly valuable chapter provides a chronology of food safety-related events. Other chapters cover issues, regulation, statistics, and careers in food safety. The chapter titled "Careers in Food Safety" offers traditional and distance-learning options, complete with contact information for specific university programs. The division on resources provides an outstanding annotated bibliography of resources and contacts in each chapter, which include "Reports and Brochures," "Books and Newsletters," "Internet and Electronic Media," "Educational Material," and "Organizations, Cooperative Extension, Hotlines, State and Local Agencies." The stated audience is any person in the food industry, dietetics, chefs, health professionals, educators, and librarians. This book will be a decided asset to any library in a university or a community college having food, nutrition, dietetics, public health, or consumer studies, as well as to consumer collections in public libraries.—**Lynn M. McMain**

HORTICULTURE

Dictionaries and Encyclopedias

P

452.   **The American Horticulture Society Encyclopedia of Plants and Flowers.** updated ed. New York, DK Publishing, 2002. 720p. illus. index. $60.00. ISBN 0-7894-8993-7.

This colorful, fascinating guide from DK Publishing is sure to delight both the professional and the novice gardener alike. The book is ideal for those planning a garden, selecting additional plants for one's garden, or identifying unfamiliar species.

The work begins with a well-written introduction to creating a garden, including aspects of style, structure, planning, using color, and providing texture. The second section, "The Plant Selector," aids the user in selecting plants specifically for their climate and their soil. It is arranged by soil type (e.g., sandy soil, clay soil, acidic soil, alkaline soil), and includes colorful photographs and symbols indicating the amount of sunlight and moisture recommended. The third and largest section is titled "The Plant Catalog." This section is over 400 pages long and is broken down into plant type, including trees, shrubs, roses, climbers, perennials, annuals and biennials, rock plants, bulbs, water plants, and cacti and other succulents. Each section begins with an introduction on how to effectively garden with that type of plant. For each plant listed a color photograph is included along with a description of the plant or tree, the amount of sunlight and moisture recommended, and its height and shape. Below the caption are cross-references to similar plants found elsewhere in the book, with page numbers and illustrations indicated. The final section is a plant dictionary that defines every genus in the *Encyclopedia* as well as 4,000 recommended plants not featured here. A color plant hardiness zone map and a color plant heat zone map are locate on the inside cover in the front and back of the volume. The work concludes with an index to common names.

This work will be an ideal addition to public libraries of all sizes. It should be one of the first resources the reference librarian reaches for when fielding a reference question on gardening or horticulture. At only $60 it is recommended for circulating collections as well.—**Shannon Graff Hysell**

P

453.   Schmid, W. George. **An Encyclopedia of Shade Perennials.** Portland, Oreg., Timber Press, 2002. 374p. illus. index. $49.95. ISBN 0-88192-549-7.

Not all shade is created equal. It can range from densely impenetrable to moments of dappling in an otherwise sunny location. As such, it represents a challenge for gardeners. Fortunately, W. George Schmid has had many years of experience working with perennials in shady gardens. His opening chapters show his appreciation, knowledge, and respect for shade gardening. The book begins with Schmid's philosophy of gardening and some brief recollections of various shade gardens he has known. A discussion of what Schmid considers to be the five popular definitions of shade is followed by remedies for common problems. The book continues with basic information on more than 7,000 species and cultivars in 184 genera. Each entry includes the plant's Latin and common names, where it is grown, and its shade requirements. This is supplemented by a description of the plant, its measurements, garden growing conditions, propagation, the plant's hardiness zones, and varieties. Where appropriate, other data, such as medicinal uses, appears. The length of the majority of the entries varies from approximately 60 to 190 words. The encyclopedia includes 500 color photographs that truly illustrate the beauty and variety of shade perennials. The work concludes with a list of where to buy shade perennials in the United States, a Hardiness Zone Map, and an index.

Overall, this is an attractive book filled with easy-to-read text and practical advice. Reading this book will give gardeners hope and inspiration for shade gardening with perennials.—**January Adams**

Handbooks and Yearbooks

P

454.   Phillips, Roger, and Martyn Rix. **Perennials: The Definitive Reference with over 2,500 Photographs.** Willowdale, Ont., Firefly Books, 2002. 476p. illus. index. $49.95; $34.95pa. ISBN 1-55209-641-6; 1-55209-639-4pa.

More than 2,500 herbaceous perennials are illustrated and described in this "reference for color and variety." Although acknowledged to illustrate only a small sample of what can be found in gardens, this collection aims to satisfy beginners and excite specialists. The section criteria for inclusion in this volume are those plants that tolerate −5 degree Celsius frost and remain outside through winter. The volume includes both commonly cultivated and rare plants. Explicitly excluded are annuals, biennials, desert plants and succulents, herbaceous perennials requiring protection from frost, and those typical in alpine and rock gardens.

The work is grouped into four seasonal sections—spring, summer, mid-summer, and late summer through autumn. Within each season the plants are arranged by family in a botanical order and then alphabetically. Plant names include the Latin scientific name (and English names for a few familiar plants), the authority, cultivar's names, and family name. The authors used the *Royal Horticultural Society Plant Finder 2000-2001* as the primary naming source. Text gives originating country, habitat, distribution and flowering times, and sometimes advice on propagation. Short descriptions accompany photographs and are intended to help in identification of plants. Photographs show plants in natural settings and gardens, as well as in groupings of species to show flower and foliage details useful for identification. The introduction to the volume and the table of contents state this seasonal grouping, but otherwise it does not appear through headings within the body of entries. A name index helps locate known plants within the text. A bibliography, glossary, and guide to gardening with herbaceous perennials, each provide brief reference resources to conclude the volume.

The two prolific and award-winning British authors, both gardeners, combine expertise of a botanist who has explored the world to collect new plants (Rix) and a plant photographer (Phillips). They provide a global breadth to the content, citing plant origins from all continents. Celsius temperatures and metric measurements are standard, although both a conversion table for hardiness zones and a note of estimated conversion from metric to feet and centimeter to inches are included.

The book is useful to identify a plant if the reader either knows its family name or browses the photographs. It offers inspiration for a gardener who seeks an individual plant addition to a garden. This is not a graphic guide for planting arrangements although several photographs and references illustrate classic gardens, primarily English ones. Included lists of places to view and obtain herbaceous perennials include many gardens and nurseries in North America. Relatively inexpensive, this book offers an attractive addition to a collection of garden books.

—**Danuta A. Nitecki**

31 Biological Sciences

BIOLOGY

Biography

C, P

455.   **Life Sciences Before the Twentieth Century: Biographical Portraits. Volume 3.** Everett Mendelsohn, ed. New York, Charles Scribner's Sons/Gale Group, 2002. 211p. illus. index. (The Scribner Science Reference Series, v.3). $80.00. ISBN 0-684-80661-4.

This series is a unique look at biographies of scientists. A search of the OCLC database yielded not many other similar works and virtually nothing in the last few years that are collected together. This volume is a collection of profiles of famous life scientists. Mendelsohn, the editor, teaches history of science at Harvard University and founded *The Journal of the History of Biology*. His research and publishing have been in this field so the authenticity of the content is assured.

The book consists of mostly text with only a few illustrations and pictures of the scientists. It starts with a timeline that runs from Hippocrates (460 B.C.E.) to Paul Ehlich (1910 C.E.). Each individual is alphabetically listed and most entries are between three and four pages long. Some, such as Darwin, are as long as eight pages. The writing in the book is really beautiful and the characterizations are fascinating. The writing is also very clear and uses language that can be handled by anyone with a high school education. However, it is not simplistic or condescending. Scientific terminology is defined in the margins so there is no need to go to a second source.

The index was professionally done and it shows it. There is a good *see* and *see also* structure and the indexer has done double posting and two levels of headings. Users can find subjects very easily. The audience for this book, and any others in the series, will be very broad. It should at least be in public and educational collections.

—**Lillian R. Mesner**

Dictionaries and Encyclopedias

C

456.   **The Facts on File Dictionary of Cell and Molecular Biology.** Robert Hine, ed. New York, Facts on File, 2003. 248p. $49.50. ISBN 0-8160-4912-2.

This dictionary is directed to students taking advanced placement science courses in high school, but is also useful to college students. Its appeal will be much broader, however. There are 2,000 entries for terms in all major areas of biochemistry, molecular biology, molecular genetics, and cell biology. Each entry includes a definition and information about the topic involved, and some are illustrated, often with a molecular diagram or in some cases a chart or graph. There are also many cross-references to related terms. Brief biographies of significant scientists are included.

The appendixes include a chronology of the major discoveries in biochemistry and molecular biology. Also provided are molecular diagrams of 20 amino acids, a chart of the genetic code, a brief list of Web pages, and a bibliography listing the major basic textbooks in the field.

Each entry is well written and clear. The illustrations are good, and there appear to be all the major terms needed for the purpose of this dictionary. One very minor point: the preface mentions tables of cell types and sizes, but this reviewer did not find any. They are, however, not listed in the table of contents. This dictionary will be very useful to students, and should be in high school and college libraries.—**John Laurence Kelland**

C, P

457.　**Life on Earth: An Encyclopedia of Biodiversity, Ecology, and Evolution.** Niles Eldredge, ed. Santa Barbara, Calif., ABC-CLIO, 2002. 2v. illus. index. $185.00/set. ISBN 1-57607-286-X.

This two-volume set takes an original look at biodiversity and ecology by focusing on how humans contribute, or more accurately do not contribute, to the Earth's delicate balance. The work begins with an introduction from the editor discussing the negative affect that humans have had on the environment. He introduces readers to the concept of "the Sixth Extinction," which can be defined as "the abrupt and devastating loss of habitat for species in nearly all the world's ecosystems" (p. xiv). Following the introduction are essays on biodiversity, the importance of biodiversity, the current threats to biodiversity, and what humans can do to divert the "Sixth Extinction."

The bulk of the work is arranged into alphabetic entries on a wide range of subjects relating to biodiversity, the ecosystem, and threats to biodiversity. Also included are entries on relevant scientists (e.g., Charles Darwin), academic disciplines (e.g., paleontology, anthropology), and threatened species. Much emphasis is placed on the effects of pollution, global warming, and the destruction of the environment. Each of the 200 entries runs several pages in length and many provide cross-references to relevant entries as well as a short bibliography. Black-and-white photographs and illustrative charts are used to illustrate the entries. The work concludes with a 30-page bibliography and an index.

This volume provides a wealth of information on the effects of human behavior on the ecosystem. It will serve well as a supplemental volume to other biodiversity reference sources, such as Simon Asher Levin's *Encyclopedia of Biodiversity* (see ARBA 2002, entry 1365), in academic libraries.—**Shannon Graff Hysell**

C, S

458.　**The Penguin Dictionary of Biology.** 10th ed. By M. Thain and M. Hickman. New York, Penguin Books, 2001. 678p. illus. $15.00pa. ISBN 0-14-051359-0.

This new 10th edition of a classic small paperback biology dictionary continues to offer what can be found in the earlier editions. The size and binding makes this volume easy to use, while it is handy in both a library collection and (where it really is useful) on the desktop. It contains over 400 entries with illustrations. The general topics covered are biology, zoology, botany, entomology, ecology, paleoanthropolgy, genetics, and cell biology (microbiology). All in all, this is an extremely useful volume, which this reviewer recommends without hesitation to all. Students will especially find this volume handy and its price is a plus.—**James W. Oliver**

C, P

459.　**World of Microbiology and Immunology.** K. Lee Lerner and Brenda Wilmoth Lerner, eds. Farmington Hills, Mich., Gale, 2003. 2v. illus. index. $150.00/set. ISBN 0-7876-6540-1.

The *World of Microbiology and Immunology* is an addition to the Gale World of . . . series. This comprehensive, two-volume reference work is a subject-specific encyclopedic guide to concepts, theories, discoveries, and pioneers in the fields of microbiology and immunology. Special emphasis is placed on current, ethical, legal, and social issues as well as those relating to biological warfare. Although microbiology and immunology are separate areas of biology and medicine, their combination provides an important understanding of human health and disease, especially infectious disease and disease prevention.

This illustrated reference work consists of 600 entries that cover a variety of topics, including anthrax, bacteria, Charles Darwin, DNA, prions, proteins, viruses, Rosalyn Yalow, and zoonoses. The entries are alphabetically arranged and cross-referenced and range from 200 to 1,000 words. This set includes a bibliography of both print and Web sources, a historical chronology of significant events in the development of microbiology and immunology, and an index. The text is written in a clear and easily understood style. The *World of Microbiology and Immunology* is recommended for purchase by academic and public libraries.—**Rita Neri**

ANATOMY

P, S

460.   **DK Encyclopedia of the Human Body.** By Richard Walker. New York, DK Publishing, 2002. 304p. illus. index. $29.99. ISBN 0-7894-8672-5.

This encyclopedia is written for a juvenile audience grades 4-7. While written simply, it does not talk down to its audience. As a result, it is also a good reference tool on the human body for any age group not familiar with how the human body is constructed and how it works.

The book is divided into seven sections, the first five dealing with the body itself and the last two being a history and a glossary. Section 1 covers the cells and microscopic level of the body. The next section covers the moving framework, including skin, bones, joins, and muscles. The third section covers the nervous system, the brain, endocrine glands, and the senses. Section 4 is called "Supply and Maintenance" and covers circulation, the immune system, the GI system, the respiratory system, and nutrition. Section 5 covers reproduction. And section 6 provides a historical timeline of key medical events and an overview of knowledge through the ages.

The book uses color very effectively to show the different parts of the body, such as the different areas of the spine. Key common diseases, such as asthma and diabetes, are highlighted. While the subject of the human body and how we have learned about how our bodies work is not covered in depth, this encyclopedia provides a very good overview for an audience with little knowledge about the human body. This book is a useful edition to a home library or school media center.—**Leslie M. Behm**

C, P

461.   **World of Anatomy and Physiology.** K. Lee Lerner and Brenda Wilmoth Lerner, eds. Farmington Hills, Mich., Gale, 2002. 2v. illus. index. $150.00/set. ISBN 0-7876-5684-4.

This is a two-volume encyclopedia of topics in classical anatomy and physiology. There are 650 articles that run from one to six columns on subjects that cover main topics, as opposed to the more specialized topics, of these disciplines. The styles of writing vary because there are more than 20 authors involved in the work. Their credentials are very good as they all have advanced degrees in their specialties. There is also an advisory board of M.D.s and Ph.D.s who provided oversight on the content in the set.

The design of the volumes is for ready reference. There is the usual encyclopedic arrangement of alphabetic entries, and that provides some access to the broad, major topics. Some additional access to information on a topic is given with the added *see* references at the end of a column, along with the bolded terms within the column. These will only be good, however, if the person using the book reads the instructions in the preface.

The editors state that they are trying to interest students who are new to these fields as well as give content for more advanced students. As said above, the slant of the content covers the classical aspects of anatomy and physiology, but the editors have also included more specialized material on developmental and reproductive biology. This is not to be considered an anatomical atlas with many images demonstrating anatomy. There are graphics and plates to demonstrate certain material, but images do not play a heavy role in the volumes. The writing does use terminology, but the writing is also very clear and explanatory. Anyone with high-school level literacy can use the set. There is some interesting additional information aside from the general topics. There are numerous biographies of people important in these fields, a 17-page historical chronology, and 11 pages of sources that were consulted in the writing of the articles. Perhaps the best part of the two volumes is the amazing 91-page index. As always, reference works stand or fall on the quality of their indexes. This helps the reader find the vast amount of information that is not covered by the general entries in the books. The terminology used in the index is appropriate for the intended audience; there are numerous *see* and *see also* references, terms are double-posted, and subheadings break down the broader topics. Working from the index to the text and back again demonstrated that the topics are fully covered and the locators are correct. This is obviously a professionally done index.

When this reviewer searched OCLC's WorldCat there was nothing found quite like this set. It will be a valuable addition to any academic or public collection that wants a reference document on these scientific fields.
—**Lillian R. Mesner**

BOTANY

General Works

Handbooks and Yearbooks

P

462.   **Handbook of North European Garden Plants: With Keys to Families and Genera.** James Cullen, ed. New York, Cambridge University Press, 2001. 640p. $130.00pa. ISBN 0-521-00411-X.

The lack of species-level information in this otherwise promising garden plant identification manual is disappointing. As the title indicates, this work covers families and genera, but not species, of flowering plants that can be grown in northern Europe and similar climates. The text is an abridged version of the six-volume set entitled *The European Garden Flora* (see ARBA 90, entry 1489, and ARBA 87, entry 1427). Perhaps the intent is for the botanist or gardener to use the "portable" handbook in the field or garden to key a plant down to the genera level, and then finish the identification process by consulting the full six-volume set. Yet, the key is of limited value to the serious gardener or botanist with or without access to the full set.

That said, the handbook is an excellent key to identification of more than 190 families and 2,200 genera of ornamental plants grown in gardens of northwest Europe and other regions with a similar climate, including eastern North America. Each genera entry contains a concise description of plants in the genera and an indication of the number of species within the genera and the number of these plants in cultivation. For example, "*Campanula linnaeus* 300/55" means that the genus Campanula is generally accepted as containing 300 species, of which 55 (represented by the species itself, hybrids, and cultivars) can be found in cultivation. Details on geographic distribution of each genus are also included. This work is only recommended for botanic garden libraries and academic libraries that support a horticulture program.—**Elaine F. Jurries**

Flowering Plants

P

463.   Clark, Lewis J. **Lewis Clark's Field Guide to Wild Flowers of Field & Slope in the Pacific Northwest.** 3d ed. Edited by John Trelawny. Madeira Park, Harbour, 2002. 108p. illus. index. $11.33pa. ISBN 1-55017-255-7.

This field guide to wildflowers covers a large territory: southern Alaska, British Columbia, Washington, Oregon, and northern California; from the Pacific coast to the western timberline of the Rocky Mountains. It is by no means comprehensive, as it lists only 107 of the most common flowering plants from sea level to about 8,000 feet elevation, but its portability will be useful to the hiker.

The fairly large color photographs are of good quality, except for a few that could have had sharper focus. Scale of reproduction is indicated for each photograph, a feature this reader would like to see in more field guides. Descriptions include common name; scientific name; bloom color, height, and other characteristics; and range.

If there is an order to the plants in this guide, this reader could not discern one; in lieu of page numbers, each photograph (one per plant) is numbered. The index displays both common and scientific names, and a one-page "glossary" diagrams the parts of the plant to aid the reader in identification.—**Lori D. Kranz**

Trees and Shrubs

P

464.   Dirr, Michael A. **Dirr's Trees and Shrubs for Warm Climates: An Illustrated Encyclopedia.** Portland, Oreg., Timber Press, 2002. 446p. illus. index. $69.95. ISBN 0-88192-525-X.

As soon as the cover of Dirr's new southern gardens book is opened, the stunning photography stands out in all its glory. Each frame has brilliance and depth befitting the image. Readers will find a selection of plants designed to enhance gardens in the warmer temperature zones. The plants selected represent close to 250 genera. While there are many more possibilities, it nevertheless is a "dealer's choice" by Dirr, whose experience in plant selection for this warm and friendly zone is beyond question. Of particular note, and a demonstration of the author's fairness, the place of prominence he bestowed on the nondescript groundsel bush *Baccharis halimifolia* is pleasing. The fluffy, silky white blossoms are always a pleasure to admire. Yet, he has selected the Georgia plume, *Elliottia racemosa*, as a plant to grace the grounds of the deep south. It seems a challenge to develop a way of propagating this very stubborn but fascinating plant, long known for its difficulty to survive early life. The selection of species for the book is a representative one and a most difficult one to make. All in all, the gentle, descriptive text; the almost perfect taxonomy (a difficult task); and the stunning photography all combine to make this book another reference to help guide the southern gardener toward perfection in their garden paths. [R: LJ, 15 Feb 02, p. 134]—**James H. Flynn Jr.**

GENETICS

C, P

465.   **The Gale Encyclopedia of Genetic Disorders.** Stacey L. Blachford, ed. Farmington Hills, Mich., Gale, 2002. 2v. illus. index. $275.00/set. ISBN 0-7876-5612-7.

What makes this reference tool readable is that it is written in layperson terms that explain clearly and in depth a genetic disorder. Each disorder includes well-defined sections on definition, description, genetic profile, demographics, signs and symptoms, treatment and management, diagnosis and prognosis, and bibliographies and Websites. The work includes several terms that are not disorders to provide an understanding of common genetic concepts and practices, such as the Human Genome Project and chromosome analysis. The compilation of this list of genetic disorders involves contributions from experienced medical writers, genetic counselors, physicians, and health care professionals. The list might not be exhaustive but it is rich enough to include rare to well-known disorders.

With each disorder, a key terms window displays related terms with annotations. Readers do not need to go far to look up specific meanings of the medical terms that are foreign to them. The thorough indexing and over 200 color graphics make the reference tool interesting and illustrative. Readers can benefit from the detailed descriptions as well as go on to other resources that list additional technical medical information. In addition, the appendix provides the pedigree charts with a symbol guide, a chromosome map, and an organizations list.

Gale does well in bridging the gap between consumer health and the complexity of understanding genetics information. The general public will find this ready-reference tool easy to use and invaluable. This source will be a good addition to public libraries as well as health sciences libraries. [R: BR, Mar/April 02, p. 62; LJ, 1 Mar 02, pp. 86-88; Choice, Mar 02, p. 1216]—**Polin P. Lei**

NATURAL HISTORY

C

466.   **Beacham's Guide to International Endangered Species. Volume 3: Non-Mammals Listed Prior to 2000.** Walton Beacham, Frank V. Castronova, Bill Freedman, and Suzanne Sessine, eds. Farmington Hills, Mich., Gale, 2001. 783p. illus. index. $105.00. ISBN 0-7876-4998-8.

Endangered species have been designated in increasing numbers over the past 40 years or so. A few have come off the federal or international lists due to extinction and many more will probably have to be included as habitats are destroyed. Simple list or annotated descriptions have been published for many individual species and regional faunas/floras (especially in the United States). A few more comprehensive works have also appeared. All of these works derive part, or most of, their information from the International Union for Conservation and Nature, which publishes the official list of threatened or endangered species. *Beacham's Guide to International Endangered Species* is a major reference source with two volumes covering mammals (published in 1997) and this one on birds (the bulk of the text), reptiles, amphibians, fishes, butterflies, freshwater mussels and clams, and a few plants. The work is taxonomically arranged, and for almost every taxon there is a good color photograph and a brief list of the species' characteristics, including diet, reproductive habits, range, and when it was listed. A longer section, about a page or so, provides more details on behavior, habitat, and threats to survival. For students at several levels, professionals, and the public this encyclopedia offers a good introduction to the diversity of endangered species and a short, but adequate, listing of references for further study of each group.

—**David Bardack**

C, S

467.   **Exploring Animal Rights and Animal Welfare.** Westport, Conn., Greenwood Press, 2002. 4v. illus. index. $128.00/set. ISBN 0-313-32245-7.

Perhaps the most important concept in the transition from elementary to secondary education is that all knowledge is not concrete, that sometimes there are gray areas and the best one can do is martial facts and information from many sources in support of an opinion. As a result, middle school teachers love to assign debates and persuasive papers, asking students to research controversial issues and argue a point of view. Animal rights is a wonderful topic for these projects, one that has inherent interest to students of this age, and one in which there are questions that emerge only as the student delves into the subject. This new four-volume set in the Greenwood Publishing Middle School Reference program includes enough detail to open students' eyes to new facets of the topic and is presented in a manner accessible to middle school students.

Each volume treats a different aspect of the issue: "Using Animals for Food"; "Using Animals for Research"; "Using Animals for Entertainment"; and "Using Animals for Clothing." Within the volumes every facet of the subject is present, from factory farming to rodeo. Although the text is written at only about a fifth grade level, the issues treated are complex, and the editors are careful to present all sides of the debate. Many chapters end with a question, urging the student to take a side and think it through. The last chapter of each volume is titled "Debating the Issue," and outlines the views of the various interest groups involved.

Each volume also includes a short bibliography and a good list of Websites and specific Web pages used as sources for the text. Students will find these volumes accessible and valuable, and teachers will appreciate the help in introducing students to the process of exploring controversial and complex subjects.—**Carol L. Noll**

ZOOLOGY

General Works

C

468.   **Internet Resource Guide for Zoology. http://www.biosis.org/free_resources/resource_guide.html.** [Website]. Philadelphia, BIOSIS. Free. Date reviewed: Oct 02.

This is an important gateway to zoological information. Provided by BIOSIS, the main categories listed on the home page are biocomplexity, biodiversity, bioinformatics, codes of nomenclature, a directory of biologists, general zoology, and systematics. From the home page one can search for animal common names, genus and species, higher taxa (class, order, family), subject terms, people (biologists), organizations and societies, or conference listings.

Under "Biocomplexity" users can find full-text articles and links to related biological disciplines. The "Biodiversity" link provides access to global, regional, and national organizations; networks; and information systems. Also covered are links to sites on bioinformatics, endangered species, environmental law, national parks, and much more.

A paragraph explains "Biological Informatics." This heading leads the user to the sites of a large number of bioinformatics organizations. The "Codes of Nomenclature" link includes the codes for zoology, botany, cultivated plants, bacteria, and viruses. There is also a "Draft Bio Code" to unite all of these.

Under "Directories of Biologists" are the directories of many specialists, such as acarologists, ornithologists, and others. "General Zoology" links to sites of popular interest along with those covering careers, directories, organizations, a taxonomic tree of life, university departments, and a great variety of types of sites. This link is also a source of color images of animals. The "Systematics, Taxonomy, and Nomenclature" link has sites explaining systematics, career information, a directory of taxonomists, glossaries, newsgroups, species counts, and more.

The *Internet Resource Guide for Zoology* easily leads the user to a very large number of excellent Websites in zoology, and a wide variety at that. Linked from the home page is the "Guide by Animal Group." This feature provides a hierarchy in grid format to phyla, classes, and orders of animals and is much better than the long lists available on other Websites. The *Internet Resource Guide for Zoology* is an essential resource for anyone researching zoology on the Web.—**John Laurence Kelland**

S

469.   Pringle, Laurence. **Scholastic Encyclopedia of Animals.** New York, Scholastic, 2001. 128p. illus. index. $17.95. ISBN 0-590-52253-1.

This volume is an alphabetical arrangement of information on 140 fairly common animals of all species, such as large bears, sand dollars, millipedes, flies, frogs, and hummingbirds. The entries range in length from two to four paragraphs. The information is presented in an interesting, but factual, manner for children and includes information on habitats, physical characteristics, diets, life cycles, and behaviors of the animals. It does not include details such as scientific names and classifications of these animals. The pronunciation of the animal's name and a color picture of the animal in its natural habitat are given in each entry. Words in bold typeface in the text are defined in the glossary, which then provides a page number reference back to the first use of the word in the body of the book. An index and a pronunciation guide are also included. Although not an extensive, nor an in-depth, reference resource, young children will be drawn to the simple arrangement; colorful pictures; and brief, easy-to-read text. This title will be most useful in collections for elementary school age children. [R: SLJ, Feb 02, p. 90]
—**Elaine Ezell**

Birds

C, P

470.   **Grzimek's Animal Life Encyclopedia. Volumes 8-11: Birds.** 2d ed. Jerome A. Jackson, Walter J. Bock, Donna Olendorf, and Michael Hutchins, eds. Illustrated by Joseph E. Trumpey. Farmington Hills, Mich., Gale, 2003. 4v. illus. maps. index. $375.00/set. ISBN 0-7876-6571-1.

Grzimek's Animal Life Encyclopedia, which surveys animal life forms from the lower organisms through mammals, has been a standard and deservedly popular reference work for 30 years. This new edition replaces the original three (relatively drab) compact volumes devoted to birds with 4 glossy larger tomes containing many more color photographs and illustrations (nearly 1,900) and colored distribution maps (1,500). All but the first volume contain identical front matter of which the most important is a user's guide. In addition, the first volume contains handsomely illustrated, brief essays on general topics (e.g., "What is a bird?"; "Birds and humans") and on such matters as avian migration, song, and flight. The exposition is lucid and nontechnical.

Organization is by taxonomic order, then family, and, finally, by selected species accounts. There are about 20 avian orders and about 200 families—all described in chapter essays. The chapters on orders (e.g., Struthioniformes [Tinamous and ratites]) offer brief narrative accounts of evolution and systematics, physical characteristics, distribution, habitat, behavior, feeding ecology, reproductive biology, conservation status, and significance to humans. Each order chapter is followed by chapters describing each of the families that constitute it. Thus, the order chapter "Struthioniformes" is followed by family chapters on tinamous, rheas, cassowaries, emus, kiwis, moas, ostriches, and elephant birds. Each family chapter is headed by a half-page "thumbnail" account, including a description, distribution map, habitat type, and the number of genera and species. The following text portion contains more detailed description, employing the same system of topic heading as that for the order chapters. This is followed by full-page illustration(s) of group portraits of the species selected for the subsequent species accounts. Descriptions of individual species are concise, rigidly formatted (in the above indicated categories), and accompanied by color-coded maps. Although there are around 9,500 birds worldwide, there are accounts of only selected representative species. To facilitate use, the thumbnail "previews" of order and species chapters are color-coded (light blue for the former; yellow for latter) on their opening pages and so labeled at the top of each page. Each chapter ends with a "Resources" section of up-to-date books and articles as well as relevant organizations and Web page addresses. The latter compensate to some extent for omitted species accounts and illustrations that could not be included for reasons of space. The common name of each species is given in English, French, German, and Spanish.

The new edition is a major improvement over the old in several ways. The graphics are far more numerous and immeasurably better in color and quality. Bird dimensions are now in both metric and traditional. Two new descriptive categories have been added: conservation status and human significance. The 30-year-old descriptive texts of the 1st edition have been revised and updated but are heavily based on the earlier versions. Each volume contains identical back matter: further reading; a list of organizations; a list of contributors to the 1st edition (much of whose material is recycled); a glossary; an Aves species list; a geologic time chart of animal life; and an index of both Linnaean and English names. These sections are indicated by visual thumb indexes spaced along the page edges.

It seems hardhearted to find fault with this splendid set, but over 150 pages from the foreword and back material in each of the four volumes is reprinted verbatim in each one. Would it not have been better to dispense with the repeated material and include more species or order and family accounts? Taken together with the elegant but oversized distribution maps, the equivalent of yet another volume could have been included in the same number of pages.

The *Grzimek* 4-volume bird set is, of course, a part of the uniform 17-volume *Encyclopedia of Animal Life*. The *Grzimek* project is, as far as this reviewer knows, unique in its coverage and lists for $1,595; bought separately, the 4 bird volumes total $375. If, however, one is interested only in aviafauna, the *Grzimek* bird volumes must take second place to Josep del Hoyo, J. A. Elliott, and J. Sargatal's *Handbook of the Birds of the World* (Lynx Edicions, 1992-), which covers and illustrates all of the world's species. Seven volumes are now available (at more than $1,700), but the passerine volumes are yet to come. While professional ornithologists will prefer the del Hoyo set, the new *Grzimek* volumes will be the popular favorite. [R: LJ, 1 Feb 03, p. 76]

—**D. Barton Johnson**

P

471.   **The Sibley Guide to Bird Life & Behavior.** Chris Elphick, John B. Dunning Jr., and David Allen Sibley, eds. New York, Alfred A. Knopf/Random House, 2001. 587p. illus. index. $45.00. ISBN 0-679-45123-4.

Three ornithological editors have coordinated the writing of 48 expert birders and biologists to make a superb handbook on North American bird life. Organized by accounts of each avian family (79 total), the book guides the reader beyond identification by discussions of taxonomy, ecology, and behavior. A family account typically includes sections on classification (taxonomic relationships), diet diversity and feeding methods of species in the family, breeding behavior (including courtship displays), and conservation concerns. The authoritative accounts are current, clearly written, and informative. Throughout the work almost 800 full-color illustrations (by Sibley) show important features mentioned in the text. A 100-page introduction actually forms an independent part of the book—a popular overview of five major topics in modern ornithology, again contributed by appropriate experts. These broad topical reviews cover avian flight, evolution, behavior, distribution, and population regulation. The birding public has a great new source of information on the biology of North American birds.—**Charles Leck**

Domestic Animals

P

472.   Morris, Desmond. **Dogs: The Ultimate Dictionary of over 1,000 Dog Breeds.** North Pomfret, Vt., Trafalgar Square, 2001. 752p. illus. index. $29.95. ISBN 1-57076-219-8.

For this delightful reference work, Desmond Morris, a consummate naturalist and former curator of mammals for the London Zoo, applies his considerable expertise to the classification of 1,000 dog breeds under 4 major headings—sporting, livestock, service, and other dogs. In the introduction, he sets out with characteristic thoroughness to define the parameters of a breed and specifies variations (i.e., feral, isolated, specialized, protected, created, and refined breeds). For the benefit of dog fanciers, researchers, students, and librarians, he organizes the text meticulously; for example, he describes each dog and their traits and varieties, and provides a country-by-country listing of examples and the page numbers on which each is introduced. Under border terrier, for example, he offers alternate names for the breed, a pen-and-ink drawing of the dog in classic stance, and a list of references in chronological order. At the end of the text, he describes wild dogs, notably the wolf, coyote, and jackal.

As always, Morris's commentary flows evenly and blends anecdote with particulars. Under Rottweiler he comments on the use of large working dogs among the Roman military, who abandoned them to local Europeans and moved on. The resulting interbreeding with German sheepdogs produced the Rottweiler, a powerful herder for cattle. The animal's value was as a bearer of money pouches. Morris states that "the neck of a Rottweiler was safer than any bank vault."

Back matter includes members and distribution of animals in the family Canidae and offers a pared-down bibliography neatly divided into general and specific reference works dating back to 1576. To the detriment of the work, he offers no guidance to electronic sources. The index consists of 20 tri-columnar pages listing animal names and indicating main entries in all capital letters (e.g., Miniature Pekingese, MINIATURE PINSCHER). Another appealing aspect of this reference works is its price. At under half what lesser works sell for, this comprehensive compendium offers the home, school, or public impeccable information, illustrations, and a long shelf life. Libraries will not want to miss out on this reference. [R: LJ, 15 June 02, p. 58]—**Mary Ellen Snodgrass**

Fishes

C, P

473.   **National Audubon Society Field Guide to Fishes.** rev. ed. By Carter R. Gilbert and James D. Williams. New York, Alfred A. Knopf/Random House, 2002. 607p. illus. maps. index. $19.95pa. ISBN 0-375-41224-7.

This attractive book is a new edition of the *National Audubon Society Field Guide to North American Fishes, Whales, and Dolphins* (1983). This edition is limited to fishes, but the plan and appearance of the 1st edition is retained. Some 696 species are included; 585 were included in the 1st edition. After an introductory section on fish biology, there are 24 photographs of fish habitats and a visual family-level key. The main part of the book is divided into a section of color photographs (3 per page) and a section of descriptions, each including identification characteristics, habitat, range, similar species, biological information (behavior, diet, life span), and a small but clear range map.

National Audubon Society field guides may be compared to the Peterson Field Guide series, which includes three fish volumes: Atlantic coast, Pacific coast, and freshwater. The Peterson books cover nearly all North American fish (about 2,300 species). Gilbert and Williams are selective, which may be an advantage as numerous rare and local species are omitted. Most, but not all, of the common fish for a given location will be included. The Peterson books use color and black-and-white paintings rather than photographs. The Peterson descriptions do not include biological information: a feature of great value.

This is a fine one-volume treatment of North American fishes. The species are well selected, the photographs delightful, and the descriptions informative. Choosing between the Peterson guides and this one is a matter of personal preference. My choice is Peterson for the field and National Audubon Society for reference. Most public and academic libraries would do well to have both.—**Frederic F. Burchsted**

Mammals

P, S

474.   **World of Animals: Mammals.** By Pat Morris, Amy-Jane Beer, and Erica Bower. Bethel, Conn., Grolier Educational, 2003. 10v. illus. maps. index. $419.00/set. ISBN 0-7172-5742-8.

This 10-volume set from Grolier is the first of a 5 part series they have planned on the animal kingdom. The next 4 sets will focus on birds (10 volumes), reptiles (5 volumes), amphibians (3 volumes), and fish (10 volumes). This set on mammals is designed with middle to high school age students in mind. It focuses mainly on animals the students will be interested in but includes some from all of the major groups—carnivores, primates, rodents, marsupials, and marine animals.

The set begins with an introduction to the set and information on the scientific naming of animals, a general introduction on how an animal is classified as a mammal (e.g., body temperature, reproduction), and information on extinction of mammals. Each volume of the set is designated a specific type of mammal. For example, volume 1 covers small carnivores, with information on raccoons, weasels, and the mongoose family. Other volumes provide information on large carnivores (e.g., cat family, dog family), sea mammals (e.g., whales), primates, large herbivores (e.g., elephant family, horse family), insectivores and bats, rodents 2 (porcupines, hares and rabbits), rodents (squirrels, mice), ruminant (horned) herbivores, and marsupials. Each volume provides colorful photographs and illustrations, sidebars with specific information on families of mammals and interesting facts, a list for further reading and a list of Websites, and a glossary specific to that volume. Each volume contains the set index.

This set will be most useful in middle school libraries and the children's collections of public libraries. Children will be fascinated by the colorful photographs and the set is written in a language that will be easy for them to understand.—**Shannon Graff Hysell**

Marine Animals

C, P

475.   **Encyclopedia of Marine Mammals.** William F. Perrin, Bernd Würsig, and J. G. M. Thewissen, eds. San Diego, Calif., Academic Press, 2002. 1414p. illus. maps. index. $139.95. ISBN 0-12-551340-2.

Marine mammals have a unique place in the view of nature. They are man's closest relatives in the oceans, yet they are very different from their terrestrial cousins because of various aquatic adaptations. Many find this combination of kinship and strangeness fascinating. This thorough and detailed encyclopedia, the only one on this subject, covers virtually every topic touching upon marine mammals. No single volume on marine mammals better fills the need to understand these wonderful creatures.

This encyclopedia is intended, in part, for scientists who wish to obtain the latest information on marine mammals, both living and fossil, so it uses technical language in most articles and has numerous references from the scientific literature. The editors have thoughtfully included a glossary of more than 1,000 terms at the back of the volume to keep the text accessible to students from beginning undergraduates on up. The volume also includes a complete species list, an extensive index, more than 50 short biographies of scientists, cross-indexing, and its own Website address for additional links and updates. No space is wasted. Even the insides of the front and back covers are used for phylogenetic trees of the marine mammals.

The articles in this encyclopedia are longer and more detailed than those in similar volumes. Most of the topics are illustrated with line drawings, black-and-white photographs, or references to color plates at the beginning of the book. The scope of this encyclopedia is generous—marine mammals are defined to include otters and polar bears as well as dolphins, whales, walruses, and the like. The articles include topics as diverse as cetacean evolution, popular culture and literature, scrimshaw, sociobiology, training, and whale lice. Most of the authors are well-known scientists. The prose style differs somewhat between selections, but is always readable. Since every community will include many who are interested in marine mammals, this encyclopedia is recommended for all college, university, and public libraries, especially since there is no other such volume.—**Mark A. Wilson**

P

476.   **National Audubon Society Field Guide to Marine Mammals of the World.** By Randall R. Reeves, Brent S. Stewart, Phillip J. Clapham, and James A. Powell. New York, Alfred A. Knopf/Random House, 2002. 527p. illus. maps. $26.95pa. ISBN 0-375-41141-0.

This book was written by a team of experts and features more than 320 illustrations, 418 photographs, and 123 maps. This new guide offers more authoritative, up-to-date, and accessible information than any book previously published on the subject. Organized by the four major groups of marine mammals (marine fissipeds, pinnipeds, cetaceans, and sirenians), the species descriptions include: full-color paintings (some depicting males and females, juveniles, subspecies, or special features); color photographs showing appearance in the wild and illustrating typical behaviors; life history data, including length and weight at various life stages and life span; range and habitat text and a full-color range map based on the most current information; facts about social organization, surface behaviors, swimming, and diving; information on mating behavior, breeding, and the rearing of young; details about food items and foraging techniques; and estimates of population in the wild plus current and historic threats.

A general introduction outlines the evolution and taxonomy of marine mammals, distribution, migration, watching guidelines, identification techniques, and organizations and laws that protect marine mammals. Introductions to groups include comparative size illustrations, discussion of behavior particular to the group, and other unique features. A useful illustrated glossary of terms and an index of species names complete the guide. Exquisitely detailed illustrations, stunning photographs, and clearly written text combine to make this an indispensable reference source for marine mammals watchers and anyone interested in the nature world. [R: LJ, 1 April 02, p. 133]—**Barbara B. Goldstein**

32 Engineering

CHEMICAL ENGINEERING

C

477. **International Petroleum Encyclopedia 2002.** Tulsa, Okla., PennWell Publishing, 2002. 256p. illus. maps. index. $160.00. ISBN 0-87814-838-8.

This encyclopedia of the worldwide petroleum industry has been published since 1968, and annually since 1986. Coverage is almost entirely on business, economic, and political aspects of the petroleum industry; there are four pages of stratigraphic charts, but very little other geological content. Articles are arranged geographically, and include many informative maps; useful statistical tables are grouped at the end of the volume. The book concludes with a listing by country of national oil companies and energy ministries, including addresses, telephone numbers, and Websites. There is a thorough index.

Some articles are tendentious. For example, the work ignores market manipulation that led to the California energy crisis, and claims that environmental risk should not be an issue in the discussion of the Arctic National Wildlife Refuge. There is no mention of proposed pipelines from Turkmenistan through Afghanistan. Nonetheless, this is a useful compilation of information and opinion. In recent years there has also been a CD-ROM version (not seen by this reviewer); the price is the same as for print edition, with a $45 discount for the combined purchase of both.—**Robert Michaelson**

CIVIL ENGINEERING

C

478. Glass, Jacqueline. **Encyclopedia of Architectural Technology.** New York, John Wiley, 2002. 353p. illus. $165.50. ISBN 0-471-88559-2.

Developed to explain how architectural design meets technology, this source is a dictionary and encyclopedia rolled into one. The more than 180 alphabetic entries are oriented to UK architectural practice and cover some of the latest developments in building services, construction, environmental design, structures, and theory of design. The subjects range from materials and techniques to architects and engineers on the cutting edge of technological developments. Some illustrations are included. A wide range of specialized practitioners contributed information. Entries include cross-referencing, but an index would be a helpful addition. Suggestions for further reading follow many of the entries, and the additional bibliography at the beginning of the book will be useful for further research on people and terms not always familiar to Americans. This book will be useful to architecture students because it provides information from a different viewpoint than an architecture textbook written in the United States. Designers and engineers could use this book as a quick reference.—**Diane J. Turner**

C, P

479.   Langmead, Donald, and Christine Garnaut. **Encyclopedia of Architectural and Engineering Feats.** Santa Barbara, Calif., ABC-CLIO, 2001. 388p. illus. index. $99.00. ISBN 1-57607-122-X.

This informative work contains selected architectural and engineering works that demonstrate the major innovations or improvements in worldwide building from ancient times to the present, including one building in outer space. Achievements that show new ideas, new shapes, new materials, or that were built against all odds are identified. There are examples of the three essential building types that were used for many centuries: post and beam, arch, and stretched filament. Added to these examples are the innovations in building that used iron; steel; and reinforced, pre-stressed, or shell concrete. Examples were chosen because they use a new material or technology, refine an existing system of building, are of social significance, demonstrate a response to an economic need, or are of an unusual scale. Entries for individuals, ideas, or institutions that move architecture or building to new limits are also included.

The entries are one-half to two pages on average and are arranged in alphabetic order by the name of the structure or building type. The description includes an explanation of what the structure is, location, date of construction, historic background, current condition, and reasons for inclusion in this work. Each entry includes additional suggested readings. This work also includes a helpful glossary and an index. Entries range from Egyptian pyramids to the World Trade Center to the Mir Space Station. Entries are carefully selected and the descriptions and explanations are well written and easy for a layperson to understand. The entries show examples from all parts of the globe, and beyond.

Langmead is a professor of architectural history at the University of South Australia and Garnaut is a research assistant in the School of Architecture and Design at the University of South Australia. Both authors have other significant publications in the field. This work is highly recommended for general and academic collections. [R: LJ, 1 Feb 02, p. 88; SLJ, May 02, p. 96; BL, 15 May 02, pp. 1628-1630; Choice, May 02, p. 1564]

—**Joanna M. Burkhardt**

33 Health Sciences

GENERAL WORKS

Dictionaries and Encyclopedias

C, P

480.   **Encyclopedia of Health.** 3d ed. Anne Hildyard, Claire Cross, and Clare Hill, eds. Tarrytown, N.Y., Marshall Cavendish, 2003. 14v. illus. index. $329.95/set. ISBN 0-7614-7347-5.

Containing a full range of information on hygiene, exercise, sports, diet, diseases, and medicines, and written specifically for middle and high school students, the 3d edition of the *Encyclopedia of Health* is an interesting and informative source for health and medical information. Topics are arranged alphabetically with full-color photographs, charts, and diagrams. Also included are 12 in-depth features, covering such topics as careers, cleanliness, drugs, mental health, and diseases. Volume 16 contains comprehensive alphabetic and topical indexes, a first aid manual, a chronology of health and medical events, a list of health organizations, a glossary, a pronunciation guide, and a list of "health heroes." Overall, it is an easy-to-use reference for students and adults alike.

—Denise A. Garofalo

C, P

481.   **Health & Wellness Resource Center. http://www.gale.com/HealthRC.** [Website]. Farmington Hills, Mich., Gale. Price negotiated by site. Date reviewed: Mar 02.

The *Health & Wellness Resource Center* from the Gale Group evolved from Gale's *Health Reference Center*. This Website provides readable medical information for both the student and the lay person researching particular diseases, conditions, and treatments. This site provides access to a variety of medical reference sources, including the *Gale Encyclopedia of Medicine* (2d ed.; see ARBA 2003, entry 1437), *PDR Family Guide to Nutrition and Health* (Medical Economics Data, 1995), U*X*L's *Body by Design* (see ARBA 2001, entry 1441), and *The Complete Directory for People with Disabilities* (10th ed.; see ARBA 2002, entry 845), just to name a few. It also provides access to more than 400 medical journals, some 200 pamphlets, and 2,200 general interest publications that discuss health and medical topics. Alternative health topics are covered here as well and include information from *The Gale Encyclopedia of Alternative Medicine* (see ARBA 2002, entry 1485) and *PDR for Herbal Medicines* (2d ed.; see ARBA 2001, entry 1483), to name only two.

This Website is easy to navigate and the information is easy to retrieve. For those seeking general information on a variety of topics the best place to start is with the "Quick Start" guide. Here, users can choose to browse topics in the "Medical Encyclopedia," "Health Organization Directory," "Drug and Herb Finder," "Medical Dictionary," "Alternative Health Encyclopedia," and "Health Assessment Tools" (which gives users access to such Websites as Cancerfacts.com and Healthanswers.com). A link to "Health News" gives users access to daily news in the health and medical worlds. Users can do more specific searches by using the "Search" button or the "Advanced Search" button. An advanced search allows the user to put in keywords and tell the database where specifically to look for them (e.g., article title). Results from each search can be printed, e-mailed, or marked with "Infomark" to save the source for later reference.

This resource provides a lot of medical and health care information in one easy-to-use site. It is most appropriate for consumer health libraries and public libraries and would be a valuable addition to both.**—Shannon Graff Hysell**

C, P

482.   **The Oxford Companion to the Body.** Colin Blakemore and Sheila Jennett, eds. New York, Oxford University Press, 2001. 753p. illus. index. $65.00. ISBN 0-19-852403-X.

Any publication from Oxford University Press produced in conjunction with the Physiological Society (United Kingdom) carries an expectation of quality, and *The Oxford Companion to the Body* does not disappoint. Editors Blakemore and Jennett are of outstanding ability and reputation, as are the section editors and the more than 350 contributors. Entries are alphabetically arranged and have *see*, *see also*, and further reading references. A detailed index incorporates commonly used synonyms, thus providing for expanded access. Lastly, a section of plates illustrate various human organ systems. Beautiful full-page photographs decorate the text intermittently and there are more than 150 illustrations, some quite historic and interesting, such as the line drawing by Christopher Wren of the base of the human brain found in the entry under the headword "Vision." The use of British spelling will be confusing for readers outside the United Kingdom. For example, to locate the entries on *estrogen* and *edema* readers must look under *oestrogens* and *oedema*. However, this does not detract from the overall superior quality of this book, which is highly recommended for secondary school, college and university, and public libraries. [R: LJ, 1 May 02, p. 92; AG, Nov 02, p. 72]—**Lynn M. McMain**

Directories

P

483.   **Medical and Health Information Directory.** 13th ed. Jaime E. Noce and Lynn M. Pearce, eds. Farmington Hills, Mich., Gale, 2001. 3v. index. $650.00/set. ISBN 0-7876-3479-4. ISSN 0749-9973.

A comprehensive source of contact and descriptive information on a vast array of medical and health-related organizations, agencies, and institutions, this three-volume set has always been a key reference in medical libraries and larger public and academic libraries. The format has remained consistent through the 13 editions, with volume 1 directing users to a wide variety of organizations, including: national, international, state, and regional organizations; pharmaceutical companies; consultants; federal agencies; and medical schools. Volume 2 profiles nearly 12,000 domestic and foreign publications, libraries, and other health-related information resources. Volume 3 is a compilation of programs that provide treatment or information on a wide range of medical conditions and issues. Each volume includes a consolidated alphabetic name and keyword index. Descriptive listings within each volume give the usual directory and contact information. Entries for organizations include brief descriptions, former or alternate names, founding date, number of members, purpose, and publications.

Despite the availability of much of this information on the Web, this work still provides a convenient, one-stop source of health-related information organized for quick access. Librarians at large medical and hospital libraries will want this resource on their shelves.—**Vicki J. Killion**

Handbooks and Yearbooks

P, S

484.   **Adolescent Health Sourcebook.** Chad T. Kimball, ed. Detroit, Omnigraphics, 2002. 658p. illus. index. (Health Reference Series). $78.00. ISBN 0-7808-0248-9.

A new addition to Omnigraphics' Health Reference Series, this volume presents holistic coverage of adolescent health issues ranging from physical, sexual, and emotional health to social concerns such as safety, education, violence, and disasters. Like others in the popular series of about 100 subject volumes, it is written in clear, nontechnical language aimed at general readers; here, especially, parents and caregivers of teenagers. The material is up-to-date, comprehensive, and mainstream, making it a convenient first-step resource for consumers wanting basic understanding (not in-depth knowledge) of health care issues facing today's youth.

The book is arranged in 7 parts and contains 93 articles and excerpts originally published by government agencies, professional medical associations, and other nonprofit groups. Chad T. Kimball, editor of several other books in the series, selected the documents. The parts are: "Emotional and Mental Health Issues Affecting Adolescents," which discusses normal development as well as specific disorders; "Physical Health Issues Affecting Adolescents," covering common diseases and health risks like loud music, tattooing, and tanning; "Adolescent

Sexual Health"; "Drug Abuse in Adolescents"; "Social Issues and Other Parenting Concerns Affecting Adolescent Health and Safety," including driving, gangs, and the Internet; "Adolescent Education," from school failure to preparing for college; and "Additional Help and Information." The latter comprises a glossary as well as contact information for agencies, organizations, Websites, and publications. A list of references and sources for additional reading, all pertaining to topics discussed in the book, is also provided. The *Adolescent Health Sourcebook* is recommended for public libraries, community colleges, and other agencies serving health care consumers. [R: SLJ, Nov 02, p. 102]—**Madeleine Nash**

C, P

485.   **Exploring Health Care Careers.** 2d ed. Andrew Morkes, Carol Yehling, and Anne Paterson, eds. Chicago, Ferguson, 2002. 2v. index. $89.95/set. ISBN 0-89434-311-4.

Including over 100 careers in the health sciences, each with its own chapter, there is a plethora of information on each career listed in this 2-volume set. The chapters have multiple sections: defining the job, describing educational and personal skill requirements, providing certification and licensing requirements, future outlook, and potential salary earnings. The unique and impressive aspect of each chapter is the "What is it like to be a . . .?" section. This section includes an interview with a person actually practicing in the profiled career, providing a perspective that goes beyond mundane data by adding a realistic and experience-based discussion of each job. Every chapter has a bibliography and a list of professional organizations with contact information. The second volume ends with three indexes: a Guide for Occupational Exploration index, an Occupational Information Network-Standard Occupational Classification (O*NET-SOC) index, and a standard job title index. This two-volume set will be a great addition to any public library, secondary school library, or a career counselor's bookshelf.
                                                                                                —**Lynn M. McMain**

P, S

486.   **Health Matters!** William M. Kane, ed. Danbury, Conn., Grolier, 2002. 8v. illus. index. $409.00/set. ISBN 0-7172-5575-1.

This eight-volume combination health encyclopedia and health class text is aimed at the middle school and high school audience. The language and reading level is fairly simple and will be easily comprehended by most students. Each of the eight volumes covers a different health-related topic, which include "Addiction"; "Sexuality and Pregnancy"; "Physical Activity"; "Weight and Eating Disorders"; "HIV, AIDS and STDs"; and "Diseases and Disabling Conditions."

Each volume starts off with a several page introduction titled "Healthy Living: Teen Choices and Actions," followed by a test for the readers to assess their own behavior relating to health issues. An alphabetic encyclopedia follows, with one to several paragraph entries on terminology, health statistics, and historical facts relating to the topic of the volume. There are numerous tables, illustrations, and cross-references to other volumes. Several appendixes to each volume relate the issue to teen life through stories of teens whose lives have been affected by health problems and question-and-answer essays on difficult topics and choices. The editor also includes glossaries and lists of hot lines, Internet sites, and organizations relating to each volume's topic.

Although this set is well written, well researched, and attractively presented, the mixture of factual information with persuasive essays and arguments may turn older, more sophisticated teens off. Teenagers have a very sensitive radar to adult preaching and may tend to doubt the factual nature of information if it is presented with a clearly stated point of view. This is always a danger when presenting such information to the young. The best teachers can present the facts and let them speak for themselves. The right balance between education and advocacy is difficult to achieve. In *Health Matters!* this balance may be satisfactory for the middle school audience but not necessarily for older readers.—**Carol L. Noll**

MEDICINE

General Works

Dictionaries and Encyclopedias

C, P

487.   **The American Heritage Stedman's Medical Dictionary.** New York, Houghton Mifflin, 2002. 923p. $27.00. ISBN 0-618-25415-3.

Stedman's Medical Dictionary was originally written in 1949 by Thomas Stedman and published by Williams and Wilkins. American Heritage is the new publisher. The dictionary contains current, accurate information about medical terms for professionals and general readers in allied medical fields, law, and the insurance industry. A special feature of *Stedman's* provides a list of more than 250 selected main entries that have subentries in traditional dictionaries as an aid for users familiar with that arrangement. The work includes more than 100 line drawings, charts, and tables and a subject index to entries. All public, college, and medial libraries should purchase *American Heritage Stedman's Medical Dictionary* for their collections.—**Theresa Maggio**

P, S

488.   **Diseases.** rev. ed. Bryan Bunch, ed. Bethel, Conn., Grolier Educational, 2003. 8v. illus. index. $299.00/set. ISBN 0-7172-5688-X.

The study of human disease is inherently interesting. In the middle school and high school curriculum, units on human disease are included in health or science classes as a sure-fire way of capturing student interest. An encyclopedia like this is a perfect starting place for the papers and other research projects students are assigned in these courses.

The eight volumes of this set contain hundreds of entries, including diseases, symptoms, and body systems. Special attention is given to diseases of particular interest to young people—from acne to sexually transmitted diseases. This is a revision of a 1997 publication (see ARBA 98, entry 1557), which has been updated to include discussions on some of the new and emerging diseases (e.g., Ebola Virus), diseases in the news (e.g., West Nile Virus), and issues of current interest (e.g., stem cells). Entries are arranged alphabetically and include pronunciation, classification (disease, disorder, symptoms), and type (infectious, environmental, cause unknown). The text for each entry is one to three pages, giving the cause, incidence, symptoms, diagnosis, treatment options, stages, and progress of the disease, and possible prevention measures. All of this is written in a very readable style with few technical terms; it is very accessible to middle school students. The graphic arrangement too is very pleasing and well organized. A clever feature is the use of icons to denote important points, such as "call an ambulance," "avoid alcohol," and so on. There is a detailed index to the entire set included in each volume—an important feature for library and class use.

There are many Websites useful in researching medical and health topics. A few are given in the introduction to the first volume of this encyclopedia, along with some other information sources such as newsletters and books. However, most of these other sources are presented in a form most accessible to adults or medical professionals. This set of books presents information at a middle school level, making it a good first step for students researching a disease.—**Carol L. Noll**

P

489.   **The Merck Manual. http://www.merckhomeedition.com.** home ed. [Website]. Merck & Company. Free. Date reviewed: Oct 02.

The Merck Manual has been a trustworthy source of information for more than a century for both medical professionals and laypersons. Now available in a full-text online version, this familiar work is made even more accessible and convenient. Users can search this source by using either a text version or an interactive version. The interactive version provides users with a "Quick Start Guide" and "A Guide for Users," both of which explain how to most effectively use this tool. The user can search *The Merck Manual* by selecting a section on the left-hand side of the screen (e.g., "Drugs," "Mental Health Disorders," "Blood Disorders") and then selecting the chapter they would like to research. There are about 10 chapters per section. Once a chapter has been selected a box of "Chapter Topics" displays the illustrations, animations, videos, and pronunciations that are available in that chapter. For instance, when researching skin disorders researchers can find photographs of dry skin disorders, an illustration of the skin layers, and a glossary of medical names for growths on the skin surface. Buttons at the top of the screen allow users to go forward and back, conduct a search, check the index, bookmark pages, and print.

This electronic resource provides all of the information of the print edition of *The Merck Manual* with the convenience of an online format. The information is updated regularly and corrections are posted. Libraries who use *The Merck Manual* regularly will want to bookmark this page for easy consultation.—**Shannon Graff Hysell**

Handbooks and Yearbooks

P

490.   **American Medical Association Complete Guide to Men's Health.** Angela Perry and Mark Schacht, eds. New York, John Wiley, 2001. 502p. illus. index. $34.95. ISBN 0-471-41411-5.

Health guides for the lay public have traditionally been directed at women's health, children's health, or family health. By focusing solely on men's health and illness, this book helps to fill a major gap in the health information and advice literature. Edited by a reliable source, the American Medical Association, the book is a comprehensive guide to health and disease issues for men across the lifespan. The reference begins with a thorough discussion of "The Healthy Man" and holistic advice on how to stay healthy. Chapters on diet and nutrition, exercise, mental health, routine health screenings, and major health risks are included. Reproductive health is covered in a separate section. The book concludes with 14 chapters discussing common medical concerns for individual bodily systems. A unique but timely addition is a chapter on cosmetic surgery. The book is written in simple language that will be accessible to a majority of lay readers. The content is accurate and timely. Individual chapters or sections could stand alone. Black-and-white graphics are interspersed, usually illustrating aspects of anatomy. A glossary of medical terms is included. The *American Medical Association Complete Guide to Men's Health* is recommended for public libraries.—**Mary Ann Thompson**

P

491.   Segen, Joseph C., and Josie Wade. **The Patient's Guide to Medical Tests: Everything You Need to Know About the Tests Your Doctor Orders.** 2d ed. New York, Facts on File, 2002. 418p. index. (Facts on File Library of Health and Living). $44.00. ISBN 0-8160-4651-4.

The tests a doctor orders for a patient can be one of the most puzzling and scariest aspects of a medical visit. And in today's managed-care environment, doctors rarely have time for detailed explanations of the reasons for a test, the possible interpretations of results, and alternatives for further testing. A source such as this handbook for the layperson can fill in the important information so that the patient can make informed decisions on what tests to undergo, how to prepare for them, and how confident to be in the results.

Although the 1st edition of this book was only published 5 years ago (see ARBA 99, entry 1455), frequent updates are necessary in this field. Many tests have been improved, some have been retired and replaced with more accurate ones, and new tests have been introduced. All are covered here, along with new information on areas of increased interest, such as Alzheimer's disease, bioterrorism, improved tests in clinical cardiology, and new forms of diagnostic imaging.

There are more than 1,000 alphabetically arranged entries in this book, each around a half a page long. Included are descriptions of each test and what it measures, what preparation the patient needs to make (such as fasting or intake of a contrast medium), the procedure the patient will undergo, and a reference or "normal" range for the results. A range is also given for the cost of the procedure and comments on precautions in interpretation and factors that could interfere with accurate results. A glossary and index help make the text more accessible. One element that is lacking is references to other sources for more in-depth information. A list of other texts, or better yet, Websites, would have been helpful, both in leading the patient to more in-depth information and in helping with updating information in such a fast-changing field.—**Carol L. Noll**

Alternative Medicine

Dictionaries and Encyclopedias

C, P

492.   **Nutraceuticals: The Complete Encyclopedia of Supplements, Herbs, Vitamins, and Healing Food.** Arthur J. Roberts, Mary E. O'Brien, and Genell Subak-Sharpe, eds. New York, Perigee Books/Putnam, 2001. 669p. index. $21.95pa. ISBN 0-399-52632-3.

This book is an official guide of the American Nutraceutical Association that was established in 1997 to provide information on nutraceuticals—the components of foods or dietary supplements that have healing or therapeutic properties. Besides including herbs, vitamins, and supplements, nutraceuticals are also known as designer foods, prescriptive foods, pharma foods, or medicinal foods. Since nutraceuticals, as opposed to pharmaceuticals, are not closely regulated by the Food and Drug Administration, quality varies and accurate data are hard to locate. This book is an excellent source to help consumers and health professionals ferret out facts about these increasingly popular remedies. The information is important and libraries of many types will want to have this most reasonably priced book available to their patrons.

The book is divided into four parts. Part 1 provides a very brief history, with quick reference charts by ailment and nutraceutical. Part 2 is a "Directory of Nutraceutical Remedies," alphabetically arranged by common disorder from acne to weight problems. This section is very well done, covering diagnostic steps, conventional treatments, and nutraceutical remedies for each disorder. Each remedy is further divided into sections on how it works, recommended dosages, and potential problems. Handy sidebars increase quick retrieval for topics like strategies for relief and symptoms of overdose.

Part 3, "The Top 200-Plus Nutraceuticals," is also alphabetically arranged and clearly presented. Each entry has subsections entitled "Role as a Supplement," "Evidence of Efficacy," "Sources," "Forms and Usual Dosages," "Potential Problems," and "What to Look For." A sample of entries in this section includes DHEA, Benecol, DMSO, oat bran, and ginseng. Part 4 covers nutraceuticals for male and female problems and aging. An appendix with purchasing tips, including recommended brand names, and a selective bibliography enhance the book's value. The editors are well-credentialed physicians. Disclaimers are prominent in the book, yet the information is as factual as current research allows.

There are many fine titles available that cover similar information for herbs and vitamins: *Prescription for Nutritional Healing* (see ARBA 98, entry 1508), *Encyclopedia of Nutritional Supplements* (see ARBA 97, entry 1349), *Nature's Pharmacy* (Prentice Hall Press, 1998), and *PDR for Herbal Medicine* (2d ed.; see ARBA 2001, entry 1483). However, none of them cover the naturally occurring, therapeutic food chemicals known as nutraceuticals to the extent of this book. [R: BL, 1 May 01, p. 1701]—**Georgia Briscoe**

Directories

P

493.   Owen, David J. **The Herbal Internet Companion: Herbs and Herbal Medicine Online.** Binghamton, N.Y., Haworth Press, 2002. 193p. index. $49.95; $19.95pa. ISBN 0-7890-1051-8; 0-7890-1052-6pa.

The old caveat "don't judge a book by its cover" certainly applies to this modest paperback with its somewhat garish cover and a title that might lead one to believe it is a list of commercial Websites where ginkgo biloba can be purchased online. What a surprise to find instead a comprehensive, authoritative guide to finding the best information about herbal medicine from respected medical and educational institutions, government organizations, and nonprofit organizations around the world. The author is a librarian and he has organized the information for efficient retrieval by focusing on 16 topics related to herbs and herbal medicine. Subjects covered include the history of herbal treatments, botany and laws, and standards and regulations. Valuable information about adverse effects and interactions of herbs is the subject of one section. Others direct the reader to consumer topics such as quackery and fraud and how to evaluate Internet herbal sites.

Each section begins with a succinct but informative overview of the subject featured. These essays serve as a point of reference to the librarian or consumer by putting the topic in the context of the field of complementary and alternative medicine. Websites are listed alphabetically by the name of the originating group or agency.

URLs are provided. Entry annotations describe the type of information to be found at the site (e.g., full text, abstracts, bibliographic, pictorial). The book is footnoted and includes a short glossary and an alphabetic index.

It is obvious that the compilation of this work was a labor of love undertaken by an expert in the field of scientific librarianship. It is unique resource that will be a valuable tool in medical and public libraries as well as a guide to practitioners and consumers of herbal medicine.—**Marlene M. Kuhl**

Pediatrics

P

494.   **Breastfeeding Sourcebook.** Jenni Lynn Colson, ed. Detroit, Omnigraphics, 2002. 388p. index. (Health Reference Series). $78.00. ISBN 0-7808-0332-9.

Breastfeeding Sourcebook, like all the titles in Omnigraphics' Health Reference Series, is a collection of freely available articles and Websites. In 8 parts and 64 chapters it covers all major areas, including rationale for breastfeeding versus bottle feeding, preparation, breastfeeding during early weeks and later in infancy, the issues of working mothers, and a variety of difficult and special situations including teenage mothers and illnesses of the mother or the infant. "Breastfeeding the Baby with Special Needs" is reprinted from http://www.lalecheleague.org. "Is it Safe to Lose Weight While Breastfeeding?" is a news release from the National Institute of Child Health and Human Development located at http://www.nichd.nih.gov. "Breastfeeding the Adopted Baby" is also freely available, although its URL (http://users.erols.com/cindyrn/24.htm) is not given.

Particularly useful is the information about professional lactation services and chapters on breastfeeding when returning to work, which includes a sample letter to an employer requesting accommodations for nursing mothers.

There is a glossary, a list of medications to avoid when breastfeeding, legal rights of nursing mothers, annotated breastfeeding resources (e.g., books, magazines, associations), and an index. *Breastfeeding Sourcebook* will be useful for public libraries, consumer health libraries, and technical schools offering nurse assistant training, especially in areas where Internet access is problematic.—**Martha E. Stone**

P

495.   **The Complete Directory for Pediatric Disorders, 2002/03.** 2d ed. Lakeville, Conn., Grey House Publishing, 2002. 1120p. index. $190.00; $165.00pa. ISBN 1-930956-62-2; 1-930956-61-4pa.

P

496.   **The Complete Directory for Pediatric Disorders. http://www.greyhouse.com.** [Website]. Millerton, N.Y., Grey House Publishing. $215.00/year subscription; $300.00/year subscription (print and online editions). Date reviewed: May 02.

Caring for a child who has a serious illness or a genetic or congenital disorder can be a challenge. *The Complete Directory for Pediatric Disorders*, first published in 2000 (see ARBA 2001, entry 1458), provides information and resources to help healthcare practitioners and parents get the support that they need. The 2d edition has 7 new chapters: "Eating Disorders," "Lead Poisoning," "Sleep Apnea," "Post-Traumatic Stress Disorder," "Physical and Sexual Abuse," "Hypertrophic Cardiomyopathy," and "Syncope." It also has several chapters covering broad subject areas, such as dental conditions and preventable childhood infections. Medical editor Alan Friedman, of Yale University, and a team of associates reviewed all of the material in the book.

The *Directory* has three major sections. The first covers specific disorders. The alphabetic entries include the name of the disorder and synonyms; a description; and information on symptoms, physical findings, related disorders, cause, treatment, and resources. The latter may include associations, support groups, government and nonprofit agencies, libraries and research centers, media sources, and Websites. Section 2 covers general resources: government agencies, national associations, research centers, libraries, media resources, and camps. Section 3 explains the human body systems. A glossary, guidelines for obtaining information, and three indexes (alphabetic, subject, and geographic) complete the work.

The Complete Directory for Pediatric Disorders is a valuable resource for medical, consumer health, and large public libraries. Although the reading level is high, it provides concise, thorough descriptions of disorders in lay language and offers help with extensive resource lists. The new edition is also available as an online subscription with continuous updates. The online edition gives the user access to more than 5,500 disorder-specific and general resources. Librarians that cannot afford it will find much of the same information available on MedlinePlus at http://www.medlineplus.gov.—**Barbara M. Bibel**

Specific Diseases and Conditions

Allergies

P

497.   Lipkowitz, Myron A., and Tova Navarra. **The Encyclopedia of Allergies.** 2d ed. New York, Facts on File, 2001. 340p. index. (Facts on File Library of Health and Living). $66.00. ISBN 0-8160-4404-X.

Millions of individuals suffer from allergies and their symptoms vary widely, ranging from sneezing to life-threatening anaphylaxis. *The Encyclopedia of Allergies* was written by an allergist and a nurse for both allergy sufferers and nonsufferers to better understand the nature of allergies. The work contains new and updated information on allergies, allergens, symptoms, tests, medications, treatments (both traditional and nontraditional), and much more, and is written in an easy-to-understand style. The entries are arranged in alphabetic order and include such topics as allergy shots, asthma, immune system, and myths about allergies and asthma. Also included are more than 40 tables that cover subjects such as occupational allergens and weeds that cause hay fever in the United States and Canada.

The *Encyclopedia* has an informative timeline of allergy and immunology that begins with the death of Egyptian pharaoh Menes from anaphylaxis after a wasp sting in 2640 B.C.E. and continues up through 2001 with the publication of Dr. Jean Ford's report on the devastating impact of asthma. Appendixes provide information on the following topics: major pollen areas of the United States and Canada, available Radioallergosorbent Tests (RAST) for allergies, allergy organizations, and guidelines for the operation of camps for asthmatic children by the Consortium on Children's Asthma Camps. A bibliography (with most of the references being published in 1992 or earlier) and an index are included. *The Encyclopedia of Allergies* is a highly informative resource and is recommended for all consumer health collections.—**Rita Neri**

Cancer

P

498.   **Cancer Sourcebook for Women.** 2d ed. Karen Bellenir, ed. Detroit, Omnigraphics, 2002. 604p. index. (Health Reference Series). $225.00. ISBN 0-7808-0226-8.

First published in 1996, the *Cancer Sourcebook for Women* has been updated to include the latest information about gynecologic cancers, cancer during pregnancy, fertility after cancer treatment, and conditions that may be mistaken for cancer. The material comes from the publications of government agencies, professional associations, and nonprofit organizations. Full citations are provided.

There are sections on breast, cervical, endometrial, and ovarian cancers, as well as chapters about conditions such as fibroid tumors that exhibit symptoms easily confused with cancer. The book also covers cancer screening and prevention, treatment options, recent research developments, and clinical trials. Information about the link between Human Papillomavirus (HPV) and cervical cancer, cancer treatment during pregnancy, and the effects of chemotherapy and radiation on fertility and sexuality will be useful for patients. The coverage of strategies for coping with treatment side effects and helping children understand their mother's illness are helpful too. A glossary, resource list, and information about the Family and Medical Leave Act complete the book. This volume from Omnigraphics' Health Reference Series is an excellent addition to collections in public, consumer health, and women's health libraries.—**Barbara M. Bibel**

Diabetes

P

499.   Petit, William A., Jr., and Christine Adamec. **The Encyclopedia of Diabetes.** New York, Facts on File, 2002. 374p. index. (Facts on File Library of Health and Living). $71.50. ISBN 0-8160-4498-8.

This encyclopedia is an outstanding example of what can happen when a highly knowledgeable medical specialist is teamed with a talented medical writer—informative, accurate information is presented in a clear, intelligible style. It begins with an overview of the history of diabetes and key historical events in the development of treatments for this disease. Entries follow that examine key issues: the variant types, medications and other therapies, associated illnesses and complications, and demographics of diagnosed populations. The volume continues with appendixes that give contact information for diabetes-related organizations, research centers, and programs; Websites for further information; medications used in diabetic care; and tables of calculated body mass indexes. It concludes with a bibliography and a very thorough index.

Written for both consumers and professionals, the goal of the authors is to educate people who have diabetes about the disease, how to control its effects, and how to avoid serious complications. The goal is to prevent its development in people not diagnosed, encourage them to help those affected, and advocate for further research. This book admirably succeeds in its goals.—**Susan K. Setterlund**

NURSING

C. P

500.   **Nursing Programs 2003.** 8th ed. Lawrenceville, N.J., Peterson's Guides, 2002. 654p. index. $26.95pa. ISBN 0-7689-0799-3. ISSN 1073-7820.

Peterson's Guides' resources for educational programs are inevitably well reviewed. In addition, ARBA's review of the 7th edition (see ARBA 2002, entry 1509) points out that this volume was more accurately titled when it had a defining subtitle of "Baccalaureate and Graduate Nursing Education in the U.S. and Canada." Other than these minor points, it should be noted that the guide remains a valuable resource for any career collection in high school, community college, university, or public libraries.

The 8th edition format follows that of the 7th, including the key fact that the American Association of Colleges of Nursing again collaborates with Peterson's in the production of the "only comprehensive and concise guide" to nursing careers (p. v). The introduction includes "an overview of the various components of the book" (p. 1), such as organization, descriptions of key data (e.g., nursing school profiles, general nursing college information), and basic information about the nursing field. Five articles grouped under the title "The Nursing School Adviser" follow the introductory section. They include choosing a nursing program, distance learning programs, a tabular presentation of nursing programs, specialty nursing organizations, and financing a nursing education.

The bulk of the guide consists of profiles of individual programs arranged alphabetically, as in earlier editions, by state or province. The last main section is titled "In-depth Descriptions of Nursing Programs," which has two-page descriptions prepared by nursing schools or departments as they choose to do so; this means that not every program profiled earlier is described. The last 44 pages of the 8th edition includes 8 indexes: "Baccalaureate Programs Offering Special Tracks," "Master's Degree Programs," "Concentrations Within Master's Degree Programs," "Doctoral Programs," "Postdoctoral Programs," "Distance Learning Programs," "Continuing Education Programs," and an "Institution Index." Taking all into consideration, the 8th edition of *Nursing Programs* continues its long tradition as a unique and valuable reference source.—**Laurel Grotzinger**

PHARMACY AND PHARMACEUTICAL SCIENCES

Dictionaries and Encyclopedias

P

501.   **The Pill Book.** 10th ed. Harold M. Silverman, ed. Westminster, Md., Bantam Dell Publishing Group, 2002. 1216p. illus. index. $6.99pa. ISBN 0-553-58478-2.

The stated purpose of this book is "to provide educational information to the public" covering the most widely prescribed medications by physicians. The editor also states that it is not an exhaustive list of prescription drugs. The information in the book is based on FDA-approved information only. This edition covers 35 new drugs recently approved by the FDA in addition to adding several dozen more entries excluded from the previous edition (2000). Again, the color insert pages of actual size pills are provided for the consumer. Each entry lists the generic name of the drug with a phonic pronunciation in parenthesis and includes the following categories: brand name, type of drug, what the drug is prescribed for, general information, cautions and warnings, possible side effects, drug interactions, usual dose, overdosage, special information, and special populations. The entries are written concisely in a readable style and in easy-to-understood terms. The index is an alphabetic listing of generic and brand name drugs. At the end of the main text is a short chapter titled "Drugs Against Bioterrorism," 20 questions one should ask either their physician or pharmacist, safety information on taking Rx drugs, and the top 200 prescribed drugs in the United States. Families who have to take a lot of prescription medications will also find it useful to keep at home; the cost is very reasonable for the information provided. Medical staff will find this a helpful guide for quick, concise drug information that is not biased by drug company literature. The new edition is highly recommended to public libraries, medical libraries, and especially to libraries doing patient education.

—**Betsy J. Kraus**

34 High Technology

GENERAL WORKS

Dictionaries and Encyclopedias

C, P

502. Collin, S. M. H. **Dictionary of Information Technology.** 3d ed. Oak Park, Ill., Peter Collin, 2002. 420p. $15.95pa. ISBN 1-901659-55-0.

The authors define a *cybernym* as "an acronym, abbreviation, mnemonic, convenient contraction, cypher, signaling code, control message or vernacular initialism used in cybernetics applications (especially telecommunications)" (p. v). This dictionary lists more than 16,000 cybernyms with over 26,000 definitions—everything from "A" for "administration" or "attenuation" or "additional" or "ampere" or "availability" to the post-alphabet symbol for "ohm." There is certainly no lack of dictionaries of computing terminology available. What makes this one unique? The subject matter includes programming; networks; the Web; databases; and computer applications of graphics, electronics, communications, and desktop publishing. There are roughly 13,000 entries contained in this volume and all are defined "using a limited vocabulary of about 500 words, over and above those words which appear in the dictionary as entries" (preface). The aim here is clarity. Entries are further clarified by the frequent inclusion of quotations from relevant magazines that put the terms in context and by boxed parenthetical comments to provide greater detail. Now in its 3d edition, Collin's *Dictionary* has its place. Libraries looking for an inexpensive, brief, basic dictionary of information technology terms would be well served by this work.—**John Maxymuk**

C, P

503. **Dictionary of Computer and Internet Words: An A to Z Guide to Hardware, Software, and Cyberspace.** New York, Houghton Mifflin, 2001. 298p. illus. $14.00pa. ISBN 0-618-10137-3.

This new edition, published by the always-reliable editors of the American Heritage dictionaries, displays their usual careful attention to detail and commitment to jargon-free definitions. The computer and Internet world is developing at a dizzying rate, with its specialized vocabulary evolving as the industry changes. Unfortunately, for the uninitiated, many of the new terms quickly become acronyms consisting of unintelligible initials. The average user oftentimes feels as if they are the lone stranger at a party where everyone else is speaking a foreign language.

The editors have addressed this need for a clear translation very efficiently. Every acronym is listed twice, once as a dictionary entry where the reader is cross-referenced to the fully spelled out entry that is cross-referenced back to the acronym entry. For example, the entry for "HTTP" also sends the reader to "Hypertext Transfer Protocol." Depending on the term, the full definition may be found under either one of the entries.

This edition has added 800 new terms that have come into current use since the earlier version. The definitions are written for both PC and Mac users. The book also contains helpful charts throughout, such as the two-page chart of the various Intel microprocessors and their attributes from the old 8080 to the newest Itanium. All in all, this small volume is well written and should prove a useful tool in assisting computer users who need to know what the computer and Internet insiders are trying to tell them. [R: Choice, Nov 01, p. 484]

—**Nancy P. Reed**

COMPUTING

C, P

504. **Computer Graphics Dictionary.** Roger T. Stevens, ed. Hingham, Mass., Charles River Media, 2002. 460p. illus. $49.95 (w/CD-ROM). ISBN 1-58450-019-0.

Like many fields, computer game design and computer generated special effects are an amalgam of several other fields including animation, photography, lighting, and video production as well as computing. This dictionary is designed to define terms from these diverse areas in one source. Definitions from how jaw muscles work, microphone types, and lighting techniques to garbage in and garbage out are included, proving the editor's contention regarding the many diverse elements necessary to work in this new area of expertise. Stevens, graphics programmer and author of several books on the topic, has collaborated with Shamms Mortier as technical editor and, in addition, has drawn from 50 other sources to create this volume.

The entries are alphabetically listed by term and include abbreviations, definitions, *see also* references, and a CD icon referring to the included CD-ROM. Some of the entries refer to specific applications such as Bryce, Poser, or others, but overall most terms found in the literature are included here. Clearly not for the beginner, many of the entries require a basic level of knowledge to comprehend.

The CD-ROM does not truly supplement the work. Aside from providing a color image of the black-and-white illustration in the text, it is often difficult to find the related entry. On the CD-ROM is an entry for "4unitcube," which could not be found in the text, and in the text there was a symbol next to "flash," but this term could not find that on the CD-ROM. The CD-ROM needs a better menu system and it should offer more than a color image to be worth including. The *Dictionary* is a useful tool, providing comprehensive coverage of the many diverse fields that have combined to make up computer graphics in a single source.—**Joshua Cohen**

C, P

505. **Computer Sciences.** Roger R. Flynn, ed. New York, Macmillan Reference USA/Gale Group, 2002. 4v. illus. index. $325.00/set. ISBN 0-02-865566-4.

This is an impressive four-volume encyclopedia that covers the world of computing from its earliest origins to predictions about future trends. Flynn states in his preface, "In this encyclopedia we aim to detail the people, activities, products, and growth of knowledge that have helped computer science evolve into what it is today" (p. vi). Each of the volumes presents computer science from a different aspect. Volume 1 deals with the foundations of the discipline, while volume 2 covers software and hardware. Volume 3 is concerned with social applications of computing and the last volume describes our computer civilization as it exists and is evolving.

The set boasts 286 entries from more than 125 individuals. The volumes are heavily illustrated with black-and-white pictures and graphs. Each book contains identical additional resources, including a timeline, a complete glossary, a list of contributors, and indexes. Each volume is arranged in alphabetic order by subject, with subtopics that are accessible from the volume index. The signed articles are of varying length, with *see also* references at the end. Technical or unfamiliar terms are printed in bold typeface with a definition included in the margin of the page and an entry in the glossary. The same formula is followed each time the term is used, so a reader gets a definition for that term each time it is used. Scattered throughout the books are lavender text boxes with additional interesting facts about the subject under discussion. Under the entry "World Wide Web" a text box informs the reader that Yahoo! is an acronym for "Yet Another Hierarchical Officious Oracle" (v.1, p.219). These boxes add interest to this already fascinating set.

The writing is straightforward, avoiding the often used computer jargon, and is geared toward the general reader. *Computer Sciences* is an excellent purchase for a reference collection, filling an existing need in the average collection.—**Nancy P. Reed**

INTERNET

Directories

P

506.   Hahn, Harley. **Harley Hahn's Internet Yellow Pages.** 2002 ed. New York, Osborne/McGraw-Hill, 2002. 939p. index. $34.99pa. (w/CD-ROM). ISBN 0-07-219251-8.

Due to the ever-changing nature of the Internet, the currency of any print resource recedes with time. However, *Harley Hahn's Internet Yellow Pages* contains a treasure trove of freely accessible resources, which are selected based on importance, usefulness, and permanency. Sites are arranged in a yellow-pages-style subject directory with 184 categories. A table of contents and index are useful for locating subcategories of the main entries (i.e., karate is a subcategory of martial arts). The quirky humor sprinkled throughout the resource brightens a seemingly overwhelming amount of raw information, and imparts intelligent advice on where to look for information or entertainment on the Internet. Each category has a brief explanation before the sites and any subcategories are listed. Overall, the sites included are stable, well maintained, interesting, and easy to navigate. The CD-ROM contains an electronic version of the book that enhances this title's usefulness.—**Denise A. Garofalo**

C, P

507.   **Resource Discovery Network. http://www.rdn.ac.uk.** [Website]. Free. Date reviewed: Nov 02.

The *Resource Discovery Network* (RDN), a multidisciplinary, collaborative effort including the British Library and coordinated by UKOLN University of Bath and King's College London, gathers in one place Internet resources that are selected, indexed, and described by local specialists in 60-plus British educational and research organizations. This mammoth effort provides both a categorized gateway and excellent bibliographic information on 65,000 high-quality Websites. Staff at separate hubs—academic, research, professional, and library institutions—identify and evaluate the sites. Each hub site has its own interface; some have been reviewed separately (e.g., HUMBUL [humanities] in September 2002 *Choice*, PSIgate [physical sciences] in October 2002 *Choice*). The design, format, arrangement, and additional services vary extremely from hub to hub, and lack of consistency in page design often makes it easy to get lost when browsing.

On the RDN entry page valuable harmony is imposed in the form of a "ResourceFinder" search box offering uniform searching over the full text of six disparate databases. "ResourceFinder" defaults to AND logic but supports OR and NOT logic, truncation, parentheses grouping, and phrase searching. The results display shows title, description, subjects, resource types, and linked URLs, and provides a clickable link to the originating hub database record. The entry page also features a Behind the Headlines (BTH) topic in the news, with a link to a BBC story (recent subjects include NATO, sex offenders, the Leonid meteor shower, North Sea Oil, and passive smoking) and descriptions of 15 or so resources pertinent to the issue. The British focus in BTH is obvious, making RDN a great place to check for that perspective, but academic disciplines are international, and the resources presented here are also useful for North American and worldwide audiences.

The scale of this project compares with that of OCLC's CORC, but RDN and its supporting sites are free to any Internet user. Search capabilities at the free (and more centralized) Scout Report archives (http://scout.wisc.edu /archives/) are arguably more sophisticated, but to fewer resources. RDN also offers free self-paced Internet learning modules in over 40 disciplines, further increasing its value as a useful tool for students and researchers starting new investigations in academic subjects.—**Susanne Bjorner**

TELECOMMUNICATIONS

C, P

508.   **Newton's Telecom Dictionary.** 18th ed. Emeryville, Calif., Publishers Group West, 2002. 859p. $34.95pa. ISBN 1-57820-104-7.

Updated and expanded, this resource remains a "virtual industry bible" for the telecommunications industry (15th ed.; see ARBA 2000, entry 1467), with its combination of definitions, facts, dates, acronyms, opinions, and brief biographies. Following the format employed previously, the dictionary section is prefaced by eight essays on everything from dollar-saving tips to practical advice (e.g., avoiding internal theft) and information about the author. Using the alphabetically arranged dictionary is an adventure as it offers the unexpected, from seemingly unrelated terms (e.g., couch potato, Christmas tree lights) to industry standards and terms designating imaginary events (e.g., foo foo dust). The volume concludes with an appendix of industry standards organizations, international calling codes, and the shapes of standard plugs and connectors.

The useful and entertaining dictionary entries vary in length from a few words or lines to several paragraphs or columns; however, the sources from which the information derived have not been indicated—clearly a problem for the chronological and biographical entries. In not annotating entries with information on their origin and use, the author has lost the opportunity to create a research tool for the ages. The dictionary, while fun, fails to develop standards and follow them with respect to acronym definitions that appear as either cross-references from the complete term to the acronym (e.g., Cellular Mobile Telephone Service, CMTS), as cross-references from the acronym to the complete term (e.g., CPC, Calling Party Control), or as cross-references from a brief definition to a longer one (e.g., Cellsite on Wheels, COW). The inclusion of event dates in the midst of number acronyms is disconcerting where a separate chronology would better serve researchers.

Despite these problems, the dictionary is inexpensive, a well-regarded tool for its primary audience, and fun to use. As such it continues to be recommended for libraries whose clientele are pursuing the telecommunications industry and the newest technologies.—**Sandra E. Belanger**

PHYSICAL SCIENCES

Chemistry

Biography

C, S

509.   Oakes, Elizabeth H. **A to Z of Chemists.** New York, Facts on File, 2002. 276p. illus. index. (Notable Scientists). $45.00. ISBN 0-8160-4579-8.

In writing a book review the first question one must ask is "Why is this work worthwhile?" One must ask if the editor has indicated the purpose in the introduction and if there are many other works on this topic currently available. In the case of the present A to Z book I must begin with criticism: the purpose of the new resource is not indicated and hundreds of dictionaries on scientists are available, although not many dictionaries are specifically about chemists. Also, the branches of science inevitably interact, so it is understandable to read in the introduction to *A to Z of Chemists* that "while the majority of the scientists in this book are, first and foremost, chemists, there is a handful of physicists, biologists, and other scientists who made significant contributions." To provide a "sense of the panorama," many dictionaries include some helpful features, such as listing the scientists in chronological order of birth, or summarizing accounts of historical developments, or providing a list of Nobel Prize winners. The additional channels of information enhance greatly the value of the resource. In addition to a main purpose, which is to provide correct and quick information, it is good if a resource reveals new data and leads to discovery of new knowledge. In comparing *A to Z of Chemists* with other dictionaries about a hundred biographies are listed over and over again in a number of resources. But in *A to Z of Chemists* there is a gap in chronological coverage from the first century (one entry: Maria the Jewess) to 1731 (Henry Cavendish). With the lack of representation from this time period it could be assumed that no scientific activity happened. Some well-known names are omitted, such as Arnold of Villanova (Spanish alchemist, 1235-1311), Bernard Trevian (Italian chemist 1406-1490), Glauber (German chemist, 1604-1668), John Hoachem Becher (Dutch chemist 1625-1682), George Ernst Stahl (German chemist 1660-1734), and Michail Vasilievich Lomonosov (Russian chemist 1711-1765). Although the introduction states the work is "comprehensive . . . featuring an international array of scientists," of the 150 chemists included in *A to Z*, 52 are from the United States.

A to Z of Chemists does fulfill its mission as a dictionary by providing clear, accurate, basic information. The book documents the stories of more than 150 chemists, including of 20 unique entries on contemporary scientists. Among those are lesser-known researchers, including women, African American, and international scientists (e.g., Bishop Hazel Cladys, Brady St. Elmo, Crutzen Paul, Fukui Kenichi, Good Mary Lowe). Also, there is a unique entry on Maria the Jewess of the first century, one of the first alchemists who is best known for having invented apparatuses, unfortunately lost in dictionaries of scientists.

Alphabetically arranged, each biographical essay is about 900 words. It includes the family information, educational background, positions held, scientific achievements, and prizes awarded. There are cross-references from individual entries to other scientists represented in the book through names in capital letters. About 50 black-and-white photographs are included. In addition to the general subject index, three other indexes are included: by country of birth, country of scientific activity, and chronological order. A bibliography consists of 62 sources and Websites.

Elizabeth Oakes has written more than 15 books, including the *Encyclopedia of World Scientists* (see ARBA 2002, entry 1305) and *A to Z of STS Scientists* (see ARBA 2003, entry 1273). This work is designed for and will be useful for high school and early college students, teachers, and general readers. [R: LJ, 1 Feb 03, p. 78]—**Svetlana Korolev**

Handbooks and Yearbooks

S
510.   Stwertka, Albert. **A Guide to the Elements.** 2d ed. New York, Oxford University Press, 2002. 246p. illus. index. $18.95pa. ISBN 0-19-515027-9.

It is easy to be enthusiastic about Stwertka's new edition of *A Guide to the Elements*, although it has not increased much in bulk since the 1st edition (1996). The author starts with an explanation of the periodic table and its development, followed by brief, one- to seven-page descriptions of each element that concentrate on their history, chemical and physical properties, and usage. Stwertka writes in a clear and nontechnical style that is appropriate for middle and high school students as well as adults with a minimal (or long-forgotten) background in chemistry. The black-and-white and color illustrations that accompanying many of the elements' descriptions add to the pleasing visual effect. A glossary, chronology of the discovery of the elements, and slightly updated list for further reading complete the volume. The 1st edition was received with enthusiasm and won several book awards. This edition has only eight additional pages, most of which are dedicated to the 1999 discovery of Element 114, Ununquadium, an epilogue detailing the 2001 retraction of the announced discovery of Element 118, and a brief list of Websites. For the updating, a paperback copy is still a worthwhile purchase for libraries with the 1st edition. While more information for young readers is available in multivolume sets such as Knapp's *Elements* (see ARBA 2002, entry 1533, and ARBA 98, entry 1600) and Newton's *Chemical Elements: From Carbon to Krypton* (see ARBA 2000, entry 1378), Stwertka provides most of the essential information within a consistent, attractive, and easy-to-read format—and at a fraction of the price. [R: SLJ, Nov 02, p. 106]—**Barbara MacAlpine**

Earth and Planetary Sciences

General Works

C, P, S
511.   Knight, Judson. **Science of Everyday Things. Volume 4: Real-Life Earth Science.** Edited by Neil Schlager. Farmington Hills, Mich., Gale, 2002. 507p. illus. index. $85.00. ISBN 0-7876-5635-6.

Volume 4 of *Science of Everyday Things* continues the main objective of this series, which is to explain scientific concepts of chemistry, physics, biology, and the earth sciences by observing common or real-world phenomena. True to this objective, this volume dealing with the earth sciences provides the reader with a thorough and yet highly readable explanation of key concepts and scientific principles in the areas of geology, geochemistry, geophysics, meteorology, sedimentology, and ecology issues pertaining to the biosphere. Employing a four-tier instructional matrix, each chapter follows the sequences of first presenting key concepts of the earth sciences, followed by a "How-It-Works" section, a "Real-Life Application" section, and concluding with a "Where-To-Learn-More" section. In this latter section, the user is presented with books, articles, and peer-reviewed Internet Websites that contain further information in the various subdisciplines of the earth sciences. The volume also has a detailed cumulative subject index for reviewing concepts and ideas explored in the other three volumes of the series. An index to "Everyday Things" is perhaps the most helpful aid to a novice of the earth sciences. This index assists the user with searching the text for specific everyday ideas, concepts, and applications without the use of the controlled or highly technical vocabulary of the earth sciences. This work, along with the entire Science of Everyday Things series, should be a welcome addition in any public, school, or college library collection.

—**Patrick Hall**

Astronomy and Space Sciences

Dictionaries and Encyclopedias

C, P, S

512.   Ince, Martin. **Dictionary of Astronomy.** 2d ed. Oak Park, Ill., Peter Collin, 2001. 235p. $12.95pa. ISBN 1-901659-72-0.

The *Dictionary of Astronomy* is a compact resource covering the discipline with more than 1,700 terms. Although effort is made to cover the vast history of astronomy, the value here is the inclusion of the most current terminology. With our ever-expanding exploration and observation efforts, new terminology inevitably creeps into the vernacular.

The definitions are concise. There are a few biographies and a smattering of illustrations. The primary use here is the quick look-up in order to illuminate a term or acronym found in an article or report. The main entry word is bold and in the style of a heading, which enables one to easily scan the page for terms. *See* references are used to link acronyms to full phrases; however, there was practically no effort to cross-reference related terms—a minor flaw. This handy resource is appropriate and recommended for school, public, and general academic collections.—**Margaret F. Dominy**

Handbooks and Yearbooks

C, P, S

513.   **Space Sciences.** Pat Dasch, ed. New York, Macmillan Reference USA/Gale Group, 2002. 4v. illus. maps. index. $325.00/set. ISBN 0-02-865546-X.

If one were to list the top events of the twentieth century, the commencement of space exploration would be right up there. Although many aspects of the human endeavor to move beyond the surface of the earth have been treated in a plethora of sources, *Space Sciences* is somewhat unique as it gathers together these many aspects in one resource. *Space Sciences*, a four-volume set of the Macmillan Science Library series, is not a typical encyclopedic treatment of the topic. Each volume has its specific theme. Volume 1 is titled "Space Business," volume 2 is "Planetary Science and Astronomy," volume 3 is "Humans in Space," and volume 4 is "Our Future in Space." Within each of these volumes, topics are listed alphabetically.

Each volume has almost the same introductory material. Each volume begins with the preface and a section titled "For Your Reference." In the latter section, the reader will find a collection of tables of data in support of articles contained within *Space Sciences*. Also, in each volume two handy timelines are featured. The first is "Milestones in Space History" and the second is "Human Achievements in Space." In addition, in volume 1 there is a third timeline titled "Major Business Milestones in U.S. History." These timelines give a convenient overview of the chronology of events. Finally, nearly three full pages of contributors are listed.

The signed articles vary in length from about half a page to several pages. The articles conclude with a bibliography for further reading as well as an Internet site or two for further enhancement. Most of the URLs are NASA or other government sites that should be stable and reliable. Each volume is generously illustrated with color photographs or artist renderings. A particularly appealing feature is the use of sidebars. Here the reader will find definitions of terms, explanations of a process, or a bit of trivia related to an article. This approach adds to the understanding of the article without necessarily interfering with the flow of the text of the article. Frequent use of cross-references between articles and volumes help tie the whole set together.

Because of the many articles on the variety of careers in the space industry and the numerous articles related to the more popular expression of space exploration, such as movies, television, and science fiction, the appropriate audience for this resource is the high school student. The assembled content is well presented and interesting. The treatment of the business of space science in volume 1 is quite fascinating and not easily found elsewhere. *Space Sciences* is highly recommended for school libraries and appropriate for public library collections. It is also appropriate for general academic collections.—**Margaret F. Dominy**

Climatology and Meteorology

C, P, S

514.   **The Facts on File Weather and Climate Handbook.** By Michael Allaby. New York, Facts on File, 2002. 290p. illus. index. (Facts on File Science Library). $35.00. ISBN 0-8160-4517-8.

This book appears to be a new title in the Facts on File Science Library series as this reviewer cannot locate a prior edition. Michael Allaby has authored over 40 books in the sciences for Facts on File and lives in Scotland. The main portion of the volume consists of a glossary of weather and climate terms. This portion forms 188 of the 290 pages in the book and contains around 2,200 entries. The glossary entries are well written and comprehensive in scope. The glossary is illustrated by small line drawings, some of which are hard to read and sometimes simplistic (e.g., low index, high index). The next portion of the volume contains 100 biographies of famous scientists associated with weather and climate. Names such as Louis Agassiz, Francis Beaufort, Daniel Bernoulli, Anders Celsius, Gustave de Coriolis, Johann Doppler, Daniel Fahrenheit, Tetsuya Fujita, John Tyndall, and Evangelista Torricelli are included. Interestingly, Allaby notes that Tyndall died after his wife accidentally gave him an overdose of a sedative. Biographies are short but contain a wealth of information on each person. Next is a chronology of important events in the field of meteorology, starting with 340 B.C.E. This is followed by 18 pages of charts covering topics such as the Beaufort Scale, the Saffir-Simpson Scale, the Fujita Scale, weather map codes, and cyclone (hurricane) names. The book concludes with an appendix containing "recommended reading" and "useful web sites." Websites checked by this reviewer were still working.

This work is a comprehensive, handy reference tool for weather and climate. The glossary is especially comprehensive and well worth the modest price of the volume. The weather map codes are hard to locate in many libraries with traditional reference sources. The physical construction of the book is excellent with the page layouts being easy to read (with the exception of some of the illustrations previously noted). This work is recommended for all reference collections.—**Ralph Lee Scott**

Paleontology

P, S

515.   Matthews, Rupert. **Dinosaurs A-Z.** Woodbridge, Conn., Blackbirch Press/Gale Group, 2002. 64p. illus. index. $24.94. ISBN 1-56711-548-9.

This thin 64-page reference source on dinosaurs is designed with elementary school children in mind. The book begins with simple definitions of what dinosaurs are, when they lived, and how they lived. It also defines what dinosaurs are not by describing the other life forms living at the same time, including birds, lizards, and turtles. Short explanations about the evolution of dinosaurs as well as the evolution of the Earth and shifting continents are then explained.

The bulk of the book consists of an A to Z listing of dinosaurs written in terms that young children will understand. For each dinosaur there is information on where they lived, how they got their name, and their eating and living patterns. Each dinosaur has a color illustration as well as a diagram showing how its size relates to that of an adult human. Throughout the book are small sidebars under the heading "Dig It!" that provide additional information on topics such as dinosaur anatomy, the Earth's evolution, and how dinosaur bones and fossils were found. The book concludes with a glossary and a two-page index.—**Shannon Graff Hysell**

Physics

C

516.   **The Facts on File Dictionary of Atomic and Nuclear Physics.** Richard Rennie, ed. New York, Facts on File, 2003. 250p. $49.50. ISBN 0-8160-4916-5.

From AAS (with a *see* reference to "atomic absorption spectroscopy") to Swiss-American astronomer Zwicky (Fritz), these definitions cover atomic theory, the structure and states of matter, spectroscopy, quantum theory, and nuclear physics, as well as new developments in particle physics and cosmology. Concepts dominate, but there are also entries for leading scientists, both classic and modern. Most of the 2,000-plus entries consist of one rather brief paragraph, although some discussions run over a page or more. Numerous cross-references result in shorter definitions, which can be a mixed blessing if one must flip back and forth between entries. Some definitions suffer from being incomplete (e.g., Hawking radiation, the triple alpha process); others, such as the Hubble Space Telescope, are weak. Those related to astrophysics seem more problematic; the age of the Universe and Hubble Constant discussions are out of date according to current evidence based on Type Ia supernovae and galaxy clustering.

As is true for other Facts on File science dictionaries, high school students are one of the primary audiences. In fact, the preface for this volume emphasizes its usefulness for students of the AP physics course or the AP chemistry course. The latter may explain why two of the four (brief) appendixes are the periodic table and a listing of the chemical elements with their proton number and relative atomic mass. Despite the weaknesses noted above, this will be an acceptable addition to high school or college libraries, particularly since there is no other current one-volume dictionary that has this specific focus within physics.—**Barbara MacAlpine**

MATHEMATICS

Dictionaries and Encyclopedias

P, S

517.   Sidebotham, Thomas H. **The A to Z of Mathematics: A Basic Guide.** New York, John Wiley, 2002. 474p. illus. $54.95pa. ISBN 0-471-15045-2.

Intended for the general reader suffering from math anxiety, this is a dictionary of basic mathematical terms including definitions, diagrams, and worked-out numerical examples. The examples are particularly useful, since, as the author wisely notes in his preface, a book on mathematics should not be skimmed like a novel; the reader must understand every detail by working through examples.

There are plenty of cross-references in this alphabetically arranged book, so the absence of an index is not a problem. The word "basic" in the title is accurate; nothing in the book is beyond the level of a basic U.S. high school program. Concepts of the calculus, and even "matrix," are absent. However, within its limits the book is a well-written, self-contained guide for the general reader. It should be useful for public and school libraries, as well as for general collections.—**Robert Michaelson**

36 Resource Sciences

DIRECTORIES

C, P

518.   Staudinger, Jeff. **The Environmental Guidebook: A Selective Reference Guide to Environmental Organizations and Related Entries.** Menlo Park, Calif., Environmental Frontlines, 2002. 294p. $59.95pa. (w/CD-ROM); $49.95pa. ISBN 0-9720685-0-3.

The Environmental Guidebook is designed to be an essential reference book profiling key environmental organizations actively engaged in environmentally related activities. The nearly 500 entries are arranged among 7 fundamental categories, including environmental nongovernmental organizations, governmental organizations, multilaterals, political organizations, other interested parties (such as labor unions, opposing view groups, and other entities). Subcategories are included. Entries include a description of the group, organization or agency (including current activities, programs, services, viewpoints, publications, and relevant financial information), and basic contact information. Two appendixes provide a summary listing of all entities profiled and a summary listing of identified key reports/publications judged to be essential reading. The *Guidebook* also includes a companion CD-ROM with a PDF version of the book that includes 3,800 Internet hotlinks built directly into the text and over 300 full-length PDF documents that are referenced in the *Guidebook*.

The coverage appears to be very balanced in that strong environmental groups such as the Sierra Club are included, as well as "opposing view" groups that are typically labeled by critics as "anti-environmental" based on their views and activities. Destructive, violent groups such as Earth First! and the Earth Liberation Front are not included in the *Guidebook*.

This resource will be valued by anyone working in an environmental area, or who is interested in where to get more information on just about any environmental agency or organization. It should be contained in the reference section of all public and school libraries.—**Michael G. Messina**

HANDBOOKS AND YEARBOOKS

P, S

519.   **Famous First Facts About the Environment.** Ronald J. Formica, ed. Bronx, N.Y., H. W. Wilson, 2002. 573p. index. (Wilson Facts Series). $140.00. ISBN 0-8242-0974-5.

Similar to other works in this series, this volume presents 3,969 "first facts" on a broad range of environmental topics, which are grouped by large subject categories that are alphabetically arranged, from "Activist Movements" to "Zoos, Aquariums and Museums." Most categories are further subdivided into smaller subject areas, and within each the entries are in chronological sequence. Geographic coverage is worldwide, although there is some emphasis on Europe and North America. No criteria for the selection of facts for inclusion have been provided, and the choices sometimes seem a bit arbitrary; for example, under "Birds—Organizations" the founding of the first Audubon Society is noted but there are no entries for any of the world's scholarly ornithological societies. There is no documentation provided for any of the data included. One factual error was noted: Audubon discovered and named the Lincoln's sparrow in 1833, not in 1883 as stated.

The work is copiously indexed: there are indexes by subject, year, month and day, personal names, and geographic names. The indexes are easy to use and very thorough, enhancing the book's reference use. This work will be of interest in most public and high school libraries. The lack of documentation makes it a marginal acquisition for academic and research libraries. [R: LJ, 15, Sept 02, p. 54]—**Paul B. Cors**

C, P

520.   Johansen, Bruce E. **The Global Warming Desk Reference.** Westport, Conn., Greenwood Press, 2002. 353p. index. $70.00. ISBN 0-313-31679-1.

This succinct book is more than a desk reference. Readable and interesting, it is not too technical, and would be useful to students or any reader who cares about this important topic. It presents information in a way that reflects the seriousness of the issue without being sensationalistic. Also, when the author comes to important topics, such as stratospheric ozone depletion, that overlap global warming, he stops to briefly review those topics. In early chapters, the author sketches out the issue, discusses the general scientific consensus, and gives an overview of the protests of global warming skeptics. However, skeptics are increasingly hard put to explain some of the obvious information presented in this book. These data include ice melting around the world, warmer seas, effects on flora and fauna, likely effects on human health, and how warming right now is affecting the Arctic's indigenous people. Finally, after a strong chapter on possible solutions, Johansen took several pages to present a postscript on very recent information. As the title implies, the book has several pages of references, many of which are up to date.—**Marquita Hill**

37 Transportation

AIR

P
521. **Encyclopedia of Flight.** Tracy Irons-Georges, ed. Hackensack, N.J., Salem Press, 2002. 3v. illus. index. $325.00/set. ISBN 1-58765-046-0.

Irons-Georges, the editor of this three-volume work, has created a very attractive collection of essays relating to flight. Aimed at the general aviation reader, the articles are written in a nontechnical yet informative style. The articles cover both animal and man-made flight. Articles cover topics such as: Air Force One, food service, Charles Lindbergh, bats, the "Vomit Comet," icing, insects, kites, the Vietnam War, and rescue aircraft. The set has a number of appendixes: a glossary; a bibliography; lists of Websites, organizations and agencies, flight schools and training centers in North America, museums in North America, international airports, air carriers, airplane types, and air disasters and notable crashes; and a timeline. There is also an alphabetic topical and subject index.

The articles are well written, signed, and contain individual bibliographies. Interestingly, the individual article bibliographies are not compiled into the general bibliography at the end of the book. There are some other minor concerns. For instance, the list of museums fails to list the Smithsonian Air and Space Museum; does not include the Airborne and Special Operations Museum in Fayetteville, North Carolina; and lists the location of the Wright Brothers Memorial in North Carolina as being at Manteo rather than its true location at Kill Devil Hills. The list of airplane types contains some Boeing and Douglas aircraft models, but it does not include the MD series and the Concorde. Furthermore, the list of air carriers omits both Midwest Express and Midway Airlines. Overall, however, the set is very readable and attractive to use. Material in the timeline is current through November of 2001 and includes some brief information on the hijackings of September 11th. The set is rather expensive but will attract a wide audience of young, college-age, and general readers. It is recommended for libraries having patrons with a general interest in aviation.—**Ralph Lee Scott**

Author/Title Index

Reference is to entry number.

Subject Index

Reference is to entry number.

St. James gd to Hispanic artists, 346
Who's who in American art 2001-02, 24th ed, 347

ASIA - POLITICS
Dictionary of the modern pol of SE Asia, 3d ed, 259

ASIAN AMERICANS
Columbia documentary hist of the Asian American experience, 110

ASSOCIATIONS
Acronym finder [Website], 1
Headquarters USA 2003, 25th ed, 22

ASTRONAUTS
Distinguished African Americans in aviation & space scis,
106

ASTRONOMY
Dictionary of astronomy, 2d ed, 512
Space scis, 513

ATHLETES
A to Z of American women in sports, 282

ATLASES
Compact Peters world atlas, updated ed, 124
Dorling Kindersley concise atlas of the world, 125
National atlas of the USA [Website], 128
Oxford atlas of the world, 10th ed, 129
World Almanac atlas of the world, 130

AUSTRALIA
History of Australia, 158

AUTHORS
Supernatural fiction writers, 383
TeachingBooks.net [Website], 377

AUTHORS, AMERICAN
American writers classics, v.1, 385
Great American writers, 372
Reader's ency of American lit, 2d ed, 387

AUTHORSHIP. *See also* **PUBLISHERS & PUBLISHING**
Oxford gd to style, 332
Writer's hndbk 2003, 331

AVIATION
Carrier aviation air power dir, 237
Encyclopedia of flight, 521

BANKING. *See also* **FINANCE**
Plunkett's financial servs industry almanac 2002-03, 61

BASEBALL
Biographical dict of Major League Baseball managers, 287
Official baseball rules 2002 ed, 288
STATS player profiles 2002, 289

BASKETBALL
Blue ribbon college basketball yrbk, 2001-02, ed, 290
Sporting News official NBA gd, 2002-03 ed, 291
Sporting News official NBA register, 2002-03 ed, 292

BIBLE - HANDBOOKS
Biblical studies on the Internet, 429
Oxford essential gd to people & places of the Bible, 427
Oxford illustrated hist of the Bible, 428

BIBLIOGRAPHY
CD-ROMs in print, 16th ed, 5
Global bks in print [Website], 4

BIOGRAPHY
Biography resource center [Website], 6
International who's who 2003, 66th ed, 7
International who's who online [Website], 8
Marquis who's who on the Web [Website], 9
Scribner ency of American lives: the 1960s, 12
U*X*L ency of world biog, 11
Who's who of Nobel Prize winners 1901-2002, 4th ed, 10

BIOLOGICAL DIVERSITY
Life on Earth, 457

BIOLOGICAL SCIENCES
Facts on File dict of cell & molecular biology, 456
Penguin dict of biology, 10th ed, 458

BIRDS
Grzimek's animal life ency: vols. 8-11, birds, 2d ed, 470
Sibley gd to bird life & behavior, 471

BIRTH CONTROL
Historical & multicultural ency of women's reproductive
rights in the US, 326

BOOK COLLECTING
Collected bks, 2002 ed, 340

BREASTFEEDING
Breastfeeding sourcebk, 494

BUDDHISM
Illustrated ency of Zen Buddhism, 430

BUSINESS - BIOGRAPHY
American inventors, entrepreneurs, & business visionaries, 45
Leading American businesses, 46
100 most popular business leaders for YAs, 47

BUSINESS - DICTIONARIES & ENCYCLOPEDIAS
Dictionary of e-business, 49
Encyclopedia of business & finance, 50
Gale e-commerce sourcebk, 51

BUSINESS - DIRECTORIES
Directory of mgmt consultants 2002, 10th ed, 76
Headquarters USA 2003, 25th ed, 22
World dir of business info Web sites 2002, 5th ed, 53

ECOLOGY
Life on Earth, 457

ECONOMICS
Worldmark ency of natl economies, 63

EDUCATION, COMPUTER NETWORK RESOURCES
CLCD instructional materials database [Website], 84
Complete sourcebk on children's interactive media 2002,
    v.10, 83
Educators gd to free Internet resources 2002-03:
    elem/middle school ed, 85
Educators gd to free Internet resources 2002-03: secondary
    ed, 20th ed, 86
EvaluTech [Website], 87
GlobaLinks: resources for world studies, grades K-8, 89
NetTrekker [Website], 88

EDUCATION - DIRECTORIES
Funding sources for K-12 educ 2002, 90
Guide to summer camps & summer schools 2002/03, 28th
    ed, 81

EDUCATION, ELEMENTARY
Using picture storybks to teach lit devices, 92

EDUCATION - HANDBOOKS & YEARBOOKS
Educational leadership, 82
Student's gd to landmark congressional laws on educ, 200

EDUCATION, HIGHER
College blue bk, 29th ed, 94
Competitive colleges, 2001-02, 96
Complete bk of colleges, 2003 ed, 95

EDUCATION, MULTICULTURAL
Institute of intl educ passport [Website], 99
Multicultural projects index, 3d ed, 93

EDUCATION, SECONDARY
Sex, youth, & sex educ, 91

EDUCATION - SUMMER PROGRAMS
Guide to summer camps & summer schools 2002/03, 28th
    ed, 81

EGYPT
Culture & customs of Egypt, 42
Usborne Internet-linked ency of ancient Egypt, 178

ELECTIONS
Congressional Quarterly's gd to US elections, 4th ed, 255
Presidential elections, 1789-2000, 256

ELECTRONIC COMMERCE
Dictionary of e-business, 49
Gale e-commerce sourcebk, 51

EMIGRATION & IMMIGRATION
Cultures in motion, 192
Facts about American immigration, 102

ENCYCLOPEDIAS & DICTIONARIES. *See also*
   CHILDREN'S ENCYCLOPEDIAS &
   DICTIONARIES
Encyclopedia Americana 2002, intl ed, 16
Encyclopedia Americana [Website], 17
Grolier multimedia ency 2002, deluxe ed [CD-ROM], 18
Oxford ref online [Website], 19

ENDANGERED SPECIES
Beacham's gd to intl endangered species, v.3, 466

ENGLISH LANGUAGE - DICTIONARIES
American English study dict, 358
American Heritage college dict, 4th ed, 14
American Heritage dict for learners of English, rev ed, 359
Cambridge intl dict of English on CD-ROM [CD-ROM], 15
Oxford advanced learner's CD-ROM dict [CD-ROM], 360
Oxford desk dict & thesaurus, 2d American ed, 361
Oxford dict of word hists, 355
Oxford world English dict shelf on CD-ROM [CD-ROM],
    20

ENGLISH LANGUAGE - DICTIONARIES - HEBREW
Modern English-Hebrew dict, 368

ENGLISH LANGUAGE - DICTIONARIES - SPANISH
Langenscheidt's new college Spanish dict, 369
University of Chicago Spanish dict, 5th ed, 370

ENGLISH LANGUAGE - FOREIGN WORDS &
   PHRASES
Facts on File dict of foreign words & phrases, 365

ENGLISH LANGUAGE - GRAMMAR
Cambridge grammar of the English lang, 356
Grammar smart, 2d ed, 357

ENGLISH LANGUAGE - SYNONYMS & ANTONYMS
American Heritage thesaurus for learners of English, 367
McGraw-Hill children's thesaurus, 363
Oxford desk dict & thesaurus, 2d American ed, 361

ENGLISH LANGUAGE - TERMS & PHRASES
Brewer's dict of modern phrase & fable, 364
Facts on File dict of proverbs, 366

ENGLISH LITERATURE
Oxford chronology of English lit, 388

ENVIRONMENTAL PROTECTION
Environmental gdbk, 518

ENVIRONMENTAL SCIENCES
Famous 1st facts about the environment, 519
Global warming desk ref, 520

ETHNIC STUDIES
Multicultural ref center [Website], 101
People around the world, 103
Peoples of Europe, 40
Racial & ethnic diversity, 4th ed, 104

PHILANTHROPY
Annual register of grant support 2002, 35th ed, 309
Funding sources for children & youth programs 2002, 311
Government assistance almanac, 2002-03, 16th ed, 310

PHILOSOPHERS
Cultural theory, 422

PHYSICS
Facts on File dict of atomic & nuclear physics, 516

PHYSIOLOGY
World of anatomy & physiology, 461

PLANTS. *See also* **GARDENING**
American Horticulture Society ency of plants & flowers,
     updated ed, 452
Handbook of N European garden plants, 462

POETRY
Contemporary American women poets, 390
Thematic gd to American poetry, 391
Young adult poetry, 392

POLAR REGIONS
Encyclopedia of Antarctica & the southern oceans, 36

POLITICAL ACTIVISTS
Jewish American & pol participation, 115
People for & against restricted or unrestricted expression, 193

POLITICAL IDEOLOGY
Political theories for students, 264

POLITICAL LEADERS
American pol leaders, 248
Who's who in intl affairs 2003, 3d ed, 240
Worldmark ency of the nations world leaders 2002, 241

POLITICAL PARTIES
Political parties of E Europe, 260
Political parties of the world, 5th ed, 244

POLITICAL SCIENCE - DICTIONARIES &
     ENCYCLOPEDIAS
Dictionary of world pol, 242
Encyclopedia of Latin American pol, 262
Oxford companion to pol of the world, 2d ed, 243

POLITICAL SCIENTISTS
American pol scientists, 2d ed, 239

POLYNESIA
Historical dict of Polynesia, 2d ed, 159

POPULAR CULTURE
Greenwood gd to American popular culture, 407
More on this day in hist, 408

POPULAR MUSIC
Early swing era, 1930 to 1941, 400

Jazz makers, 401
Parents aren't supposed to like it, vols. 4-6, 398
Tin pan alley song ency, 399

POST - COMMUNISM
Political parties of E Europe, 260

PRESIDENTS - UNITED STATES
Facts about the presidents, 7th ed, 246
Presidential elections, 1789-2000, 256
Presidents, 3d ed, 247
Scholastic ency of the presidents & their times, updated
     ed, 249

PROVERBS
Facts on File dict of proverbs, 366

PSYCHOLOGY
Depression sourcebk, 275
Encyclopedia of psychology [Website], 268
Encyclopedia of psychotherapy, 269
Gale ency of mental disorders, 270
Internet mental health [Website], 271
Psychology, 277
Psychology of humor, 278

PSYCHOLOGY - DIRECTORIES
Complete mental health dir 2002, 3d ed, 272
Complete mental health dir [Website], 273
Insider's gd to mental health resources online, 2002/03 ed, 274

PUBLIC RECORDS
Public record research system (PRRS) [Website], 253

PUBLISHERS & PUBLISHING
American bk trade dir 2002-03, 48th ed, 228
Checklist of American imprints 1820-29, 230
International literary market place 2002, 229

QUILTS
Vintage quilts, 342

QUOTATIONS
America in quotations, 153
People on people: the Oxford dict of biogl quotations, 28

RADICALISM
Encyclopedia of modern American extremists & extremist
     groups, 144

READERS' ADVISORY SERVICES
Now read this II, 380
What do children read next?/What do YAs read next? v.4,
     373
What do I read next? 2002, v.1, 381

RELIGION
Dictionary of religious orders, 424
Encyclopedia of cults, sects, & new religions, 2d ed, 281
Usborne Internet-linked ency of world religions, 425

RELIGION - CHRISTIANITY
New ency of Christian martyrs, 433
World Christian ency, 2d ed, 432

RELIGIOUS LEADERS
American religious leaders, 423

RENAISSANCE
Renaissance, 166
Renaissance & reformation: almanac, 167
Renaissance & reformation: biogs, 168
Renaissance & reformation: primary sources, 169

RIGHT TO DIE - LAW & LEGISLATION
Living wills simplified, 206

ROMAN HISTORY
Roman Emperors [Website], 164
Usborne Internet-linked ency of the Roman world, 170

RUSSIA
Historical dict of medieval Russia, 175

SACRED MUSIC
Encyclopedia of contemporary Christian music, 402

SCIENCE - DICTIONARIES & ENCYCLOPEDIAS
American Heritage student sci dict, 441
Encyclopedia of sci & tech, 443

SCIENCE - HANDBOOKS & YEARBOOKS
More sci projects for all students, 445
Science activities, 446
Science experiments index for young people, 3d ed, 447

SCIENCE - HISTORY
Scientific revolution, 442

SCIENTISTS
A to Z of chemists, 509
Cambridge dict of scientists, 2d ed, 438
Life scis before the 20th century: biogl portraits, v.3, 455
Nobel scientists, 439
Portraits of great American scientists, 440

SEWING
Encyclopedia of sewing machine techniques, 343

SEX INSTRUCTION FOR TEENAGERS
Sex, youth, & sex educ, 91

SHORT STORIES
Thematic gd to popular short stories, 384

SKIING
Skiing USA, 4th ed, 299

SOCIAL CONFLICT
Alphabetical listing of word, name, & place in N Ireland
    & the living lang of conflict, 41

SOCIAL POLICY
Blackwell dict of social policy, 267

SOCIAL SCIENCES
Dictionary of the social scis, 29
Gallup poll, 2001, 30

SPACE SCIENCES
Dictionary of astronomy, 2d ed, 512
Space scis, 513

SPANISH LANGUAGE DICTIONARIES
Langenscheidt's new college Spanish dict, 369
University of Chicago Spanish dict, 5th ed, 370

SPECIAL LIBRARIES
Directory of special libs & info centers, 27th ed, 223
Subject dir of special libs & info centers, 27th ed, 225

SPIES
America's military adversaries, 140

SPORTS. *See also* **ATHLETES**
Canada: our century in sport 1900-2000, 283
Quick ref dict for athletic training, 284
Sports & games of medieval culture, 286
Sports & games of the ancients, 285

STATISTICS
CQ's state fact finder 2002, 319

STOCK MARKET
NASDAQ-100 investor's gd 2002-03, 59

STYLE GUIDES
Oxford gd to style, 332

SUBJECT HEADINGS
People, places & things: a list of popular Lib of Congress
    subject headings with Dewey nos, 227

TECHNOLOGY
Encyclopedia of inventions, 444
Encyclopedia of sci & tech, 443

TEENAGERS - HEALTH
Adolescent health sourcebk, 484
Drug info for teens, 312

TELECOMMUNICATIONS
Newton's telecom dict, 18th ed, 508

TELEVISION
Encyclopedia of American TV, 415

TERRORISM
Bioterrorism & pol violence Web resources, 212
Encyclopedia of terrorism, 209
Encyclopedia of terrorism, 211
Terrorism: almanac, 214
Terrorism: biogs, 215
Terrorism: primary sources, 216